# Studies In Nidderdale – Primary Source Edition

## Joseph Lucas (F.G.S.)

*Frontispiece.*

THOS. KELL & SON, LITH 40 KING ST. COVENT GARDEN.

# STUDIES

## IN

# NIDDERDALE:

UPON NOTES AND OBSERVATIONS OTHER THAN GEOLOGICAL,
MADE DURING THE PROGRESS OF THE GOVERNMENT
GEOLOGICAL SURVEY OF THE DISTRICT, 1867—1872.

BY

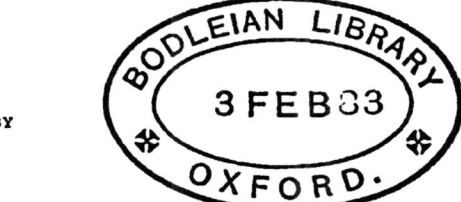

## JOSEPH LUCAS, F.G.S., F.M.S.,

*Telford Medallist of the Institution of Civil Engineers.*
*Associate of the Institution of Surveyors.*

LONDON:
ELLIOT STOCK, 62, PATERNOSTER ROW.
PATELEY BRIDGE: THOMAS THORPE.

PRINTED BY T. THORPE, PUBLISHER, PATELEY BRIDGE.

# STUDIES IN NIDDERDALE.

## ERRATA.

| PAGE. | LINE. | | | | | |
|---|---|---|---|---|---|---|
| 13 | 26 | The words " or the name may like Watch'em be from the word of command—" Rak " drive (see Glossary)," in lines 29—30, should follow the word 'dog' in line 26. | | | | |
| 16 | 20 | *for* | ' degression ' | .. | *read* | ' digression.' |
| 21 | 5 | ,, | ' imparts ' | .. | ,, | ' imports.' |
| 28 | 4 | ,, | ' Whan ' | .. | ,, | ' Wham.' |
| 30 | 10 | ,, | ' passin.' | .. | ,, | ' passin." ' |
| 31 | 3 | ,, | ' ah,ve ' | .. | ,, | ' ah've.' |
| 32 | 9 | ,, | ' *Styre, Stire* ' | .. | ,, | ' *Styrc, Stirc*.' |
| 37 (col) | 6 | ,, | ' Uu ' | .. | ,, | ' Un.' |
| 51 | 6 | ,, | ' have the ' | .. | ,, | ' have of the.' |
| 58 | 14 | ,, | ' Manmum ' | .. | ,, | ' Mannum.' |
| 63 | 4 | ,, | ' that have " gates " ' | | See Introd. p. xviii., and Glos., p. 254, s.v. GEEAT. | |
| 70 | 11 | ,, | ' vale Denbighshire ' | | ,, | ' vale in Denbighshire.' |
| 76 | 6 | ,, | ' Lib.' | .. | ,, | ' Tib.' |
| 78 | 20 | ,, | ' by doth ' | .. | ,, | ' cry dost.' |
| 80 | 33 | ,, | ' *Deel to division*.' | | ,, | ' [*Deel to division*].' |
| 84 | 1 | ,, | ' Britian ' | .. | ,, | ' Britain.' |
| 89 | 28 | ,, | ' off ' | .. | ,, | ' oft.' |
| 92 | 23 | ,, | ' islet ' | .. | ,, | ' inlet.' |
| 96 | 29 | ,, | ' on ' | .. | ,, | ' an.' |
| 97 | 7 | ,, | ' as ' | .. | ,, | ' has.' |
| 97 | 9 | ,, | ' bekkjr ' | .. | ,, | ' bekkja.' |
| 97 | 21 | ,, | ' pertinentiis Snis ' | | ,, | ' pertinentiis snis.' |
| 97 | 24 | ,, | ' Lost hourrs ' | .. | ,, | ' Losthonrs.' |
| 101 | 15 | ,, | ' cover ' | .. | ,, | ' Cover.' |

| PAGE. | LINE. | | | | | |
|---|---|---|---|---|---|---|
| 101 | 29 | *for* | ' probably ' | .. | *read* | ' probable.' |
| 112 | 13 | ,, | ' besides ' | .. | ,, | ' beside.' |
| 116 | 10 | ,, | ' Blasyhaw ' | .. | ,, | ' Blayshaw.' |
| 123 | 21 | *erase* | ' it.' | | | |
| 124 | 4 | *for* | ' King ' | .. | ,, | ' Kring.' |
| 128 | 14 | ,, | ' TRIPLIATA ' | .. | ,, | ' TRIFOLIATA.' |
| 141 | 15 | ,, | ' clangornm ' | .. | ,, | ' clangorum.' |
| 145 | 2 | ,, | ' Wharedale ' | .. | ,, | ' Wharfedale.' |
| 153 | 2 | ,, | ' Laweslight ' | .. | ,, | ' Lawslight.' |
| 156 | 24 | ,, | ' Kennit ' | .. | ,, | ' Kennet.' |
| 176 | 6 | ,, | ' EASTERLEY ' | .. | ,, | ' EASTERLY.' |
| 176 | 24 | ,, | ' cover ' | .. | ,, | ' Cover.' |
| 182 | 11 | ,, | ' gentlemen ' | .. | ,, | ' gentleman.' |
| 197 | 1 | ,, | ' in ' | .. | ,, | ' on.' |
| 200 | 1 | ,, | ' flashed ' | .. | ,, | ' flash.' |
| 249 | 35 | ,, | ' heet ' | .. | ,, | ' breet.' |
| 267 | 45 | ,, | ' Zanors ' | .. | ,, | ' Yarrow.' |
| 271 | 35 | ,, | ' Gr. ϝflug ' | .. | ,, | ' Ger. pflug.' |

# CONTENTS.

# LIST OF ILLUSTRATIONS

# STUDIES IN NIDDERDALE.

—◆—

## Introductory Commentary.

—◆—

While hesitating to tax the patience of the reader, by introducing the subjects of these studies in the form of a commentary upon the text, a justification for this course is found in the Gaelic word ' Strath,' upon the very first page.

This brings us to perhaps the most important, the last, and certainly the least expected outcome of these Studies, viz. :—the former existence of a GAELIC population upon this area. That such a result was unexpected, may be shown by the effort in the footnote, (p. 1) to treat ' Strath ' as Welsh, and by the fact that in the enumeration of the successive races, that have populated the District, (Study IX, p.p. 69-87) there is an omission of any mention of the *Gael*. It was not till the long list of words in the Glossary had been carefully worked out, that it became evident, not only that several of them are Gaelic, but that from their nature, it is impossible that they could be imported words. Lovers of Dialects have long been familiar with the Gaelic word (Ná) *nor* for *than*, but its presence in England has not been accounted for. Several place names are Gaelic; names of pastures are especially Gaelic, and from their general character and local application forbid the idea of importation. Further particulars will be found in the commentary on the Gaelic element in the Glossary.

A curiously similar observation to that in line 8, p. 8, was made by Robert Brown, in 1799. To wit, ' Corn has already been cultivated there, for all the low fields have at one time or other been ploughed.' This proves the change older than the end of last century. The true key is found in Laveleye, (*Prim. Prop.*, 1878, p. 254-5) who shows that it took place at the end of the 15th, and all through the 16th century.

Local legends respecting *Dun Bulls* (p.4.) must give place to the fact related by Barker, *(Hist. of Wensleydale, p. 12, note)* that they are one of the badges of the Nevilles. In ' The Rising of the North,'

> ' Lord Westmoreland his ancyent raisde,
> The *Dun bull* he raysed on high.

That the years 1795 and 1797 were *historical* ' bad harvests,' gives additional interest to the tradition recorded on p. 6, as to Ryebread.

It should be mentioned that ' Bakewell ' was the name of a celebrated breeder of Leicester sheep, and that the ' Bakewell ram,' (p. 8, *note)* is in fact only a ' Leicester Tup ' called after him, which proves that the modern cross did originate as stated in the said note. (P. 15,) Old Tusser gives a curious note regarding *Tems,*

> ' Some mixeth to miller the Rye with the Wheat
> TEMS loaf on his table to have for to eat.' *Sept. Husb.* v. ii.

The name *tems loaf* bears out the suggestion respecting *tommy cake* (p. 15, *note*).

The Chimler-hoal (p. 20), which enabled the stars to be counted by persons sitting in the room, (p. 21.) figures in Herodotus, (VIII, 187), who says, ' the rays of the sun reached into the house down the chimney.'—' The lad...traced a circle on the floor of the house round the sun's rays.' Beckmann infers from this passage the orifice in the roof, which is prettily introduced by Tegner, in his beautiful Swedish version of Frithiof's Saga

> .  .  .  .  .  .  .  .  .  .  .   ' And adown the airy chimney
> ' Wakeful stars, celestial friends ! resting, viewed the festive circle.'

(W. Strong's *Transl.*, Canto III).   The great festoons of soot, (p. 20) have suggested another beautiful verse to the great Swedish poet, (Canto XI, v. 18) where in describing Angantyr's house in Orkney as Frithiof saw it, he says,

| | |
|---|---|
| Ej midt paa golfvet glöder | No fire on mid-floor glowed |
| Den muntra brasans sken, | Or brazier's bright flame shone, |
| Men emot vagg sig stöder | But at the wall there stood |
| Kamin af marmor sten. | Chimney of marble stone. |
| Ej rök i sal sig lade | No reek, the hall o'erspread, |
| Ej sågs der sotad ås, ; | Sooted the Rannel-balk ; |
| Glasrutor fönstren hade, | Glass panes the windows had |
| Och dorren hade lås. | And the door a lock. |

Were this contemporaneous, the reference to chimneys would be very interesting, but Tegner's version is modern, while the " invention of chimneys " is put down in Haydn at " 1200, when they were confined to the kitchen and large hall."

"One thing " says Leland, 1549, " I much notyd in the haull of Bolton howe chimeneys were conveyed by tunnels made on the syds of the wauls betwyxt the lights in the hawll ; and by this means, and by no *covers* is the smoke of the harthe in the hawle wonder strangely convayed."—By the ' covers ' are meant the ' hood.'   Harrison (*Descrip. of Britayne* in Holinshed, 1577), says " Now we have manye chimneyes......then, we had nothing but reredosses, and yet our heads did never ache"— thus proving their general introduction in the 16th century. King's ' *Vale Royal*,' 1656, says of the Cheshire farm houses, ' till of late years, they used the old manner of the Saxons, for they had their fire in the midst of the house against a hob of

clay, and their oven under the same roof, but within these forty
years they have builded chimneys.' Barker (*Hist. of Wensleydale*,
1856, p. p. 76) says, 'It is a fact that the last farm house of
this ancient construction was standing in the township of Tong-
with-Haugh near Bolton, in Lancashire, within the last sixty
years.'  In connection with this ' central fire,' the reference in
the above verse to Angantyr's house, and again (Canto III),

" Central placed, with constant blaze, were the halmfed embers burning
Cheerful in their walled hearth."

fall in with the Valle house (p. 20) and Lambe's note in Percy,
(p. 241 below).  The curious will find further information in
Rogers's *Agriculture and Prices*, V. 1, c. 18, p. 421.

A parallel to *Pferdich* or *Pferdisch* and *paddock*, (p. 34)
will be found in *Pfälung* and *paling*, *pfund* and *pund*, (*pound*)
and many others.  Andrew Borde (*Boke of the Introwduction
of Knowledge*, 1542) gives a list of Cornish numerals which differ
slightly from those on p. 88 below.  They are ' Ouyn, Dow,
Tray, Peswar, Pimp, Whe, Eth, Naw, Dec, Unec, Dowec,
Fredeec, Peswardeec, Pympdeec, Whedeec, Sythdeec, Ethdeec,
Nawdeec, Igous.'  According to Mr. Leyland, of Kettlewell,
' Sheepscoring numerals ' are unknown in Wharfedale, where
' Sheep are counted on the fingers in silence, or a little pebble
dropped every score.' (Orally, Sep. 7th, 1881).  This reminded
me of the following passage—' Bargains among the Indians are
conducted in the most profound silence, and by merely touching
each other's hands.  If the seller takes the whole hand, it
implies a thousand rupees or pagodas; five fingers import five
hundred; one finger, one hundred; half a finger, fifty; a single
joint only ten.' (*Hist. Acct.* of Travels in Asia, Hugh Murray,
in Simpson's *History of the Gypsies*. p. 311, *note*).  Simpson
also cites Bruce's account of two Indian brokers concluding a
bargain as to the purchase of cargoes.  ' After about twenty
minutes spent in handling each other's fingers, below the shawl,
the bargain is concluded, say for nine ships, without one word

ever having been spoken on the subject, or pen and ink used in any shape whatever.' (Bruce, *Travels*).

In addition to Study VI, (p. 51-5) there is a short article on the 'Garth' in the Glossary, p. 253. 'Sulh' the A.S. name for the plough, which figures so largely in Study VII, is still in use in Somersetshire. *Pers.* Kulba, a plough.

A glance through Amyot's *Mantchou-Tartar* and *Fr.* Dict. will reveal several familiar words, which are probably of Mongolian origin. In connection with the 'Helm,' the subject of Study VII, the Mantchou-Tartar 'Helmen' *the shadow* of an opaque body, is very striking.

Accurate figures, as to the rural populations 'early in the century,' (p. 62) from a remarkable paper 'on the Increase of Population in England and Wales,' by Mr. R. Price Williams, C.E., read before the Statistical Society, 15th June, 1880, show that 'the increase in the population of the rural districts of England and Wales during the first decade of this century, was 12·11 per cent., or very similar to that of the smaller towns, and as in that case, the maximum rate of increase (14·74 *per cent*) was reached in the following decade, (1811-21) from that time, down to the census of 1851, the increase of the rural population was relatively very small...the decrement in the rate of increase being rapid and continuous. From that period, however, up to 1871, there was a rapid and continuous increment...The cause of the slow increase of the rural population between 1821 and 1851, is evidently in a great measure due to immigration into the towns ; this will at once be seen in referring to the diagrams,' [which show] ' that the periods of greatest increase in the town populations are coincident with those of greatest decrease in the case of the rural population. This is especially noticeable in the decade, 1841-51.'...' The population of the towns, which up to this period was considerably less than that of the rural districts, equalled it about the middle of the decade, and at the end considerably exceeded it.' *(Journ. Stat. Soc., Sep.,* 1880.)

In Col. A. H. Ouvry's translation of E. Nasse, 'Agricultural Community of the Middle Ages,' 1871, (p. 19) the passage from the *Laws of Ine*, c. 42, (p. 62) is given and translated. I had printed this part of the Studies before meeting with a copy of Nasse. He says 'Price and Schmidt remark very justly, that there is a hiatus after ' næbben,' (p. 63, line 1, first word) which they fill up from Ine, c. 40, ' & recen heora neahgebures ceap in ' *(Ouvry* p. 19). I had filled it up in the text with the words ' their cattle,' (p. 62, line 2) which is all that is required. In the next clause, however, (line 4) for ' have " gates " ' read ' that gap own.' The ' commotions ' mentioned in Mavor's note (p. 64) are explained by the following. ' Commencing with the great insurrection of the peasants in 1549, there were numerous local risings throughout the 16th century, all with the same object, the destruction of the enclosures which deprived them of their lands.' *(Prim. Prop.*, p, 256*).* Anent Mr. Atkinson's note, p. 65, on ' Sheep gates,' in France, under the system of common pasturage, a common flock of sheep receives from each inhabitant a number of heads, determined by the quantity of land which he possesses in individual ownership.' I must again refer to *Mantchou-Tartar.* ' Tchop' means exactly the same as *Welsh* 'Cop' *Eng.* ' Top,' summit of a hill, (p. 69). *Wel.* ' Tran' (p. 70) is in *Gael.*, 'Treann,' a field. ' Kist' (p. 72) is classed as being of immediate Welsh descent into this dialect, because, being a Latin word, probably of monastic origin (see Gloss.*)* it would be in use among the Celtic inhabitants long before the Angles came. ' Hull,' (p. 70) another Welsh word, appears in a 'Terrier of Glebe Lands' of the Chapel of Middlesmoor 1809— ' A little swine-hull, in length three yards, and breadth one yard and a half, covered with slate.' Grainge, *(Hist of Nidd.*, p. 165.*)* Cleasby, or perhaps I ought to say Vigfusson, *(Icel. Dict.)* has 'Hask-wind' which is evidently wrong. *Welsh* Asgellwynt, is *lit.* ' the wing of the wind,' (p. 72,) as I am informed by the Rev J. G. Roberts.

Few readers will have the dates of the Roman Emperors (p. 75) at their fingers' ends. They are Nero, A.D. 54-68; Galba, 68; Otho, 69; Vespasian, 70-79; Titus, 79-81; Domitian, 81-96; Nerva, 96-8; Trajan, 98-117; Adrian, 117-38. Very interesting is the account in Hobkirk's *Hist. of Huddersfield*, 1868, (p. 491) of the discovery at *Cambodunum* of the bronze companion medal to the silver 'Juda' denarius, found in Steanbeck, which medal is mentioned on page 75.

The bulk of Study VIII was written in 1871. Page 80 was printed off before the early months of 1881, when the Irish Question brought to light the *Rundale* system, still in use in Ireland. Some excellent plans or maps of the 'Rundale Villages,' with their radiating *stripes* of land, appeared in the Illustrated London Papers of that date. Nevertheless, the word seems to be O.N. Rönd, a *rim, border, stripe*, and deel, *division*, which like Mere, a *boundary*, and Mark or March, a *boundary*, has given its name to the village land. *(Russ.* Mir, *Ger.* Mark.) 'Ray' or 'Wray,' (p. 82) is certainly *Gael.* Rae, a *pasture*, probably the same word as 'Reoh' and 'Rough' in Surrey.

To the A.S. place names 'Bolton' must be added. The Domesday *Bodelton*, shows it to be A.S. Bótl, or Bótel an *abode, hall*, etc, and *ton*—a name still preserved intact at 'Bootle,' Liverpool.

To p. 89 we may add Chaucer's line,

'Whereas they made him at the quernë grind.'

*Rani* (p. 90) occurs in the form 'Hrani' as a man's name in the Incantation of Hervor, v. 2. '*Sleet*' (p. 91) occurs in Somerset in 'Sheep-slate'='sheep-walk.' Therefore also the 'slate' upon our houses is the same Gothic word, and means 'flat.' In addition to the Gothic forms given on p. 91, I find one apparently foreign word in Welsh, *Ysletan, any flat body*, or vessel, a *flat*, a flat bottomed boat. ' *Huntari*,' the ' hunting grounds,' or the district over which a tribe had the right of hunting, affords another example of a name being transferred to a newer form of the same thing. The venerable name of *Mark*, which in *Dan.* now simply means a *field*, occurs again half a mile east of MalhamTarn, in ' Gans High *Mark*,' ' Bordley Hall High *Mark*,' ' Cote High *Mark*,' fields ranging from 1400 to 1500 ft., and in ' Clapham High *Mark*,' 1650 ft. For ' Ketywell,' (p. 95) see p. 161. ' *Iwdenbec* ' (p. 96) is evidently Doubergill Beck, which flows down through Wath. Roger de Mowbray gave by Charter, to the Abbot and Convent of Fountains all the land between ' Pateleigate and Iwdone,'—*(Hist. of Nidd.* p. 89). Mr. Grainge adds in a footnote " This *Iwdone* is evidently not the place now called *Yeadon.*" But it certainly is, Mr. Grainge himself proves it. The *Carta* (p. 96, bottom) shows that Fountains Earth originally extended from *Iwdenbec* to *Beckermote*. Mr. Grainge *(Hist.*, p. 175) says, that it still extends " from a short distance above Beggarmote Scar, to where Doubergill falls into the same river, [Nidd] near the hamlet of Wath." He says again, " Doubergill divides it from Bishopside." The place really in doubt is ' Pateleigate,' which must have been the name of a road or track at the *northern* extremity of Fountains Earth= the ' Pateley road.' ' Mote ' is a commoner name than appears in the north. There is an old Cumbrian rhyme which says,

> " The Esk and the Liddle
> Run a striddle
> And meet at the Mote."

which I take from Mr. Palmer's charming work, (*The Tyne and its Tributaries*, C. xiv, p. 157).

As regards the suggested Græco-Latin origin of *Buskr*, a *bush*, Lat. Boscus, (p. 104). ' By Inquisition, *post mortem*, (26 Ed. 1), Roger de Mowbray held ' Nidderdale Chacea,

Baggworth *boscus*, Glomescalle boscus ' which were within the Manor of Kirkby Malzeard,' (*Hist. of Nidd.*, p. 175).

Two Papers of mine, on " The Vestiges of the Ancient Forests of part of the Pennine Chain," have been published, one by the British Association, 1881, and the other in the beautifully printed publications of the " Geological and Poly-technic Society of the West Riding of Yorkshire, 1881." Both are founded on Studies XIII and XIV. For more about Charcoal-burning, (p. 117) see Rogers *(Agriculture and Prices,* V. 1, c. 18, p. 421.) ' Terraced Reins.' (p. 120) are of world-wide invention—' At Murichon, a small village in Bhotan, which occupies a spot of even ground at the top of a mountain, the farmers level the ground they cultivate in the slopes of the hills by cutting it into shelves, forming beds of such size as the slopes will admit,' (Capt. Turner in Hamilton's East India Gazetteer, 1828. V. 2, p. 262).

To Mr. J. G. Baker, F.R.S., of Kew Herbarium, the author of ' North Yorkshire,' with whom I had the pleasure of walking over some of the ground treated in these Studies, when I had the honour of conducting the excursion of the British Association from York to Brimham Rocks, 1881, I am indebted for the following notes on Study XV. The Modern Botany, (p. 121). " *Primula Elatior.* The Yorkshire Oxlip is not *P. Elatior,* which is confined to Essex, Sussex, and Cambridge, but a hybrid between the *Primrose* and *Cowslip. Euonymus Europæus* ascends to Leyburn Shawl, 700 feet, and Aysgarth Force." The ' London Pride,' (p. 122) " Dr. Lees, in his ' West York-shire,' treats it as a true native in Heseltine Gill." *Melampyrum Sylvaticum* should be *M. Pratense* var. *Montana.* The Surrey plant is no doubt *M. Pratense,* which has a larger flower. *Rubus Chamæmorus,* the Nowt-berry, " marks off beautifully in *N. Eng.* the lower boundary of Watson's Arctic region." *Oxyria Reniformis,* " this must be a mistake, *Oxyria* is one of the few plants frequent amongst the lakes of Westmoreland and Cumberland, not known in Yorkshire." I bow to this opinion. My herbarium contains several specimens, all of which I may have brought from Norway. *Trientalis Europæa,* " plentiful on our hills above Thirsk, specially at Boltby."

Mr. Reason has stuffed at Wath, a most life-like group of *Merlins,* (p. 137) cock and hen and five young birds covered with dirty grey down, which were taken on Sigsworth Moor, 1878. 'Tits,' (p. 130) *Russ.* Ptetzei, *birds.* Mr. Leyland, (Sep. 7th, 1881) has stuffed at Kettlewell two Kingfishers, shot there. Professor Max Müller has fulfilled his promise, (p. 141). The passage nows reads (*Ed.* 1880, Vol 2, *Lect.* 10) " The Emperor Julian, (Misopogon, init.) when he heard the Germans singing their lays on the borders of the Rhine, could compare them to nothing but the shrill cries of birds." Mr. Newbould has stuffed at Drygill, a *Greater Spotted Woodpecker,* (p. 143) shot near Pateley Bridge, (Sep. 6th, 1881). ' Ket Crow,' (p. 142) *i.e.,* ' Kite Crow,' for *Kite* means ' belly,' and *Ket* means ' offal.' This explains *Kite* the falcon.

Some further comments upon the text will be found in the Glossary.

---

## THE PATE.

The Pate, brock, or badger, which gives its name to Pateley (but see Glossary for all I know about the word), has long been quite extinct in Nidderdale and Wharfedale. Mr. John Tennant of Low Green, told me the following respecting the Pate. " Fifty five or sixty years ago, when I was a boy, Pates were common about Goldsborough and Knaresborough, and used to eat and destroy considerable quantities of corn and potatoes. We used to hunt them at night. They cannot run.very fast, on account of the difference in the lengths of their legs." There is a great difference in length, between the fore and hind legs, but I can bear witness to the fact, that in Nidderdale, several persons of undoubted intelligence credit the story, that the legs on one side, are longer than those on the other! They were formerly common in the Dales. Old John Wilkinson was living September 5th, 1881, with his wife, who was just over 92 years of age, and two months his senior, at his son's house at Heathfield. They had been married upwards of seventy years, and seemed to be enjoying a peaceful old age, after a long life's work, quite content sitting side by side on the settle, with all they wanted in each others company, though they were both too deaf to converse easily, but in other respects in full possession of all their faculties. When I asked John Wilkinson, whether he had ever killed a Fomud or a Pate, he replied, ' Aye, scoores,' and his son, himself an old man, entertained me with the following relation. " About forty years ago, I was crossin from Heathfield with fadther, to lay wait for a man that we thowt was like to be out poachin. We did not want ta cross t' brig, and, as t' Nidd was varra low, I greed to hug fadther across t' watter. When I had taken ma stockings off, and had got inta t' middle, we heard a splash, and saw something swim across t' Nidd. So I maks back, and when it got ta t' bank we saw it was a Pate, so we gave chase, and as they cannot run sa varra fast we seean catched it."

Mr. John Leyland, of Kettlewell, related to me another personal experience. " A Badger was killed at Starbotn, [Wharfedale] about forty years ago. I and two brothers all rode on one horse to see the Badger-bait. We made a tunnel about 20 or 30 feet long, with a tub at t' far end Seven or eight fox terriers tried to draw the Pate, which was killed by Roger Tattersall's dog." " Mr. Leyland also told me that the last Pates known in the district, were a family, which were all, including young ones, caught in Doubergill above twenty years since, by Frank Bentley." The ' Basons,' on page 188, are evidently Badgers, as the Yetholm Gypsies call the Badger ' Burran.'

Mr. Thorpe tells me (June 1882), " That the last Pates seen or known in Nidderdale, were a male and female, and they were killed about 28 years ago in the Tenement Wood, Fountains Earth Township, by two men named respectively Mat Nelson, and Frank Bentley. Within my recollection, I have known many Pates to have been killed at the Tenement by two brothers, Jack and Harry Blake. The Tenement was the stronghold of the Pate in Nidderdale. I also remember several Badger-baits, in the back yard of the Bay Horse Inn, Pateley Bridge."

Some works that have previously gone over part of the same ground as the present work are referred to in the course of these Studies, but the ' Northern Tour ' of Arthur Young, ' North Yorkshire,' by J. G. Baker, and ' The Danes and Norwegians in England,' by Professor Worsaae, require special notice. As regards the last, large numbers of the words and names, which the learned Professor referred to the Danish, are identical with Old Norsk words, a circumstance that may be explained by the want of the very excellent Dictionaries of that Language which we now possess.

The outline of these Studies was published in the Zoologist for September and October, 1879, under the title of " The Naturalist in Nidderdale."

# LIST OF ABBREVIATIONS.

* Published by Thos. Thorpe, Pateley Bridge.

EDITION.

*Lang.* Languedoc.

*Lye.* Saxon and Gothic Latin Dictionary. Ed. Lye, and Ow. Manning.          1782.

*C. Molbech.* Dansk Dialekt Lexicon.          1841.

Dansk Ordbog.          1859.

*Nid. Al.* Nidderdill Comic Almanac. *          1880.

*Ormul.* Ormulum. 1190. Ed. White.          1852.

*Ow.* Welsh-English Dictionary. W. Owen.          1803.

*Prompt. Parv.* Promptorium Parvulorum. (The first English Latin Dictionary).          1864.

*Riola.* How to Learn Russian. Henry Riola.          1878.

*Russ.* English Russian Dictionary. A. Aleksandrov.          1879.

*Sax. Chron.* Anglo-Saxon Chronicle, *Ed.* Ingram.          1828.

*Shakspear.* Hindustani Dictionary.

*Skeat.* Mœso-Gothic Lexicon. W. W. Skeat.

*Skin.* Etymologicon Anglicanum.

*Somn.* Dictionary Saxon-Latin-Anglicum. Gul. Somner. 1659.

*Spel.* Glossarium. Spelman.

*Stratm.* Old English Dictionary. Stratmann.

*Ulf.* Mœso-Gothic Bible of Ulfilas. (Lye and Skeat).

*W.* or *Wel.* See *Ow.*

*Wedg.* Dict. of English Etymol. Hensleigh Wedgwood. 1859.

*W. of C.* (p. 247). William of Cloudesley.

*Williams.* Sanscrit English Dictionary. Monier Williams.

* Published by Thos. Thorpe, Pateley Bridge.

# STUDIES IN NIDDERDALE.

## I.

In Yorkshire there are three well-known hills that bear the name of Whernside, all about 2000 feet in elevation. Two of these—Great Whernside, 2300 feet, and Little Whernside, 1984 feet—lie together, fourteen miles south-east of the third Whernside, which sends down feeders to the Ribble, the Lune, the Ure, and the Wharfe, on the backbone watershed* whose waters descend to the North Sea on the one side, and the Irish Channel on the other. Great and Little Whernside lie near the head waters of the Cover,—a tributary which joins the Ure near Middleham, twelve miles north-east from its source—and the Nidd, a tributary of the Ouse, which joins the main river near York, thirty-five miles south-east from its source. On the west, Great Whernside looks down upon the village of Kettlewell, in the far-famed dale of the Wharfe, and up the lovely Langstrothdale;† whilst above these, in the middle distance, looms the stupendous Pen-y-gent, having the truncated sugarloaf shape characteristic of all the millstone-grit eminences on the Pennine Chain.

This part of the valley of the Wharfe derives its beauty from being cut deeply into the mountain limestone, whose regular terraces and lines of cliffs form one of the most pleasing features

---

* The actual watershed passes to the east of Whernside.

† Pronounced "Langsterdale"—Lang *Strath*. This common Scotch word only occurs in England in the name "Langstrothdale."—J. R. D. Strath is Welsh YSTRAD a *vale, bottom*, or *valley*. It forms the names of many places in Wales—as "Ystrad Yw," "Ystrad Tywi."—(Owen.) Strath may also be contained in the name Col-ster-dale.

in the dale.   Though this limestone reappears in the valleys to the east, it is too low in their beds to give a character to the scenery.    With these exceptions all the hills and slopes are formed in the millstone-grit formation, which ranges on a huge anticlinal line from Derbyshire into Scotland.   It is this formaton that supports upon its sandstones and shales that remarkable extent of heather-covered moor and peat which occupies a belt of country, broken only by valleys, for a length of 200 miles, being in places thirty miles wide.   The line of demarcation between the vivid green grass of the limestone and the black heather-covered peat of the millstone-grit is generally as well defined as that of the formations themselves.

The basin of the Nidd above Hampsthwaite includes an area of eighty square miles ; and though some allusions will be made to the more southerly part of this area, it is the more northerly and more elevated parts that will be particularly described. For sixteen miles from Great Whernside the valley proper is nowhere more than one mile wide from ridge to ridge, and is from 500 to 800 feet deep, forming, as it were, a deep groove in the vast easterly-sloping heather-covered moorland.   South of that the valley becomes more open, the height of the surrounding hills falls, and the moors—which retreat to the west— disappear altogether on the east side.   Save for the magnificent Brimham Rocks, the valley below is tame, but by no means uninteresting.

## II.

Between the Wharfe near Otley and the Nidd below Pateley Bridge, there is a great extent of wild half-cultivated land, almost all of which has formerly been under the plough. Some of this tract is yet wild moorland, in which lies the ancient enclosure of Haverah Park, but the rest has long since been turned into grazing land. Over this and surrounding districts, farms fitted up for agriculture are now standing half ruinous, and it is no uncommon thing to see a little shed of logs, thatched with hay for the shelter of a few calves, put up in one corner of a large roofless barn built for the reception of hay and grain. Fences have been allowed to go to ruin, or gaps have been intentionally formed in them to give the herds of cattle now grazing there a larger run.

Till about fifty years ago long-horned cattle were kept in the dale. They were black-and-white, and blue.* These dun cattle

* " The horned cattle of this district may be classed under four different heads. 1.—The Short-horned kind, which principally prevail in the east side of the Riding, and are distinguishable by the names of the Durham, Holderness, or Dutch breed. 2.—The Long-horned or Craven breed, which are both bred and fed in the western parts, and also brought from the neighbouring County of Lancashire. These are a hardy sort of cattle, and constitutionally disposed to undergo the vicissitudes of a wet and precarious climate. 3.—There is another breed which appears to be a cross between the two already mentioned *and which we esteem the best of all.* A great number of milch cows of this sort are kept in Nidderdale and the adjacent county, which are both useful and handsome. They are perhaps not altogether such good milkers as the Holderness cows, but they are much hardier, and easier maintained. They are at the same time sooner made ready for the butcher, and are generally in good order and condition even when milked; and besides these, there are numerous quantities of Scotch cattle brought into the county, which beef sells higher than that of the native breed."—Agriculture of West Riding, Rob. Brown, 1799, pp. 178—179.

are now very scarce in England, but are common enough in the
dales of Norway.  A tradition of them is preserved in the sign
of " the Dun Cow,"* which is found in the mountainous parts
of the North of England.  They were replaced by shorthorns,
whose chief merit lies in the fact that in a year and a half they
will put on as much flesh as an ordinary beast will in three.  In
addition to this. they " feed " better, and grow fat on pastures
where an ordinary cow would remain poor.  For these reasons
they are well adapted for keeping for a year and a half or two
years on these moorside farms.  Since the decline of agriculture
in the dale their numbers have very much increased all along
this part of the lower slopes of the Pennine Chain, which may
truly be called the nursery of the famous breed of Yorkshire
shorthorns.  The cattle are subject to a disease which causes
them to swell up about the eyes and tail, when they are said to
be "betwenged."†

* In Mardale is a well-known " Dun Bull," familiarly called " Dunny,"
which got its name thus :—The owner and landlord were standing talking
together about what the Inn should be called, when a man came along
driving a *Dun Bull*.  This story was told me by the son (I think) of the
man in question—so that the tradition which the name carries is not
always ancient.—J. R. D.

† The Rev. J. C. Atkinson, the learned author of the Cleveland Glossary
suggests, " TENG, to sting, to affect by injected venom ;" a word which he
surmises may be " *sting* with the *s* removed."  He has " TENGED, stung.
An animal of the ox kind is liable to an affection, which by the Dales'
people is attributed to the venom of a small insect; ' a small red spider,'
*Whitby Glossary* says, 'attacking the roots of the tongue.'  The symptoms
are swelling of the parts, and copious and excessive discharge of saliva,
Tongue-tenged is the customary expression."  For the ascribed cause in
Nidderdale, see Glossary.  Remember Cleopatra's hair-pin (see Glossary
' BELLONED').  Mr. Atkinson says further, in a letter—' As for the *w* in
*betwenged* compare the parallel forms ' thwack' and ' thack' to drub or
thrash.  Your friend's " bewitched " is the old, old notion that is involved
in many a term applied to cattle ills of divers kinds—a notion neither more
nor less ' superstitious ' than that of the venomous insect, or ' small red
spider' of the Dales people in this district in connection with ' tenged ' or

Quitting the zone of cattle-grazing country we may now turn to Nidderdale proper. For the first six miles from Great Whernside the valley takes an easterly course, and both sides are marked by lines of fine escarpment—*à propos* of which it may be observed that this kind of scenery, terrace rising above terrace, which has been so faithfully depicted by Turner, is peculiar to the valleys of the Pennine Chain, not only as regards England, but Europe, as neither Norway, the Hartz, nor Switzerland show anything of the kind. To return, however—below this the valley turns to the south, after which only the eastern side continues to be steep. The margin of each terrace is frequently marked by a line of wood, but the slopes and terraces are grazing land. Nearly all the enclosed land on the sides of the dale as high as Woodale, 1000 feet, has been ploughed. It was ploughed straight up and down. No doubt this was necessary, as the slopes are so steep that heavy showers would wash away the soil.*

Agriculture has never been a complete success in the dale, and within these twenty years the last of the ploughed land in the dale north of Pateley Bridge has been " swathed." Several late harvests, and some never got at all, have the credit, locally, of having contributed to this result; but the true explanation demands a wider view. The dalesmen themselves say that oats often failed, and wheat would not ripen; but that, as oatmeal was almost their only article of food, they and their fathers were obliged to put up with bad crops and imperfect success, as they were too poor to fetch oatmeal from the better districts.

Grose quotes an ancient proverb " A famine in England begins at the horse-manger," and remarks " If oats fail, there is

' tongue-tenged.' Your own account of ' betwenged' is sufficient to prove the extreme improbability that it ever could have been a household word with that part of the folk who must have originated the term, if it ever was originated." Grose (1790) has " Teng, to teng; to sting or bite; as the bee, wasp, or adder.—North."

* See Author's remarks.--Transac. Inst. of Surveyors, Vol ix., p. 154.

generally a bad crop of every other kind of grain ; indeed, oat-meal makes a great part of the food of the poorer sort of people in the north." This was written in 1790, had it been 1880, he would have added many peers and royal personages to the list ; for a more wholesome and beneficial article of food was never vouchsafed to the human race ; nor perhaps was there ever a time when oatmeal was more in demand for porridge than it is at present.†

Though from such names as " Rye Close " one would infer that rye had once been cultivated in the dale, there has been none grown for the last eighty years, and all the old inhabitants say that they never heard of any being grown. However, in the winter of 1799-1800 wheat bread was very dear, and the inhabitants of Lofthouse fed upon rye bread.

* In the East-Riding oatmeal is not used as man's food commonly; oat-cake is unknown. This may account for the Norwegians (whose communication with England is principally by Hull) being so incredulous that the English eat oat-cake.—J. R. D.

## III.

NIDDERDALE is now one large grazing field. Not only are the young shorthorns nursed here, but vast flocks of sheep are reared on the moors. "Sheep-gates," or the right to turn sheep on to the moors, are let in specified numbers with each farm, and now it is difficult to get " gates," though thirty years ago there were not sheep enough in the dale to stock the moors. At that time they were nearly all *Scotch* wethers, now there are few Scotch wethers in the dale. Nidderdale has its own breed, formed by crossing Scotch ewes and first-rate Leicester tups, called in the dale " mugs."* (A. S. *Mug, muga, mucg,* a heap, round mass, stack, mow, in reference to the same feature that gives the name Tup. See Glossary.) The name " ram " is never used, and by many not understood. It occurs only once in the A. S. Laws—viz. :—in the Introduction to the Laws of Æthelstan.—" *an ram weorthe* iiii *peningas*." In the older laws
one ram worth 4 pence.
it was called *hrytheru*. " *Twá euld hrytheru oththe tyn wetherus*."
Two old rams or ten wethers.
—Laws of Ine., c. 70. " Wether " occurs once or twice.
" Ewe " was also an old Saxon name, but " Lamb " although a Gothic word used by Ulfilas appears to have been used by him in the general sense of *sheep*. " *Hairdeis ist lambe*."
Herder is of sheep.
John x. 2.—" Is the shepherd of the sheep ;" and, although an A. S. word occuring several times in the A. S. Bible, never appears in the A. S. Laws. Thus—" *Eowu bith mid hire geonge*
An ewe with her *young*

---

* *Scotch Ewes and Leicester Tups.* This crossing is the common mode of breeding in all the dale country. In Westmorland, about Mardale, they rear ' Herdwicks.'—J. R. D.

*sceápe scill. weorth, oth thæt feowertyn niht ófer Eastron."*—L.
*sheep* is worth a shilling, till a fortnight       after Easter.
Ine., c. 55. The result of crossing the mugs and Scotch sheep
is a sheep known as the "half-bred," with plenty of wool and
mutton—commodities largely in demand in the manufacturing
districts of Leeds and Bradford.\*

The wethers are now nearly all "half-breds" or "Nidderdale Breed," the advantage of which over the Scotch breed is
shown by the fact that when the wethers were "true Scotch"
they were kept until they were three or four "shears." Now it
is common to sell the "half-bred" at one or two "shears."
Wether mutton is the best mutton in the market. Large fortunes have been made in Yorkshire out of breeding sheep and
cattle, with a view to meeting the ever-increasing demand for
food and clothing. The true secret—successfully accomplished
by the skill of the Nidderdale farmers—is in bringing forward
your beast or your wether so as to carry the largest possible
amount of flesh, or wool in the case of sheep, in the shortest
possible time, and on the cheapest possible food, viz.:—Pasture.

There was a time when wool for clothing purposes was a
scarce article in this country. In the Laws of Ine. (A.D. 688-
728), c. 69, we read—" *Sceáp sceal gongan mid his flyse oth*
                    A sheep shall    go    with his fleece until
*midne sumor, oththe gyld thæt flys mid twam peningum."*
mid summer,    or    pay for that fleece with two    pence.

---

\* The origin of this cross is apparently contained in the following
passage of the great Agricultural Survey of 1793, p. 186. " Sheep.—The
sheep bred upon the moors in the western parts of the Riding, and which
we presume are the native breed, are horned, light in the fore-quarters,
and well made for exploring a hilly country where there is little to feed
them but peat and ling. These are generally called the Penistone breed,
from the name of the market town where they are sold. . . *We suppose
crossing ewes of this sort with a Bakewell ram would produce an excellent
breed for the low country pastures, as the Bakewell herds have usually
the properties that the Penistone wants.* There are great quantities of
Scotch sheep from Teviotdale, &c., fed in this county."

From this it would appear that Midsummer would be the time when the fleece would be at its prime, and the man who cut it before that was fined for wasting material. Again in the Laws Æthelstan (A.D. 924-940), c. 15.—"*We cwædon that nán scyld*
We command that no shield
*wyrhta ne lecge nán sceápes felle on scyld, and gif he hit do*
maker lig (lay) any sheep's skin on a shield, and if he it do
*gylde* xxx *scill.*"
let him pay 30 shill.

When sheep are to be salved or sheared they are laid on a proper frame called a "sheep-cratch" shaped like a broad ladder, and erected horizontally, one end being supported upon two legs, and the other gradually curving down till the ends rest upon the ground.

FIG. 1.

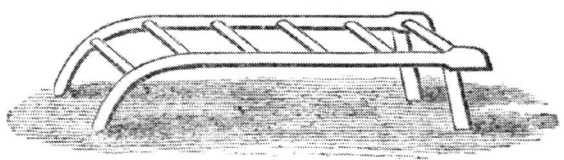

THE SHEEP-CRATCH.

All the spring and summer the sheep run on the moors, each farmer turning out as many sheep as he has "gates" for. In November the farmers near the dale-head send their sheep down to winter in Haverah Park. Two or three flocks are joined together under the charge of one man, who drives them down and remains with them all the winter, and brings them back on the approach of spring, late in March. They graze on the ling in Haverah Park, or on the sweet land that has been formerly ploughed and again "swathed." All the sheep, how-ever, do not go down. The fields in the upper parts of the dale in winter are full of sheep that have been brought down from the high moors. Though these undulating fields, with their ridges and hollows, are admirably adapted for wintering sheep, they can only accommodate a certain number ; many die

B

in cold nights, when they contract a disease known as "black-water."

In the spring the sheep feed greedily on the flowers of the moor-silk (cotton-grass), or, as it is termed in the dale, "Moss-crops and cutthroats."* Many hundreds are lost on the moor during the summer by casualties, such as falling into holes in the peat, by getting entangled in the heather, by getting bogged, and sometimes by getting drowned. At all times of the year losses occur through the sheep getting "rigged," that is laid on their backs or "riggs" in a little hollow, so that they cannot get up again without help. (See Glossary.)

These half-bred sheep possess a habit common to all animals that live among mountains, and which seems to attach to the quality of sure-footedness, viz.—that when they walk they place one fore-foot in front of the other. Even the horses that go much upon the High Fjeld in Norway acquire this habit, which keeps the animal well-balanced, and prevents it from sprawling about. The hind legs on the contrary move straight forward, so that, in the result, the animal leaves a track which has taxed the perspicacity of several of my friends during the last ten years. This track is what the shepherd hopes to find on the snow when he is searching for a missing sheep, not indeed upon the rough high moors, but upon the bents and upland pastures. Sheep are said to "rake out" when they form into a line on being first disturbed by the shepherd, and the sheep-tracks which they make walking single file are called "sheep-rakes." Danish *Rœkke* means a "row."

Sheep breeding has been practised here from the most ancient times, and it is probable that the " Scotch " or " black-faced sheep" are the descendants of the primæval British stock. I now give side by side—

* Spring is said to be "bad times" for sheep. They then feed so greedily, after winter short commons, on rark grass that they get diarrhœa, or otherwise sicken and die. I have noticed that in spring one meets with more dying, or recently dead sheep than at any other time.—J. R. D.

1.—" An ancient form of counting sheep in Nidderdale," supplied by Mr. T. Thorpe, Pateley Bridge, "which," he remarks, "you will probably be aware, are counted and sold in scores or half-scores."

2.—"Swaledale numbers," supplied by my friend Mr. J. R. Dakyns, M.A., Trinity College, Cambridge, of H. M. Geological Survey, who says " they are also used in a Knitting Song," on the authority of Mr. J. G. Goodchild, H. M. G. S.

8.—" Welsh numbers," from Owen's Welsh and English Dictionary (1803).

4.—" English numbers."

| 1 | 2 | 3 | 4 |
|---|---|---|---|
| Yain | Yahn | Un | One |
| Tain | Tayhn | Dau | Two |
| Eddero | Tether | Tri | Three |
| Peddero | Mether | Pedwar, Petwar, Ir. Cethir | Four |
| Pitts | Mimph | Pump, Pimp, Ir. Coic | Five |
| Tayter | Hithher | Cweç * | Six |
| Later | Lithher | Saith | Seven |
| Overro | Anver | Wyth | Eight |
| Coverro | Danver | Naw | Nine |
| Dix | Dic | Deg | Ten |
| Yain-dix | Yahndic | Un-ar-zeg | Eleven |
| Tain-dix | Tayhndic | Deu-ar-zeg | Twelve |
| Eddero-dix | Tetherdic | Tri-ar-zeg | Thir-teen |
| Peddero-dix | Metherdic | Pedwar-ar-zeg | Four-teen |
| Bumfitt | Mimphit or Mumphit | Pymtheg | Fif-teen |
| Yain-o-bumfitt | Yahn-a-mimphit | Un-ar-bymtheg | Six-teen |
| Tain-o-bumfitt | Tayhn-a-mimphit | Deu-ar-bymtheg | Seven-teen |
| Eddero-o-bumfitt | Tether-a-mimphit | Tri-ar-bymtheg | Eigh-teen |
| Peddero-o-bumfitt | Mether-a-mimphit | Pedwar-ar-bymtheg | Nine-teen |
| Jiggit or Giggit | Jigit | Ugain or Ugaint | Twenty |

These numbers have been handed down from generation to generation, and remain, with the exception of a few single words, the sole surviving remnant of the ancient Cymric

* Welsh " ç " is a guttural like Germ. ch., Span. x, Gr. ch.

dialect of the Pennine Chain—though those are hardly cold in their graves who spoke it fluently in Swaledale.

In times of snow, from their habit of sheltering in the hollows, sheep often become buried in the drift. When this is the case a good dog will " set " them, and, if his master is there, he will recover the sheep; but, what seems most strange, however good the dog may be, if he is alone he will be certain to worry* the sheep. None of the dogs on these moors are to be trusted when they go by themselves, as they are all—the best of them—apt to turn on the sheep. The dogs on these moors do not attain to the same perfection as they do in Scotland, probably because the runs are smaller; but many dogs are sent up to be trained here.

The capacity of the dogs for managing the sheep is very different in different individuals. Some seem to be born to the work, others would never learn. A dog must be obedient, quick at understanding, swift, strong, and able to stand the fatigue of running over the uneven ground of the heather-covered high moors. He must be able to learn to know all the hundreds of sheep under his charge individually, and to detect a stranger's, so that if two flocks get mixed, he can single out his own from the stranger's. They have to do this repeatedly on the open moors. A wave of the hand is sufficient to send a good dog long distances in search of a missing sheep.

The sheep dogs in Nidderdale are referable to four distinct varieties. One, a thin long-bodied dog, smooth-haired, black and tan, long sharp head, long tail, sometimes tall; very strong, swift, and clever. A second kind is a smaller dog, smooth, silver-grey, with dark grey blotches; always wall-eyed, light eye in lighter patch; bark snappish; barks in a skulking way, with its tail between its legs; cowardly. A third kind, handsomer than the other two, and generally larger, is a long-haired shaggy

---

* Worry—Kill (See Glossary).

dog, with a mass of long hair about the neck ; colour black and white, being black over the back and sides ; has a white ring round his neck, (whence he is generally called " Ring ") ; ears sharp, short, erect ; face short, triangular ; tail hairy. The fourth type is a noble-looking dog, rough-haired, terrier like, large ; colour dark slaty blue above, light ochreous brown below ; tan legs ; face hairy ; ears small, partly erect, then drooping ; tail large, dark above, light under ; bark loud—a good honest announcement of the presence of a stranger. Though there are some few dogs that do not fall under any of these types, by far the larger number of the sheep dogs in Nidderdale do ; and though the points of difference may appear to be trifling, they are extremely characteristic and distinctive. A great many of these dogs are imported from Scotland, a few from Craven, and elsewhere.

The following are some of the very old dog's names in the dale:—Bute (said to be for Beauty), Corby, Cort (after Corton in Craven), Crab, Craft, Daisy, Fan, Fleet, Flora, Gade, Gess (*pronounced* like guess), Glan, Harry, Houve, Jessie, Jockie (said for Jock), Jos, Laddie, Lassie, Lady, Luce, Morna or Mourner, Nell, Rake, Rap, Ring (type 3), Rock, Roy, Sam, Shep, Spot, Sprat, Sweep (type 1), Swift (type 1), Tip, Tossel, Trip, Turk, Watch, Watch 'Em, Wench, Wenny, Whip, Wily, Yarrow. Some of these are eminently suggestive of high antiquity. " Rake " probably has a Scandinavian origin, *Rakki* being the Old Norsk for a dog. We may fairly conclude that the name of " Rake " is at least 1000 years old in the dale. " Shep " may be A. S. *Scep*, a sheep, but *Seppi* is an Icelandic pet name for a dog ; or the name may, like Watch 'Em, be from the word of command—" Rak," *drive* (see Glossary.) Similarly "Hoov" is the Welsh *Hwv* (the Anglo-Saxon *Hôf*) a hood (pronounced *Hoov*), and was probably given as a name to a dog in allusion to the shape of the hair on the head, or to its colour, presenting the appearance of a hood. The word

"Hove" (a hood) was still in use in the time of Chaucer, and is, in fact, used by him in the "Canterbury Tales":—

"  .  .  .  .  .   And some deal set his hove,"—V. 3909.

The name "Hoov" may therefore be 1300 years old in the dale. Many of the others are equally interesting. Some are obviously imported from Scotland.

## I V.

It is probable that we are more dependent upon animal food than we used to be. In their early days, the present generation of dalesmen fed almost exclusively upon oatmeal ; either as "hasty pudding," that is Scotch oatmeal which has been *ground over again* so as to be nearly as fine as flour, boiled smooth and eaten while hot with milk or treacle ; or "lumpy," that is, boiled quickly and not thoroughly stirred ; or else in one of the three kinds of cake which they call "fermented," *viz.*, "riddle cake" (see Glossary), "held-on cake," or "turn-down cake," which is "made from oatcake batter poured on the bak' ston' from the ladle, and then spread with the back of the ladle. It does not rise like an oatcake." Or of a fourth kind called "clap cake." They also made "tiffany cakes" of wheaten flour, which was separated from the bran by being worked through a hair-sieve *tiffany*, or *temse*, south of England *Tammy*,* with a brush called the *Brush Shank*. Brachet refers the Fr. *Tamis* to a German origin from Dutch *Tems*, but Wedgwood takes us to the Italian and Latin—"Fr. *Tamis*, It. *Tamigio, Tamiso*, a sieve, Fr. *Estamine* the stuff tamine, also, a strainer (Cotgrave), It. *Stamigna*, a strainer made of Goat's hair, from *Stame*, Lat. *Stamen*, the fixed threads in a loom, woof, yarn"—reasoning apparently upon the words. The fact however that we have the Dutch name *Tems*, would rather indicate that the Temse came into the North of England from the Netherlands, for otherwise

* "Tommy" is a common term for food among workpeople. As the "tiffany" gave the name "tiffany-cake," so, probably, the Fr. "Tamis" may have given "Tommy-cake," shortened to "Tommy." If this be so, the name "Tommy" carries a tradition of the time when oatmeal was the principal if not the *only* article of food, and so came to mean "food" generally.—J. R. D.

we should have expected *Tammy* as in the South. Again, if the Dutch had derived their *Tems* from a French or Italian source, why should *we*, who got our *Tammy* from the French, have gone to the Dutch for our *Temse*? That is, why should we have gone to two markets for the same article, the one being the original and the other a second-hand source? It is true that the great commercial enterprise of that nation may explain the difficulty, under the light of an historical account of the invention, which I have not before me.

Stone ovens were formerly much used for baking, and a few are still in use. They are called "yewns," and are about two feet high by two feet square, vaulted, and have a square door. They are made about breast high in the wall of the comfortable room on one side of the fire-place. The gude wife burned ling in this yewn till it became quite red-hot, when she raked out the ling and put in the dough to be baked. Dough is frequently called *Doof* and I remember, when a little boy at school at Blandford, in Dorsetshire, how we all hated a hot currant bunn, which went by the elegant cognomen of *Figgy-duff*. Pardon the degression, but on our way back to Yorkshire, it may be interesting to note that on that very charming and beautiful range of hills, known as the Lower Greensands, in Surrey, stone ovens are still in use. Peat is there extensively used for fuel, and what is still more delicious, the small sticks and branches, picked up in the extensive plantations of Scotch Firs, are used as well as heather for heating the ovens. Sweet, indeed, is the fragrance of burning peat, but the scent of the pale blue smoke from the Scotch Fir boughs, with the leaves attached, is sweeter still.

The *Bakstone* was once an important thing in Nidderdale. It has given its name to several large Gills from whence they have been, and still are obtained, and that not only in Nidderdale, and the surrounding dales, but all along the Pennine chain. From Bakstone Gill, near Lofthouse, the stone is a very fine bedded soft micaceous flaggy sandstone. It will stand fire quite as well as fire-brick, which at the Dale Head is an expensive article. It is still used for lining all the limekilns, ovens, boilers, etc., and is laid horizontally. It is left thicker in the middle for baking, so as to stand the heat better. It makes sweeter cakes than iron plates. This stone is useless for any other purpose, as it shives off with frost, on account of the extreme thinness of the layers.

Mr. Atkinson cites "Hire cake bearned o' the *stàn*," from *Hali Meidenhead*, (*Ed* O. Cockayne, p. 37,) which he claims to mean hearthstone, in support of his untenable suggestion of O. N. *Bakstjàrn* as the derivation of Bak'stone. That could never have named the Gills, however, from which the Bak'stone is actually dug.

The word *Bakstrjarn*, moreover, referred to as O. N. is Icelandic, meaning "*an iron plate for baking sacramental wafers*," and occurs in an Icelandic church M.S. of the fourteenth century, called after a Bishop, *Vilkins-Màldagi*, 15. 37. This, were the other evidence less conclusive, would effectually dispose of the suggestion that Bak'stone is the result of a "transition of sound" from "the O. N. original" Bakstrjarn.

The Bakstone is still in use for baking, but has generally been supplanted by an iron plate, which retains the old name Bakstone like *iron milestones*.

It is now many centuries since the iron "bakstone" first came into use, and, indeed, I can throw no light upon the actual date at which this took place. All I know is, that Sir John Froissart in his immortal Chronicle, which is a model of patience and careful attention to details, in an account of the manners of the Scots, and how they carry on war, tells us that "in their invasions into England, they are all on horse back, except the camp followers who are on foot. The Knights and Esquires are well mounted on large bay horses," (the ancestors no doubt of the

C

now nearly extinct *Cleveland Bay*,) "the common people on little galloways," (still the commonest kind of horse in Nidderdale,) "they do not carry with them any provisions of bread or wine; for their habits of sobriety are such in time of war, that they will live for a long time on flesh half-sodden, without bread, and drink the river water without wine. They have therefore no occasion for pots or pans, for they keep the flesh of their cattle in the skins, after they have taken them off, and being sure to find plenty in the country which they invade, they carry none with them. Under the flap of his saddle each man carries a *broad plate of metal; behind the saddle, a little bag of oatmeal*; when they have eaten too much of the sodden flesh, and their stomachs appear weak and empty, *they place their plates over the fire, mix with water their oatmeal, and when the plate is heated they put a little of the paste upon it, and make a thin cake like a cracknel or biscuit*, which they eat to warm their stomachs; it is therefore, no wonder that they perform a longer day's march than other soldiers."—Cap. xviii. This was in the reign of Edward III., who was crowned A.D. 1826. The kind of cake they made was no doubt " clap-cake,"—Dan. *Klappe-bröd*, or thin cakes beaten out with the hand. Mr. Grainge points out that though the name of " clap-cake " is retained in Nidderdale, the old method of making it—from which it took its name—has been given up.*

The Bakstone, whether of stone or iron, is laid upon a frame called the Branderi, (*pron Branderee*,) which consists of four iron bars, upon two of which, a fifth, the slott bar, slides parallel to the remaining two, *Branderi* is used at and above Lofthouse, *Briggs* is the general name in the Dale. (A. S. *Brieg, Brig, Bric, Brycg, Brygc, Bryc*, a Bridge, Dan. *Brig)*. ·

* *Nidderdale*, p. 223, 1863.

FIG. 2.

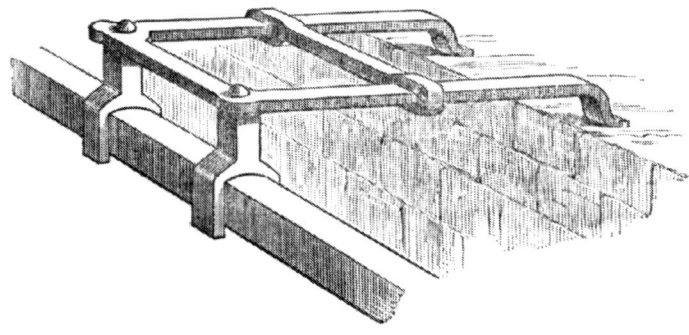

THE BRANDERI.

The Branderi is made to fit on to the fire place, so that stones or vessels of any size, by shifting the sliding bar, can be placed upon it. The Branderi is unmistakeably of Danish introduction, (Dan. *Branderi*; O.N. *Brandreith*,) and is not at all used in the south of England. It is a great addition to the open range.

There was formerly in common use a round iron pan, about 10 inches deep, and 18 inches across, with a tight fitting convex lid. It was provided with three legs. *The Kail Pot*, as it was called, was used for cooking pies. etc., and was buried bodily in burning peats. As the lower peats became red hot, they drew them from underneath and placed them on the top. The Kail pot may still be seen in use on a few farms. The name is, doubtless, from Kale a cabbage. The Kale pot was probably originally designed, and used for cooking vegetables.

The *Swape* or *Beak* is a crane over the fireplace on which hang the *Reckons*, or pieces of iron having several hooks to hang pots on. The name of Swape is Scandinavian, from *Sveipa* to sweep round, " hann *Sveipadi til Sverdinu*," he *swept round him with the sword; Sveipr*, a *Swape*, that which sweeps round, an oar,—so a long oar used for working a Keel on the Tyne is still called,—but I suspect that the Norsemen gave a new name to an article, which they found in some more primitive form, existing

in this Island at the time of their settlement, because I cannot
find that the name is used, or ever was used, for the same article
in Norway. *Beak.* the other, and probably the older name, is
Cymric or Welsh.—Beçyn a little hook, *dim.* of Baç a hook.
This carries us back to something more primitive than the
kitchen range, however antiquated ; and that is the tripod, such
as Gipsies use, made of poles meeting at about 5 or 6 feet above
the ground, and having a pot suspended from a hook above the
blazing wood fire. It also shows us that the name of Beak, a
hook, has survived the change, and like *Bakstone* has attached to
the more " civilised " substitute that took its place. Upon the
*Swape* or *Beak* hang the *Reckons*, or pot-hooks, pieces of irons
hanging down, with several hooks, one above another, to hang
pots on.

No doubt in England there were formerly plenty of houses
with a mere hole in the roof, such as I have seen in Norway and
Shetland, the roof and beams being hung with great festoons of
soot, that must have taken years to accumulate. In Shetland I
noticed that the fire was sometimes at one end of the room, and
the hole in the roof at the other, so that the smoke had to travel
all along the roof before it could find exit. This was for the sake
of creating a regular draught, the cold air sinking into the room
at one end, while the smoke rose at the other. When the hole
(as in the cases mentioned by Percy, cited below,) is directly
above the fire, the cold air sinking on to the smoke breaks the
column, and tends to dissipate the smoke, and spread it about
the house.

A tradition of this hole exists in the name *Chimler-hoal.*—In
the old Scandinavian houses the fire was in the middle of the
room, and, in fact, some of these may still be seen. One of the
oldest houses in Norway is at Valle, in Setersdal,—at least it
existed in 1870, when I went over it.—In it the fire-place was
in the middle of the room. When near the end or side however, the large flagstone stood well out in the room, so that

people could sit all round it except on the side by the wall.

The next progressive improvement was the large chimney, such as may be seen in the kitchens of many Abbeys, large enough to allow several people to sit round the fire under the chimney itself. The Chimney, as its name imparts, was introduced by the Norman French. *(Fr. Cheminée. Ital. Camminata, dim of camino;* Lat. *Caminata, dim of Caminus,*—whence also Dan. *Kamin,*—used by Vitruvius for a chimney; Gr. Káminos an oven, also *a flue.* Probably from *Kaio, Káo* to burn.—Lid. & Sc.) (Bra.)

This was shaped in its lower part like a hood, whence arose as I suppose, the name of *Hoodend,* which though still in use for " that side of the fire opposite to the yoon where there is no boiler " in modern houses, is clearly a tradition of these large hood-shaped chimneys. These chimneys were found in even very small cottages, when they had only a *but* and a *ben,* as well as in farm houses in the North of England and Scotland. The appearances of one of these cottages is thus graphically described in the little story of " Dicky and Micky Date ;"—

" They yuse ta git sat roond t' oade fire-plaise—t' father at yah side an' son at tother— · · *·coontin stars hoot o' t' chimler top fer a wager as they sat,* for it wer yan o' *thease oade fashun'd chimlers* 'ats rarely to be'y seen noo-a-days. *Ye cud see hoot o' t' top fra onny part o' t' harstan.* Doon t' chimler hang a gert chean fra t' *rannel boak* o' witch they yuse ta *hing t' poddish pan,*t' fryin pan, t' kettle, er howt else 'at wantid ayther boilin er fryin.

The name of *Rannel Boak* tells a tale. It literally means *house-beam ; Ranns, gen. sing., Ranna, gen. pl.,* of O. N. *Rann,* a house, *Bálkr,* a beam. This requires a word of explanation, as it is evident that a beam across a chimney of the kind described, would never have received the distinctive appellation of the house-beam. On the south side of the High Street in Redcar, there still stands a small white cottage. If one enters it, he will see just inside the door, some strong beams slanting at an angle from the bottom of the present outside wall, and running right up to the middle ridge of the roof. On ascending into the upper storey, a parallel series of similar beams will be seen slanting on both sides, from the base of the outside walls, up to the medial line of the roof, where they all rest *against one beam*— in sooth, the *Rannel-boak*, or *house-beam*, upon which the whole structure depends. If the upper surfaces of these slanting beams be further examined, they will be found covered with the marks of where there were formerly horizontal laths, not nailed on to them, but fastened on by wooden pegs. On these laths the roofing material, whatever it was, was laid. The structure of the house was exactly as if a span roof, were built upon the ground, without any walls except end walls—of course the present side walls are modern. On the noble and wild estate, that formerly belong to the Elwes family, in Eskdale, Cleveland, in the years 1873 to 1875, a large number of old farm houses and other buildings, most of which had fallen into a wretched state of decay, were under repair. I then saw several skeletons of these old roof-wall houses laid bare, so that it was evidently the common mode of building houses some centuries ago. In one case, the house had been for centuries an outhouse, for there was a very old farm house near it, which had been built to take its place, when it was made into an outhouse. These old beams were black with the soot and smoke of fires that had burnt beneath them, when they supported the roof-walls that sheltered the farmer and his family, before the old farm house close by was built. This proves that there was no chimney but that, in all probability, as in Shetland, the fire was at one end of the house, and the chimler *hoal* at the other. Such then was the *Rannel-boak*, or house-beam. In the little story of "Dicky an' Micky Date," it says that "they had a jackass called Jerry,"—they all three "liv'd tagether in a oade thakt buildin i' t' loanside,—Dicky an' Micky occupied t' maist o' t' buildin, *Jerry hevvin a corner tav hissen i' yah end.*" Now

I have repeatedly slept in Norway, close to the partition between the house and the lair, and heard a cow eating within a foot or two of my head. In fact the cottage here described, is precisely similar to those which are found everywhere in Norway, but especially in the *Sæters*, or high up the dales. Now this end of the house, which is inhabited by the donkey, is called in Denmark, the *Fremmers*, from *Fremrage*, to project. "The *Fremmers*," says the Rev. J. C. Atkinson, "in old fashioned country-side houses, in several parts of Denmark, was a projecting end or portion of the building (whence the name,) which contained the oven, and gave shelter to one cow, or more, beside some sheep and the fowls." "In some cases the great or cooking fire of the establishment was also in the *Fremmers*, and where this was the case, meat, salt or fresh fish, and the like, were hung *i raan*." "Dan. D. *raan, raane*, or *rân, rane, raande*, the *space below the roof* in the *Fremmers*."

Now from this Dan. *Raan*, Mr. Atkinson derives the Rannel in Rannel Boak. The question then arises, "Is *Raan* the same word as the O. N. *Rann*, differently applied? or is it a different word? The oldest form in which we find the word *Rann*, is the Goth. *Razn* a house, but especially a ceiling, a roof *(Lye)* a structure, an edifice, something erected, that which is raised, probably a corruption of the *part. pass. Raisgans?* of Goth. *Raisgan*, to raise. This passed into A. S., in the forms, *Ræsen, Ræsn*, a *covering, roof, ceiling*, also, according to Somner, *a beam in a roof or ceiling*, or in fact *Rannel-boak*. The word did not survive in English, as the word "roof" proved the stronger of the two. In O. N., as in A. S., it was a borrowed word from the Gothic, but it here underwent a marked change. Instead of *Razn*, it became *Rann*, of which Cleasby remarks, "the assimilation of *zn* or *sn*, into *nn*, is peculiar to the Scandinavian language." Not being a word of native growth, this word had little more life in Icelandic than in A. S., only remaining now as a poetic word. In Dan. instead of *Rann*,

*Razn* appears to have beome *Raan*, and in this case to have never grown in meaning beyond its first sense of *roof*. Thus the two derivations are in reality one, but I believe the immediate source of the Rannel Boak in the English Dialect, to be the O. N. *Rann*, because of the association with the O. N. *Bálkr*, a beam.

To return, however, after this long digression upon *t' Rannel-boak*, to the chimneys and fires in the farm-houses of the North of England and Scotland.   When that witty libertine, King James V. of Scotland, (who died December 13th, 1542, aged 33,) had successfully accomplished an unusually audacious feat of gallantry with a country lass, under the disguise of a travelling tinker, he immortalized the scandalous event in a rich little ballad entitled " *The Gaberlunzie Man*."   He called at a farm house, wi' monny " Good eens,"

> " Saying, ' Gud-wife for your courtesie,
>     Will ye lodge a silly poor man ? '
> The night was cauld, the carle was wat,
> And down *ayont the ingle* he sat."

Now upon this Percy has the following note :—" Ayont the ingle, beyond the fire,"—(see sketch of Ling Hall,)—" *the fire was in the middle of the room*.   In the west of Scotland, at this present time, in many cottages they pile their peats and turfs upon stones in the middle of the room.   There is a hole above the fire, in the ridge of the house, to let the smoke out at.   In some places are cottage houses from the front of which *a very wide chimney projects like a bow window;* the fire is in a grate like a malt kiln grate, round which the people sit, sometimes they draw this grate into the middle of the room.—*Mr. Lambe.*"

Here we have another form of *Hood*, which name we will leave with the remark that *Hood end* meant no doubt originally the Hood end of the *Langsettle*, which stood out at right angles to the wall.

Such were some of the older forms of fire-places and chimneys in respect of which, several highly interesting existing names, of modern appliances, were originally given. We will now continue our account of this part of the subject, as it at present exists.

The *pore*, *tengs*, and *showl*,—poker, tongs, and shovel,— complete the furniture of the fire-place. We appear to be indebted to the Dutch for our pokers, or at least for the name of the process, Dut. *poken* to poke. For tengs we may thank the Scandinavians, with a strong probability that we are not giving them more than their due, for *Tengs* is the Swed. *Täng.* and *Tongs* is the O. N. *Taung, Töng*, Dan. *Tang*, meaning *tied together*, from O. N. *Tengja* to tie or fasten together,—originally with bands of pliable wood, ash or hazel, as we see in any smithy to-day. In one corner stands the creel (O. N. *Krili* a basket,) full of " peats." At one side of the fire stands the *Langsettle*, *settle*, or " squab." Settle is the A. S. *Setl, Settl, Setel, Setol; Sedel, Sedl, Gesetl*, a settle, bench, stool, but *Squab* although now synonymous with *Settle*, was originally a *stuffed cushion*. Formerly when beef was killed it was hung to dry on a frame called the *beef-case*, shaped like a ladder with broad steps. The beef-case was hung horizontally on the ceiling above the fire-place. Ling Hall was about the last house in the dale in which the old style was to be seen,—as late as Christmas, 1871—at which date I heard that the venerable occupants were under notice to quit, and the house was to be pulled down. Ling Hall was one of the last of the old cottage farms, and it so happened that my kind landlord, at Lofthouse, supplied the household with milk. Knowing the interest I took in all matters connected with Nidderdale, and in everything and everybody in the dale, he offered one night, shortly before Christmas, to introduce me. The snow was thick on the ground at the time, and had been lying about three weeks. Between six and seven o'clock in the evening we walked up from Lofthouse, by the light of the snow, and a lantern. Ling Hall was a very small house, and not in itself so interesting as many older ones in the dale. But on

D

entering, had I been shown straight in to the presence of the
Great Mogul, I could not have felt more awe struck. There was
no light in the house but that of the peat fire, which was burning upon a flag-stone that stood well out in the room. The
night was a very dark one, and the general impression was that
of entering a wood shed in the dark in which a man was lighting
a pipe. When my eyes had become accustomed to the weird and
lurid light, I was aware of two venerable Dames, bent nearly
double with age, and resting with both hands upon high sticks
with crooked handles. On their heads they wore high caps,
having an enormous frill over the top of the head, and rising
behind into a very tall rounded peak. They wore short waisted
dresses, and short skirts. " Ayont the ingle " I also conjectured
that there was some one to whom a pair of thin legs, in tight
fitting breeches and leather gaiters, belonged, visible close to the
fire. On perceiving us a thin old gentleman roused himself, and
bent forward close to the fire to inspect me. There was no
modern humbug in that face—true as steel, and as straight as an
arrow, was written on every line of it. 'Strangers not admitted,'
could not have been more plainly seen had it been painted up in
large white letters, but my landlord having introduced me as
" My friend, Mr. Lucas," the old people gave me a very cordial
reception. I now observed that the old Dames leaned upon their
sticks in a particular manner, which I will be careful to describe.
The right hand rested upon the handle, and the left grasped the
stick about eight inches lower down.

On the ceiling, which was not ceiled by the way, hung the
*fleak*, loaded with fresh made oat-cake, and over the fire was the
*beef-case*.

Wooden spoons are not used at all, at or above Lofthouse.
They use a flat piece of wood called a *Thivel* or Spurtel, for
stirring *Gwl*, or *Hasty Pudding*, and a small round Thivel for
stirring cream. The *Thivel*, or *Thithel*, is of A. S. origin,
from *Thyfel* a shrub, thorn, *Thythel* a bush, bough, branch ;

so is *Spyrtle*, A. S. *Sprytls* a stick, a sprout ; A. S. *Sprytan* to sprout.

There was formerly in use in Nidderdale a *Rush Stand*, originally made by splitting a stick, and in fact this sort of rush-stand was in use down to the time when the farmers gave up making their own candles. An important kind was made of iron, with a spring to compress the holder upon the candle. Of this kind, I give a sketch, which I made of one belonging to Mrs. Ryder, of Middlesmoor.

FIG. 3.

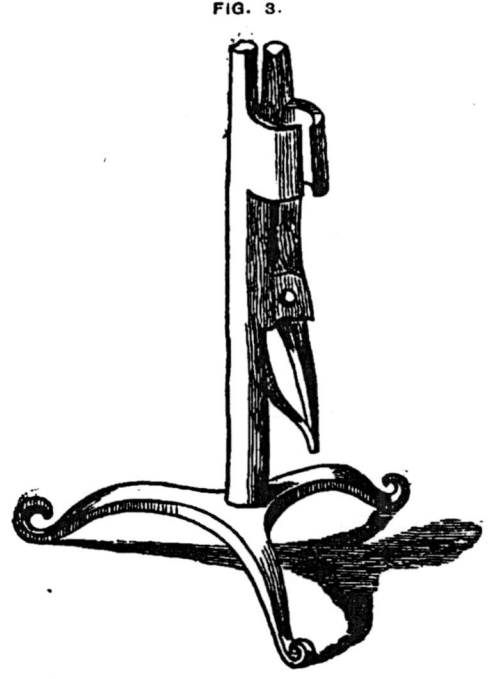

THE RUSH STAND.

The seaves were gathered at certain places on the moors by parties of gatherers, who went out to get them—in the autumn, or late in summer. They chose the largest and strongest, from which they stripped off the outer skin; so as to enable the

tissues to imbibe the melted fat into which they were dipped.*
As the same places were visited year after year, they were
known by names, such as "Fleet Seaves," "Seavy Hill,"
"Seavy Whan," "Seaves," etc.

The *Bukker, Bink* or *Binch*, is a large flagstone " which is
leant against the side of a wall," and is used to "bray" sand upon
for floors. The name *Bukker* (*pron.* Booker) is here misapplied,
as it properly belongs to the instrument with which the sand is
brayed. Swed. *Bokare*, a *breaker, Boka*, to bray sand—whence
Fr. *Bocarder*. It is probably from *Bok*, beech, the original
Bukker being a beech stump, from its hardness. Brocket gives
'*Bucker*, an iron instrument with a wooden handle, used in the
country to bray sand with.' In this we see the beechen stump
shod with iron. Bink or Binch, first meant a *mound*,
*Knob*, then a *seat, bed*, then that of which the seat was made.
Thus O. N. *Bingr*, a heap of corn, bed, bolster ; Swed.
*Binge*, a heap, and Dan. *Banke*, a bank, hillock, are natural
seats ; A. S. *Benc*, O. N. *Bekkr*, Dan. *Bænk*, a bench,
binch (flagstones,) artificial ones. This gives the name to
*Binks* Wood, where they are, or have been dug.

Wooden floors have to a great extent replaced the old stone
floors, so that the Bink, or Bukker, is not so much used as
formerly. Wooden floors are washed, but stone floors were
at one time never washed; they were merely sanded, and the
sand swept away.

In the dairy department, there is the *kern*, (O. N. *Kirna*, a
churn,) now a revolving barrel or tub, on a horizontal axis ; the
*sile*, (O. N. *Sahl* a sieve,) and *Sine*, (A. S. *Sihan*, to strain
[through a *Sihan ?*], O. N., *Sia* a sieve, for *Siva* or *Sifa* a sieve.
*Sine* is A. S., probably, from the *pron.*) and the "lile roond
thithel" for stirring cream. Last, but not least, the *blake* butter.

* The Gipsies strip off two opposite sides, leaving the alternate ones to
support the pith.

A cheese press is still used in the upper part of the dale, which consists of two uprights fixed in the ground, and joined at the top by a crossbar. One third of the way up, is a shelf, on which the cheese to be pressed is placed. Above this there is an arrangement of handles for raising a heavy stone, or lowering the same, so as to press the cheese, as shown in the figure. A is a wooden peg for holding down the handle, so as to raise the stone weight, when the cheese is being put in or taken out.

FIG. 4.

THE CHEESE PRESS.

## V.

## THE FARM.

Ah've tell'd ye summat aboot t' hoose, noo ah'se boon ta tak ye'y roond t' farm.  First,—t' *Garth, (yard)*,—leak ! tharr's t' last *cletch* o' chickens, (O. N. *Klekja* to *hatch*,) call them, " chuck, chuck, chuck, *(pron. chook, chook, chook,)* and they come running, all but the *reckling*, pooer lile thing, its nobbut wa'ak.  (O. N. *Reklingr* an outcast).  Thats t' lang stee (O. N. *Stigi*, a ladder) 'ats reear'd up agean t' coo hoose (*mistal*) tharr. It hez yah stower, (O. N. *Staurr* a pale stake,) an' twa rungs (O. N. *Röng)* brokkan, t' oade meear gav it a gert *kelk* (O. N. *Kelk*, a kick, found in compos.,) as she'y wor passin.  I can make nothing of *Mistal*, if it be not O. N. *Myki*, dung ; Dan. *Mög* ; Germ. *Mist*, dung,—in fact it looks more like a German word—and O. N. *Stallr* ; Dan. *Stald;* Germ. *Stall*, *;* stall, stable,—Dung stall.*

From the stable comes a sound as of ʃ *reasted* (a *stupid* horse that won't draw or work) horse, and a voice says, "Hod t' still er ah'le gie the' a *twanck*," (the whip, A. S. *Thwang*, a thong.) Tharr's t' oade gallowa' see ye, they're *fettlin* it (O. N· *Fetill;* A. S. *Fetel,)* ta gan ta t' station.  Lisan at yon *coaf*, (O. N. *Kálfr)* hoo it bawls, lets gan ta t' lair, (O. N. *Leir*, clay, originally a clay building) an' hev a leak at it, fer its a grand 'in.  " Trunnel t' *coop-barrow* hoot o' t' road John William.  Mally, we want ta lewk at t' *coaf*."  " Why'a, wait wal ah've dun *milkin*, an' then,"

* I find that Atk. Cl. Gl. conceives the same idea, but refers it to A. S. *theox*, *myx*, *mix*, dung, and *stæl*, *steal*, *stall*, stable, stall.  It is, however, very much a north country word, on which account, I prefer to refer it as above.

(O. N. *Mjólka* to milk.) " D'ye hear Mally's *clogs*, hoo they clatter when she'y walks," (Welsh *Clog* ). "Hev ye'y nearly dun Mally ? " " Ah'se naain far off, ah,ve gitten *tweu skeels* full, ah've nobbut t' 'umal'd coo to strip an' then ah've dun." (A. S. *Tweo*, *Tŵio*, two.) (O. N. *Skjóla* a pail). " Wa'ahs brokkan t' *beild*, lass ? " " Nay ah dewnt knaw ah'se sewer, its nut me ah knaw." (Welsh *Beiliad* ). There you see the *Redstake*, (prob. A. S. *Wræd*, a wreath, band, tie,—see Gloss.) in the *Bewse*, (A. S. *Bos*) to which the *Kye* (A. S. *Cy*, cows) are fastened ; and, round the beasts' necks, the *Coo-bow* ; (O. N. *Bogi*, bow) a large horseshoe-shaped wooden collar, generally of ash, to fasten cows up by, to the *Redstake* in the *Bewse*. The two ends hang downwards, and are joined by a crosspiece of wood, with a knob at either end, by which it catches, and remains fastened by the elasticity of the bow. Sometimes, instead of a piece of wood, a loop of hazel bough is made to fasten the ends together.

When the *Kye* are feeding up i' t' *Far Pastoor*,* (O. Fr. Pasture) they are milked at the *High Lathe*, (O. N. *Hlatha)* and as that is some 600 feet above the house, and a mile or more *fra heeam*, (Dan. *Fra*, from, *hjem*, *hiem*, home,) he takes the *Backcan*, or Budget, a large oval tin can, with a tight-fitting lid, which is carried on the back, fastened on with straps, like a knapsack, exactly the same as may be seen in Norway, except those are of wood as these formerly were. Are you looking at that stick hanging there ? that is the *Beast-stang* (O. N. *Stöng*, gen. Stangar, Dan. *Stang*,) which is thrust through the hind legs of calves when they are killed, to hang them up by. Mind in turning round that you do not trip over the end of the *Sheep-cratch*, (O. N. *Kraki* a looped and branched stem ; used as a staircase in Icel.) Some people call it the *pig cambril*, (O. Fr. *Cambré*, curved) because pigs are killed upon it. Now you shall see the *Stack-garth*, (O. N. *Stakk-gardr)*. That *Helm* (O. N,

---

* Pastoor above Lofthouse, lower down, Paster.

*Helma*, straw, *Hjálmr*, a barn ; A. S. *Healm*, straw, *Hælm*, a shed) wants fresh *thack*, (O. N. *Thak*, ͂thatch) but we sa'ant be able to get at it till t' back end o' t' week, as t' barns (O. N. *Barn*, a man) are agate making new *limmers* (O. N. *Limir*) for hooer *conveyance*, and some new *sealh* (A. S. *Sealh*. willow) shafts for t' *fleäing spades*. There in the *toft*, (O. N. *Topt*, *Toft ;* A. S. *Toft*, home field) are the *hogs*, (*hog*, a lamb a year old, cp. Wel. *Hogen*, *Hogyn*, in Glossary)—sum of thease *Hogs* er worth £2 or mair—and sum *Stirks* (A. S. *Styre*, *Stire)* o' wer awn breedin. That *Stott Stirk* (Dan. *Stud*, an ox) hez just been seld for 1000 guineas ta gan tav America, and thease *Heifer Stirks* are worth £600 apiece.* It t' clooase yonder ye'll see wer oade *Mugs*, (Leicester Tcäps) we've maaide a deär streight into t' ship'n for 'em.

Noo if yer nut tired, ah'le tak ye doon ta t' *Parks*, ta see hooer *Stags*. (A. S. *Pearruc*, a parruck, paddock, enclosure,) (*Stag*, a colt. O. N. *Steggr, prop.* a mounter, from *Stiga*, to mount ; the application is obvious.) Ye see its varra *banky* i' this countrie. We can ayther gan doon to t' *beck* an' ower t' lo' brig, or cross *a lile bit hisher up t' daal* be'y t' hippins, but ah doot it'll be runnin ower t' steeans ; if it is, we can gan up o' this side be'y t' *Intaks* an' ower t' bank top, ta t' new Intak. (O. N. Inn-tak, that which is taken in, Dan. *Indtage*, to take in.) Its nobbut lately *swathed*, we lime'd it weel, but ah doot it'll mak a pooer *gersin field ;* it lewks sa *benty*. Will ye gan be'y t' beck ? Varra weel, then we'll gan doon through t' *Hee Boon*, an' t' *Low Boon*, (? Dan. *Bund*, a meadow, *bottom*, as I do not see how to explain it by the *Boonservice ;* moreover it appears to me that the latter word proceeds from the former— as the *alms* in the old ecclesiastical sense proceeded from *helm*.) and then be'y t' carrs an' alang t' *breah* top, (A. S. *Breah*, the broken bank of a river) doon through t' *Nar Sleets*, (Nar, near,

---

* The prices here quoted are no fable, I am reciting an actual experience.

O. N. *Slétta*, a level field) ta t' *Wath*, aboon t' Lo' Holm.
(A. S. Wath, a way, O. N. Vath, a ford.) A Holm is a flat
meadow by a river, especially a small one, isolated from other
fields by the sides of the valley approaching each other, and
being steep and wooded on both sides to the River, so as to nip
out the Holm at both ends. (O. N. *Hólmr*, Dan. *Holm*.) Its
varra *slape*, (O. N. *Sleipr* slippery,) tharrs sa mitch rain o' t' *Fog*,
(Welsh *Fwg*, O. N. *Fok*. Fog in Nidderdale is the young grass
that springs up after a field has been mowed, the aftermath,)
it maks it *blashy* as weel, tharrs been sa mitch pelsh lately.
I mun cut a *grip* doon this *croft*, (A. S. *Grep* a furrow;
A. S. *Croft* a small enclosed field). This *hoose* (O. N. *Hús*
a house) is whar me'y *hind bides*, (O. N. *Hine Hina* a servant;
A. S. *Bidan* to remain). Thar he cums wi' t' *lea*," (O. N. *Lé*
a scythe, a large heavy scythe with a straight handle, and
blade flat with the handle, unlike those of the south, which
are smaller, and the blade is turned at an angle. The mode
of using the lea is quite different from that of mowing with
a south country scythe. Instead of being able to work himself into an even swing, taking short steps, the mower with the
lea takes a gigantic stride, and as he does so, bends down very
far forward, at the same time taking in a far larger sweep than
is possible with the south country scythe. It has the appearance
of being far more laborious, than mowing with the common
scythe, as the mower stops between each sweep, and has to raise
himself upright to make a fresh start for every stroke. In
addition to this there is no quick " recover " with the lea, which
is too heavy for that, and at the end of the stroke has to be
pulled back *towards the mower* after a check, and then carried by
a fresh effort over into position to commence the next sweep.
Nevertheless, those who are used to it do formidable work with
it, but I cannot say by which method a given area of *gers* could
be cut quickest.) " Tharrs t' oade stud meeare asleep, ah reckon.
Coa-up, coa-up, oade woman; coa-up, den, me'y lass! What

E

deead! Deng my buttons if she'y hezzant torfled i' t' neet. She'ys ben a rare gud meeare fer me i' her time. Bud noo we mun gan heeame, fer ye'le be tired, ah've na'ah doot."

My thanks are due to Mr. T. Thorpe for revising this chapter, and making the spelling of all words, and orthography, to agree with the usages of the Dale.

We have had occasion to mention the word Park. Brachet says : " The word Park is from Lat. *Parcus.*" This is a common mistake. Wedgwood gives, apparently in no methodical order, " Fr. *Parc* enclosure, sheepfold, fishpond ; Dan. *Fisk-park*, a fishpond ; It. *Parco*, A. S. *Pearroc*, O. H. G. *Pferrich*, Germ. *Pferch*, park, enclosure ; Bret. *Park* an enclosed field ; Lang. *Parghe*, a fold for cattle ; *Parga*, *Parghejha*, to fold cattle on the ground,"—omitting W. *Parc.* Wilkins,— referring to the various forms of the word,— in his Glossary to the A. S. Laws, observes under *Parcus*, " omnia a Sax. *Pearruc* fluentia ;" but under the word *Pundbrece*, he says " Aut a Gallor. *Parc* aut a Sax. *Pearruc*, *Parcum* vocabamus." " We took the word Park either from the Welsh Parc, or from the Saxon Pearruc." Park in Coverdale and Wensleydale is an enclosure, field *for horses*, and this, I doubt not, is the original meaning of the word. The O. H. G. *Pferrich*, *Pharrich*, M. H. G. *Pferrich*, *Perche*, (*Gottes*) *Pfirch*, *Parche*, and Eng. *Paddock* (*P(f)addock*) are evidently the same word ; *Paddock* being a corruption of a form [*Pferdich?*] represented by the mod. Germ. *Pferdisch*, relating to horses, from *Pferd* a horse. [*Pferdich?*] changed into *Pferrich* in Germ., *Contr. Pferch*, gave the parallel A. S. form *p(e)arroc* contr. *parroc*, *park*, so that we have in English, side by side, the two forms, *paddock* and *park*, proceeding from the same word, meaning "*for, or belonging to horses.*" It was so used in the Germanic Laws :—' " Qui gregem *equarum* (a troop of horses) in *parco* furatus fuerit ' says the Lex Bajuwariorum,—a passage which Brachet actually quotes against himself. All the other forms proceed from the

O. H. G. From meaning simply an enclosure for horses, *park* came to mean enclosures of various kinds ; and because the boundary was frequently a *bank of earth*, so it even came to mean a *fishpond*, which was made by throwing a bank of earth across a valley. Cowell says : " Parcus autem est locus ad ferarum custodiam *palis aut alitei circumseptus*."—" A park is a place for keeping deer in, surrounded by palings, or some other kind of fence." The only other kind of fence possible formerly was an earth bank, probably between two ditches, a cam-fence.

" Bedrifon    hie  on ænne *pearruc*."—Sax. Chron. Anno. 918.

They drove them into  one      park

" On thisum lytlum *pearroce*."—Boet, 18. 2.

in     this      little   enclosure.

———:o:———

*The chapter of the Farm would be incomplete without an Abstract of an elaborate Paper on*

## SHEEPSCORING NUMERALS ;

*By the Rev. T. Ellwood, B.A., Rector of Torver, Coniston.*

I was not aware until long after the earlier part of these Studies were printed off that the subject of sheepscoring numerals had been previously treated. However, in two able papers upon the subject, read before the Cumberland and Westmorland Antiq. Society, by the Rev. T. Ellwood, B.A., Rector of Torver, the author gives no less than fifteen different versions of the same numbers, three of which are from North America, having been formerly used by North American Indians, who learned them from early English, or Welsh Settlers. Mr. Ellwood points out that the numerals " run in pentads," or sets of five, and refers this to the primitive method of counting upon the fingers. He then shows that in only one of the divisions of the Celtic speech, the Cymric, and in only the Welsh dialect of the Cymric " do the numerals proceed by fives up to twenty. In all the other systems sixteen is represented by 10+6. In the Welsh there is a separate word *pymtheg* for fifteen, and then it proceeds *un-ar-bymtheg*, &c., differently from all the other Celtic systems ; and in this it exactly corresponds with the numerals of the Lake Districts. They have *bumfit* for fifteen, and *yen-a-bumfit* for sixteen, &c. Now this *ar* of the Welsh, according to Pugh's Welsh Grammar, means *over*, or *in 'excess of*, . . . . and thus *yen-a-bumfit* means *one over fifteen*. But *bymtheg*, or *bumfit*, is really itself a composite word, and is made up of *pimp*, or *pump*, = 5 and *dec* = 10, so that *yen-a-bumfit* really means 1 in excess of 5 + 10, &c."

It is most rarely that leave is so readily accorded to make the fullest use of published matter, as that most generously given to me by the Rev. Mr. Ellwood, in reference to his valuable and widely known paper. Unfortunately I had not the opportunity of communicating with the other gentlemen, from whom Mr. Ellwood derived part of his materials. Their names are mentioned herein, and to each and all of them—but particularly to Mr. Ellwood—I acknowledge the fullest obligations for the greater part of the following Table, in which all the versions are brought together under the eye.

NOTE.—"Ever since the publication of my paper on the Sheepscoring numerals I have continued to receive information on the subject, which tends to confirm the opinion that they are not a recent importation into the northern districts in which they are found, but have come down orally from time immemorial. The many cognate Celtic names of places in those same districts form an additional testimony to this. The missing link, however, in the chain of evidence was whether any Celtic dialect had ever been spoken in any of those secluded districts of Yorkshire and Lakeland, in which the numerals have been found. In looking over the proofs of the present volume of Mr. Lucas, I find this question answered, as I thought, in a convincing manner. He says that in one of the valleys of Yorkshire "they are hardly cold in their graves who spoke such a dialect." This being the case, the numerals are I think the relics of a language formerly spoken in the Celtic kingdom, which occupied these parts, and which is generally known as the kingdom of Strathclyde."—Rev. T. Ellwood.

| | 1 Sanscrit. | 2 Hindustani. | 3 Gipsy. | 4 Old Welsh. | 5 Modern Welsh. | 6 Breton. |
|---|---|---|---|---|---|---|
| 1 | Eka | Ek | Yek | Un | Uu | Unan |
| 2 | Dui | Du | Dui | Dau, Dou, *Fem.* Teir | Dau Dni Dan | Daou, *Fem.* Diou |
| 3 | Tri | Trin | Drin, Trin | Tri, *Fem.* Teir | Tri | Tri, *Fem.* Teir |
| 4 | C'atur | Char | Stor | Petuar *or* Pedwar, *Fem.* Peteir | Pedwar | Pevar Peder |
| 5 | Pancan | Panch, panj | Pauge *or* Spange | Pump, Pimp | Pump | Pemp |
| 6 | S'as | Tscho, Chaye | Tscho, Shove | Chwech | Cweç | Choueoh |
| 7 | Saptan | Sat, Saath | Efta | Saith, Seith | Saith | Seiz |
| 8 | Astan | Aute, Aoth | Octo | Wyth | Wyth | Eiz |
| 9 | Navan | Noh, Nu | Enia *or* Henya | Naw, Nau | Naw | Nao |
| 10 | Dasan | Des, Das | Desh, Des | Deg, Dec | Deg | Dek |
| 11 | Ekadasan | Ekadashi | Desh-a-yek | Un ar-dec | Unarzeg | Unnek |
| 12 | Dvadasan | Dwadash | Etc. | Deudec | Deuarzeg | Daouzek |
| 13 | Tray-o-dasan | Tray-o-dash | | Triardeo | Triarzeg | Trizete |
| 14 | Tchatur-dasan | Chaturdash | | Petuarardec | Pedwararzeg | Pavarzek |
| 15 | Pantsch-a-dasan | Panchdah | | Pymthec | Pymtheg | Pemzek |
| 16 | Sho-dasan | Sho-dash | | Un-ar-pymthec | Unarbymtheg | Chouezek |
| 17 | Sapta-dasan | Satrah *or* Sattarah | | Deu ar pymtheo | Deuarbymtheg | Seitek |
| 18 | Ashta-dasan | Hazhdah | | Tri ar pymtheg | Triarbymtheg | Triouech |
| 19 | Nava-dasan | | | Petnar ar pymtheg | Pedwararbymtheg | Naoutek |
| 20 | Vinsati | Bjs | Besch | Ucent | Ugain *or* Ugaint | Ugent |

| 7 | 8 | 9 | 10 | 11 | 12 |
|---|---|---|---|---|---|
| Cornish. | Manx. | Knaresborough, Yorkshire. | Nidderdale. | Swaledale. | Kirkby Stephen, Westmorland. |
| Un, onen | Unnane | Yah | Yain | Yahn | Yaan· |
| Dean | Jees | Tiah | Tain | Tayhn | Tyaan· |
| Tre, Trei | Three | Tethera | Eddero | Tether | Thed'·ere |
| Peswere | Kiare | Methera | Peddero | Mether | Maed'·ere |
| Pemp, Pymp | Queig | Pip | Pitts | Mimph | Mimp |
| Huik | Shey | Seezar | Tayter | Hithher | Hai·tes |
| Seith | Shiaght | Leezar | Later | Lithher | Sai·tes |
| Eath | Hoght | Cattera | Overo | Anver | Hao·ves |
| Nau | Nuy | Horns | Coverro | Danver | Dao·ves |
| Deg, Dek | Jeigh | Dick | Dix | Dic | Dik |
| Ednack or Uznack | | Yah-dick | Yain-dix | Yahndic | Yaan·edik |
| Dewthek | | Tiah-dick | Tain-dix | Tayhndic | Tya·n·edik |
| Tardhuk or Trethnk | | Tether-a-dick | Eddero-dix | Tetherdic | Taed·eredik |
| Peswrthack | | Mether-a-dick | Peddero-dix | Metherdic | Maed·eredik |
| Pymthek | | Bumper | Bumfitt | Mimphit or Mumphit | Boon, Buom, Baum |
| Huetag or Whettak | | Yah-de-bumper | Yain-o-bumfitt | Yahn-a-mimphit | Yaan·eboon |
| Seitag or Seytek | | Tiah-de-bumper | Tain-o-bumfitt | Tayhn-a-mimphit | Tyaan·eboon |
| Eatag or Eythek | | Tether-de-bumper | Eddero-o-bumfitt | Tether-a-mimphit | Taedere·boon |
| Nawnzack, Naunthek | | Mether-de-bumper | Peddero-o-bumfitt | Mether-a-mimphit | Maelere·boon |
| Igans or Ugens | | Jigger | Jiggit or Giggit | Jigit | Buom·fit or Buum·fit |

| 13 | 14 | 15 | 16 | 17 | 18 |
|---|---|---|---|---|---|
| Middleton, Teesdale, Durham. | Coniston, High Furness. | Borrowdale, Keswick. | Millom, Cumberland. | Eskdale, Cumberland (Foot of Scawfell). | Wasdale Head, Cumberland. |
| Yan | Yan | Yan | Aina | Yaena | Yen |
| Tean | Taen | Tyan | Peina | Taena | Taen |
| Tether | Tedderte | Tethera | Para | Teddera | Tudder |
| Mether | Medderte | Methera | Peddera | Meddera | Anudder |
| Pip | Pimp | Pimp | Pimp | Pimp | Nimph |
| Sezar | Haata | Sethera | Ithy | Hofa | |
| Azar | Slaata | Lethera | Mithy | Lofa | |
| Catrah | Lowra | Hovera | Owera | Seckera | |
| Horna | Dowra | Dovera | Lowera | Leckera | |
| Dik | Dick | Dick | Dig | Dec | |
| Yan-a-dik | Yan-a-dick | Yan-a-dick | Ain-a-dig | Yaen-a-dec | |
| Tean-a-dik | Taen-a-dick | Tyan-a-dick | Pein-a-dig | Taen-a-dee | |
| Tether-a-dik | Tedder-a-dick | Tether-a-dick | Par-a-dig | Tedder-a-dec | |
| Mether-a-dik | Medder-a-dick | Mether-a-dick | Pedder-a-dig | Medder-a-dec | |
| Bumfit | Mimph | Bumfit | Bumfit | Bumfit | |
| Yan-a-bum | Yan-a-mimph | Yan-a-bumfit | Ain-a-bumfit | Yaen-a-bumfit | |
| Tean-a-bum | Taen-a-mimph | Tyan-a-bumfit | Pein-a-bumfit | Taen-a-bumfit | |
| Tether-a-bum | Tedder-a-mimph | Tether-a-bumfit | Par-a-bumfit | Tedder-a-bumfit | |
| Mether-a-bum | Medder-a-mimp | Mether-a-bumfit | Pedder-a-bumfit | Medder-a-bumfit | |
| Jiggit | Gigget | Giggot | Giggy | Giggot | |

| 19 | 20 | 21 | 22 | 23 |
|---|---|---|---|---|
| W. Browne, Esqre., Tallentire Hall, (Collected by). | Epping, Essex. | Maine. | Hebron, Connecticut. | Cincinnati, Ohio. |
| Ein | In | Een | Een | Een |
| Tein | Tin | Teen | Teen | Teen |
| Tethera | Tethera | Tother | Tudhur | Tother |
| Wethera | Fethera | Fither | Fedhur | Feather |
| Pimp | Fip | Pimp | Pip | Fib |
| Hatus | Lethera | Een-pimp | Sat | Soter |
| Latus | Methera | Teen-pimp | Latta | Loter |
| Sour | Co | Tother-pimp | Poal | Poter |
| Dowr | Debera | Fither-pimp | Defri | Debber |
| Dics or Dix | Dick | Gleeget | Dik | Dick |
| Ein-a-dic | In-dick | Een-gleeget | Een-dik | Een-dick |
| Tein-a-dic | Tin-dick | Teen-gleeget | Teen-dik | Teen-dick |
| Tethera-a-dic | Tether-a-dick | Tother-gleeget | Tudher-dik | Tother-dick |
| Wethera-a-dic | Lether-a-dick | Fither-gleeget | Fedhur-dik | Feather-dick |
| Bumfit | Bumfit | Bumfra | Bungki | Fib-dick |
| Ein-a-boon | In-a-bumfit | Een-bumfra | Een-bungki | Een-bumpteg |
| Tein-a-boon | Tin-a-bumfit | Teen-bumfra | Teen-bungki | Teen-bumpteg |
| Tether-a-boon | Lether-a-bumfit | Tother-bumfra | Tudhur-bungki | Tother-bumpteg |
| Wether-a-boon | Mether-a-bumfit | Fither-bumfra | Fedhur-bungki | Feather-bumpteg |
| Jiget or Giget | Gigot | Frith-en-y | Gigit | Unick |

## Notes to Tables of Sheepscoring Numerals.

COLUMN 1, up to 10; COLS. 4, 6, 7, 8, 9, and 12—20, or fifteen out of the twenty columns are taken from Mr. Ellwood's Paper.

COL. 2 is from Forbes's Hindustani Dictionary.

COL. 3, up to 5, from the Gypsies on Mitcham Common, above that from Grellmann and Hoyland.

Cols. 5, 10, and 11, see page 11.

Col. 12 was given to Mr. Ellwood by A. J. Ellis, Esq., Ex-president Philolog. Society, who changed the Spelling from that of a copy taken down by Mr. J. A. H. Murray, from the mouth of Mr. W. H. Thompson, of Kirkby Stephen.

Col. 13, obtained by Mr. Ellwood "from Mr. Ellis, who obtained it from Rev. W. F. Bell, Laith Kirk Vicarage, Mickleton, Barnard Castle, who had it from a youth, who learnt it from his grand-mother, a person of about 80, now living at Middleton," (1877).

Col. 14 is on the authority of Mrs. Ellwood, who learned it from her mother, a native of Coniston. These numerals have been known in Coniston from time immemorial.

Col. 15 was obtained about 1818, from the shepherds of Borrowdale, by the Ponsonbys, of Barrow Hall, who gave it to Mr. Browne, of Tallentire Hall, who gave it to the Rev. T. Ellwood, 1878.

Col. 16 was obtained by Rev. T. Ellwood, from Mr. J. Hellon, of Dunnerdale, Seathwaite.

Col. 17, given to Mr. Ellwood by Dr. Kendall, of Coniston, who got it from a servant, a native of Eskdale.

Col. 18 was obtained by him from Mr. Ritson, of Wasdale Head.

Col. 19, taken by W. Browne, Esq., of Tallentire Hall, from the dictation of a female traditioner, who got them as a girl, thirty years since, from a woman of fifty years old, who got them from an old woman of eighty years of age, when the woman of fifty was about 15. That makes $30+35+$ say $65=130$.

Col. 20, given to Mr. Ellwood, "by R. S. Ferguson, Esq., Editor of Transact. Cumberland and Westmoreland Antiquary Society, who got it from A. Harris, Esq., who obtained it 42 years ago from an old lady in Epping, Essex," (1878).

Col. 21, "used by the extinct Wawenocs in Maine, as written by Dr. Ballard. Sent to Mr. Ellis by Dr. Trumbull, Hartford, Connecticut; was well known by residents in the Wawenocs territory as early as A.D. 1717.

Col. 22, written in Glossic by Dr. Trumbull, from the dictation of a gentleman of Hartford, Connecticut, about 60 years old, who had been taught the scoring when a child, by an old Indian woman, who used to come to his father's house in Hebron, Connecticut,

F

## YULE IN NIDDERDALE.

" About Yule quhen the wind blew cule,
  And the round tables began."

YOUNG WATERS I. I.

T'ool clog is provided by selecting a large log and getting it well dry. In some cases the fag end of last year's yule clog is used to light the new one, which in its turn is saved for a like purpose against the following year. The yule clog is lighted on Christmas Eve, which is called " *Fromarty neet.*" Fromarty is a preparation of sodden wheat, and is eaten at tea on Christmas Eve. (I do not know that Fromarty, which is called the same, is eaten in the south at any other time of year than at harvest time, when the gleaners, who have not gleaned enough wheat to make it worth while to have it ground, " shuck " it with their hands, and boil it in water to eat at breakfast.) In addition to frumarty, " *Spice Cake*" is eaten at tea, and " *T'ool Cake*"—sweet cakes with currants, sugar, etc. One Yule Cake is given to each member of the family and each servant. I now give, side by side, the method of making the Yule Cake, as made in Nidderdale and in Denmark at the present day,

20 miles south east of Hartford, to sell baskets, brooms, etc. "She must have been," says Dr. Trumbull, " a Narragansett Piquot, or Mohegan Squaw." The woman used to stroll the country gipsy-like, to sell the articles of her own manufacture.

COL. 23, To " A. J. Ellis in February, 1875, by Mr. H. Jenner, British Museum, who had heard it that day from Mr. E. A. Guy, Cincinnati, Ohio, U.S., who was visiting the Museum. He said he learnt it from his mother, who learned it from the white hunters and trappers, who came in from the forests. They were said to be used by the Miami Indians, now extinct, formerly living in South Ohio. These numerals have no affinity whatever to the systems of numerals used in the Native North American Indian languages, which are very complete in themselves.

the former supplied by Mr. T. Thorpe, Pateley Bridge, the latter by a Danish friend of mine :—

### YULE CAKE.—*Nidderdale.*

" 3¼ lbs. of flour ; ¼ lb. currants ; 1 lb. raisins ; 2 oz. candied lemon—chopped fine ; a little cinnamon ; 2 eggs ; 2 pints of luke-warm milk—the eggs to be beaten in the milk ; ¼ a tea-cup-full of yeast ; 8 oz. of butter ; and 1 lb. of sugar. Mix well. The paste is then dropped from a spoon on to a cake-tin—generally four on a tin. After they are baked, mix a little brown sugar in milk to glaze the cakes with. When finished, they are hardly so large as a tea-cake."

In shape they are like the Danish *Jule Kage*. On Christmas Eve one Yule Cake is given to each member of the family, along with a piece of Christmas cheese. As a rule, part of it is left for Christmas morning, and eaten at the breakfast.

### JULE KAGE.—*Denmark.*

" 1¾ lbs. of flour ; 6 oz. of butter ; 6 cardamoms ; 2 oz. raisins ; 2 oz. mixed peel ; ¼ lb. sugar. Beat the cardamoms with the sugar, and mix with the flour and fruit. Dissolve a little yeast (about a halfpenny worth) in a good half pint of luke-warm milk. Mix well, and beat with the hand until the paste is quite smooth and does not stick to the dish. Then let it rise for a couple of hours. When well risen, work the butter in—do not rub or roll it. Put it into the tins, rise again, and bake."

The Danish *Jule Kage* is a flat cake, about an inch or more thick in the middle, and 8 or 10 inches across, getting rather thinner towards the edges. It is powdered with white sugar, and when broken, is very light and well aërated.

It is customary for the tradesmen to give each of their customers a candle at Christmas,—and I use the word advisedly, for this candle is part of the Christmas, and not properly of the Yule, and in consequence, the custom is found in the south, as well as in the north,—called T'ool Candle, or, T' Yule Candle. Thus one house is often provided with twelve or more candles. Sometime after tea, in the evening of Christmas Eve, these are all lighted together, and the members of the household hold them in their fingers alight for about ten minutes, when all but one are

extinguished.    This one is left to cut the cheese by.    A whole
cheese is always provided for Christmas, and is cut for supper on
Christmas Eve by the master of the house.    After dark, on
Christmas Eve, no person may take a light out of doors, not
even a pipe alight, as it is considered unlucky to do so.    After
twelve o'clock at night, that is, the first thing on Christmas
morning, people go round singing Christmas Carols.    As early
as five o'clock on Christmas morning, " t' lile barns " come
round, holding each a sprig of green hollin, and saying, " Browt
ye gud luck."    They receive a trifling present.    The first comer
gets most, sometimes as much as sixpence, while those who
come after only get a penny.    Grainge says : " He who enters
his neighbours house first on the morning of Christmas Day
is styled "the lucky bird ;" should a female enter first it is
regarded as an evil omen."    There is no further celebration
of Christmas Day.    They do not even have a Christmas pudding.
This proves that the plum pudding is part of the Christmas,
and not of the Yule.

The earliest mention of Yule in the A. S. Laws, is in the
Laws of Alfred, (A.D. 872-901) " oththe on Geól." c. 5.
                              or    at   Yule.
From another passage in the same laws, it also appears that the
Yule feast lasted twelve days with the Saxons, " xii dagas en
Gehhól," c. 89.    This was the great feast of heathen times on to
which christianity grafted Christmas.    As to the meaning of the
name, there are eight or nine different theories with regard to
that, and I shall not go into them, farther than to remark, that,
as regards that one which makes the name to have meant ' feast',
and to have been used of various other feasts in the year, a
curious passage occurs in the Ballad of ' The Boy and the
Mantle,' in Percy's Reliques.

> " In the third day of May
> To Carleile did come
> A kind curteous child . . "
> [To King Arthur's court].

" Forth came an old Knight
Pattering ore a creed.
And he proffered to this little boy
Twenty markes to his meede,
And *all the time of the Christmasse*
Willinglye to ffeede."

The word *Christmasse*, here applied to a feast held in May, may be substituted for the word *Yule*, in an older ballad.

———:o:———

## THE SWORD DANCE.

Mr. Grainge, in his *History of Nidderdale*,* says : " The graceful and martial " *Sword dance* " is yet practised at Christmas Tide by the young men of the Dale. Their dresses for this purpose are of many colours, and their persons are adorned with a profusion of ribbons and other ornaments." He has kindly supplied the following for these Studies :—" My recollections of the sword dance—as performed some forty years ago—are, that the performers were from eight to twelve in number. They were young men, one dressed like a clown, with a wooden sword, the others all in white trousers, and jackets of red, yellow, or some very showy colour, decorated with sashes and rosettes of ribbon, their caps were also decorated with ribbon. Along with the dancers was always a fiddle. First, the performers stood on one side of the room in a line, with their swords in their belts ; the clown then—as the leading man—walked round and began his nominy, something in the style of the boys Christmas play of St. George of England, telling the audience that he is some wonderful great man,—Sampson for instance,—and that he has brought his valiant sons to make them sport. Then he calls on the first by the name of Alexander the Great, or some other mighty man, to follow him. Alexander draws his sword and follows his leader ; the same process is repeated until all the

* T. Thorpe, Pateley Bridge, 1863.

performers are on the floor following each other with drawn
swords ; when, at the words of their leader they face each other,
clattering their swords against each other above their heads, at
the same time dancing round in a circle.  Afterwards each man
grasps hold of the point of another's sword when held horizontally
say two feet above the ground, when they all jump over them
in quick succession,—a feat requiring much agility.  This
continues for some time.  Afterwards one of them holds his
sword upright, when by some means the others interlock theirs
with his, and form the whole into a kind of square lattice work,
which the leader holding up carries round the ring some twice or
thrice, dancing all the time ; then he throws down the lot in the
centre, and each man regains his own sword.  Lastly, they clatter
them against each other above their heads, as at the beginning,
and after continuing this for some time the dance ends.  The steps
are timed to the music, which all the time keeps rattling away.
I have no recollection of any particular song, although some of
them sung all together at the end of the performance, something
like the following rhyme :—

> Now ladies fair and gentlemen,
>   Our dance is at an end,
> We do our best to please you,
>   We come not to offend.
> We thank you for your kindness,
>   We thank you for your cheer ;
> We wish you all a merry christmas,
>   And a happy new year.

I have seen many parties of sword dancers, but the best and
most respectable was trained at Grantley, and George Watson,
who once kept the George Inn, at Pateley Bridge, and his
brother William, were two of them, and the music man was
" Fiddler Leeming," of Sawley."

Mr. Grainge has also obligingly communicated the following
*Notes on the Sword Dance*, from Brand's " Popular Antiquities :"

There is a curious and very minute description of the *Sword Dance*
in Olaus Magnus's History of the Northern Nations.  He tells us

that the Northern Goths and Swedes have a sport wherein they exercise their youth, consisting of *a dance with swcrds* in the following manner . First, with their swords sheathed and erect in their hands, they dance in a triple round ; then, with their drawn swords held erect as before : afterwards, extending them from hand to hand, they lay hold of each other's hilts and points, and while they are wheeling more moderately round and changing their order, throw themselves into the figure of a hexagon, which they call a rose; but, presently raising and drawing back their swords they undo that figure, in order to form with them a four-square rose, that they may rebound over the head of each other. Lastly, they dance rapidly backwards, and, vehemently rattling the sides of their swords together, conclude their sport. Pipes or songs, (sometimes both) direct the measure, which at first is slow, but, increasing afterwards, becomes very quick towards the conclusion.

Henry, in his History of Britain, says : "The Germans, and probably the Gauls and Britons, had a kind of martial dance which was exhibited at every entertainment. This was performed by certain young men, who, by long practice, had acquired the art of dancing amongst the sharp points of swords and spears."

A writer in the Gentleman's Magazine in 1811, states that in the North Riding of Yorkshire, the sword dance is performed from St. Stephen's Day till New Year's Day. The dancers usually. consist of six youths dressed in white with ribbons, attended by a fiddler, a youth with the name of " Bessy," and one who personates a doctor. They travel from village to village. One of the six youths acts the part of king in a kind of farce, which consists of singing and dancing, when the Bessy interferes while they are making a hexagon with their swords, and is killed.

Wallis writes that the *Saltatio armata* of the Roman Militia on their festival *Armilustrium*, celebrated on the 19th October, was practised by the common people in the neighbourhood of Northumberland on the annual festivity of Christmas, –the yule-tide of the Druids.—young men march from village to village, and from house to house, with music before them, dressed in an antic attire, and before the vestibulum or entrance of every house, entertain the family with the *Motus incompositus*, the antic dance, or Chorus Armatus, with swords or spears in their hands erect and shining. This they call the *Sword Dance*. For their pains they are presented with a small gratuity in money, more or less, according to every householder's

It is quite evident that the modern celebration of the Sword Dance comprises another feast formerly celebrated on Plough Monday, as appears from the following description : "The first Monday after Twelfth Day is called Plough Monday. On this day the people went in procession to gather money for Plough Lights, or candles kept burning before certain images in churches, to obtain a blessing on their work. The reformation put out

ability ; their gratitude is expressed by firing a gun. One of the company is distinguished from the rest by a more antic dress ; a fox's skin generally serving him for a covering and ornament to his head, the tail hanging down his back. This droll figure is their chief or leader. He does not mingle in the dance.

Strutt, in his " Sports and Pastimes of the People of England," says : " There is a dance which was probably in great repute among the Anglo-Saxons, because it was derived from their ancestors, the ancient Germans ; it is called the *Sword Dance*, and the performance is thus described by Tacitus : ' One public diversion was constantly exhibited at all their meetings, young men, who, by frequent exercise, have attained to great perfection in that pastime, strip themselves, and dance among the points of swords and spears with most wonderful agility, and even with the most elegant and graceful motions. They do not perform this dance for hire, but for the entertainment of the spectators, esteeming their applause a sufficient reward.' "

To these Notes I add the following :—

The Rev. G. Young says: " There was usually an extra band of six to dance the *Sword Dance* at Whitby. With the music of violin or flute, they formed a ring with swords raised in the air. They then went through a series of evolutions, at first slow, afterwards quick. Towards the close each one catches the point of his neighbour's sword, and various movements follow, one of which consists in forming or plaiting the swords into the form of a hexagon or rose in the centre of the ring, when one holds it up above their heads. The dance closes with taking it to pieces, each man laying hold of his sword. During the dance two or three *Toms* or *Clowns* make antic gestures, while another set called Madgies, or Madgy pegs, dressed like women, collect money."

the lights. But till lately the festival was kept up. A plough,
called the *Fool Plough*, was decorated with ribbons. Thirty or
forty swains, with their shirts over their jackets, and hats and
shoulders covered with ribbons, dragged it from house to house,
proceeded by one in the dress of an old woman, called *Bessy*,
who carried the money box. There was also a *Fool* in fantastic
attire. Occasionally some reproduction of the Ancient Scandinavian Sword Dance added to the means of persuading money out
of the pockets of the lieges. One of the mummers generally
wears a fox's skin in the form of a hood. The feast originated
probably with the priests as a means of collecting the Plough
Alms, or money for maintaining the Plough Lights."*—(Book of
Days, Vol. I., p. 94-96.) When the feast of Plough Monday
fell into disuse, part of the ceremony appears to have been
grafted on to the festivities of Yule, and the Sword Dance.

* See Study VII.

—————:o:—————

## THE NEW YEAR.

By many people New Year's Day is thought more of than
Christmas, at least in the upper part of the Dale. At Lofthouse,
I was told that Carols were sung before one o'clock in the
morning, but Mr. T. Thorpe writes : " Carol singing is not much
observed in Nidderdale." New Year's Eve is called " *T' Watch
Neet.*" Meetings are held in Methodist Chapels on that night.
On New Year's Morning, the first person who enters a house
must be a man. At Lofthouse a *boy*, but generally a man, with
dark hair, is considered the luckiest, or, as it was told to me,
" They dont reckon to let one in with ginger hair." Arrangements are often made beforehand as to who shall " *let t' new
'ear in.*" As a rule, the door is kept locked, and if any one
knocks who is known to have " *leet*" hair, he is greeted with :

G

" We cannot let the' in till Matty comes in becos thoo hez leet
hair, etc." This custom seems to me to carry a tradition of
hatred felt by the Celts, of Strathclyde, for the fair-haired
Angles, their conquerors, and may have originated while they
yet indulged a hope of casting off the yoke, and regaining their
freedom.

# VI.

# THE GARTH.

A Garth in Nidderdale means a small enclosed field close to a house. Calves, sheep, or pigs, are put in it. It corresponds with Dan. *Vænge* and *Toft*. It occurs in the name of *Haver Garth*, near Pateley Bridge, which is synonymous with *Haver Close*, north of Middlesmoor; and means *oat-yard*.

Perhaps the oldest form we have the word, is the *Gothic Gards*. It is used several times by Ulfilas in his Bible, of which Lye gives chapter and verse. Thus—

*Mark 3, 25.* "If a *house* be divided against itself, that *house* cannot stand." The word here is inclusive, and means all that belongs to one lord or master, a *freehold estate*.

*Luke 19, 46.* " My *house* is the *house* of prayer,"=Temple, synagogue, cathedral, church, chapel, etc.

*John 12, 3.* " And *the house* was filled with the odour of the ointment,"=a dwelling-house.

*Matt. 8, 6.* " *in Garda*," in *domo*, "Thy servant lieth at home sick of the palsy.=dwelling-house. " *us Gardd in gard*," from *house* to *house*,=dwelling-house.

The meanings of Garth by itself, are thus illustrated, (1) house, (2,) freehold estate, or manor, (3,) church.

*John 18, 1.* " *Aurtigards*," orchard, Lat. *Hortus*, " over the brook Kedron where there was a garden." Goth. *Aurti gards*=O. N. *Jurta-gardr, Urta-gardr* ; M. H. G. *Wurz-garte* ; A. S. *Vyrtgeard, Ortgeard* ; Eng. *Orchard*, or *wort-yard*, an enclosure for ' worts' i.e. vegetables, a garden.—(Wedg.)

John 10, 1. " *Gards-lambe,* " *Domus orium,* " He that entereth not *by the door into the sheepfold,* but climbeth up some other way, the same is a thief and a robber."

From the *Gothic* we may pass to examine its meanings in O. N., and Icelandic.—*(Cleasby's Dict.)*

I.  FIRST, then it means *a yard,* (an enclosed space) especially in compos., as *Kirku gardr,* a *church yard; Stakk gardr,* a *stack-garth; Dyra gardr, a deer park;* gardr alone is a *hay yard,* (round the hay ricks.)

SECOND, a *court yard, court and premises.*

THIRD, esp. in Norway, Denmark, and Sweden, a *house* or building in a town or village, (Dan. *gaard,* Icel. *bær.*)

FOURTH, *a stronghold.*

FIFTH, in Icel. a heavy snowstorm is called *gardr.*

II.  In Icel. *a fence* of any kind; *legja gardr,* to make fences, especially around the house field. *Grjót gardr,* a *grit garth,* i.e. a *stone wall. Torf gardr,* a turf fence. *Haga gartk,* a *haw garth,* hedge around a pasture. Eb. 132.

*Garda-riki* or *Garda-veldi,* is the name of the Scandinavian— Russian kingdom, of 10th and 11th centuries, parts of which were Hólm gardr, Kæmi gardr, Nov-gorod, etc.; the name being derived from the castles and strongholds *gardar* which the Scandinavians erected among the Slavonic people, and the word tells the same tale as the Roman ' Castle ' in England. The Mod. Russian *gorod* and *grad* are the remains of O. N. Gardr, a castle. e.g. *Novgorod, Belgrad.*

This gives a lively interest to the name of " *Hardcastle Garth,*" near Birstwith, because it was so called after a Mr. Hardcastle, a farmer, who formerly lived there.

We will now trace the word in Welsh.—*(Owen's Dict.)*

*Garz,** an enclosure, a garden ; *garz yd.* corn yard ; *garz wair,* hay garth ; *garz ragai,* a nursery.

*Garth,* 1, a fold ; 2, a buttress, rampart, a fort ; 3, a cape, ridge, spur of a mountain. Gives the name to *Garth beibeo, Penarth,* etc.

In Mod. Dan. the meanings of *Garth* divide themselves into three groups :—

1.—*Gjord* and *Omfang,* circumference.

2.—*Tykkelse* and *Omfang,* extent, compass.

3.—*Vænge* and *Gaard.*

The word *Garth* includes the transitional ideas which they keep separate. *Girth,* or circumference, *thickness* or bulk (of solids,) *area enclosed,* (of surface).

*Rosing's Dict.*

1.—*Gjord,* girth.

2.—*Omfang,* circumference, extent, compass.

3.—*Tykkelse,* thickness.

4.—Gaard : 1, *yard, court* ; 2, *house* ; 3, *farm* ; 4, *freehold* ; 5, *manor ?*

5.—Vænge, inclosed field.

*Fiske-gaard,* a dam or weir for catching fish.—(Imp. Dict.)

| English. | | Danish. | |
|---|---|---|---|
| Girth. | | Gjord | |
| (in a limited sense) space enclosed, thickness. | | *Tykkelse.* | |
| Enclosed field. | *Extent, compass.* | Vænge. | *Omfang.* |
| Yard, court. | | Gaard. | |
| House. | | Gaard. | |
| Farm. | | Gaard. | |
| Freehold. | | Gaard. | |

*Skjær-Gaard* in Norway is the *fringe of islands* along the coast.

* Welsh z is pronounced like TH, hard.

*Gjerde*, a fence, hedge.
*Gjerde*, to fence, make a fence.
Omgjerde, to enclose, surround with a fence.

Gjord, girth, a girdle.
Gjorde, to girde.
Omgjorde, to surround with a girdle.

The meanings of gjord and gjerde have stopped short, not performing the transition from the thing enclosing to the thing enclosed, like garth, else we should have yard at once from either of them.

The transition from girth to thickness is natural, and from *thickness, a measure in one direction,* the transition is easy to *extent, compass, in every direction,* never losing the idea of an ultimate limit. There the limit of meaning seems reached as regards solids.

From Girth or circumference the transition is easy to the space enclosed or area, but in this sense the meaning was limited to an *enclosed field.* When the cattle had trampled down the grass it became a yard, this was muddy and therefore paved, so it became a *court yard* of a house, then the name passed to the *house* itself, then to the *whole farm,* and ultimately a *freehold estate.*

In Nidderdale *Garth* has only one meaning, an enclosed field near a house. In Denmark it is represented by five words, the last of which, Gaard, has four meanings.

The sense of *fortress* is found in Old Scandinavian and in Welsh, while its descendant *Gorod* in Russian means a town.

# VII.

# THE HELM.

The name of Helm, and the size of the old barns themselves, are interesting as pointing back to a bygone age, and to very ancient customs, but also as regards the word alms. *Helm, Barn, Lathe*, and many other names of sheds are used now quite indiscriminately, though originally they possessed very different meanings.

Barn is strictly the *Barley house*, from A. S. *Bere*, Barley, and *Ern, ærn*, a place, house. *Berern, Beren, Bern, Bærn,* barn. If Cleasby be right in suggesting that the A. S., Eng., Hel., and Germ. *Helm*, O. N. *Hjálmr*, a *helmet*, also a *hay-house, barn, helm,* may be derived from hylja to hide, then we have two totally distinct words meeting in the sense of *helm* a barn. The distinction and derivation of ·Hjálmr is not, however, clear or at all established, whereas the senses of *Hjálmr* may well be derived from Hálmr, because thatch is used to cover, so *a cover,* a helm, a helmet.

Whether *helm* came to mean barn from one or both of these sources, however, it is clear that it did and does mean a *store-house for the produce of the farm.* This brings us to the point respecting *alms*. After the advent of Augustine, it was first ordained in the *Laws of Ine*, (A.D. 688-728, c. 61,)  " *Be*
About

*cyric sceattum*     *Cyric*     *sceat*     *mon sceal agyfan*     *to* church first fruits.   Church first fruits one shall give from *tham* HEALME, *and*    *to*    *tham heorthe the se man on hith to* the    *helm,*    and from the house that the man is in at

*mildan wintra.*" Next in the *treaty between Edward and Guthrun,*
   mid  winter

(A.D. 924-940,) we find : " *Gif    hwá    ful-hælmyssan*
                  If    anyone   do not give full

*ne sylle.*"—c. 6.  Next, in the *Laws of Æthelstan,* (924-940,)
helm-fruits.

Introd. where the difficulty first arises.  " *& ic wille  eac  thæt*
                                & I will   also  that

*mine gerefan gedón thæt man agyfe tha cyric   sceattas  & tha*
  my  sheriffs cause that one yield the church  first fruits & the

*sawl  sceattas to tham stowum    the   hit mid rihte to gebyrige,*
  soul first fruits to  the    places which  they rightly belong to

*& SULH-ÆLMESSAN on  geare.,*'
& the *plough alms* of the year.

In the *Laws of Eadmund,* (A.D. 940-946,) we find c. 2,
*Be  Teothungum &  cyric-sceatum.*
About   Tithes   & church-first-fruits.

*Teothunge we bebeodath ælcum Chistenum men, be his Cristendome,*

Tithes we ordain for every christian man, by his christianity,

*& cyric-sceat,  & ÆLMES-FEOH.  Gif hit hwá dón nylle*
& church first fruits, & alms money.  If anyone will not pay

*sy he    amansumod.*
let him be excommunicated.

Here we may have *the first mention of tithes paid in money,*
though the meaning of feoh is uncertain, for in the *Laws of
Æthelstan,* Introd. it expressly says : " *agyfan tha teothunga*
                                give   the   tithes

*ægther ge on cwicum ceape ge on thæs geares eorth wæstmum.*
either  in live  cattle or in  the  fruits of the earth for the year.

This I mention because sulh-ælmessan is the word used in
the same passage.

Next we find in *Canon.* 49, temp. *Eadgar,* (A.D. 959-975,)

" *And we lærath that ælc fæsten beo mid* ÆLMESSAN *gewurthad,*
And we ordain that each fast be honored with alms
*that is, that gehwá on Godes est* ÆLMESSAN *georne sille,*
that is, that whoever for love of God gives *alms* amply and cheerfully,
*thonne bith his fæsten Gode the gecwemre.*"
then his fast will be the more acceptable to God.

Here for the first time the word ÆLMESSAN *stands alone,* and here it evidently means *money* as well as *kind.* In *Canons.* 54, 55, 56; we find,—*Can.* 54, " *And we lærath that Preostas*
And we ordain that Priests
*folc mynegian thæs the hig Gode dón sculan, to gerihtan*
remind folk of that which they should do for God, to be correct
*on teothungum & on othram thingum, ærest* SULH-ÆLMESSAN
in tithes & in other things, especially the plough-alms
*XV night on ufan Eastron. & geoguthe teothunge be Pentecosten.*
XV days after Easter. & tithes in young cattle by Pentecost.
*& eorth westma be Omnium Sanctorum. & Rom feoh be Petres*
& earth fruits by All Saint's Day. & Rome fee by Peter's
*Massan & ciric sceat be Martinus messan.*"
Mass & church first fruits by Martinmas.

Here Sulh-ælmessan clearly cannot mean fruits of the year's plough. Bosworth says :—" *Plough-alms,* or the penny which was given to the poor for every plough, and for every such portion of land as would employ one plough."

*Can.* 55, " *And we lærath that Preostas swá dælan folces*
And we ordain that Priests so divide folks
ÆLMESSAN, *that hig ægther dón ge God geyladian, ge*
alms, that they both cause God to be pleased *and*
*folc to* ÆLMESSAN *gewænian.*"
reconcile folk to alms giving.

*Can.* 56, " *And we lærath that Preostas sealmas singan*
And we ordain that Priests sing psalms

*thonne hi tha ælmessan dælan.   & tham thearfan   georne*
when they distribute the alms.   & for the poor we earnestly
*biddan that hig for thæt folc thingian."*
bid   that they intercede for the people.—In return, I suppose
for the alms.

Next we find in the section of the Canons relating to
Repentance. *Be dæd bétan*, c. 13, *" Dæd bóta sind gedihte*
Expiatory deeds are arranged
*on mistlice wisan,   & micel man mæg mid* ÆLMESSAN *alysan."*
for in various ways, & *much one may redeem by alms giving.*
And again, c. 15, *" & sece mid his* ÆLMESSAN *cirican gelome."*
& seek with his   alms   the church after.

Afterwards occurs *Ælmes leohte,* "alms candles." (*Be
Mightigum Manmum, c. 3.*) SULHÆLMESSAN. (*Lib. Constit.,
Parag. 5*) and "HÆLMESSAN" in the general sense of alms.  *" &*
&
*on hwam mæg huru æfre ænig man on worolde   swythor*
in what may indeed ever any man in the world more exceedingly
*God wurthian thonn on cyrcan   & on* HÆLMESSAN,  *& eft on*
worship God   than in church and in   *alms,*   and lastly in
*gehalgedan healican hadan."*
high   holy   orders.

That fruits of the earth are here meant as well as *alms* in
the other sense appears from the succeeding section. *Be cyric
grithe*, par. 14, *" his teothunge, aswá seó sulh   thone teothan*
his   tithes,   as well the plough as the tenth
*æcer."* And by *Sulh-ælmessan* in par. 19. *Sulh-ælmessan*
acre.
occurs again in the *Concilium Ænhamense* par. 17, (about
A.D. 1010.)

Up to the Tenth Century *Hælmysse* was used in a certain
sense, when another word, *Ælmesse*, of ecclesiastical introduction, a corruption of the Greek *eleemosunê*, came into use *in the*

*same sense.* The probability is that in the lapse of centuries the origin and meaning of *Hælmysse* was forgotten, and that the *Bishops* regarded it as a corruption of *Ælmesse,* which may account for the corrupt form HÆLMESSE. Whether or no, *Ælmesse* at that time drove out *Hælmysse,* and literally took its place. Hælmysse, which occurs in the sense of *Ælmesse,* in Lib. Con., A.D. 1008, was not wanted, indeed, for Tithe was used inclusively; and on the other hand, Ælmesse had the sense of *alms,* charity, which *never* appertained to *Hælmysse.* But though *Hælmysse* was driven out of the leading dialect, its meaning has survived to the present day in the sense of a *cart load,* the second sense of *awmous,* which derives its pronunciation from the O. N. *almusa, ölmusa,* alms.

# VIII.

# THE  REINS.

Up to the early days of the present generation, (1871) the dalesmen lived upon the agricultural produce of their land.  In Nidderdale, much of the upper part of the dale consists of property farmed by the landlords,* and in this respect Nidderdale differs from parts of the surrounding county.  There is no trace of the former existence of a village community in Nidderdale,— though I am far from asserting that such never existed in the dale—or of any other state of things than that of individual ownership.

In Nidderdale, a *Reean* is the strip that was formerly left unploughed around a ploughed field.   The farmers used to allow the men who worked for them, to graze their cows on these strips during the winter.   Since the introduction of the steam-plough, however, they plough much closer to the hedge, and these *Reeans* are not now left.  This gives us, as nearly as possible, the original meaning of the name which was *a strip of land left Rein, i.e. undug or unploughed* between two adjoining parties, whether freeholders or commoners.  Thus we find in O. N. *Rein*, a strip of land.....................*Hreinn*, pure, clean.

Dan. { *Reen.*                            [two fields.†] } ......*Reen*, pure, clean,
         { *Ager-reen*, a small ridge between }

Swed. *Ren*, a boundary.............................*Ren*, pure, clean.

Germ. *Rein*, a strip of land......................*Rein*, pure, clean.

* The original " Statesmen," in fact, from whom the leaders in Parliament derive their title.

† A bank of earth surrounding Bishop Burton Park, near Beverley, in the East Riding, is called " The Rein " to this day.—J. R. D.

A *Rein* is the only kind of boundary which it was practicable for the occupiers of adjoining land to make, where there were no stones, and few labourers. The Danes brought the institution into these dales with them, as they did to Normandy, where I believe they are still in use. In Wharfedale, Coverdale, Wensleydale, and on the slopes of the hills to the east of Nidderdale, the country is covered with little step-like terraces called "reins," *(pr. reeans)*. Some of the best examples are those at Wardermarske, of which I give a plan on a scale of 6 ins. to the mile, showing also the modern fences, and the contours of the ground at 25 ft. intervals.

FIG. 5.

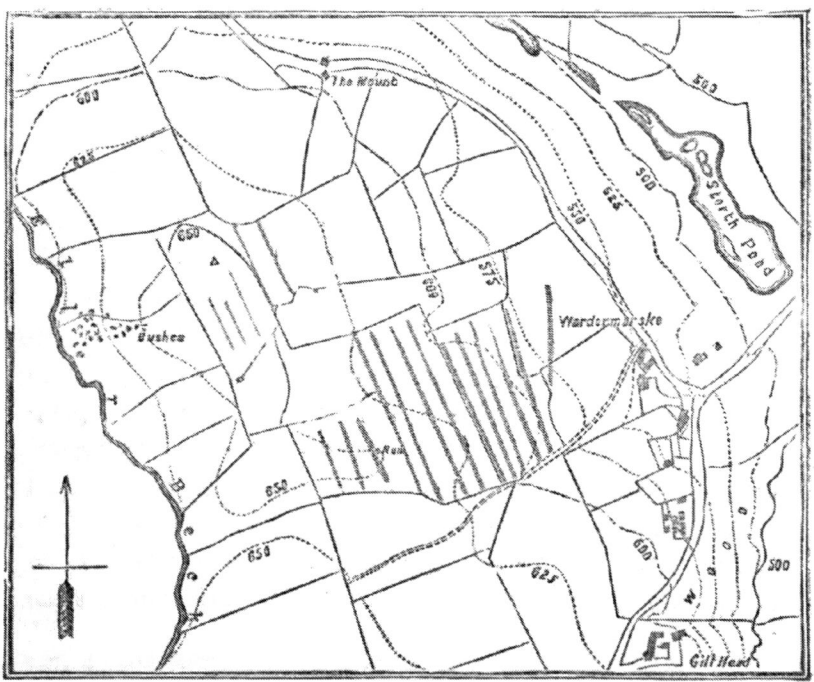

THE WARDERMARSKE REINS.

The sides of the limestone slopes of Wharfedale are covered with them, each being twenty or thirty or more yards long, and two or three yards wide, and though they almost always there run horizontally, yet occasionally they lie up and down. These "reins" lay on land which belonged to the village communities of the dale, and each man in the village had one. One man held a "rein" for three years, when he exchanged for another. This system was in full working order down to the time of the grandfathers of the present generation of men about fifty years old.* With the decline of agriculture and the increase of grazing farming, consequent upon the departure of manufacturing, power to enclose was applied for, under the Enclosure Act [6 and 7 William IV., cap 115], 1886, which gave power to enclose, without a special Act, "open and common arable and pasture lands, and lands commonable during part of the year only, by Commissioners with consent of two-thirds in number and value of proprietors, or, without Commissioners, with consent of seven-eights in number and value." Long stone fences were built, and the "ranes" remained as the monuments of a bygone age. This was followed by a rapid depopulation of the dales. The stream of emigration set in to the great manufacturing towns of Leeds and Bradford: so that the population of the dales is not now one-third of what it was early in the century.

There is an interesting passage in the *Laws of Ine*, which throws considerable light upon the ancient usages in regard to common land, cap. 42. *Be ceorles gærstune.* "Gif ceorlas
                Of farmers gers fields. If farmers
hæbban gærstún gemænne, oththe other gedal land
  have a gersin-field amang 'em, or other common land
to tynanne, & hæbben sume getyned heora dæle,† sume
to be fenced, and some have fenced their part some

* I doubt the system of Reins, as part of the village community having been "in full working order" so recently. Some reins may have been still used at that time, but the village community, if any, had died out long before.—J. R. D.

† *Dale, a division.* In Wharfedale, near Buckden, a certain piece of

næbben & ætten heora gemænan æceras oththe
have not and their cattle eat the common arable or

gærs, gan tha thonne the thæt geat agan &
grass fields let them then *gan* that have "*gates*" and

gebete thæm othrum the heora dæle getyned hæbben
compensate them others that have fenced their part

thone æfwyrdlan the thær gedón sy, & abidden him
the damage that is done to them, and beg them off as

æt thæm ceápe, swylc riht swylc cyn sy. Gif
regards those cattle, as formally as is proper. If

thonne hrythera hwylc sy the hegas breco, & gà in
however a beast there be which breaks fences, and goes in

gehwær, & se the hit nolde gehealdan se hit agø oththe
anywhere, and if he that owns it is unwilling to hold it or

ne mæge, nime se hit on his æcere gemete & ofslea
cannot, let him take it to the 'reean' of his piece and kill it

& nime se agen frigea his flæsc, & tholige thæs othres."
and let the owner take again its carcase and lose the other part.

Here the people had a common grazing field, and each commoner
had to make so much of the fence. Adjoining this field they
had another, in which each commoner had a portion of land
alloted to him, and was obliged to make so much of the
common fence, but each allotment was not fenced off from
those about it. Every commoner had "*gates*" for so many
cattle in the grazing field,—whose trespasses occasioned the
law.

Tusser who published the 1st edition of his " Five hundred
points of good Husbandry," in 1557, writes very sarcastically
about the ' evils' of the common field system, but at that time
it was so much part of the national system, that he was

ground is called *Buckdendales* meaning I suppose a number of divisions
for meadow among the different families, though it is not divided now,
Again a certain narrow field is called *Sykedale.*—J. R. D.

apparently alone in his opinion.    The grounds of his objection
are thus quaintly expressed.

> " Some commons are barren, their nature is such,
> And some over layeth their commons too much.
> The pestered commons small profit doth give,
> And profit as little some reap, I believe."

> " Some pester the commons with fowls and with geese,
> With hog without ring, and sheep without fleece.
> Some lose a day's labour with seeking their own,
> Some meet with a booty they would not have known."

On this W. Mavor, L.L.D., who published an Edition, 1812,
has the following note : — " The right of commons, though per-
tinaciously insisted on by those who possess claims, is nevertheless of comparatively little value, especially to the poor.    That
lazy industry, that beggarly independence, which are created by
the miserable stock which the poor man can command, and
which is generally seen on commons, are as injurious to himself
as to the community.    The prevalence of *enclosures, to which the
good sense of our Author rendered him partial, though the age in
which he lived was not ripe for such an improvement,* as may be
learnt from the commotions excited about that period, has
diminished the evils of the common field system, but till every acre
of ground is in severalty, Agriculture cannot be said to have
reached beyond the first stage of perfection."

How sad a conclusion ! but reserving comments, we see
from this that two and a half centuries after Tusser's time, the
system was still vigorous enough to call forth such a note as the
above.    We have indeed more authoritative statements on this
head in the report of the great agricultural survey of 1799.—
*Agriculture of the West Riding*—which are as follows : —

> From Ripley to the western extremity of the Riding, nearly all the good
> land is kept under the grazing system, and seldom or never
> ploughed.... During the time we were in that part of the country
> we hardly ever saw a plough, and a stack of corn is a great rarity.

Upon the higher grounds, there are immense tracts of waste, which are generally common among the contiguous possessors, and pastured by them with cattle and sheep. Some of these are *stinted pastures,*⁎ but the greatest part are under no limitations, the consequences of which are, the farms are oppressed, the stock upon them starved, and little benefit derived from them by the proprietors." P. 77.

4th. *The Common Fields.* These are most numerous in that part of the country to the eastward of the great north road from Doncaster to Boroughbridge. It is impossible even to guess at the quantity of land under this management, in general, it may be said to be extensive, and from the natural good quality of the soil, and the present imperfect state of culture, great room is afforded for solid and substantial improvements being effected upon all land coming under the description of common field. P. 78.

5th. *The Moors.* These lie in the western part of the Riding, and perhaps contain one eighth of the district. Upon them sheep are chiefly bred, and afterwards sold to the graziers in the lower parts of the country. A great part of these is common, which lays the proprietors under the same inconveniences as are already pointed out, and which might easily be remedied by dividing and ascertaining the proportion which belongs to the respective proprietors. P. 78-79.

The first fruits of this Report was the Enclosure Act of 1801, [41 Geo. 3. c. 109] which though perhaps inoperative, was the thin end of the wedge, and served to facilitate the passage of that of 1836. This latter has so far swept away the common fields, that few men under 40 years of age can remember them.

Regarding them as a part of the commune, one must regret the lost institution of the Reins.† Not satisfied with an equal division of land, the commoners caused a change

⎯⎯⎯⎯

⁎ " Mr. Atkinson says in Cleveland the Sheep-gate is as much connected with the farmstead as the fields or farm buildings. You cannot separate them, and you cannot create new ones. It is all a bit of what we speak of as 'common right,' and the association is with the front stead,—i.e., the site on which a house stands, or has formerly stood." A consideration of all the passages quoted in these Studies, shows how the Sheep-gates grew up and the reason for their existence.

† The physical reason for the TERRACED Reins will be given in Study XIII.

I

every three years following the triennnial rotation of crops, in
order to insure absolute fairness in regard to fertility of soil,
and that each man should take the good with the bad.   One man
grew potatoes, another wheat, (where possible,) another oats, and
so on.   By means of " cowping " potatoes for oats, each man
actually did live upon the produce of his Rein, and all went on
well for nearly a thousand years after the first settlement of the
Danes.   But as the population increased, notwithstanding that
they added to the number of Reins, the struggle became
harder and harder till at last the resources of the Dale were
insufficient to maintain the inhabitants.   With the difficulty of
making a living at home, the impossibility of maintaining the
home manufacturer in competition with Leeds and Bradford, and
the certainty of obtaining good wages in those and other centres
of industry, there came the final blow in the Enclosure Act, 1836.
The commoners of Kettlewell speedily availed themselves of this
Voluntary Act, with the results stated above.—(See p. 62.)*

In Nidderdale other causes tending to depopulation have been
working concurrently with that which operated in Wharfedale.
The farmers engage their servants by the year, paying them so
much wages, and finding them board, lodging, and paying their
washing.   In a farm house, in addition to the farmer, his wife,
and family, there are all the servants of the farm.   When I
enquired what became of these servants,—mostly young men,—
I was told that those who save a little money take farms of their
own and marry, but that the improvident marry as farm
labourers, and, as there are no cottages out of the villages, live
at Middlesmoor, Lofthouse, or Ramsgill.   If overburdened with
children, they ultimately move to a manufacturing town, where

* In the Russian *Mir* " two thirds of the votes of the peasants are
necessary to pronounce the dissolution of the community, and to divide the
soil into permanent individual property."—*Primitive Property*, Laveleye,
p. 11, (1878.)  This provision may have been preserved by tradition in
England from ancient times, and so found its way into the Enclosure Act,
cited on p. 62.

they get their children into a mill, and themselves obtain employ-
ment of some kind from the manufacturers.    That is one cause.
There is another.    Though much of the upper part of the Dale
consists of property farmed by the landlord, the bulk of it lies
in larger properties.    It has been of late the practice on these to
throw two or three small farms into one.    They pull down all the
habitable structures on the farms except one, to drive the tenants
off, and prevent a possibility of any returning.    Thus the same
number of hands that formerly managed the small farms, now
manages the larger one.    It is true there has been a change
from agriculture to grazing, and that on that account so many
hands are not required to work the same area of ground, but
capital is destroyed inasmuch as two of the three families who
formerly lived upon the three farms, have to seek their living
elsewhere, and become a burden to some already overburdened
source of subsistence.    "It's all very well," says the landlord,
"but *I* was keeping them, now that they are gone, I get a larger
rent for the single farm than I did for the three farms, and the
land is far more profitable for grazing than it was for agriculture."    All this is very true, but the public is the loser, to the
extent of having two families and their servants to keep, or find
occupation for, where they had none before, while the landlord
and the large farmer are clear gainers by the difference between
the yield of the large farm and the three small ones, and the
keep of the two ousted families and their servants.    Few of these
people take fresh farms.    Most go to one or the other of the
manufacturing towns, where the difficulty of finding food enough
for the teeming thousands is already terribly felt.

The absence of "reins" in Nidderdale is not the only
distinctive feature that isolates it from the surrounding country.
Though woolcombing was the staple trade till very recent years
of Masham,* West Burton, and Aysgarth, in Wensleydale, there

---

* Masham, "In spinning of worsted a woman earns, if industrious,
sixpence or eightpence a day."—ARTHUR YOUNG, *Northern Tour*, 1770,
v. 2, p. 279.

never were any wool-combers in Nidderdale, unless on the borders of the Dale at Greenhowhill. Blackah makes one of the miner's wives say—(p. 30.) :—

"Ah've been carding and spinning all day."

Weaving and spinning "line" A. S. *Lin* (flax) employed women till about forty years ago. They made sheets, huckaback table-cloths, and towels, many of which are still in use. At Ramsgill, the birthplace of Eugene Aram, they wove cotton with a machine they call a "leäm" (loom). A man came from Hebden, in Wharfedale, bringing them the raw material, and took back what they had woven. He paid them for their work, and left them as much cotton as he thought they could finish before his next visit. But "t' oade harden looms, sowlin can, an' t' windin' wheel amang t' rest," are things of the past. "Garn" O. N., Dan., Swed., *Garn;* A. S. *Gearn,* (yarn*) is still spun in the Dale for knitting stockings; but all signs of manufacturing activity has long since been absorbed by the great centres, and disappeared from the Dales.

## ADDENDUM.

In Switzerland and Russia, the system of Community, under which the Reins existed, is still flourishing. It formerly prevailed throughout the Aryan Nations. In Russia, the body of inhabitants of a village owning common land is called the *Mir.* All the arable land is divided into zones round the village....Each zone is divided into narrow strips from 5 to 10 yards broad, and from 200 to 800 yards long....A partition of the soil was effected every year, or every three years, after each triennial rotation....In some places, partition takes place every six years, in others every twelve or fifteen, every nine is the most usual period....The hay meadows are divided into fresh lots every year, and each family mows its own parcel, (dale) or else the whole is mown in common, and the hay divided.—*Primitive Property,* Laveleye, c. 2.

* There is a fine valley of land called Nidderdale......very populous, and the inhabitants are much engaged in the linen manufacture. They generally bleach the yarn before it is wove.. ..." etc.—*Agric. Surv., West Riding,* 1799.

# IX.

# THE CELT.

Nidderdale lies in the ancient district of Kymry-land, and the kingdom of Strathclyde, and the evidence of names of places shows that the country immediately to the south of it, and west of Leeds, was well populated by Celts. Thus, in *Billing* Hill, an eminence between the Wharfe and the Aire, falling sharply both ways from an exceedingly narrow ridge, is found the W. *Byl*, a brim or edge.—*Byliawg* having a rim or edge. Otley *Chevin*, a long hog's back shaped hill, which pre-eminently features that locality, overhanging as it does with its steep wooded sides, and gigantic scars the broad flat meadows of the sluggish Wharfe,—is W. *Cevyn* the back; a ridge; a long extended mountain. Pannal* is W. *Pannel* a *dingle*, a *slope* or *fall*. In *Washburndale*, *Pendragon Castle*, the name of a house high up on Jack Hill, was, probably in Roman times, the site of the abode of a Pendragon, or chief leader of the Cymri. *Cop Cray* (near Brandrith Crags) at the summit of the moor, is a name of two Welsh words, *Cop* the top, summit; and *Craig*, a rock. *Craddock*, the name of a house, is Welsh, being the name of the successful Knight at King Arthur's Court.

> " *Craddocke* wan the horne
> And the bores head ;
> His ladie wan the mantle
> Unto her meede."

*The Boy and the Mantle*, vv. 191-194.

More properly written *Caradoc*, as in *Caer Caradoc.*

* Pannal. (anciently called Rosehurst.)—ALLEN, *Hist. of Yorks.*, *v.* vi., p. 187.

On the moors (Wharfedale side) north of Greenhowhill, "*Coombes* Hush," and "*Coombes* Marsh," 1500 ft., may contain a Welsh name. *Coombs* appears again on Arnagill moor, 1100-1200 ft. (W. *Cwm*, a hollow, a place between hills, a dingle or deep valley.)* Meugher, *pron.* Mewfa, a conspicuous conical hill over 2000 ft., on the watershed ridge between the Wharfe and the Nidd, and on the moors S.E. of Great Whernside, is probably Celtic. In Surrey, south of Godalming, there is a lofty hill called "Mervel Hill," but *pron.* by many Mi'erva Hill, exactly as we should *pron.* Minerva without the *n*. *Myvyr Elian* in Mona, and *Glyn-y-Myvyr*, a vale Denbighshire, are names which bear a striking resemblance to the present. *Myvyr* means *contemplation, study*, and is so explained in the above names by Owen. I can find no better explanation of the name of this lofty hill.

"*Slack*," in "Foulcauseway Slack," as Kex Gill Moor, "Sough Slack," near Libishaw Hill, "Hey Slack," near Hudstorth, in Washburn, and especially "Clack Gill Beck," and many others,—a boggy hollow in a moor as a place name generally because a road crosses it,—(W. LLACA *slop, mire, mud, dirt*, is more in accordance with fact than O. N. SLAKKI a *slope* on a mountain edge, (*Cleas*) which is perhaps more tempting). That magnificent hanging wood, "The Shawl," at Leyburn, (W. *Gallt* a woody cliff, or steep; GWYZALLT *a woody cliff, from* GWYZ *woody, overgrown, wild*, and GALLT.—In Wales this forms the names of several places, as "Y ZUALLT," "GALLT-Y-CRIB," "PEN-YR-ALLT," &c.) "Rather Standard" is the name of a sloping ridge or plateau, 1500 to 1650 feet, on Grassington Moor. (W. RHATH a *cleared spot*, a plain; YSTAIN that spreads or extends. "Tranmire" is generally an elevated moorland plateau, and seems to me to be a compound word. It has a wide range, however,—from N. Wales to Cleveland—which is rather against a compound origin. W. TRAN a *space* or *stretch*,

* On Pateley Moor, situate in a hollow, is a house called *Coombes* cottage. The "Cam holes" of the Ordnance Map of Great Whernside is called "Coomb holes."

a *district* or *region.*) " Crundell Hill," a small round knoll on the face of the hill above Braithwaite, near Middleham.—(W. CRWN round, CRON round. CRONELL a globe, CRONELLU to glomerate. CRYNDER roundness, CRYNAU to round, etc.) " Round Hill " is not an uncommon name for a similar feature. " Jonaman" a rock on Roova Plain.="*Jona Stone,*" (W. MAEN a rock, block of stone.) " Tarn " occurs several times in the Dales of the Pennine Chain, as the name of single houses far removed from any small lakes so called. In this case the word is probably Cymric, and may indicate a site of an ancient royal residence of some Chief of a clan or petty King. (W. *Teyrn* a King.) *Pen* in *Pen Hill,*—which Arthur Young writes " Pennel," *(Northern Tour,* v. 2, p. 459, 1770,)—and *Pen-y-Ghent,* is W. *Pen* head, summit. Respecting the latter name I have never heard so much as a plausible explanation of that, but it seems likely that we have the same word as in Kent, (spelt *Chent*\* in Domesday Book,) and Canterbury, viz., W. *Caint* a plain, or *open country,* also a *field of battle.* There are many places called by the appellation of *Caint,* as *Caer Gaint,* Canterbury. Similarly *Pen-y-Gaint* would mean *summit of the open country, i.e.* not wooded. Mr. Dakyns suggests that *Malham* may be Keltic, as it is pronounced *Mawm,* and " Maum is used in Ireland now to denote a connecting mountain gap or pass."— (Kinahan " Valleys," p. 122.) *Madhm* is Keltic for *the hollow of the hand,* so any hollow. The name would apply to the " cove." The name *Malham Cove* would then be a reduplication, as *Pen Hill,* etc. In the " Confirmation of gifts " to Fountains Abbey by Richard I., we find " Malghum cum toto Malghmore et Malghwatre," and in an enumeration of the possessions of the Abbey, " Malghum or Malham."

In the Nidderdale districts proper, (assuming that some of the unexplained names are really Cymric) there is at least a marked absence of Celtic names, and the one or two that can be

---

\* Spelt " Caent " in *Laws of Hlothær,* c. 16.

proved lie on the moors.   We know that the Britons worked the
lead mines at Greenhowhill, but there is nothing to show that
the Celts ever made any settlement in Nidderdale.   I question
whether there are thirty Cymric words in the Nidderdale
vocabulary.   There are *Beak* and *Beild*, utensils ; *Bogle* and I
suppose *Boggart ; Brat*, an apron ; *Bray*, BREUAN ; *Brawn* the
place where trees branch ; *Cabin; Clog, (t'ool clog)* a log ;
*Cluther*, (Greenhowhill) ; *Fog*, aftergrass ; *Hippings*, stepping
stones; *Hog*, a lamb; *Kist; Toppin ;* and *Yewn*, to bully, *Hull*,
a small hovel or shelter, a very small shed, such as a tool-house,
W. *Hul* a cover, covering.   *Ask*, in the phrase an " *Ask wind*,"
a hard dry biting wind like the east wind, may be simply a
corruption of W, ASGELLWYNT, a side wind, or it may be connected with *Asg*, a splinter ; *Asgor*, to divide ; *Asglodioni*, to
shiver, etc., and so mean a *sharp, cutting* wind.—For others see
Glossary.   Some of these are confined to Greenhowhill, and
some only used by the lowest stratum.   The most that can be
urged on the strength of them is that there may still exist the
descendants of a few Celtic slaves in the district.   The statement
at the head of page 12 that a Celtic dialect was till recently
spoken in Swaledale, was inserted on high authority.   Mr.
Goodchild however, who has more recently studied that district,
in answer to a question, replies, " I have no well proved Celtic
element at all in Swaledale."   There is certainly a well proved
Celtic element in Nidderdale, to the extent shown above, and
generally over the districts on which the numerals are found.

————:o:————

# THE ROMAN.

Of the *Roman occupation* Grainge mentions that two pigs of
lead bearing the inscription
IMP. CÆS : DOMITIANO. AUG. COS. VII—BRIG.
were dug up at Hayshaw Bank, in 1735.   This shows that they
were cast A.D. 81.

In addition to this, Roman coins have been discovered. The account of the discovery was thus narrated to me by the finder, Thomas Jackson, a carpenter, at Lofthouse.*

" I was playing with another boy up How Stean, when I crossed to "Tom Taylor's Chamber," the other boy was afraid to cross. I fun a small coin like a fourpenny piece, on the lowest floor of the cave. Then I held it up and showed it to the other boy. "Now wont you come across!" says I. So he came across. Then we traced 'em, one by one, stuck in the floor, and in the crevices of the cave. Others were stuck on their edges, and had been pushed into the cracks so far that we could not reach them. We were climbing out of the gill when we met a gentlemen. "This is a curious place," says he. " Ay, an' its been a rich 'un yance," says I, as we each pulled out a handful of coins and showed them to him. " What'll ye tak for em ?" says he. " Ah'll tak a shillin fer my sharr," says I. "An' what'll ye tak for yours ?" says t' gentleman. " Six shillings," answers the other boy. So he sed he'd only give five shillings. " Ye sal hev 'em then," we sed. I went back t' next day and taaike a pair o' pincers wi' me'y an' pulled hoot them 'at wer fast i' t' cracks 'at ah cuddant draw t' day afoar. We fand altogither thirty-five silver pieces, and four bronze. When I had got 'em all, " Fetch me'y black coit" says I, "Ah'll work na marr !"

* The same man who found these coins also told me the following little anecdote :—" I was a little boy, when I found a small coin. I took it to school, and was showing it to the. other boys, when t' maister calls out " What hev ye'y got thar, Tom ?" So he maks me tak it up t' him and taks it away. " Oh," says he, looking at it, " I'll tak it to be magnified." *An' its magnifying yet.*"

Mr. Ormerod's father found, when a little boy, fifteen crossbar guineas of William and Mary, near Newhouses. He took them to his father, who was ploughing. "See," says he, "what curious buttons I've fun." His father went with him to the place, but they could find no more, Some few years ago, Mr. Ormerod's brother ploughed up a crossbar shilling in a field near High Lofthouse.

J

In explanation of this curious story, it may be added that How Stean Beck runs through a very narrow cleft in the limestone, in places 70 feet deep or more, with vertical or overhanging sides. When the sun is shining, a rich effect of light and shade, is produced in the liquid atmosphere, by the shadows of the leafy trees, marvellously suspended overhead, playing upon the grey limestone, or lost in the dark recesses of its numerous caverns ; at the bottom runs the beck, now tearing its way in narrow strips of foam through the tortuous crevices of its adamantine channel, now checked in its velocity in some deep basin, through whose pellucid waters a rich pencil of light may steal down to illuminate the collection of stones by which the eddying torrent has excavated it.   Between the summer level and the flood line, the surface of the limestone is worn smooth by the water, and has, by chemical action, become covered by a thin film of redeposited silica, which has the appearance of a high polish, and makes the rock as slippery as glass.  Added to this, the edges frequently slope toward the rushing torrent at such an angle as to afford no hold to the booted foot.  At one of the points, where all these unfavourable conditions combine to render the passage of the beck all but impossible, is the cave called "Tom Taylor's Chamber," which at that time was not easy of access.   Mr. Metcalfe, the owner of Stean Beck, has obligingly communicated the following :—"Friday, June 12th, 1868.  A few days prior to the above date it came to my knowledge that two boys at Lofthouse had found in the rock upon my property, at Stean Beck, a number of old coins.  On inquiry I came to know that they had been met accidently by a gentleman, who informed me that when in Leeds, as yesterday, he had sold them to a person in the central market, a general broker. On this Friday evening I found the broker, who had the coins in his pocket.  He demurred to my demand upon him for them, stating they were under offer to the curator of the Leeds Museum.  I, however, prevailed upon him to sell them to me for £8 5s. They consisted of Thirty-two Silver pieces, viz. :—

| | | | | |
|---|---|---|---|---|
| One Coin | - | - Nero. | Four Coins | - Domitian. |
| Two ,, | - | - Galba. | Two ,, | - - Nerva. |
| One ,, | - | - - Otho. | Nine ,, | - - Trajan. |
| Three ,, | - | - Vespasian. | Nine ,, | - - Adrian. |
| One ,, | Titus, (Juda Coin.) | | | |

Three others I had obtained in Lofthouse, besides four Bronze pieces. The Lord of the Manor, John Yorke, Esq., hearing of this find, presumed he was the rightful owner, and called upon me to look at them. I gave him ten silver pieces, (duplicates,) he giving me a Pig of Lead, found buried in the earth about 18 inches under the surface, in his land near the gate coming into Castlestead."

Mr. Metcalfe has also added the following Notes on the Inscriptions on the Coins ;—

1.—NERO—came to the throne A.D. 54.

*Obverse.*—Nero Cæsar Augustus.

*Reverse.*—Jupiter Custos.

As regards the " Juda" Coin mentioned in the above list, the owner furnishes the following extract from Dr. Kitto's Bible :—

" ' She being desolate, shall sit upon the ground.'—This is strikingly illustrated by the attitude, in which the captive daughter of Zion, is represented upon the medal struck by Ves., to commemorate the taking of Jerusalem, (A.D. 70.) The obverse contains the head of the Emperor, while the reverse represents a woman sitting in a mourning posture under a palm tree. The inscription J. CAP., precludes any misapprehension of its meaning. So striking is the analogy, that some think the idea of the device on the medal was purposely taken from this probably at the suggestion of Josephus, who was then at the court of Ves. and enjoyed his favour. The same event is also commemorated in a silver *denarius*.* of the same Emperor, in which the mourning female sits more markedly *on the ground*, while behind her rises the military trophy, which signalizes the triumph of the conquerors, and her own desolation."

As regards the probable date at which these coins were hidden, we read in the Saxon Chronicle (MS. Cot. Lib., which was written A.D. 977.) " A.D. 418—This year the Romans collected all the hoards of gold that were in Britain, and some they hid in the earth, so that no man afterwards might find them, and some they carried away with them into Gaul."

* This is the coin in question.

# THE ROMAN'S FAREWELL.

### *A Study in Verse.*

### I.

Briton, while summer on these mountains gilds
And wraps in verdure all the dales below,
While yet thy glad eye, feasting on these wilds,
Marks pleased the brown hills dappled with folds of snow—
Ere yet their winter-stricken summits go
To bury their heads in all pervading ice,
Ere yet to floods the swollen torrents grow—
Rome will have quit thy shores, moved by the imperative cries
Of grim barbarian hordes beneath fair Italy's skies.

### I I.

Down this deep rift alone in cool seclusion,
Hid from the hot rays of the scorching sun,
Where thick trees shade, and herbs in wild profusion
Cast flowers around, and winding creepers run,
With doubting mind I peer the vista through,
I see the bright flowers to the daylight turning,
I see the sky above, whose bright dark-blue
Tells how fiercely aloft the midday sun is burning.

### I I I.

And bitterly I regard my own fresh tear
That mingles dripping with the dark springs under,
To think that I must eke deposit here
The accumulated hoards of many a year
And sally forth again to bear the brunt and thunder.

### I V.

Here in this little clint I thrust these moneys—
Safe to remain till we have eke chastised
The insolent Goth that with his Myrmidones
Stands menacing Rome—then straightway back to the prize
Eftsoons I will return, and spend my treasure
All in a life long spell of vengeance-sweetened pleasure.

## V.

Ye rocky dales where many a mountain stream
With hoarser whisper vies the mountain's breath,
Where crag born echoes, wakened from their dream,
In distant answer carry the eagle's scream
Up to the moorland solitudes and down to the dales beneath.

## V I.

Ye dales of woodland and secluded farms,
Of rills and ripples and of forest shade,
Of bleakest summit sides, and mountain arms,
Of deep-cleft gills where murmuring becks cascade—
In you, ye dales, not Rome, my heart is ever laid.

## V I I.

Lo, where a kingly heron from the beck
Doth, rising loft, add grandeur to the grand;
With stately feet outstretched, and bended neck,
And pale wings that the sable crest-plumes deck,
He flaps his slow high flight toward the far marsh-land.

## V I I I.

Majestic bird! alike of youth and age
Beloved, and fitly favorite of kings,
Thy swan peer delicate on lake let feedeth,
A prince's child thy cousin gentle leadeth,
Whilst thou with fierce wild by doth flap thy slow-arched wings.

## I X.

Majestic bird, farewell! Sweet dale farewell!
Farewell ye moorlands, fare ye well my flowers,
Yet hear how often on the heath-clad moor
I listened to the golden plover's pipe,
I watched aloft the curlew and the snipe—
How often, when the summer day was ripe,
I lingered for a moment more
To catch the sun's alternate stripe
That lit and dimmed on Middlesmoor.

### X.

How often, when the night was nigh,
I wandered out upon the hill
To see the lines of daylight die,
How oft have sat in dear July
All night besiden Arna Gill,
And listened to the corncrakes cry,
That made the stillness doubly still,
Or spoiled the blackcap's melody.

### X I.

Great Jove, amongst the Gods most high !
Methinks I hear the hoarse war-cry.
Een now I feel my heart's blood burn,
And I mun to the battle fly.

### X I I.

With the rising sun
Hack the painted shield,
Now to the bath of blood,
With the greedy goshawk
And the sallow kite,
Call the grey wolf of the weald.

### X I I I.

Let the vulture hoarse,
And the swarthy raven
With horny neb,
And the eagle swift
With yellow feet,
Raw to devour
Find the mangled corse.

### X I V.—Farewell !

The Roman here painted is the degenerate Roman of the fifth century, and a Colonist. Having once parted with his coins he finds courage, and as he does so, the metre shortens, till he finishes in the mocking savage strain of the older Teutonic Heroic poetry. Verses XII. and XIII. are in fact little more than adaptations of verses in the Death-song of Regner Lodbrog, and in the Saxon Chronicle, year 988.

## THE ENGLE.*

The Dale was first *populated* by the Engles.   The great kingdom of Northumbria was founded by Ida the Engle, in 547, but the great influx of Engles into England on the north and east took place about A.D. 559, under Ella.   They appear to have taken possession of the dale, at least as far as regards its upper half.   The interior slopes of the hills, the villages, farms, pastures, sheds, one wood, the springs, tributary streams, and the main river itself, bear generally Anglo-Saxon names.   Thus " Raydale Knotts " is the name of the interior side of Little Whernside.   The occurrence of this name and that of *Prydale,* a field on Lodge Farm ; as well as Rundleside, (*Rundale Side*) the interior slope of the dale between Lodge and Woodale ; of *Woodale* itself; and probably of others in which the name *dale* is limited to fields or woods, induce me to withdraw the statement on P. 60.   " There is no trace of the former existence of a Village Community in Nidderdale," and to suggest that in Anglian times there probably were such, or *at least one family Community* near the Dale Head.   In this limited sense, *Dale* is an A. S. word, Dæl, used (as I have shown on P. 62) in the Laws of Ine, of divisions in common land (gedal land).†   The word Dale meaning the valley, is O. N., and was introduced later.   "Thorpe" or "Thrope," probably the *Thorp sub bosco,* or ' Thorpe Underwood' of Fountains Abbey, and " Stæn," villages ; " Limley " (lime-field) being situated upon the narrow strip of

* The earliest use of the word Englishman I have found is in the Laws of Ine, c. 24, (A.D. 688-728.)  " *Englisc mon,*" next in " Treaty between Alfred and Guthrun," c. 2, A.D. 878.  " Engliscne and Deniscne," next in " Treaty, Edward and Guthrun," *introd.*  "Engle and Dene."  I therefore prefer ENGLE to Angle.

† In Germany, under the system of the *Mark* or Commonland, the fields were anciently " divided into long strips, all bordering on one side on the road left for Agricultural purposes.  These parcels were called DEEL, *Deel* is the Danish for a *division.*  *Schiften,* in the North ; in England Oxgang," etc.—*Prim. Prop.,* p. 111.

limestone in the bottom of the dale a farm; "Tiedera Wood,"
*tiedera* being a pure Anglo-Saxon adjective meaning "thin,"
most descriptive of the thin hanger of birches upon a steep cliff
of limestone to which the name applies; with such names as
"Wising (*wisung*, guiding) *sike*," "*Haga* sike (hedge or fence, *i.e.*,
boundary), "Twisling" *(twislung*, tributary, ad.); "Thornit"
*(thorniht*, thorny, or abounding in thorn-bushes); "Mere
Dike" *(meera*, a boundary, being the boundary between
Stonebeck Up and Fountains Earth) applied to streams, as well
as "Hëaning" to fields (Anglo-Saxon *heán*, high; *iny*, field),
as in the field called Hëaning Top, on High Lofthouse Farm,
also Heaning, a flat meadow by the Ure, near Kilgram, which
may be O. N. HEGNINN, *fenced*, enclosed." Other physical
features demanding notice are Gladstones, a wreck of large
grit blocks lying strown on the hill side below the scar at
which they must formerly have made an imposing crag;
(A. S. *Glad* slipped). Compare 'Slipstone Crags,' Colsterdale.
Throstle Hill, a little conical eminence on Masham Moor, may be
called after the Moor Throstle, or Ring Ouzel.—(See Glossary.)
In the *Carta* of Roger de Mowbray " de recompensatione de
Niderdala," in the 'Register of Fountains Abbey,' *Fol.* 143. 6.,
given in Dugdale, Throstle How is thus mentioned as a point on
the boundary of Fountains Earth :—" et sic usque ad Frostilde-
hou, et de Frostilde-hou usque ad Hameldon," [here the initial F
is apparently a mistake for T] " et inde usque ad Dalhagha et
totum Dalhagha (Dallowgill)......et inde transversum moram
deversus *Scheldene*," etc. From the latter part of this passage,
however, we have valuable hints as to the correct etymology of
Dallow, also written *Dalagh* in the ' Confirmation of Gifts' by
Rich. I., and in the enumeration of the possessions of the abbey
temp Hen. VIII. and of Skell, evidently the same word as
' Schelde' a river in Belgium. " Pony well," at Middlesmoor,
may be A. S. *Ponne* a pan, partly because the term Pony is
not used in the dale, Galloway being the term, and partly
because of the celebrated enactment of King Edwin, (A. D. 627,)

K

King of Northumbria, that wherever there were clear wells by
public roads, cups of brass should be suspended upon posts for
the refreshment of way-goers.—(Bede *Hist. Eccles.*, *Lib.* 2, c.
xvi., 187). If so, of course the name is 1250 years old.
"Heathfield," A. S. *Hæthfeld.* "Slade" near Blubberhouses,
"Hanging Slade," "Slade Wham," a bog on moors, twice.
Slade only occurs in Washburn and Wharfedale, A. S. *Slæd* a
slade, plain, open tract, but it seems to have meant a clear
place in the forest as in Robin Hood and Guy of Gisborne :—

> "And John is gone to Barnesdale,
>   The "gates" he knoweth eche one ;
> But when he came to Barnesdale,
>   Great heaviness there he hadd,
> For he found two of his own followers,
>   Were slaine both in a *slade*."—L, 56.

"Hen Stones" recurs several times as the name of groups of
rocks on the high moors.   They are always on the highest ridges
in the locality.   "Hen Stones" on Pockstones Moor, 1360 ft.;
"Hen Stones" on Barden Fell, 1500 ft. ; "Hen Stones Ridge,
1250-1350 ft., N.W. of Greenhowhill ; "Hen Stone Band," the
watershed ridge between Wharfe and Nidd, 1750 ft., S.E. of
Meugher Hill.="High Stones."   A. S. *Héan*, high.   *Band* in
"Henstone Band," "Long Band, " means an elevated ridge on
the high moors, but it only occurs in this one locality.   I think
"Ray" or "Wray" in "Raydale Knotts," "Raygill," "Wood-
man Wray," (a bog at the head of Black Sike,) is the equivalent
of what on the Lower Greensand in Surrey are called "Roughs,"
*e.g.* "Perton Rough," near Abinger, (A. S. RÆOH rough,
*uncultivated*).   These give but a faint idea of the extent to which
the Engles stamped their image upon the higher parts of the
dale during the three centuries of their possession of it before
the Danish invasion.

Of the appearance of the Engles we know nothing from themselves, but we gain some notion of their looks from a graceful

picture bequeathed to us in the time honoured anecdote, related partly by the venerable Bede, and partly by Antoninus, Archbishop of Florence, in his "Summa Historiahs." When Gregory was a Monk at Rome, years before he became Pope, some merchants, having just arrived at Rome, exposed many things for sale in the market-place, and many people went there to buy,—among others Gregory himself. Amongst the other things for sale were some boys " *candidi corporis ac venusto vultûs capillorum quoque formâ egregiâ,*" white in body, of beautiful countenance, and with fine fair hair. Having inspected them he asked from what country they were brought, and he was told that they were from the island of Britain, whose inhabitants " *talis essent aspectûs* " were all like them. Then he asked whether those Islanders were christians or pagans, and was told that they were pagans. " Alas," said he, drawing from the bottom of his heart a long sigh, " what a pity that the author of *Darkness* should possess men " *tam lucidi* vultus,"—of such open, frank, and fair countenances, and that such *external grace* should be unaccompanied by *inward grace.*" He then asked again what was the name of that nation. The answer was that they were called "Angli," Angles. "Right," said he, "for they have the faces of angels, " *angelicam habent faciem,*" and it is fitting for such to be coheirs with the Angels in heaven. What is the name of the Province from which they are brought?" The answer was " Deiri." " Truly are they *de ira,*" said he, " withdrawn from wrath and drawn to the mercy of Christ,— (" *Bene* " inquit " *Deiri de ira eruti,*" etc.) What is the King of that Province called?" The answer was " Ælla." And he playing upon the name said " Alleluia, the praise of God the Creator must be ' Sunge in yᵗ countrey yᵗ so feyre chyldren were born in.' "—Bede, *Hist. Eccles.,* Lib. 2, c. I., 89 ; Fabian. *Chron.,* c. cviii. Gregory lived to be Pope A.D. 592, and sent Augustine A.D. 596, 156 years after the coming of the Angles, and before his death we hear him exclaiming, " Behold a tongue of Britian, which knew nothing else but to utter barbarian speech, already in the divine praises of the Hebrews, has begun to resound ' Alleluia.' "

———:o:———

## THE DANE.

Centuries before there was any permanent settlement of the Danes or Northmen from Scandinavia in North England, their name had become the dread and terror of Saxon, Engle, and Celt, in these islands. Whatever spirit the Saxons once had they soon lost, and the Chronicle sounds one long wail of a slothful, shiftless, spiritless people, without resource, organization, or grasp of mind enough to tackle with the quick movements and fertile resources of the Danes. Fabian quaintly recites one of the superstitions that sprang up after the terrible Dane had hacked, hewed, and burned his way from north to south, and from east to west, through the length and breadth of the land, maiming or hamstringing his prisoners, and leaving them to die of starvation, or to fall a prey to the wolves which then abounded in many parts of this island. Brightricus, first King of West Saxons, began his reign A.D. 678. "About the ii year of Brightrycus, was seen in Great Brytaygne, a wonder syghte, for sodenlye, as men walkyd in the strete, crossys lyke unto bloode fell upon they clothis, and blood fell from Hevyn like droppis of rayne : this after some exposytours betokened ye comynge of ye Danes into this londe ; the which entred shortly after. For, as witnesseth POLYCRONICA, about the ix. year of Brigthicus, the Danes fyrste entered this londe."—FAB. CHRON., *cap. clvii.* King Regner Lodbrog, one of those invaders, was King of Denmark early in the ninth century. He was taken at last, in battle, by Ella, King of Northumberland. In his Deathsong, he or his Scald, or Poet Laureate, records all the valiant achievements of his life; and threatens Ella with vengeance, which history tells us was effected by his sons. The following shows the irrepressible fiery energy of these bloody men : —

| | |
|---|---|
| " Hinggom ver med hianrvi. | " We hewed with the sword. |
| Haurd kom ríd á skiauldo | Hard came stroke on shields, |
| Nár fell nidr til jardar | Corpse fell down to earth |
| A Northymbra-Landi. | In Northumberland. • |
| Var'at um eina ótto | There was not at the eighth-hour |
| Aulldom thaurf at fryia | Need for man to waken        [blade |
| Hilldar-leik, thar er hvafsir | Hilda's game,✝ there-where‡ sword. |
| Hjálm-stofn bito skiómar. | Bit skull through bright helmet. |
| Var at sem unga eckio | Was it not as young widow |
| I aund-vegi kista'c." | At high-table kissed I." § |
| Lodbrokar Quida, *v.* 14. | |

Piracy was the recognised occupation of the North men.

Piratical invasions went on from time to time, until Harald Haarfagr, King of Norway, A. D. 860-933, by a new system of unbearable tyranny, drove from Norway all the more independent of the aggrieved freemen whose allodial holdings he taxed, and otherwise meddled with.‖ The fugitive was no slave. He had left the home of his fathers, where he thought no freeborn man could now care to live, and scattered over many lands. " But of all countries," says Sir G. Dasent, " what were called the Western Lands, were his favourite haunt," [among these] " England, where the Saxons were losing their old dash and daring, and settling down into a sluggish sensual race."

• Northumbria.

✝ Hilda's-laik,=Battle. HILDA, Goddess of War.

‡ At which time—eight in the morning.

§ Was it not as pleasant as when I kissed the young widow at the high-table.

‖ There still exists a descendant of this Harald Haarfagr, Tofte by name, at a farm called Toftemoen, far up among the Fjelds in the heart of Norway. The King dined at his house on his way to be crowned at Trondhjem, in 1860.

Towards 867 an organised expedition of Norsemen under Ingvar and Ubba, two of their kings, landed in Northumbria, in which district, in the beginning of Alfred's reign, or about 872, Halfdene rewarded his followers with grants of land. The settlement was something like the Norman Conquest two hundred years later, and its extent may be gathered from the fact that in the four counties of Yorkshire, Lincolnshire, Cumberland, and Westmoreland, there are nearly one thousand places which have Dano-Norwegian names against less than four hundred in all the rest of England.* If the names of farms and physical features were taken into account, this number would be greatly extended. Among other places the Danes settled in Nidderdale. We may now consider the meaning of the name Nidderdale, and of Nidd the river in it. Several attempts have been made to derive this from a celtic source, but I believe unsuccessfully.

Near the end of the twelfth century, the *Carta* of Roger de Mowbray, above-mentioned, "de recompensatione de *Niderdala*," goes on " Scilicet totum *Niterdale*," and writes the name of the river NID. About a century later, or in 1284, the " Statute of Westminster the Second," [13, Edward I., c. 47,] writes the name of the river *Niddiore*. The abstract of Roll 32, Henry VIII., Augmentation office, given in Dugdale, has *Nedirdale*, while Camden, 1607, writes *Nidherdale*, and the name of the river *Nidde*.

About four miles from its source the Nidd sinks into its limestone bed, and for two miles takes a subterranean course,—like the Mole in Surrey, which does the same between Dorking and Leatherhead, and the Churn in Gloucestershire. It would have been strange if this phenomenon had escaped the notice of the dwellers in the dale, to which it gives a distinctive character. We find the Anglo-Saxon word NIDER, NYDER, meaning " down,"

* Pearson's ' Early and Middle Ages,' ed. 1861, p. 107 ; Worsaae's 'Danes in England,' p. 71.

" below," which may have been given in allusion to this descent
and subterranean course, as a name to the river, and the A. S.
word *geótend*, the " down-pouring " or " channel, " to the
second swallow through which the water flows. This is now
called " Gooden Pot," (W. *Pot*,) or " Goydin Pot." It has been
attempted to give this word a Celtic derivation. The modern
pronunciation of " Nidderdale " is as nearly " Nitherdil " and
" Netherdil " as it can be written in modern English, but the
modern name of the river is Nidd. This is, doubtless, one of
the modifications introduced by the Dano-Norwegian invaders
on their settlement in the dale three centuries after the coming
of the Engles, for Nid is the name of a river which flows
through Throndhjem, in Norway, and gives the name of Nidar-
óss to a famous old town at its mouth. Similarly " Nidderdale"
may be Norsk, Nidar-dalr, the dale of the Nid, but the earlier
explanation seems preferable, considering the three centuries'
occupation of the Engles. However this may be, the modern
name of Nid certainly seems to be Norwegian or Danish.

## X.

# THE QUERN.

From Nidderdale, Great Whernside and Little Whernside appear as two distinct hills, two miles and a half distant from each other. The name of Whernside is itself of doubtful origin (A. S. *cwærn*, O. N. *hvern*, a quern ; and A. S. *sid*, O. N. *sida*, side ; the first, given by A. S., seems best), but this much about it is certain, that the whole hill takes its name from a part of it, *viz.* the Wharfedale side, which is so called. Here are quarries from which the stone may have been dug to make querns. The Nidderdale side, however, is called Blackfell. In other words, the hill seen from Wharfedale, is called " Whernside," and from Nidderdale "Blackfell."* Similarly the slope of Little Whernside in Nidderdale is called " Raydale Knotts," and that in Coverdale " Cowside,"—a common name for Pennine slopes,†—while it borrows its general name from the larger hill. Whernside is pronounced " Whairnsid" which favours the A. S. origin. " Quernside " has been changed into Whernside, in the same way as " Quarrel"—*i. e.*, Quarry—has been softened into '· Wharrel'" in the name Wharrel Crags on the moors east of Coverdale.

I received information of the discovery of two querns in Nidderdale, one in the flat field at the bottom of the hill below Middlesmoor, between the road and Stean beck, and immediately east of the confluence of Whitbeck with Stean beck ; and the

---

* The map in Camden's Brittannia, 1805, writes " *Great Wharne-side* " for the northern end, and *Blackfell* for the southern end of the hill, but this is wrong. (See below under Fell and Fieldfare.)

† The name *Cowside* is very ancient, and must have belonged to the unenclosed hill pastures of the Village Communities in A. S. times. It is most common on the grassy limestone fells.

other in the flat footpath field close to the Nidd, immediately south west of Low Sykes.

The quern, or handmill, among the Greeks and Romans was worked by slaves. The labour of using it was exceedingly arduous, nevertheless the toil was imposed principally upon women. The smallest farmers, however, ground their own meal, rising before daylight to prepare enough for the requirements of the day. The graphic description of Virgil renders it unnecessary to draw upon our imagination, to picture the quern in use. The right hand turned while the left kept feeding the grain,—" Læva ministerio dextra est intenta labore"—or *vice versâ* when the right hand required rest. Cowper thus translates the description in " The Salad."

> " Simulus poor tenant of a farm
> Of narrowest limits".... [having risen
> before the lark] " opes his granary door.
> Small was his stock, but, taking for the day
> A measured *stint* of twice eight pounds away,
> With these his mill he seeks. A shelf at hand
> Fix'd in the wall affords his lamp a stand
>
> . . . . . . . . . . . . .
>
> And with a rubber for that use designed
> Cleansing his mill within, begins to grind.
> Each hand has its employ ; labouring amain,
> This turns the winch while that supplies the grain.
> The stone revolving rapidly now glows,
> And the bruised corn a mealy current flows,
> While he to make his heavy burden light,
> Takes off his left hand to relieve his right."

That the quern was still worked in this country by female slaves in Anglo Saxon times, appears from a passage in the Laws of Æthelbirht, c. 11., " GIF SIO GRINDENDE THEOWA SIE," " if she be a *mill girl*," which incidentally alludes to them. It also appears from the same laws that the mill girl was not of the lowest rank, being compensated at a higher rate than the King's nurse, and the ' THRIDDE' third or lowest rank. I believe the quern is still in use in the Highlands of Scotland, or, if not, it has only very lately gone out of use. We owe our water-mills to the Romans, by the way.

L

## XI.

# PHYSICAL FEATURES,

*With Norsk Names.*

That tract of moor included between the Nidd and How Stean
Beck bears the name of " In Moor " and " Middlesmoor "
(Middel mór).    " Middlesmoor " by the analogy of several
Icelandic names compounded with middle would appear to be
O. N.    The same must be said of " In Moor " as opposed to
Owster Bank, O. N. *Austr* eastern, *Bakki* bank, the elevated
ridge which forms the eastern watershed ridge of Nidderdale
opposite In Moor, and from which a magnificent view is obtained
over the whole of the vale of York and Mowbray, and of the
Cleveland Hills.    The summit of In Moor forms a conspicuous
hill, 1488 feet in altitude, which now bears the name of " Rain
Stang."    " Rane-stang-en " is the name of a mountain in
Norway on the watershed between Valders and Hallingdall.
" *Rani* " is the old Norsk for a hog's snout, a hog-shaped hill,
or " hog's back," and " stang " the Danish for a pole or post,
W. *Ystang*.    The name " stang " occurs many times on hills in
Yorkshire, as " Kettlestang Moor " and " Stang Brae," near
Carlesmoor in the Laver basin, and " Stanghow " (Cleveland).
Besides " Rainstang " to its summit, the Danes gave various
names to other parts of " Middlesmoor," of which they took
possession : *e. g.*, " Armathwaite " (O. N. *thveit*, a clearing,
detached piece of land), while Middlesmoor was eventually
retained only as the name of the village.    Armathwaite occurs
several times on the Pennine Range and in Westmoreland.
Other Norsk names of hills and eminences are " Bull brae "

(Icel. *bula*, to tear asunder ; Norsk *brae*, hillside), the name
of a part of the north side of the dale from which there
has been a large slip, " Haden Carr " near the dale head, a
plateau 1500 feet ending in a steep escarpment (O. N. *hæd*, hill,
height ; *Kjarr*, bog covered with brushwood), " Jordan Moss "
(Dan. *jord*, earth, peat ; *en*, the ; *mos*, moss, the peat-bog),
peat-bogs on Braithwaite, near Greenhowhill sike, and Lofthouse
Moors. " Blue Burnings," the name of a steep hillside above
Lofthouse, (O. N. *blåberne*, the blæberries), formerly a wood
famous for bilberries ; also " Blubberhouses " (Blåber-husum)
Washburndale ; " Trappen Hill," the steepest part of the hill-
road that runs up by Blue Burnings, (Dan. *trappe*, staircase, *en*,
the—*trappen*, the staircase). Before the road was made it is
probable that steps were here cut in the soil ; they are common
enough at the present day. " Arna Nab " (O. N. *arna*, gen.
plur. of *örn*, an eagle ; Nab, Dan. *næb*, projecting point of a hill,
eagle's point) ; " Arnagill," a picturesque rocky gill at the
southern extremity of the Colsterdale basin. " Brown Ridge "
(O. N. *brún*, brow of a hill), the northern watershed ridge of
Nidderdale, 1500 feet ; " Acora Scar " (O. N. *akr*, arable land ;
as opposed to *engr*, grass land). " Sleets," a flat field ; " Sleet
Moor," an elevated flat moor, 1500 feet, east of Grassington
Moor ; " Nar Sleets=near Sleets " (O. N. *Ná* near,) and
" Hunters Sleets," a flat moor, 1500 feet at Coverdale Head.
probably also " Slight Hill," (375 feet) N. W. of Thornton Hall,
and " Sleights" a village near Whitby ; (Goth. *Slahits* flat, level,
O. N. *Sléttr*, Dan *Slet*). In the names " HUNTER'S Sleets" and
" HUNTER'S Stones," (near Jack Hill) we seem to have another
vestige of the village *Commune*. " The *Marken* [or districts of
the Communes] were called *Geraiden* in Alsace, or *Hundschaften*
or HUNTARI, among the Alemanni. They included cultivated
land, pasturage, wood, and water." *(Prim. Prop. p. 101).*
So also in the names of " MARKENFIELD, MARKINGTON."
" Horse Helks," a confused pile of slips and Rocks on the dale

edge, 1000 feet; opposite Ramsgill, (O. N. *Háls* a neck, also a hill, ridge between two parallel dales, a pass; *Hölkn*, a rough stony field).* "Kelds" springs, and "Kell" at Greenhowhill, "*Kills* Wham," etc., (O. N. *Kelda* whence, A. S. *Keld* a spring). "Stainin Gill Beck," (three O. N. words,—*Steinn* stone, *inn* the *Gil & Bekkr*) "Bain Grain Beck,"=near branch beck—three O. N. words,—(*Beinn*, near, *Grein*, a branch, Dan. *Green*, & *Bekkr*), also "Grainings," "Crag Grainings," "Grainings Gill," and many others. "Green *Nook*," a *knoll* on Stean moors, 1550 feet, (O. N. *hnjúkr, hnúkr*, a knoll, peak). "High Fleak," an elevated flat moor, (O. N. *Fláki* same). "Flask," on the north west side of Barden Fell; "Half Flask," etc., (O. N. *Flask* a green spot among bare fells, also written *Flas, Fles*, in which form it appears in the name "Flesh Beck," East Witton, and "Flasby Fell." "Fell," O. N. *Fjall*, Norsk *Fjeld*, Gr. *Phellos*.—See Glossary. "Carle Fell," "Blackfell," "Barden Fell," "Blashaw Fell," and "Segsworth Fell." "This common North of England word," says Mr. Dakyns, "does not occur in Scotland save in composition. In Yorkshire it is not found south of Skipton, Flasby Fell being the most southern "Fell" in Yorkshire, but in Lancashire it reaches a little further south."† The word Hope, (O. N. Hóp) properly *a small land-locked bay or islet*, occurs in England only in composition. In addition to the Northumbrian and Durham names *Kilhope, Stanhope, Ryhope*, etc., we find

* "*Horse*," Hause, Hawse, hass, a ridge between two dales.—Se in "*Horsehouse*" in Coverdale, "*Horsehead*" between Wharfedale and Littondale, *Hawes*, properly "The Hawes," (*pron.* T' Hars) Wensleydale. Here you pass over from east, to west England,—either by Widdale to Dent, Ingleton, or Settle; or by Garsdale to Sedbergh (*pron.* Sebber or Sedber); or by Mallerstang into the Vale of Eden—five different routes. This is therefore *par eminence* "*The* Hawes." *Helks*, in Wharfedale, surfaces of bare limestone cut up by joints into numerous rhombs.—J. R. D.

† For further remarks on the word Fell see under *Field fare*.

"Widdop" in Yorkshire, north of Todmorden; "Gate-up," north east of Grassington; "Bac-up," in Lancashire; in which *op* and *up*=HOPE. To these we may add "Lead-up Beck," on the east side of Coverdale. "Woogill Tarn" and "Coverdale Tarn," two large ponds in the peat, 1690 feet, on the plateau of the North Moor west of "Great Haw," (O. N. *Tjörn.)* "Priest Tarn," about 1700 feet, on Grassington Moor. "This northern word," says the same authority, "too only extends south about as far as Fell does—the most southern Tarn being a pool near Keighley, called 'The Tarn.'" "Flamstone Pin," a rock 1350 feet, on the flat elevated plateau of Braithwaite moor, (O. N. *Flœmi* a waste open place.) "The Three Howes" often recurring on the moors on elevated ridges, (O. N. *Haugr* a mound, *burial mound).* "Storth's Hall" near Huddersfield. "Hoodstorth," Washburndale, (O. N. *Storth*, a young plantation). "Swinsty" (O. N. *Svinsti*, swine sty). "Hammer," "Hammer End," a hill bank near East Witton, (O. N. *Hamarr*, a hammer shaped crag, a crag). The river "Burn" (O. N. *Brunnr)*, but "Burn Gill"=Burn's Gill, after a farmer who formerly lived up there, where are now the ruins of farmstead and field-walls. "Gir Beck" Coverdale, (O. N. *Geiri*, strip of grass among rocks). "Birk Gill Beck," Colsterdale, three O. N. words. Scale Gill = Shale Gill, that part of its course being between cliffs of blue shale. "Fuley Gill," a deep cleft in high Colsterdale moors, (O. N. *Fjálfr, Fjálbr* an abyss). "Roova Crag," "Roova Trough," East Scrafton Moor, 1500 feet, (O. N. *Hrjúfr*, rough). "Wilder Botn," a trough in the plateau of the same elevated range of moors, on the Coverdale Shed and "Starbotton" Wharfedale, (O. N. *Botn*, the head of a dale). "Grey Yaud," a crag above East Witton, (now a large quarry). "Yaud Head," the rocky gill in which lies Eavestone Lake. "Rowan-tree Yards," crags on the moor near Hummerstone, Washburn—dubious. "Sourmires," part of Masham Moor, 1250 feet.

"Sour Ings," a field Colsterdale. "Sower Beck," high moors near Henstone Band, 1500 feet, (O. N. *Saurr*, mud; *Myrr*, moor, bog, swamp). "Vollens Gill," Coverdale. "Volla Wood," South of Sawley (O. N. *Völlr*, a field, a close or paddock. *Dat. plu. völlum*). "Clint Gill"—clint, narrow cleft in limestone. "Griff," trib. of Clint Gill, (O. N. *Gröf* a pit, hole dug—for limestone). "Hummerstone," Washburndale (O. N. *Hömul*; Norse *Humul*; heaps of earth-fast stones—*Humul gryti*).* "Gollinglith," *pron.* Gownley, (*Gula* is a local name in central Norway. *Hlith* a slope, mountain side). Golling lith is a long spur in Colsterdale. "Gollinglith Foot" is the village at the foot of the slope. "Swidney" in Colsterdale, (O.N. *Svida*, in Norway, woodland cleared for tillage by burning. Swidney looks a dative or locative, in Icel. *Svidnur* is a local name where sea-weed was burnt for salt making). "Melmerby," by the termination, is Dan., ' by ' being a *town, village*, or *farm*— so with all places ending in 'by.' Places ending with *um* are generally Danish. We find "Kilgram" on the Ure, "Angram," and "Angram Cote," the latter at Ellingstring. "Toldrum" twice—houses south of Evestone Lake and west of Winksley. "Brandstone Scar," "B. Beck," etc., three O. N. words meaning "hearthstone scar," i.e., the scar where the hearthstones were dug, and probably still are dug. Old English "brand" and (O. N. *Brandr*, the hearth.) *Comp.* "Bakstone Gill." Langbar, that fine ridge of moor that overlooks the ings of Bolton, from a height of 1250 feet="Long Ridge, " or "long edge." (O. N. *Barth*, the *verge, edge* of a hill, freq. in local names in Icel. *comp.* "Langbarth" in Cleveland). "Bale Bank," a slope of grit grass covered—725-975 feet, (O. N. BALI a *grassy bank*). "Ivin Waite," a farm house="Ivy Thwaite." "Water Gate"=a ford where a road crosses the beck. "Blea Beck," "Red Beck," "Brown Beck,"—the two former near East

---

* Also "Homerstone grit," a coarse sandstone with large quartz pebbles.—J. R. D.

Witton—are all O. N. names; the last O. N. *Brún*, a brow, edge of a moor. "Bak'ston Gill," trib. of Long Gill, "Bak'ston Gill," trib. of Birk Gill Beck—both in Colsterdale. "Great Gill," in reality a very little gill, O. N. GRJOT, grit from coarse sandstone forming a part of its bed. Grit is generally *pron.* "Greet." "Beldin Gill," a very little gill on the moors rising on Great Haw. I cannot explain Beldin—such a man's name is unknown to me. "Brown Rigg"=moor ridge, (O. N. BRUN, the *brow of a fell, moor*, etc., HRYGGR, a ridge, as in Fjall-hryggr a mountain-ridge.) "Braithwaite" is a compd. of Bræ and "thwaite," *the clearing on, beneath, or beside the bræ*, a common man's name. "Braithwaite Banks," near Middleham, are 400 feet high. "Strutt Stear," a crag about 1250 feet on the same spread of high moors as "Flamstone Pin," and "Wharrel Crags;" O. N. STRUTR, as a local name, a "*strut*" *formed fell* in Icel. *Strut, a hood jutting out like a horn;* also *Stryta a cone formed thing.* STÖRR, *Bents*, bent grass. Strut Stear is therefore "the Bents with the 'strut' formed crag." This interpretation would make the name rather that of the immediate part of the moor on which the crag is situated, than that of the rock itself, which would be simply 'Strut.' "Middle Tongue" occurs several times as a name of *the mountain spur that runs down between two becks*, O. N. MEDAL, *Middle*, TUNGA, meaning the same as above, cp. "MEDAL FELL" Middle fell, MEDAL-LAND Middle Land, etc., and our "Middlesmoor," written MIDLESMORE in possessions of Fountains Abbey, and MIDDLEMORE in Camden's Brittannia, 1607, Lib. vii., 68.

The names of well known Northmen who settled in Yorkshire, enters into the composition of the following :—"Ulfers Crags" and "Ulfers Gill," Coverdale, O. N. ULFR man's name, *lit* "Wolf." "About the time of King Canute the Dane, Ulph, the son of Thorold, a prince of that nation, governed in the western part of Deira."—*(Camden's Brittan).* "Kettlestang," "Kettle-sing," and "Kettlewell," spelt "Kettelwel" in the possessions of

Fountains Abbey ; O. N. KETILL, man's name.  " Baxley,"
Coverdale, and " Barnley," Colsterdale, moorland pastures, seem
by their terminations to be Norsk.   O. N. *Hlith*, a slope,-*comp.*
" Gownley "=Gollinglith.   " Great Stockiner " and " Little
Stockiner," large moorside pastures in Coverdale, from the kind
of fence by which they were enclosed, (O. N. *Stokkr*, a stock,
stake, *the beams laid horizontally* above *a loose stone wall*, a mode
of fencing much used in the Dales of the Pennine chain.   These
horizontal bars are supported by upright posts, and do not rest
upon the wall.   They are to keep sheep from jumping the wall and
knocking it down.   They are only necessary where the only
available walling stones were *round*, and for that reason easily
knocked down.   " Stockiner "means "*the Stock fence enclosure,*"
*dat. sing.* with *def. art* STOCKINUM *nom. plu.* STOKKARNIR, *the*
*Stock fences.*   The name is either the *nom. plu.* or a *dat* of place.
" Seavy Wham " a moorland bog, two O. N. words.   " Foss
Rakes " the ford in " Greet Gill," on the moors near Roova
Crag, just above a " foss " or waterfall, (O. N, FORS ; *Icel.*,
*Swed.*, and *Dan.*, Foss ; and Rake a footpath.—See Glossary.)
" Fosse Gill," etc.   " Pockst'ns " a group of rocks and crags
on the high moor east of Barden Fell, (Dan. PAK, a 'group),
" Mosscar Beck " three Norsk words, trib. of " Brandstone
Beck," also Norsk.   " Brown Beck Swang," a bog on Agra Moor,
Colsterdale, (O. N. *Brún* a brow, edge ; *Svangr* a hollow place).
Blazefield occurs three times—always high, bleak, bare ridges.
Blaze is dubious, but field is certainly Norsk FJELD, as there
are no fields, but open moor in two of the three cases, and only
modern [?] enclosures in the third.

Another physical feature of great interest that bears on old
Norsk name is " Beckermote Scar," a steep cliff in limestone
at the angle of the Nidd at which it first sinks in volume into
the ground at a place called " Manchester Holes."   The *Carta*
of Roger de Mowbray " *de recompensatione*," etc., mentions this
place.   " De Iwdenbec sursum in longum Nid usque ad BECKER-

MOTE." In Cumberland there is a place called " Beckermet," and in Langstrothdale "Beckermonds " is the name of the tongue of land between two rivers at their confluence. Beckermote (pronounced " Beckermort ") is O. N. *bekkja*, gen. plu. of *bekkr*, beck, and *mót*, meeting; but it does not mean a meeting of the waters, for there is no meeting of any waters. It simply means a " juncture," and as the same sense as in *alda-mót*, the end and beginning of two centuries ; *missera-mót*, the meeting, juncture of the seasons, where one ends the other begins ; so *bekkjr-mót* means the point at which the river on the surface ends, and that below ground begins. Beckarmote* Scar is opposite Tiedera* Wood, which is on a similar limestone cliff, but bears an Anglian name. The true explanation of the meaning of this interesting name shows how necessary it is to *visit a place and see the nature of the spot* to which a name is given. " Manchester " refers to the same event, and may be It. *manchézza*, loss, defect.

It is interesting to note the collection of *Danish* names as opposed to old Norsk, on the east side of the Nidd near Lofthouse, which is itself Danish. It is thus mentioned in the oft-quoted *Carta* of Roger de Mowbray " Et preterea totum LOFT-HUSUM cum pertinentüs Suis. Lofthusum is the *dat. plu.* of *Loft hus*, a dative of place or *locative*, precisely as used and spelt in Denmark and Norway. The " Confirmation of gifts " by Richard I., writes it " Lost hourrs," in which a " *long* s " has been put for " f," and " rs " for " se." These Danish names probably indicate that the settlers there were of a later date than the original Scandinavian invaders who settled on the west side of the Dale.

* Mis-spelt on the 6 IN. ordnance map—" Beggarmote" and "Thedera" respectively.

## XII.

## CRAGS AND SCARS.

Several Crags on the moors bear Anglian names.
" Ewe Crags " occurs as a name several times, A. S. Ewe Eʌ,
water.  These crags always have a spring issuing from their
base.  Several sets of crags on the moors take their names from
having been used as guide-marks for shepherds or others.
" Owing to the steepness of the hills, and the spongy and
desolate nature of the surrounding moors," says Mr. Grainge,
" the approaches to the dale were always difficult, and at some
seasons of the year dangerous"......" The road from Kirkby
Malzeard, to Fountains Earth and Pateley Bridge, even to the
commencement of the present century, was nothing but a track
across the moors, *indicated to travellers in misty weather*, and *in
winter*, by tall upright pillars of stone, some of which yet
remain." (*Hist. of Nidd. p. 11.*)  Everyone who goes much on
the moors, will know how suddenly a Scotch mist comes on,
and how utterly lost he is with no landmarks, once let him get
sight of " Wigst'ns (A. S. Weg, a way) or of " Raygill House
Wigstones," or of the " Wising Crags," or of " Wising Gill,"
(A. S. Wisung, *guiding*) or, where there are no natural crags,
of the " Long Stoop," a stone post sometimes eleven feet high—
or let him find the straight line of large stones on the Great and
Little " Stangate "='stone way,' i. e., ' the way by the guide
stones,' an elevated flat topped ridge in How Stean basin, and
he will soon find his way down to the dale.  Now *Weg & Wising*
have possible alternative derivations and meanings.*  It is the

* Wising Gill occurs twice, " Wising Gill Sike," trib. of Stone Beck at
Angram, and " Wising Gill," trib. of How Stean Beck at West End
Houses.  Both have a short steep course, the former three quarters of a

rarest thing, however, to find a crag, or solitary stone on the moors, without a name. They are all, and always were, used as land marks. " Whey Crags," *pron.* " Wy Crags," seems to be the same as Wig, but Dan. *Vei,* a way.

Other crags take their names from the sun, or points of the compass. " Twelve O'clock Stones," about 900 feet, on the moor to the south of that wild gorge, west of the Washburn, through which the Harrogate and Bolton Road passes.—" Noon Stone," on the flat moor south of Bewerly, 1000 feet.—" Summer Lodge Stone," on the north side of the dale, not far from Woodale.

It may be generally remarked, that crags on moors and solitary stones, *always* have names, the exceptions being so rare, that I do not hesitate to use the strong adverb. Crags in dales, even though, conspicuous, and near villages, frequently have no names. The reason is of a practical nature. On the moors

mile, the latter a mile, with a fall of in the former, 400 feet, and in the latter 600 feet. Some part of the course, in each case, is on the peat covered plateau of the moor, and the remainder, precipitous. Both are exceedingly small ' grooves,' the latter being the larger. Wising Gill Sike deflects the contours of the hill side in a very slight degree. Neither has the characteristics of a swamp, except on the open moors, where they both have that character in common with the other slight hollows on the moor. I am particular, because Mr. Atkinson writes anent this name, " a place near Guisbro' called " The Weises," sounded Wyzes. I referred my enquiring friend to the word spelt ' weeze ' in my Glossary, and meaning " to ooze out," and gave besides some German and other analogies and connections, e.g., O. N. VEISA, a swamp, morass ; O. Sw. *wäsa*, a swamp ; Germ. WIESE, a moist meadow, &c., the place know as the ' weise' or ' wises,' being just in moist weather, a water-logged field, with coarse herbage, which grows in such places. Dont you think *oozing* sike a better explanation than *guiding* sike ? " Wising Gill, How Stean, it should be mentioned is quite in a line with the Stangate, up to which it leads. On the other hand we have " Sypeland," the name of a large bog on Fountains Earth Moor, which is unquestionally " SIPE, to *drip, ooze.* The difficulty about the Wising Gills is that the physical character is not that of Sypeland.

they are the only landmarks, in dales the roads and paths avoid
them.    Thus in Nidderdale, above Lofthouse, there are *twelve*
considerable sets of crags, of which only *two*—Gladstones, and
Summer Lodge Stone—have independent names.    Four others
have borrowed names,—Maiden Gill Crags, Wising Gill Crags,
Haugh Crags, (from Great Haw, on the south slope of which
they stand) and Whin Pasture Crags, while the remaining *six*
have no names.    Now it is these crags that give the dale its
character.    They are the setting, the jewel, the diadem, which
brings into harmony the dark, somewhat savage, moors above,
and the quiet dale below.    (See " The Clifford Fragments "
below).

The complement to a crag is a scar.    A scar is a hollow
cliff left behind a place from which there has been a landslip, or
above an angle of a river which has eaten away part of a hill side.
Scars are conspicious features in a dale.

While Brimham Rocks may be instanced as the noblest
example of a crag, Guyscliff is the finest instance of a scar.    And
I cannot pass over these two remarkable Physical Features with-
expressing my undiminished admiration of their unique beauty,
and of the stupendous scale upon which they are formed.    A
Scar is an object of very great beauty.    The clean cut section of
the rocks with their alternating bands, and rich colouring, the
vestige of the native forest that clings to the verge of the cliff, or
that shoots up on the screes or sprouts from the inaccessible face
of the rock wall, give to a Scar a kind of beauty quite different
from that which characterises a Crag.    Above Lofthouse there
are *fifteen* considerable sets of Scars, of which only *four* have
independent names, The Old Scar, Beckermote Scar, Boysoak
Scar, High Scar ; and *two* have borrowed names, Woodale Scar,
and The Scar, by Scar House,—which name evidently reflects
upon The Scar from which the house takes its name, i. e. if
Scar House had not been built, " The Scar " would probably
have been classed among those which have no name.    Of these

Scars, Woodale Scar and the Old Scar are very large, coming only second to Guyscliff in point of size and beauty.

Men's names enter into the composition of the following :— " *Haxby* Hippings," stepping stones in the Nidd near Darley, from a farmer who first placed them there. " *Burn* Ground " and " *Burn* Gill." " *Eylin* Hole," a cave in Stæn Beck, from the owner of the land. " *Turner* Car," generally spelt " Turnacar," and " Turnacar Gill." " *Ruscoe*," (pron. Roosca,) a small farm house, "Ruscoe Beck," etc. " *Oliver* High Lathe," " *Oliver* Scar," etc, near Stæn. " *Kay* Head Allotment" *Kay* is Welsh or Cymric, as it is an Arturian name. " *Bales* Hill," Colsterdale. " *Lobley* Crags," near there. " *Day* Ash " near Thornthwaite. " *Bird* Ridding," Coverdale. " *Mall Reynolds* Wham," and " *Tom Claypham* Bogs," bogs on Moors, Colsterdale. " *Pickering* Dub," a sheep-wash in the cover. " *Backhouse* Gill," " *Jemmy* Dike," " *Hardcastle* Moor," " *Hardcastle* Garth," " *Palley's* (Polly's) Crags," " *Jack* Hole," peat pits. " *Abraham* Crags," " *Nanny* Black Hill," " Black Hill,"=" Bleak Hill," is common. Nanny=Nanny's Black Hill, is thus distinguished from another Black Hill close by. " *Nanny* Pasture," rocks, with grass between. " *Hood* Gap," " *Oddy* Ridge," a rough strong ridge, may be from a man's name, but the name " Oddy" is the O. N. ODDI, a *point* or tongue of land, Dan. ODDE, so that the meaning is the same. In Iceland and Norway it is frequent in local names. " ODDI," as a man's name, also written *Oddr*, means a *leader*. The name " Odd Stones," similarly placed at the end of a ridge on the moors, not far west of Henstone Band, is certainly Oddi, ODDE, a *point of land*, which so far makes it probably that the name Oddy Ridge was not a man's name, but the Norsk name for that feature in the landscape. " *Hardisty* Hill." These are but a drop in the ocean. It will be observed that the men's names are all genitives, but without the *s*, thus Haxby Hippings=Haxby's Hippings.

Mythical names may enter into the composition of the following :—" Frèia Hèàd,"*pron.* " Freeya Heead," a lofty ridge on the Wharfe and Nidd watershed, about 1800 feet, S.E. of Great Whernside.    A. S. *Freâ* the Teutonic Venus—in O. N. *Freyja*— " and Freia," says Pearson, " at once Cybele and Aphrodite Demosia."—*Middle Ages*, p. 74.

" Hurders Edge," *pron.* " Hurthers Edge," on Black Fell, the eastern side of Great Whernside, about 1600 feet, O. N. *Höthr*, the blind brother and slayer of Baldr.   So also " Huddersfield " is *pron.* locally and spelt, on the map accompanying the Agric. Survey of the West Riding, 1799, " Huthersfield."

## XIII.

## BECKS AND GILLS.

Thus far attention has been drawn to the names of Physical Features, but there are one or two more most interesting points connected with names of places that should on no account be passed over without mention. It has already been shown that most of the streams in the upper part of the dale bear Anglian names. For the highest eight miles of the dale, or as far down as Stæn Beck, there is not one Danish name applied to a stream.

In How Stæn basin however, the names of the tributaries seem to be almost all O. N. and Danish, thus on the south side BAK'ST'N GILL, fed by " BAKSTONE GILL Great WHAM," a spongy bog, 1750 feet, on the north side of Meugher FELL, " Great Blawn GILL BECK," Little do., " Sandy Sikes GILL," " STAINING GILL BECK," " AYGILL BECK," " BUSKAR BECK," O. N. BUSKAR bushes, *nom. plu.* of BUSKR, a bush.—Dan. BUSKER, *nom. plu.* of BUSKER,) and lastly, ARMATHWAITE GILL. This derivation of Busker Beck has been contested, and the Mediœval Latin " Boscus " suggested in its place. It is therefore desirable to state that all the above-named tributaries lie wholly on the high moors, except Buskar Beck and Armathwaite Gill, which is much lower down the valley. Busker Beck springs in the peat on the table land at about 1400 feet, and descends through a short course of three quarters of a mile to How Stean Beck, at a point rather below 1000 feet above Sea level, rather more than half its course being through moorside pastures, in which the sheds are called LATHES, also O. N. The whole valley is bare of trees above 900 feet, save for a few bushes of thorn, etc., scattered here and there in that part of the course of Buskar Beck, in which it cuts through the " Edge " or " Nook " of the dale, and is in consequence deep enough to afford them shelter. Now if we look to the meaning of Boscus we shall at once see that it would be wholly inapplicable here. Boscus, It. *Bosco*, Fr. *Bois*, means a *wood*, also a *part of the forest*, a *woodland pasture*, (Du. Cange), and this last was a special meaning of Boscus. Again, Boscus in this country was a monastic, and so a legal word, not one in use amongst the remote dalesmen. Moreover the Abbey of Bylands, in whose Forest of Nidderdale this remote beck lay. held the wild and extensive district of Stonebeck Up and Stonebeck Down, which contained many places in its lower parts to which the name Boscus would have been very properly applied. I apprehend also that the name Boscus was a generic one like " Wood " or " Pasture," and by itself or simply prefixed to Beck would define no place in particular, whereas Buskar defines the only Beck at that altitude near which there were and are bushes. Buskar Beck has a south-east exposure. More might be added, but to my mind the evidence given is conclusive.

In the highest eight miles of Nidderdale, above Stean Beck, there are forty-two streams, including branch tributaries, of which twenty-seven are named. Of these twenty-seven, six retain their original Anglian names unchanged, as "Stand Sike," " Hagga Sike," " Maddering Sike," " Mere dike"; and twenty-one do so with the interpolation of the word " Gill," as in " Skitter *Gill* Dike," " Wising *Gill* Sike," " Twisling *Gill*," " Thornit *Gill*." " Gill " (O. N. GIL, a deep narrow glen with a stream at the bottom,) being the name, not of the stream, but of the narrow valley which contains it. The English, who came from the Low Countries in which *rivers* are the most strongly marked physical lines, were careful to name their rivers and streams, the water- shed ridges being low, flat, and ill-defined ; but the Norseman, who dwelt in a land where the watershed ridges form the great physical barriers, or lines of *division*, called the included area

DALE, *dale,* or *division,* (Goth. DALUR, DALEI, *dale,* DAILJAN, to divide ; A. S. DÆL, a *division,* a *dell ;* GEDAL, *divided ;* O. N. DEILD, a *division ;* Germ. THAL, *dale,* THEIL, a *division ;)* making the name of the river subordinate.

For this reason a dale frequently bears one name and the river another, as Sœtersdal in Norway, river Otter ; Wensley-dale in Yorkshire, river Ure ; Colsterdale, Yorkshire, river Burn. Therefore, when the Norseman found himself in the Yorkshire hills, he applied the cognomen of " gill " and " dale " to the smaller and larger valleys, which the English had been content to know by the name of the river or stream.

There is one more point worthy of mention. The English, or Engles, settled in the whole dale ; whereas the Norseman, and at a later date, the Dane, obtained a footing here and there. Thus " Angram," at the Dale head, is a Norwegian settlement, (O. N. ANGRUM, written " ANGROME grangia " in *Abstract of Roll 32,* Henry VIII., *Augmentation Office,*—dat. plu. of *Angr,* a bay (?), these datives, the representatives of the old Aryan locative, have the force of " in " the place). It is right to mention, however, that the name ANDGRYM appears in verse 3, line 2, of the Incantation of Hervor, (Hervarer Saga).

" There was originally, in all the Aryan languages," says Max Muller,[*] " a case expressive of locality, which grammarians call the *locative.* In Sanscrit, every substantive has its locative as well as its genitive, dative, and accusative." It has been suggested that the *um* termination represents an old word meaning *home.* " The element ' Ham,' " says Latham,[†] " is found all over Germany. But it is not found in the same parts, [by which I suppose he means that it is not found everywhere in the same form] it is *Heim* in some ; in others, *hem* ; in others *um* ;—

[*] Lect. on Science of Language, Second Series, p. 218.

[†] The English Language.—LATHAM.—P. 136.

N

Oppenheim, Arnhem, Husum." My friend, Mr. Berg, Director of Education in Færoe, from whom I have derived much information, in answer to a question as to how this termination is understood by the Danes, gave the following illustration of its form. " Where do you live ? " " Húsum," i. e., in the place ' Húse,'=houses. In olden times the plural was frequently used when referring to a single house, (Cleas). Single houses frequently consisted of groups of buildings within one wall.

" At Angram we have the words " thwaite," and " laith" or " lathe," for shed, (O. N. *hlatha*, a barn) :—

> " Whyne had thou put the capel in the *lathe*."
> CHAUCER, ' *Canterbury Tales*,' v. 4085.

On the next farm, Lodge, an Anglian settlement, all the sheds are called " barns," an Anglo-Saxon word which prevails all the way down the valley to Stean Beck, at which stream we again find the word " laith." At Stean the word " shipn " is used .—

> " The shepen burning with the blackë smoke."
> CHAUCER, ' *Canterbury Tales*,' v. 2002.

Perhaps no word in the English language offers a readier, more perfect, and more completely satisfactory, *apparent* etymology than shipn. In A. S. we find the forms SCIPEN, SCYPEN, SCEPEN, SCIPPAN, SCIPAN, SCYPPAN, SCEPPAN, SCÉOPPAN, SCEAPAN, SCAPPAN, SCAPAN, a stall, stable, shed ; also SCEPEN-STEALL, a sheep stall. We also find SCEP, SCIP, SCÆP, SCEAP, SCEOP, a sheep, for the first half of many of those various modes of spelling the word, and PEN, PIN, PINN, a fold, for the latter half=sheep pen. Yet nothing could be farther from the truth. Shipn probably means ' a small barn,' though it is evident from the eleven different ways of spelling the word used by the Anglo-Saxons, and since shipn with them meant a stall, a stable, as well as a barn, that the real origin of the word was lost and unknown to the authors who wrote those various editions of it. It is also clear that they spelt it on the erroneous theory of the

above derivation and etymology. But it may be roundly stated
that it is found spelt eleven different ways *because* its real
etymology *was* unknown. Some of the terminations are AN, not
EN, a fact which at once raises the question as to the final half
PEN. This termination is neither the result of ignorance nor
accident, for the termination of the original word is AN, and not
EN. All the various modes of spelling are phonetic. Shipn in
its various forms is a corruption of another word, which the
Anglo-Saxons could not, or would not take the the trouble to
pronounce. Welsh u sounds like English ɪ in *ship*. YSGUBORAN,
a small barn, *dim.* of *Ysgubawr*, a barn, a place to store sheaves,
from *Ysgub*, a sheaf of corn, is the true full form. The process
of contraction is obvious.

The words "with" (O. N. *vidr*, a wood) and "royd" (O. N.
*rjódr*, a clearing in a wood), so common south of the Wharfe
and to the east of Nidderdale, do not occur in the dale, above
Hartwith. In Washburndale 'Blaywith Wham' is over 1000
feet and on a southern slope on the open moors. There are no
trees there now, and I believe there are none at Grimwith. This
raises the curious question, were there trees there since the
Danes settled in this part? Some light may be thrown upon
the answer by the parallel case of "Shaw," *a wood*, a
word apparently exclusively Danish in this sense, as it is
common in Jutish Kent. O. N. SKÓGR; Swed. SKOG; Dan.
SKOV, a wood. The *Shaws* were great places for the outlaw and
hence originated several Norsk terms. The analogous words,
A. S. SCÚA, O. N. SKUGGI, Dut. SCHAWE, mean *shade, shelter.*
Shaw is common in the Ballads, and Chaucer,

> " Gaillard he was as Goldfinch in the *shawe*."
>
> CHAUCER, ' *The Cook's Tale.*'

> " Whither ridest thou under this green *shaw*? "
>
> CHAUCER, ' *The 'Friar's Tale.*'

> "In somer when the *shawes* be sheen,
>   And leves be large and lang."
>
> ROBIN HOOD.

"I rede that we drawe
Into the *wode shawe*
Your heddes for to hyde."

And many others that might be cited leave no doubt that Shaw meant and means a *wood,* and therefore it is interesting to note that it occurs many times on the open moors, far above the present limits of tree-vegetation. In such positions "Shaw" is generally a craggy or rocky place. There are no trees or bushes in " Shaw Gill," (about 1200 to 1580 feet,) or " Shaw Gill Sike," (1150 to 1400 feet,) tribs. of Trows Beck, at the dale head, near Lodge, nor in Trows Beck, (which probably is itself A. S. TREOW a tree). There are no trees on " Feather Shaw," (1250 feet,) Colsterdale Moor, on " West Shaw," (1200 feet,) on " Foulshaw Crags," or " Foulshaw Crags Wham," (1000 feet,) on Bewerley Moor, or on " Shaws Ridge," N. W. of Greenhowhill. Mr. Dakyns adds—" ' Collishaw Ing,' 1125 feet, (but the presence of Great and Little Collishaw Hills suggests for this case a man's name,) " Hem Gill Shaw," swamp up to 1950, just below Red Scar, head of Coverdale, close by " Slape Gill Shaw," 1700, also under Little Whernside, " Lords Gill Shaw," 1500 feet and over, " Outershaw," a hamlet 1125. Artificial clearance is out of the question here. " Firth," a wood, is common over the watershed to the east, but does not occur in the upper parts of the dale. "Wham" is a common name for a swamp on the moors, as " Great Wham," 1750 feet (O. N· hvammr, a swamp) which possesses a rich flora; also " Sandwith Wham," on the moors to the east of Nidderdale. The branch of a stream is called the " grains " or " granes " (on the moors), as " Agill Granes," (O. N. *qrein,* Dan. *green,* a branch). One of the oaks below the High Scar, Bak'stone Gill, being split upwards as far as the branches by a landslip upon the edge of which it grew, was said to be " roven up to the *grain.*" This point is also called the " brawn," (W. *Brawn,* that abounds with growth).

————:o: ————

## THE NORMAN.

Of the Norman we see few traces. Such as there are are probably of monastic origin. Grange tells us that Roger de Mowbray gave Brimham with Hartwith and Winsley, Dacre with Bewerley, and Fountains Earth to Fountains Abbey within a century of the Domesday Survey, and to Byland he gave the district now constituting Stonebeck Up and Stonebeck Down, so that the whole valley was held by three proprietors, the Archbishop of York, and the Monasteries of Fountains and Byland.*

The pronunciation of the old French word " PASTURE " (pastoor) is well preserved in the upper part of the dale, while the small list containing the names of " Haver Close " (Danish *haver*, oats, French CLOS) and " Hazel Close ;" *arran,* a spider (old French ARAIGNE); " Heronsew " (old French *Heronçeau,* a Heron); " Fromarty " (old French FROMENTEE, sodden wheat,) &c., indicates that the Norman invasion touched Nidderdale lightly. A few more will be found in the *Glossary.*

* *History of Nidderdale, p. 9.*

# XIV.

## VESTIGES OF THE ANCIENT FOREST.

Nidderdale and its moors have formerly been covered by an extensive forest.  Many trees lie buried in the peat upon the moors.  In the thousands of sections made by little water-courses the birch appears almost everywhere predominant.  Hazel, "sealh" (willow), thorn, oaks, &c., also occur, but the birch must have formed a thick and almost universal forest by itself, such as may be seen on the west coast of Norway at the present day.  The upper parts of the moorland gills, and much of what is now the moors, must formerly have made a beautiful appearance with its light gauze-like forest of birch and mountain ash.  The last surviving example on any considerable scale is preserved in Birk Gill, a tributary of the river Burn.  The run of the Gill is N. W. to S. E.  The Gill is about 400 feet deep at its mouth, and half a mile wide from ridge to ridge.  Like all other valleys at the same elevation in these hills, it is boat-shaped in section, the beck running in a deep ravine at the bottom. The sides of the Gills are wild heathery moorland, crowned with fine lines of crags down to the edge of this ravine in which the native forest is preserved.  There is no cultivation in the Gill, the bottom of which is 600 feet above sea at its mouth.  The belt of wood clothes the sides for 200 feet, or up to 800 feet near its mouth, and ends where the stream reaches 900 feet, in a distance of rather more than a mile.  Above this the stream is called Barnley Beck.  The wood consists of Mountain Ash, Alder, Oak, Ash, Birch, Holly, and Thorn, running above the edge of the cleft with a delightfully irregular and feathery margin on to the ling-covered moor. Above 900 feet, the following stragglers were noted, in ascending the stream :—

| | ASPECT. | FEET. | SOIL. | |
|---|---|---|---|---|
| Mountain Ash<br>Alder. Oak. | } E. | 900 | Grit | |
| Alder. Birch. | | 925 | ,, | A few stragglers of M. Ash, a Salix up to 950 on side. |
| Holly | | 940 | ,, | South side of Gill. |
| Alders | N | 950 | ,, | Highest living Alder. |
| Birch | N | 975 | ,, | South side of Gill. |
| Salix | N | 970 | ,, | ,, ,, |
| Birch | S | 975 | ,, | North side. ,, |
| Holly | N | 1000 | ,, | South side. |

### Scale Gill, N.W. and S.E.

| | | | | |
|---|---|---|---|---|
| Thorn | S | 1050 | Grit | North side nr. stream Highest living Thorn. |
| ,, | E | 1100 | Shale | South side. |
| Mountain Ash | E | 1125-1175 | ,, | Highest living Tree. Highest living M. Ash. |

### Barnley Beck, S.W. and N.E.

| | | | | |
|---|---|---|---|---|
| Birch | N.E. | 1050 | Sandstone | East side. Sheltered from East. |
| Holly | Protected | 1050 | ,, | West side. |
| Salix | ,, | 1050 | ,, | East side. Sheltered. Highest living Salix. |
| Mountain Ash | ,, | 1100 | Shale | West side, high up. |
| Thorn | ,, | 1080 | Sandstone | In bottom. Highest living Thorn. |
| 2 Mountain Ashes | ,, | 1120 | base of Sandstone | On Scar. |
| Birch | ,, | 1125 | . ,, ,, | ,, ,, Highest living Birch. |
| Mountain Ash | E | 1175 | Sandstone | On trib. near stream. West side, 50 feet above Barnley Beck; highest living M. Ash. |
| Holly | E | 1130 | Shale | In bottom nr. stream. |
| ,, | E | 1150 | ,, | ,, ,, ,, Highest living Holly. |
| Mountain Ash | E | 1150 | ,, | ,, ,, ,, Highest living M. Ash. |

Colsterdale presents a similar picture.

### House Gill.

| | | | | |
|---|---|---|---|---|
| Mountain Ash | E | 1150 | Shale | 20 feet above beck; on moor; highest living tree. |

### New House Gill.

| | ASPECT. | FEET. | SOIL. | |
|---|---|---|---|---|
| Mountain Ash | S | 1175 | base of Grit | Steep bank; close to stream, ; 100 feet above river Burn. |

### River Burn.

| | | | | |
|---|---|---|---|---|
| Thorn | | 1175 | Grit | On tongue at junction of Long Gill. Highest living Thorn. |

### Long Gill.

| | | | | |
|---|---|---|---|---|
| Birch | S | 1175 | base of Grit | Highest living Birch. |
| Mountain Ash | E | 1225 | Grit | 25 feet above stream. |
| „          „ | W | 1210 | „ | Besides stream. |
| 2 Mountain Ashes | E | 1250 | „ | Highest living tree. |

### Backstone Gill.

| | | | | |
|---|---|---|---|---|
| Mountain Ash | S.W. | 1275 | Grit | Highest living tree. |

### Steel House Gill.

| | | | | |
|---|---|---|---|---|
| Mountain Ash } Bullace | E | 1375 1375 | base of Sandstone | Edge of Gill; on moor. |

### River Burn.

| | | | | |
|---|---|---|---|---|
| Mountain Ash | N | 1225 | base of Sandstone | South side of Burn; 120 feet above river. |

### Thorny Grane.

| | | | | |
|---|---|---|---|---|
| Mountain Ash | E | 1200 | base of Sandstone | Highest living tree. |

### Deep Gill.

| | | | | |
|---|---|---|---|---|
| Mountain Ash | N | 1255 | Sandstone | On South side, slightly sheltered by Middle Ridge. |

Now let us compare the highest elevations at which the Birch, Mountain Ash, Thorn, Oak, Hazel, and other trees now grow, with the elevations at which their remains lie buried in the peat. First it may be desirable to premise that the highest six miles of Nidderdale runs due east from Great Whernside, and that the northern edge rises 400 feet above the Nidd in three quarters of a mile. This grand slope, having a southerly exposure, of course gets all the sun there is. Nor is this all. Throughout this six miles the dale has a northerly curve, the greatest convexity towards the north being at Lodge, and Woogill. Lodge owes its existence as a farm to this fact, and the fields of Lodge Farm are the highest anywhere in the district—their upper edge being about 1500 feet above sea level. One field called "Bewtcher Newking" runs over the dale edge up to the 1700 feet contour. I may here observe that a newk or nêåk is far from being the sheltered corner that it is in the south, but a bleak shoulder or " edge," a bold sharp feature running along the side of a dale. (O. N. Hnjúkr, and hnúkr, a knoll, peak, Cleas).

It must also be observed that, after they have been made a few years, these elevated mountain pastures tend strongly to run back to moor. Ling begins to grow upon them, and it would be too expensive a matter to repeat the original process of burning ploughing, and limeing, to keep them up. In this way the wanderer along the skirts of the northern moors may see hundreds of old enclosures or "Intaks," that have been thus lost as pastures. Bewtcher Newking will ere long have reasserted its right to be classed with the moorland around it.* The shelter from the north-west, north, and east winds, and the sheltered exposure to the full warmth of the southern sun, has also preserved in Woogill several relics of the ancient forest at higher elevations than they are found anywhere else in the district.

## WOOGILL.

| Hazel .... | 1350 | Grit | Deep Wooded Gill in moor, highest living hazel anywhere in the district. |
|---|---|---|---|
| Birch .... | 1275 | ,, | |
| Salix .... | 1375 | ,, | |
| M. Ash .. | 1400 | ,, | |
| M. Ash .. | 1450 | ,, | |
| M. Ash .. | 1550* | Base of Grit | Highest living tree; Gill gets out on to moor. |

*1600 in a note made 1871.

* In Arthur Young's *Northern Tour*, 1770, I find the following observations on the Moors, made during his visit to Swinton :—" There are tracts of land that have in process of time been inclosed from the moors and thrown into small farms, but I should observe that scarce any

O

When a great elevation is attained by the stragglers, they are always found at the base of a bed of Grit or sandstone, from which there is a perennial ooze or spring.

Next I will exhibit the *general* Tables of observations on the elevation of the highest stragglers of each kind of tree.

## BIRCH.

| Locality. | Aspect. | Elevation. Feet. | Soil. | Ordnance 6 in. Map. | Remarks. |
|---|---|---|---|---|---|
| Burning & Rye Close | E. | 1525 | Peat | 117 (S.W.) | Dead birch stems buried in peat. |
| Do. do. | ,, | 1200 | ,, | Do. | Do. do. |
| Arna Knab Wood | S.W. | 1000 | | | Highest living birches on the steep hillside on borders of moor. Others, trees in wood an oak, ash, heck-berry, thorn. |
| High Scar, Bak'stone Gill | S. | 1100 | | 100 (S.W.) | Scar left by slip, most thorns, then birch, & only two small oaks. |
| Fox Crag, do. | | 950 | | Do. | Elder, birch, hazel, sycamore, holly, & one small oak. |
| Foul Sike | E. | 875 | Sandstone | 101 (S.W.) | Highest living birch, with M. ash. protected ; at a water fall ; alder a few ft. below. |
| Cot Gill | N. | 850 | Sandstone | 101 (N.W.) | Highest living birch, 24 ft. lower down are two thorns & a hollin, open ling-cov'd moor. |
| Greenhow Sike | | 1050 | Peat | 135 (S.E.) | Dead birch & oak stems in peat. |
| Carlesmoor Beck | E. | 800 | Sandstone | 118 (N.W.) | Close to the stream ; living. |
| Far Beck | S.E. | 900 | Do. | 118 (S.W.) | Highest living birch, sheltered. |
| Sandy Sikes Gill | + | 1725 | Peat | 99 (S.E.) | Top of flat moor ; dead stems in peat. |
| Wising Gill Sike | + | 1560 | Do. | Do. | Do. do. |
| Woogill | | 1375 | Sandstone | 99 (N.E.) | In deep gill, protected ; M. ash ascends to 1550. |

+ Means exposed all round.

of these inclosures have been made of late years, they are all old farms. Many of these contain very large fields of moorland,—an hundred acres and upwards in a field,—that are all overrun with ling," &c., &c., in as wild a state as any moor, and differing from it in nothing but in the being inclosed."—*Vol. II., p. 283.*

| Locality. | Aspect. | Elevation. Feet. | Soil. | Ordnance 6 in. Map. | Remarks. |
|---|---|---|---|---|---|
| Fleet Seaves | | 1025 | Peat | 118 (N.W.) | Dead stems in peat. |
| Long Gill | S. | 1175 | At base of Sandstone | 84 (S.W.) | Highest living birch, in deep gill, sheltered. |

### MOUNTAIN ASH.

| Locality. | Aspect. | Elevation. | Soil. | Ordnance Map. | Remarks. |
|---|---|---|---|---|---|
| Woogill | S (Protected) | 1600 | Sandstone | 99 (N.E.) | Highest living M.Ash: at base of grit: protected. |
| Scale Gill | E. (,,) | 1175 | Do. | 84 (S.W.) | Highest living M. Ash, some thorns at 1100. |
| Bak'stone Gill Long Gill | S. | 1350 | Do. | 84 (S.W.) | Highest living M. Ash, Birch at 1175 in Long Gill. |
| Skell Beck | S.F. | 900 | Do. | 118 (S.W.) | Highest living M. Ash, |
| Carlesmoor Beck | E. | 875 | Do. | 118 (N.W.) | Do. do. do. Birch at 800. |
| Foul Sike | E. | 875 | Do. | 101 (S.W.) | Highest living M. Ash, at base of grit. |
| Trib. of Wandley Gill | E. | 975 | | | Highest living M. Ash. |

### THORN, 1870.

| Locality. | Aspect. | Elevation. | Soil. | Ordnance Map. | Remarks. |
|---|---|---|---|---|---|
| High Scar, Bak'stone Gill | S. | 1100 | Shale | 100 (S.W.) | Most of the trees are Thorns (see Birch). |
| Cot Gill | N.E. | 825 | Do. | 101 (N.W.) | Highest Thorns, Holly at 850 (see Birch). |
| Sike, from Sandwith Wham to Stock Beck | E. | 800 | Do. | 101 (S.W.) | Highest Thorns. |
| Greenhow Sike | Protected | 1050 | | 135 (S.E.) | Do. do. with Ash, Plum, & Sycamore. |
| Long Gill | E. | 1175 | | | Highest Thorns. On point at junction of Long Gill & River Burn. |
| Scale Gill | E. | 1100 | | | Highest Thorns. |

### JUNIPER.

| Locality. | Aspect. | Elevation. | Soil. | Ordnance Map. | Remarks. |
|---|---|---|---|---|---|
| Lul Beck | | 925 | Peat & Grit | 117 | On Grit Crags; sheltered; narrow cleft in Fountains Earth Moor. |

Next to compare with these I will put in a Table showing some
of the elevations at which I noted

### DEAD BIRCH STEMS IN PEAT.

| Locality. | Aspect. | Elevation. | Soil. | Thickness. Feet. | Remarks. |
|---|---|---|---|---|---|
| Steel House Moor | | 1600 | Sandstone | 5 | Head of valley, in moor, Colsterdale. |
| Kay Head Allotment | E. | 1570 | Grit | 8-10 | Nidd Basin. |
| Little Blowing Gill Beck | N.E. | 1725 | Grit | | Nidd Basin. |
| Burning & Rye Close | E. | 1525 | | | Nidd Basin. |
| Fleet Seaves | N. | 1025 | | | Nidd Basin. |
| Greenhow Sike | S. | 1050 | | | With dead Oak stems. |

It will be observed that the highest living hazel is in Woogill, at 1350 feet, but there was a time when the hazel not only grew, but ripened its nuts, at 1650 feet, on the moor east of Henstone Band, at the head of *Gate Up Gill*. There I found, buried in the peat, hazel nuts, many of which were bored by a maggot, proving that the nut came to maturity, and the kernel was eaten out by the moth before it ate its way through the shell. (Our word *moth*, the name of the mature insect, is taken from the Gothic *Matha* a worm, caterpillar).

There are many oaks in the peat bogs between Blasyhaw Gill and Brown Rigg, 1000 to 1250 feet, easterly aspect, exposed ; and a very large oak, thirty feet long, was dug up at Biggin Grange, Kexmoor (550 ft.) In Sykes Moss, most of the buried trees are sealhs, oaks, and birches. The birch is easily recognised by preserving its bark so completely, and an old sealh is known by its red wood. The wood of the young sealh is white. The wood of the sealh is much sought after, as it will last under water longer than oak. It is used for making spade-shafts, the sides of sleds, etc,

Unlike the northern side, the southern side of the dale in the neighbourhood of Woodale, rises only 200 feet above the Nidd till the " edge " is reached. Under the edge, however, west of Woodale Scar, it is called " Wintersides," and there is a house (Scar House) upon which,—it is said,—the sun does not shine for thirteen weeks in winter. This is by no means an uncommon thing in similar situations. The effect on the vegetation is to lower the limit of trees to the extent of—sometimes—hundreds of feet.

From the remains of the lost forest we can distinguish two zones, that of *oaks* up to about 1200 feet, and that of *birches* above that level. No doubt there would be no difficulty in constructing a fairly good map of their distribution, if one had time to devote to it.

The birch and thorn covered the upper part of the sides of the dale, what the Angles called the " Edge," while in the bottom of the dale there flourished the sycamore, ash, holly, hazel,

alder, bullace, elder, wych-elm, "heckberry" (bird-cherry),
&c.; the last especially in the neighbourhood of Lodge, near
the dale head. There is now a fine avenue of planes (sycamores)
at Woodale, 1000 feet, with heckberry, common ash, and alder,
with *Petasites vulgaris* along the river bank. At Rough Close,
925 feet, there are hazel, holly, ash, sycamore, bullace; on
Bekkamót Scar, 725 to 900 feet, there are ash, hazel, holly,
bullace, thorn, the ash being the commonest. All the large trees
on the Scar are ash, with a strong undergrowth of hazel. All
along under Thwaite House nearly all the trees are ash, with the
remains of hazel undergrowth, and a few fine "hollins" (hollies,
A.S. *Holen, Holegn*). On Boysoak Scar, 700 to 750 feet, there
are ash, alder (at bottom), holm, ivy, and elder; and along the
river bank south of Thrope* House, 600 to 650 feet, there are
ash, alder, hazel, heckberry, plum (sloe, A. S. *Slág, Sláge, Slág-
thorn, Sláh-thorn*). In the same field there is a remarkable old
birch, with very small leaves, not pendulous. Though there are
now hardly any beeches to be seen in the dale, I am told by the
old people that they formerly abounded, but have been gradually
all felled. Bekkamót Scar and Boysoak Scar are limestone, but
all the rest of the dale is sandstone and shale, or the covering of
drift clay and gravel that lies upon them.

With these may be compared the limestone slopes of Wharfedale. A little above Netherside, on a steep slope below the road,
is a natural wood of birches. At the top of the sides of the
valley for miles are remains of extensive thorn scrub. Lower
down the sides and along the bottoms, many sycamores. The
valley has, however, been much cleared of trees by agriculturists.

Birch and "eller" (alder, Dan. *eller*) were formerly extensively exported from Nidderdale to supply the bobbin-makers, but
this trade has nearly ceased. Some years ago, when the
"scrogs" (Dan. *skrog*, trunk, stump) were cleared off Thrope
Edge to make room for a large plantation of larches, known as
"Thrope Plantation," a great deal of charcoal was burnt, and
was sent to Masham to heat the combs of the woolcarders: this

---

* Spelt as generally pronounced. Sometimes *Throp, Thorp, & Trope.*

was not commonly practised, however in the dale. Blue Burn-ings Wood, which formerly existed near the spot (1000 to 1200 feet) consisted of birch and hazel scrub. Blæberries abounded there : this being a most capricious plant in the matter of ripening its fruit, it may be well to state that the site is a steep hillside running north-west and south-east, and facing south-west, at the elevation given, the slope of the ground being 1 in 44, or an angle of fourteen degrees. Most part has been ploughed within the last seventeen years, (1871), Turnips and potatoes succeeded there ; oats would hardly ripen, sometimes not at all. Blue Burnings now belongs to different proprietors ; part is glebe land. Before the enclosure the same proprietors ran sheep on it, each having so many gates.

The peat on the moors, viewed broadly, is now undergoing a process of destruction. Except in the " Whams" the conditions for its formation do not exist. In summer, on the higher ranges, the peat becomes very dry and dust-like, when it is swept away by the strong winds, all along the lines of the dry beds of what are, in the autumn and winter, watercourses. This process is best seen in the ascent of Great Whernside from the south-east, where acres together of bare rock have been thus denuded.

The peat on these moors does not run to a great thickness, as may be seen from the subjoined table.

| Locality. | Aspect. | Elevation. Feet. | Subsoil. | Thick-ness. | 6 in. Map. | Remarks. |
|---|---|---|---|---|---|---|
| Carle Fell | + | 1650 | Shale | 6 | 99 | Elevated sandstone pla-teau, |
| Carle Fell | + | 1700 | Sandstone | 5 | 99 | Do. do. |
| Deadman's Hill | + | 1750 | Sanst & Shale | 8 | 99 | Most elevated nab of same |
| Kay Head Allotment | + | 1525 | Grit | 4 | 99 | Elevated sandstone pla-teau, gently sloping E. |
| Agill Beck | + | 1550 | Grit | 5 | 99 | Do. do. |
| Riggs Moor | E. | 1775 | Grit | 8 | 99 | |
| Blayshaw Gill | E. | 1625 | Shale | 6 | 116 | Nidd Basin. |
| Moor at head of Bain Grain Beck | N.E. | 1825 | Shale | 8 | 116 | On watershed between Wharfe and Nidd. |
| Great Blawn Gill Beck | N.E. | 1775 | Shale | 6 | | |
| Moor E. of Henstone Band | S. | 1650 | Sandstone | 8 | 116 | On watershed between Wharfe and Nidd. |
| Hazel Nut in Peat | S.W. | 1650 | Sandstone | 8 | 116 | Highest living hazel is in Woogill, 1350. |
| Rochard Dike | N. | 1260 | Shale | 6 | 135 | Washburndale. |

The villages have their common land on the moors from which the inhabitants may fetch peat. Middlesmoor has one hundred acres of peat common for the village. The top spit of the peat is cut with a spade with a long bent handle, called the flaying (pronounced *fleäing*) spade, into pieces sometimes a yard long and eight or ten inches wide. These strips are called "flouts." They are not used for burning when "peats" can be got, but blacksmiths use them for heating the tires of wheels. For this purpose they are better when cut from sandy ground, as the sand makes them grow hotter.

In the process of gathering peat they first cut slices the shape of a thin brick, about eight inches or so long, in May. These they call "peats." The peats are laid to dry and harden on the moor a few hundred paces from the place where they are cut. After about a fortnight the cutters "set" them, which is standing three pieces together, one piece on its side edge, slightly leaning over towards two others resting endways against it. After another fortnight they "hut" them, which is setting six or eight more peats round these, and laying two or three flat on the top to shoot the rain off. After a time, sometimes as much as a month more, they pile them into stacks, which are called "ruckles." Last of all, the process of bringing them down to the farm in a cart is called "leading" peats. They are then stacked, generally in the open air, ready for use. Of course all this has to be done in the dry weather. If a person puts off getting his peat till late in the season, he runs risk of not having any for the following winter, and indeed this sometimes happens. It is useless to try and get them when the wet season has once set in. The process of gathering his peats occupies a man for a period not complete under about two months.

NOTE.—I will now give the physical reason for the TERRACED REINS promised on page 65, as after the picture just drawn of the Ancient Forest, we are now in a position to understand it. The smooth slopes of limestone in Wharfedale, were the only places not covered with a dense forest vegetation, until one rises far above the limit of cultivation.  They were clothed with short green turf, but were so steep that terraces had to be made, to prevent the heavy rains from washing down the soil.  Similar terraces formed the ' terraced gardens ' of the early Jewish Kings, near Jerusalem.  They were formed under the Incas in Peru on a noble scale, (Prescott, *Peru*, Vol. 1, *cap.* 4, 3rd Ed.) by the co-operation of Agrarian Communities, (Laveleye, *Prim. Prop.*, P. 133), also (Wiener, *Perou et Bolivie*, 1880.)

## X V.

# THE MODERN BOTANY.

To the botanist the district of which Nidderdale forms a part possesses a fourfold interest. While its higher parts ascend into the arctic region of Watson, its lower portions lie far down in the agrarian zone. The line marking the upper limit of grain crops divides the district into two parts, in the higher of which many northern types occur, while in the lower we have representatives of the Midland and Southern English, and of the Germanic types of distribution. The district lies upon the border-land of several provinces, both as regards zones of elevation and areas of distribution.

The Germanic is represented by the rare *Primula elatior*, or oxlip, which ranges up to 750 feet east of the Nidd, but up to 900 feet or more in Wharfedale; and in Wharfedale by the still rarer and more beautiful lily of the valley, *Convallaria majalis*, which grows in the woods near Netherside in large beds like garlic, and at Arncliffe.

The Southern English type is represented by the daffodil (here a rare plant), *Narcissus pseudo-narcissus* (which grows at Azerley, at 300 feet), *Colchicum autumnale* (in meadows by the Ure near Tanfield, 200 feet) *Euonymus europæus*, the spindle tree (one bush by the Ure near Low Mains, in Masham parish, 250 feet, exceedingly rare) ; while to the British English type, or those which, though occurring throughout Britain, are yet more plentiful in the southern counties, belong Herb-Paris, *Paris quadrifolia* (wood near Azerley, 250 feet, very rare), and Hang-

ρ

how Pastures, 720 feet, in small wood, steep hill side, north aspect, south of Middleham, and *Gentiana amarella* widely scattered, but rare, and exceedingly pretty with its pale rose-coloured flowers.

The Midland, or Intermediate type of distribution, is represented by the nearly extinct *Cypripedium calceolus*, or lady's slipper, which still grows at one or two favoured stations in Wharfedale, very properly "not for publication;" *Polemonium cæruleum*, Kirskill Wood, Arthington, 350 feet, sheltered, N. aspect, June 10, 1870; and *Primula farinosa*, one of the most beautiful of plants. Its flowers are a pale lilac-purple, with a yellow eye; the leaves are mealy, pale green above, and silvery beneath. Its habitats "stream-bogs," or bogs not stagnant.

The British Intermediate type, or those which, though occurring throughout Britain, are most plentiful in the Midland district, is represented by the cranberry, *Vaccinium oxycoccos*, a fastidious fruiter.

The Scottish type, or those which range as far south as the North Midland districts, is represented by *Trollius europæus*, the globe-flower, which ascends to 1400 feet, on Greenhowhill; it likes shallow valleys by running streams. *Prunus padus*, the heckberry (Danish *hekkebær*, hedge-berry); or bird-cherry, which is common in the upper part of Nidderdale, from 800 to 1200 feet. Towards the end of May, the long white racemes of clustering flowers that adorn this mountain-loving species add a strange and characteristic beauty to the pleasing wildness of these subalpine dales. The London-pride, *Saxifraga umbrosa*, grows wild on the limestone of Greenhowhill, at 1400 feet, where it carpets for acres the gently sloping grass fields on the northern side. The is no reason for doubting that this is as true a British species as the very grass that grows with it. Who, it may be asked, would take the trouble to carry it up to a wild Yorkshire hill and plant acres of it 1400 feet above sea-level? Surely such an enterprising person would have chosen a locality better calculated to bring him some reward for his trouble. "Mr. Tatham," says Mr. Watson, in his 'Cybele Britannica,' "deemed it wild in Heseltine Gill, West Yorkshire; and according to Mr. Brand, it grows ' on Craig-y-barns, a hill to the northward of the Park at Dunkeld, covering acres, and in some places to the exclusion of everything else, forming the entire turf. But for the occurrence of *Hypericum calycinum*, and other introduced plants, it would have been considered native.' But against this fairly given testimony of Mr. Brand there is something more positive than the suggestive counter evidence of *Hypericum calycinum* and its associates. In the 'Correspondence of Sir J. E. Smith,' we find a letter from Mr. Winch, expressly stating that the *Saxifraga* was introduced into the woods of Blair Athol by the gardener. Whether his introduction extended as far as Craig-y-barns does not (from memory) appear in the letter." Now a gardener would probably be the very last person to plant it on Craig-y-barns, though he might to adorn ornamental woods; and the natural conclusion is that he introduced it into the woods *from Craig-y-barns*, its native habitat. *Melampyrum sylvaticum*, whose small deep yellow flower is often the only one to be seen in the woods, it is plentiful from Huddersfield northwards. In Nidderdale it is plentiful in the woods near Fellbeck, 600 to 700 feet, sheltered; also at Hag Pits, 500 to 600 feet, sheltered. I have since found this northern plant in oak woods, at 600 feet, southerly exposure, on the Lower Greensands of Surrey, one mile N.W. of Leith Hill, fairly plentiful. If of accidental introduction with the Scotch firs, it has flourished well.

The Scottish-British type, or those which, though occuring throughout England, are most plentiful in Scotland, is represented by *Pyrola minor*, lesser wintergreen, which grows in leaf-mould in Hackfall, 360 feet, a noble wooded gorge through which the Ure flows between Masham and Tanfield. The Wintergreens are noticeable plants in the woods of Norway. The name is Scandinavian, (*Dan.* Vintergrön; *Swed.* Wintergröna). In Bp.

Tegner's beautiful Swedish version of Frithiof's Saga, (*Canto* 12)
it is thus introduced :—

> ................"och Vintergrönt
> King offret hänges,"
> "And Wintergreen around the victim hangs."

*Parnassia palustris*, grass of Parnassus, and *Pinguicula vulgaris*,
the butterwort, adorn many of the wet bogs generated by springs
on the hillsides.    The green-veined wax-like flowers of the former,
and the noble appearance of the plant, call forth the admiration of
the botanist who for the first time lights unexpectedly upon them in
their native hillside bog; and the recollection of the inexpressible
pleasure felt on first finding *Parnassia palutris, Pinguicula
vulgaris, Drosera rotundifolia, Narthecium ossifragum, Rubus
chamæmorus, Myrica Gale, Trollius europæus, Saxifraga umbrosa,
Botrychium lunaria, Ophioglossum vulgatum,* and many other rare
and beautiful plants, has remained fresh in the memory, affording
a never-failing source of pleasure through many after years of the
rough battle of life.    The young botanist who yet has before him
the pleasurable emotions attendant upon the discovery of some
new or rare plant for the first time may well be envied that
rapture.    *Botrychium lunaria* is rare.    It grows in grass fields,
and is difficult to see.    It grows in Nidderdale near Clark's Carr
Wood, at 600 feet, sheltered.

The Scottish Highland type, or those which, though occurring in the northern counties of England and Scotland, are yet
limited to the mountains, is represented by *Empetrum nigrum,*
the crowberry, which grows sparsely among the ling on the moors
up to 1800 feet; *Vaccinium Vitis-idæa,* cowberry; *Arctostaphylos
Uva-ursi,* the bear-berry, which is very rare on these moors, occurs
on Great Wham, 1750 feet, and on Little Whernside; *Rubus
chamæmorus,* the smallest tree, the cloudberry, locally the ' Nowt-
berry,' with a beautiful white blossom, is scarcely six inches high,
and grows sparsely on the high moors, but is very local in its distri-.

bution on them; *Oxyria reniformis* is common on moorside pastures and streams; while *Trientalis europæa* is exceedingly rare. This last occurs also on the moors of Cleveland.

The British type, or those that are fairly equally distributed throughout this island, is represented by many rare and interesting plants. *Drosera rotundifolia*, which is found on the peat on the moors in abundance; the juniper, which is very rare, but of which a few bushes are preserved in sheltered gills on the borders of the moors, as in Lul Beck, at 1000 feet; the asphodel, which is very rare, grows under Brimham Rocks, at 850 feet, and on Conistone Moor, about 1750 feet: the golden yellow flowers of this exquisite little plant are some of the most beautiful things in nature. *Menyanthes*, bogbean, fairly common in bogs; *Myrica Gale*, not common, moorland bogs; *Calluna vulgaris*, the ling, characterises the moors, but does not ascend above 1800 feet, often replaced by green grassy moors, called *Bents*; *Erica tetralix* and *cinerea* occur among the ling; *Gymnadenia conopsea*, sparsely, up to 1200 feet, in grass fields; *Corylus avellana*, in the valleys, up to 1200 feet; *Vaccinium myrtillus*, local, but not uncommon, especially in moorside woods and in sheltered damp places on the moors on which the sun shines, when it fruits best; *Draba verna*, scarce, Pateley Bridge, 500 feet, and Galphay 400 feet; *Ophioglossum vulgatum*, exceedingly common in places occurs right up the dale to Lodge, 1250 feet, in grass fields; *Digitalis purpurea*, sparsely; *Mercurialis perennis*, less plentiful than south of Wharfe, where it is most common; *Primula vulgaris*, 1800 feet, on Pen-y-Gent, in flower May 7th, 1871, very dwarf; *Cochlearia officinalis*, Carrier Pasture, near Kettlewell, grassy boggy moor, 1600 feet, north-east aspect, same day; *Adoxa moschatellina* and *Asplenium viride*, on north slope of Pen-y-Ghent, 2000 feet, both very dwarf.

The following table shows the stations of several of the more interesting plants of the district.

## TROLLIUS EUROPÆUS.—GLOBE FLOWER.

| Locality. | Aspect. | Elevation. Feet. | Soil. | 6 in. Ord. Map. | Remarks. |
|---|---|---|---|---|---|
| Linton Bridge, Wharfedale | | 600 | | 135 | Fl.[May 27th, 1869. |
| Hollin Close Dike, Nidderdale | | 800-850 | | 135 | Near Haver Garth; shallow valley on high ground. |
| Above Carlton, Coverdale | | 900 | | 83 | |
| By River Cover | | 620 | | 84 | Steep wood to Cover. |
| Grantley, Skell | | 350 | | 136 | Alluvium of Skell; one plant; very small and meagre. |

## DROSERA ROTUNDIFOLIA.—SUNDEW.

| Locality | Aspect | Elevation | Soil | Map | Remarks |
|---|---|---|---|---|---|
| North Gill Beck | E. | 1025 | | 117 (N.E.) | Aug. 16, 1870: S.E. of Hambledon Hill wet ground close to stream. |
| Gowthwaite Moor | E. | 1575 | Peat | 117 (S.W.) | Wet bog called Burning and Rye close. |
| Cot Gill | N.E. | 800 | ,, | 101 (N.W.) | Bog beside stream. |
| Between Cot Gill and Brandrith How | N.W. | 800-850 | ,, | 101 N.W. | Boggy Sike: near boundary of Masham moor. |
| Carle Top | E. | 1000 | | | Hill Top, exposed. |
| Sike from Sandwith Wham to Stock Beck | N. | 800 | | 101 S.W. | On a slip: boggy. |
| Stock Beck | S.E. protected | 725 | | 101 S.W. | Bog by side of stream. |
| Blayshaw Gill | E. | 1625 | ,, | 116 (N.W.) | Near head of Gill: on hill top. |
| Seaves | S. | 1025 | ,, | 135 | Edge of Braithwaite Moor. |

## PARNASSIA PALUSTRIS.

| Locality | Aspect | Elevation | Soil | Map | Remarks |
|---|---|---|---|---|---|
| Near Hard Gap | E. | 1150 | Boulder clay | 117 (N.W.) | Sep. 2, 1870, Fl: bog on edge of grassy moor. |
| Sike, south of Whitbeck | E. | 1250 | ,, | ,, | Aug. 25, 1870, Fl.: boggy ground. |
| Blayshaw Gill | Protected | 1050 | ,, | ,, | Aug. 24, 1870, Fl.: small bog on stream bank. |
| ,, ,, | ,, | 950 | ,, | ,, | Aug. 24, 1870, Fl. |
| Fountains Earth Moor | W. | 1000 | ,, | ,, | Aug. 23, 1870, Fl.: bog at spring on steep hill side. |
| Near Moor Lane Plantation | S. | 650 | ,, | ,, | In a little bog. |

## COMARUM PALUSTRE.

| Locality. | Aspect. | Elevation. Feet. | Soil. | 6 in. Ord. Map. | Remarks. |
|---|---|---|---|---|---|
| Bogs in Skell and | E. | | . | 118 | Below moors : with Menyathes trifoliata. |
| Laver Basin | E. | | | 136 | |

## RUBUS CHAMŒMORUS.—CLOUDBERRY.

| | | | Peat | | Scattered along the high moors above 1700 feet, among the ling. |
|---|---|---|---|---|---|

## PETASITES VULGARIS.—BUTTER-BUR.

| | | | | | Common on the sandy banks of the streams in the millstone grit. |
|---|---|---|---|---|---|
| *Coverdale.* | | | | | |
| Arkleside | | 850 | | 83 | |
| *Colsterdale.* | | | | | |
| Pott Beck | | 500 | Sandy drift | 100 | Burgess Bank Wood, Deep valley. |
| Agill Beck | | 675 | Alluvium | 100 | Very narrow, wooded gill. |
| *Nidderdale.* | | | | | |
| Woodale | | 840 | Alluvium | 100 | Sandy bank of Nidd. |
| Low Sykes | | 500 | Alluvium · | 117 | Alluvium close to Nidd. |

## CAMPANULA LATIFOLIA.

| | | | | | |
|---|---|---|---|---|---|
| Banks of Nidd above Lofthouse | | 575 | Limestone | 100 | At bottom of dale, here 750 ft. deep : not uncommon. |
| Above Carlton, Coverdale | | 700 | | | |

## ARCTOSTAPHYLOS UVA URSI.—RED BEAR BERRY.

| | | | | | |
|---|---|---|---|---|---|
| Moor near Little Whernside | N. | 1750 | Peat | 99 | Rare ; High moors : among the ling. |
| Great Wham | N.E. | 1750 | Peat | 116 | An extensive swamp, on high moors. |

## PYROLA MINOR.—LESSER WINTERGREEN.

| | | | | | |
|---|---|---|---|---|---|
| Hackfall | | 400 | Leaf Mould | 101 | Fl. June 23, 1869, a deep gorge in Millstone grit. |

## CHLORA PERFOLIATA.

| Locality. | Aspect. | Elevation. Feet. | Soil. | Date. | Remarks. |
|---|---|---|---|---|---|
| Sutton Limestone Quarry | N.E. | 275 | Mag. Lim. | June, 1870, | The only one I saw in the district. |

## GENTIANA AMARELLA.

| Locality. | Aspect. | Elevation. | Soil. | Date. | Remarks. |
|---|---|---|---|---|---|
| Field E. of Great Wood | S.W. prot. | 400 | Sandstone | 136 | Grass field north of Nidd. |
| Near Brimham Rocks | | | | 136 | Fl. Sep. 24th, 1869. |
| Wike Fields | S.W. | 360 | | 188 | Grass field, side of narrow valley; S. of Harewood. |

## MENYANTHES TRIPLIATA.—BUCKBEAN.

| Locality. | Aspect. | Elevation. | Soil. | Date. | Remarks. |
|---|---|---|---|---|---|
| Several Bogs | | | | 118 | In Skell basin, below moors. |
| Bog near Lady Hill | | | | 118 | |
| Below High Fish Pond | | | | 118 | With Comarum Palustre., bottom of narrow valley. |
| Bog near Sutton | | 325 | Mag. Lim. | 102 | Sheltered, on Drift. |

## PINGUICULA VULGARIS.—BUTTERWORT.

| Locality. | Aspect. | Elevation. | Soil. | Date. | Remarks. |
|---|---|---|---|---|---|
| Kettlewell | | 800 | Limestone | | Deep Gorge with Prim. Farinosa. |
| Arkleside Force | N.W. | 900 | | | Coverdale. |
| Gir Beck | S.E. | 900 | Drift | 84 | On Agra Moor; Gravelly Drift. |
| Tranmire Bog | E. | 875 | Do. | 84 | Gravelly Drift, on moor. |
| Azerley | | 300 | | 118 | With Prim. Far. |
| Bog near Lady Hill | | | | 118 | With Menyanthes trifoliata & Comarum Palustre. |
| Bog nr. St. John's Well and St. Helen's Well | N.E. | 175 | Peat | 102 | In valley on Magnesian Limestone. |

## PRIMULA FARINOSA.—BIRD'S EYE PRIMROSE.

| Locality. | Aspect. | Elevation. | Soil. | Date. | Remarks. |
|---|---|---|---|---|---|
| Kettlewell | | 800 | Limestone | | Deep Gorge, near bottom. |
| Linton, Wharfedale | E. | 600 | Drift | 134 | ½ mile above Linton Bridge; bog in small landslip in field by Wharfe, fl. May 27th 1869. |
| Grassington, do. | W. | 700 | Do. | 134 | Fl. June 15th, 1869. |
| Field south of Azerley | | 300 | Do. | 118 | Bog in valley, green fields, lie low. |
| Bog nr. St. John's Well and St. Helen's Well | N.E. | 175 | Peat | 102 | In valley on Magnesian Limestone, not far from Ripon, with Pinguicula Vulgaris. |

## PRIMULA ELATIOR.—OXLIP.

| Locality. | Aspect. | Elevation. Feet. | Soil. | Date. | Remarks. |
|---|---|---|---|---|---|
| Litton, Wharfedale | S.W. | 875 | Limestone | May 6th, 1871 | Flower; at foot of wood N.E. slope of valley. |
| Netherside, do. | | 625 | do. | ,, 15th, do. | Flower. |
| Carlesmoor Beck | Protected | 750 | Sandstone | 118 (N.W.) | |
| River Skell | | 415 | | | On Alluvium; near Hungate. |
| River Laver | | 300 | | | At foot of North Wood. |
| Winksley | | 350 | | Field | Beside a little stream which joins the Laver at Rough House. |
| R. Laver | | 270 | | | On Alluvium. |
| Granny Bank | N. | 650 | | | 84 Steep wooded bank by River Cover. |

## NARTHECIUM OSSIFRAGUM.—ASPHODEL.

| Locality. | Aspect. | Elevation. Feet. | Soil. | Date. | Remarks. |
|---|---|---|---|---|---|
| Head of Gateup Gill | S.W. | 1650 | Peat | | 116 Exposed; face of ridge; high moors. |
| Below Brimham Rocks | N.W. | 850 | | | 136 Bog; hill slope; spring fed. |

## XVI.

# THE FOMUD.

The first time I ever saw a Fomud was during a never-to-be forgotten visit to my venerable friend, Col. Crompton, at Azerley Hall. It had been shot in the woods there a few years before.

One hot afternoon in the summer of 1870, about three o'clock, as I was walking with Plato down High Ash Head Moor, at the height of 1200 feet above sea level, on a northern exposure, my dog, who was a few yards ahead of me, suddenly stopped. When I came up to him I found that he had at bay a most beautiful and courageous animal, in shape like a gigantic Stoat, in colour russell, and with a head like that of a Fox. It was crouching with its fore quarters down, and its pretty face turned up showing the sharpest white teeth, its ears erect, and beautiful eyes rivetted on its Leviathan assailant. My dog was burning to attack it, but I restrained him, when, taking advantage of the opportunity, the beautiful creature shot swiftly away. Its general appearance was that of a fox, with a long thin body and a very small head. In fact it more resembled a fox than any other animal. As I did not then know what the animal was I described it to the next man I met on the borders of the moor, who told me that it was the *Fomud*. This was all the enlightenment I could get, and I was obliged to rest satisfied with it for sometime afterwards when I learned from the late Mr. Wood, the intelligent keeper at Bewerley, that it was a Marten. He said " The Foul Mart." Herein, however, my poor friend was mistaken, in common with everybody who has written about this name,—than which no word has given rise to more confusion or originated more mistakes. *The Fomud is not the Foul Mart,* which is a name of the Polecat. A Polecat would often be called a *Foul Mart,* but never *Fomud.*

These are the salient facts. We have in England only one species of Marten,—*The Pine Marten,*—*Martes Sylvatica,* generally called *Martes Abietum.* This is the now accepted determination of Mr. E. R. Alston, in a paper "On the specific identity of the British Martens," published in the *Proc. of the Zoological Society,* 1879, *p.* 468, of which I now give an abstract.

" Two European species of Martens have been generally recognised since the days of Albertus Magnus and Agricola, although Linnæus and others regarded them as identical."

" *Martes Sylvatica.*—Outer fur rich dark brown ; under fur reddish grey with clear reddish yellow tips ; breast spot usually yellow, varying from bright orange to pale cream colour or yellowish white. Breadth of the skull across the Zygomatic arches rather more than half the length ; the arches highest posteriorly, whence they slope rather suddenly downwards and forwards. Sides of muzzle nearly parallel, etc."

" *Martes Foina.*—Outer fur dull greyish brown ; under fur greyish white. Breast spot smaller than in M. Sylvatica, pure white. Breadth of the skull across the Zygomatic arches much more than half the length, the arches regularly curved, broadest and highest near their middle. Sides of muzzle slightly converging, etc."

" The young Pine Marten has a bright yellow throat, which fades in old individuals to white or greyish-white, or pale grey mottled with brownish."

" *Martes Foina is not and never was a member of the British Fauna.* During the last ten years I have traced out every supposed Beech Marten I could hear of from various parts of England, Wales, Scotland, and Ireland, and *everyone has proved to be Martes Sylvatica.*"

"The Pine Marten, although greatly reduced in numbers by persecution, still maintains its ground in the wilder districts of Scotland, the north of England, Wales, and Ireland, and occasionally specimens are killed in counties where the species was thought to have been long extinct. In Scotland it is perhaps the most abundant in Sutherlandshire and Rosshire, especially in the Deer Forest. In the Lowlands a Marten is now a great rarity. In the north of England, Mr. W. A. Durnford* says the species is "still plentiful" in the wilder parts of Cumberland, Westmoreland, and Lancashire.

W. Harrison, (*Description of Britayne*, Bk. iii., c. vii., p. 108, in *Holinshed*, 1577, V. i.,) in a chapter 'Of savage beasts and vermines,' says,—"But it shall suffice that I have named them [Bevers] as I dœ also the Martern, although for number I worthily doubt whether that of our Bevers or Martens may be thought to be the lesse."

In Bp. Tegner's beautiful Swedish Version of Frithiof's Saga, the Marten is effectively introduced in the pretty lines—

> "Som en mård han flög
> Uti   Masten opp."—*Canto* x., *v.* 8.

which is, literally translated,—

> "As a mart he flew
> Up the mast aloft."

Upon this passage Strong has a Note :—"*Mustela Martes*, the Pine Marten. In proof of the facility with which this little animal scales the yet unfelled masts of the forest, it may be stated on the authority of Buffon, that it usurps the nest of the Squirrel and of the Buzzard, and dislodges the Woodpecker from its mine."—*Strong's Transl.*—Note, p. 137.

The *Wood Marten*, *Pine Marten*, or *Fomard* is not an offensive animal like a Stoat and a Polecat, and has no smell, but on

* *Zoologist*, 1877, *p.* 291.

the contrary, the skin is used by furriers and it is even called the *Sweet Mart*, in contradistinction to the *Foul Mart* or Polecat. Therefore the Fomard *is not the Foulmart*. Fomud is always assumed to be a contraction of Foulmart, but Fomard seems to be a name complete in itself—from O. N. *Fóa* a fox, and *Mördr*, Dan. *Maard*, a Marten,=the Fox-Marten,—as we say the Marten-Cat, etc.

O. N. *Fóa* a Fox, O. H. G. *Foha*, Goth, *Fauho* pl. *Fauhons*, (*Ulfilas*. Matt. viii. 20), and A. S. *Mearth*, *meard*, also *mærth*, Germ. *Marder*, Dan. *Maard*, O. N. *Mördr*, a Marten, are from Gothic *Matha* a worm, (which also gives us our word *Moth*, from the caterpillar state,) as we call them Vermin from their worm-shaped bodies, Lat *Vermis* a worm.

While Fomard is thus quite a different name from Foulmart this latter is equally an independent name, and is simply the two A. S. words *Fúl* foul, and *mærd*, *meard*, *meard*, a Marten, weasel, stoat, etc., a generic name. This I gather from the old spelling of Foul without the *o*, as in King's *Vale Royal*, 1656, p. 18, " Foxes, *Fulmards*, Otters, Basons, and such like ; " and the beautiful lines cited by Brockett.—

> " The hart, the hynd, the doe, the roe,
> The *Fulmart*, and false fox."
>
> *The Cherry and Slae.*

Brockett says " *Fulmart* in Sherwood's Dict., and some of our old writers use *Fulimart*." The title was conferred upon the Polecat in recognition of the eminent qualities by which it is distinguished, and save under the book-learned idea that Fomard is a corruption of Foulmart, is never applied to the Marten cat.

By a similar assumption, Foulmart has been made the same name as Fr. *Fouine*, the Beech Marten, a third distinct species, which is also a Sweet Marten, *but which does not occur in this island*. In Cotgrave we find " *Fouine, Fouïnne*. The *Foine*, Wood-Martin, or Beech Martin. Foüant a *Muske-cat*, or as *Fouïnne. Fou* a Beech tree."

It is clear therefore that Foüant and Fouïnne in O. Fr. means the *Polecat* as well as the *Beech Marten, Martes Foina.*, but an impassable gulf exists between Fouïnne, and the good old English word Fúlmart. So far from our being beholden to the French for our English name, the very name of *Martre* in French was borrowed from our Forelders on the Continent. The Med. Latin *Martes* is doubtfully used by Martial (EP. x. 37). This gave *Martalus*, found in some late Latin texts. Ital. *Martora*, whence *Martre* (Bra). Again, Fouïnne would appear to be corrupted by German influence. For the O. Fr. *Fou* a beech tree, from which Fouine comes, is apparently changed from its original form *Fau* under the influence of the Germ. *Buche.* Faîne, *Beech mast*, is from Lat. *Fagina.* Now the word Fagina is used for the Beech Marten in an Article of the *Council of Tarragon*, "Nulli canonici

Let no canons

vel clerici......vestes rubeas vel virides nec forraturas pellium

or clergymen presume to wear red or green garments or furs of skins

de martis, de *faginis*......portare præsumant."—(*Cit* by

of Martens or of Fouines.

who says Fouïne was formerly Foine, and originally Faine).

We here see a distinction made between two Martens, which were not called by the same name, i.e. the *Pine Marten* was not called *Fouïne* in France, where both kinds exist. Far less should it be called Fouïne in England where the *Fouïne* proper does not occur. It is therefore abundantly clear that three quite distinct names, *Fomard, Foulmart,* and Fr. *Fouïne*, applied to three quite distinct animals, respectively the *Pine Marten,* the *Polecat,* and the *Beech Martin,* which last is not a British species, have been confounded and treated as one.

As regards the cognomen *Cat* in "Marten-Cat." O. N. *Köttr* gen. *Kattar,* Dan. *Kat,* Swed. *Katt,* O. H. G. *Chatza,* Germ. *Katze,* Gael. *Cat,* Wel. *Câth,* meant originally the Marten Cat or Weazel, ermine, wild-cat. The cat was not domesticated in the tenth century among the Scandinavians, (Cleas.)

though, as Darwin shows, they were domesticated in the East and in Egypt more than 2000 years ago.*

From O. H. G. *Chatza* comes Fr. *Chat*, Lat. *Catus*, a cat. But what is Lat. *Catta.* Riddle translated it " *a kind of bird, doubtful.*" When the passage is carefully read however there is little doubt that Martens are intended.

It is necessary to state that Martial, who was born A.D. 43, published his 12th Bk. A. D. 103, and the passage in question occurs in Bk. xiii., Ep. lxix.

> " Pannonicas nobis nunquam dedit *Cattas*
> Mavult hæc domino mittere dona Putens."

> " [Umbria] never gave us Pannonian Martens
> Pudens prefers to send them as presents to our Sovereign."

Rather than keep them himself, they being new to him, and on account of their novelty deemed worthy as presents to the Emperor. Pannonia was a province containing modern Hungary and part of Austria, whence they were sent as curiosities to Pudens, who was in Umbria. There is little doubt then that *Catta* and *Catus* both come from the German.—In Latin there was already the word *Feles* meaning a Marten, Polecat, etc., Welsh *Bele*,—and that our compound Marten-Cat is a similar one to Fóa-mödr, Fomard, Fomud.

* Animals and Plants under Domestication, v. 1, p. 43, 1868.

# XVII.

# THE BIRDS OF NIDDERDALE.

Pateley Bridge lies at the centre of a circle of somewhat over forty miles radius that passes through several points on the eastern and western seaboard.    Thus it is forty-one miles from the Tees-mouth, forty-three from Morecambe Bay, forty-seven from the Ribble near Preston, and forty-five from the Humber at Goole.    This central position, taken with the great vertical range of the district, 100 to 2300 feet, is eminently favourable for the occurrence of birds, resident, marine, migratory, and casual. Sea-birds occasional find their way across, and perhaps I should say not uncommonly, if all the occasions on which they have done so had been placed on record.    In the summer Gulls slowly flap their way all along the eastern slopes of these hills.    In June, 1868, I saw one above Billing Hill, in Airedale ; on July 29th, 1869, one over Haverah Park ; and on May 11th and 13th, 1871, a Lesser Black-backed Gull at Kettlewell, in Wharfedale.    A young Gannet, in speckled plumage, was found on Bewerley Moor (1000 feet) in 1858, and is now in the possession of Mr. Yorke, of Bewerley Hall.    ' Gannet , is an A.S. name, as appears from the beautiful line, " OVER GANOTES BÆTH," over the Gannet's bath, i.e., the sea, Sax. Chron., A.D. 975.

In the absence of any recent record of the Golden Eagle in the district, the names of " Arna Nab," " Arncliff," "Arnagill," indicate that it formerly bred on these hills.*    Buzzards are occasionally seen on the moors.    At Christmas, 1868, Mr. Yorke's keepers trapped a Common Buzzard on Gowthwaite Moor (1200—

* See page 91.

1500 feet). Mr. Ormerod shot a Rough-legged Buzzard on the moors near Lofthouse about 1861. The Rough-legged Buzzard is said to be commoner here than the Common Buzzard. The Merlin Breeds on the moors. On February 22nd, 1868, I saw one a few miles west of Bradford ; on June 12th, 1869, one on the moor behind Guys Cliff (1100 feet), a magnificent cliff with a northerly exposure, over 100 feet in height, in the lower part of Nidderdale. Its flight is swift, low, and graceful. As it flies its wings seem sharper than a Kestrels, and its tail thinner, approaching the appearance of a Swift. The last week in June, 1869, Mr. Yorke's watchers found a Merlin's nest on Ramsgill Moor (1250—1500 feet, N.E. exposure), with four young birds.

On July 1st, 1869, I saw a Red-backed Shrike at Hole Bottom (950 feet), a dell full of trees and bushes, slightly exposed to the S.E., chattering and making a great noise. It is here a rare bird, as I have no other record of its occurrence. Says Chaucer, in ' The Friar's Tale ':—

.   .   .   . "As full of Jangles,*
As full of venom be these *Wariangles*."—V.6990.

The Wariangle (Germ. *Würgengel*,) is now a rare bird. I believe the name is still used in some West-Midland Counties. Mr. Speght (*Edit*, Chaucer, 1597—1602,) explains "Wariangle" to be " A kind of birds full of noise, and very ravenous, preying upon others, which when they have taken, they use to hang upon a thorne or pricke, and teare them in peeces, and devour them."— A faithful description of the habits of the Red-backed Shrike. Cotgrave's " French Dictionary," published 1650, translates *arneat* by "The ravenous bird called a Shrike, nyn-murder wariangle." The Anglo-Saxon "*Scric*" is rendered by Manning, in Lye's " Gothic and Anglo-Saxon Dictionary," by " *Turdus*," i.e., *Turdus viscivorus*, the Screecher. The Old Norsk *Skrikja* is rendered by Cleasby, in his "Icelandic Dictionary," "The

* "Chattering."

R

Shrieker," and *Sól-shrikja* (*i.e.*, sun or day-shrieker), " Shrike, butcher-bird," ("Itinerarium, or travels of Eggert Olafsson," 1772, p. 582), while the modern Swedish *Skríkja* is the Jay, another " screecher." " Skrikes Wood," near Bewerley, pro-bably takes its name from either the present species, or the Jay.

These birds commence their autumnal migration in July, when they are to be seen along the coast of Sussex. On July 30th and 31st, 1867, I saw two at Heene, and on August 7th and 8th S. F. Lucas (alas! gone to a too early grave,) shot two migrating.

The Tits, at least the Great Tit and the Blue Tit, are clever mocking birds. On January 26th, 1868, I heard the Great Tit uttering a cry like that of the Wryneck, but not so loud and sweeter. I have noticed the same note in the Lesser Spotted Woodpecker, and a young Kestrel. In 1867 there was an extra-ordinary abundance of holly-berries at Heene, Sussex. The Blue Tit (August 9th) was constantly in the holly bushes, in company with a Blackbird, cutting off the berries, the ground being strewn with them. On Sunday, October 25th, 1868, at Pool, Wharfe-dale, I watched from inside my window a Blue Tit busily engaged in pecking at the apparently bare bark of a trained cherry tree, on the young shoots and buds, and when he had gone I looked to see what kind of food he had been eating. The extremities of the young branches and buds were covered with the Aphis, much changed in colour, very few being the light green they are in summer ; they were dirty brown and black. The Blue Tit, through the autumn, goes in flocks with the Cole Tit and Great Tit, together numbering perhaps fifty birds. They like the sheltered deep valley of the Washburn, where all three kinds abound. The Blue Tit has a powerful, sprightly note like "Chick-weed, chickweed, chickweed," quickly repeated. The Long-tailed Tits go in little flocks of six or seven ; they have a sweet little single note, a straightish flight, stronger than one would expect, with their long tails stuck out behind. It is uncertain whether one of the Tits is meant in the lines :—

> " *Parus* enim quamvis per noctem *tinnipet* omnem
> At sua vox nulli jure placere potest."*

" Tit " is the O. N. Tittr. The A. S. names were *Col-máse,* *Frœc-mase,* and *Spic-máse ;* O. N. *Spiki.* The species to which these severally applied are not identified. *Tinnipet* seems to be formed upon a noun *Tinnipe* from the some root as Tit. In the *Legend of Good Women,* about A.D. 1868, we find—

> " As doth the *tidife* for newfangleness."—V. 154.

And again in the *Squire's Tale,* about A.D. 1390.

> .   .   .   .   .   . " false fowls
> As be these *tidifes,* tercelets and owls."—*Cant. Tales, v.* 10962.

"Skinner" says Tyrwhitt, "supposes it to be the Titmouse," and rightly, I think, from its Etymology. Lat. N frequently $=$ Eng. D as Tener, Tenera$=$A. S. Teder, Tedera ; also Lat. P Eng. F, therefore Lat. Tinnipe$=$Eng. (or O. Fr.) Tidife, which might probably contract to " Tit, but the pre-existence of O. N. Tittr in the north, and the invasion of Tidife on the south rendered the extinction of the A. S. names, in part at least, and the acceptance of " Tit " a matter of certainty.

The pied Flycatcher breeds in Bolton Woods, near Barden

---

* From a very beautiful little Latin poem of the third century, called " Elegia de Philomela," written by Albus Ovidius Juventinus (about A.D. 210). It expresses the cries of forty-one different birds by appropriate verbs, and is the sole authority for the meaning of several of the Latin names. It is to be found in the " Anthologia veterum Latinorum epigrammatum et poematum." Henricus Meyerus, Lipsiæ, 1835. Several pretty verses are cited in the present work.

Tower, Wharfedale; at Bewerley and at Harefield Wood,
Pateley Bridge, Nidderdale; and at Hackfall, near Masham, on
the Ure. All these are deep wooded valleys. They rear two
broods in the course of the summer; the first brood is brought
off in May. On July 15th, 1869, the second brood flew from
the nest at Bewerley. At Harefield Wood the site chosen was in
an old wall, which can be entered in three ways, two of which
are easy to the bird, and the third so narrow as to cause it to
squeeze very flat to go in or out; nevertheless this is the one
generally chosen. The cock appeared to build the nest, and used
to prevent the hen from approaching till it was ready. Harefield
Wood is on the west side of the hill, is admirably protected from
the north and east, and is itself cover from the west. Accor-
dingly it is one of the very few places in the district of which it
can be said that it abounds with Whitethroats, Lesser Whitethroats, Spotted Flycatchers, Redstarts, Robins, Chaffinches,
and at least two pairs of Pied Flycatchers. The Pied Flycatcher
has a melancholy little "tweet," very like the Spotted Flycatcher.
They dart from the wall, &c., just as the Spotted Flycatcher
does. They are a trifle more sprightly, not quite so downcast-
looking as the latter, and evidently have the mastery of it.
They are naturally very tame. The Spotted Flycatcher is far
from common. In 1868 I did not see one till May 8th, when I
saw one in Jonas Wood, near Farnley Hall, Wharfedale. This
bird feeds its young after they have left the nest. It utters a
weak, piercing note.

The Kingfisher is very rare, I should say almost extermina-
ted. On March 4th, 1868, I saw one on the River Aire near
Bingley; and on November 9th, 1870, one at Burrill Wood
(350 feet), in a narrow "clough" with well-wooded sides,
sheltered, and one at Mickley (175 feet), on the River Ure, where
it flows through broad meadows.

The Raven,* which has given its name to a great many places, is now confined to the wildest and most elevated parts of the West Riding. I have only seen it twice. On July 23rd, 1868, I picked up a young Raven at Carlton, on the south side of Otley Chevin ; and one hot day (May 6th, 1871), after a wearisome climb to the summit of Pen-y-ghent, J. R. Dakyns and myself watched a pair wheeling about, croaking hoarsely, at a great height above us, doubtless taking us for carrion as we lay motionless upon our backs enjoying their beautiful evolutions.

* Max Müller remarks. " The Emperor Julian, when he heard the Germans singing their popular songs on the borders of the Rhine, could compare them to nothing but *the cries of birds of prey*." The original (in the " Misopogon," written about A.D. 352), has *tois chrôgmois tôn trachù Boônlon òrnithôn*, and the Latin translation in the Leipsig edition of 1693 has " clangornm quos aspere clamantes aves edunt," while Eugene Talbot, in his French translation, 1863, gives " cris ranques de certains oiseaux,' but boldly adds in a foot-note, " *Les corbeaux*." See Voltaire, " Essai sur les Mœurs," Preface. *Clangorum* is not a good rendering of *Chrôgmois* for the " Elegia de Philomela," which was written 140 years or so before Julian wrote the " Misopogon," says, " *Clangunt* porro Aquilæ. . et *crocitat* Corvus." Crocito is for *crocio*, Greek *Crôzô, Crôxô*, to croak as a Raven or Crow, from which *Chrôgmos*, a croaking noise. In 1879 I was induced to write to Professor Max Müller concerning this passage, when he courteously replied, " The passage from the ' Misopogon ' is too general to allow of any conclusion being drawn as to what kind of bird Julian intended. I shall alter the wording of the passage in my Lectures to which you refer."

## XVIII.

## THE BIRDS OF NIDDERDALE,

*( Continued.)*

I have never known the Hooded Crow to breed on these hills, nor even to stay the summer. In 1868 I saw the first on October 20th, at Yeadon Ghyll, and on the moors near Lanshaw House (800 feet) ; in 1869, on October 13th, at Appletreewick, Wharfedale , in 1870, on October 28th, in some fields near Newton House, in the flat country of the Vale of Mowbray (110 feet). These birds are very plentiful in Norway, where they breed in the summer, as I have observed in 1870 and 1871. The Hooded Crow is a noticeable bird, and has attracted my attention when quite two miles off. It has far greater power of wing than a Rook.

My late revered friend the Rev. J. W. Warter, Vicar of West Tarring, Sussex, gave me the following note about this bird :— "He is wild, wary, and often savage. In the year 1849, one pecked out the eye of a lamb at Heene, and some years ago one remained near Courtlands till some half-bred wild ducks belonging to the owner of that estate were out of their shells. These he killed by turning them on their backs, after which he pecked out their insides. Having been caught in the fact, he was shot. 'He had no business,' said my informant, 'to have stopped behind.'"

The Carrion Crow in Yorkshire is called " Ket Crow." " Ket " means *offal*. In Westmorland they are called " Doup Crows." Rooks begin to build in February. They rob old nests to build the new, and apparently wage war upon each other's colonies, as they both bring twigs to and carry twigs away from the same rookery. Rooks begin to take long flights at least as early as September, when they fly to the salt marshes by the sea. They are seen during the summer high up on the moors, often when there are no other birds visible. "May 23rd, 1871. Many Rooks about Angram to day. I hear they have been shooting young Rooks at Woodale." At Woodale is the highest Rookery in the dale. The Jackdaw is a bird of the low country, but the Magpie goes up the dales and gills, only stopping short of the moors.

> "Pica loquax *varias concinnat gutture voces,*
> Scurrili strepitu quidquid et audit ait."

The Jay also keeps to comparatively low country ; it occurs in some of the large "falls," or "hangers," in Airedale, as in Calverley Wood, at 225 feet, and in large woods throughout the district.

The Nuthatch is rare ; I have seen it only once, in the deep wooded gorge of Hackfall (500 feet). The Wryneck and the Tree Creeper, common in the south of England, I have never seen anywhere in the district. In December, 1868 or 1869, Mr. Ormerod shot a Lesser Spotted Woodpecker in Bak'stone Gill, near Lofthouse ; but it is a rare bird here.

The Cuckoo, Fr. *Coucou,* W. *Côg,* is locally called "Gowk," (O. N. *Gaukr,* a form allied to Dan. *Giöy,* Swed. *Gök,* and A. S. *Geac,*—like the "Jack" in "*Jack* Daw," onomatopœic names).

The Cuckoo ranges from sea-level up to the high moors, where they ascend as high as Ring Ouzels or Titlarks are found to make nests for them. In spring, up to 1200 feet or higher, there are few places on the moors in which it is possible to be out of hearing of a Cuckoo. Cuckoos begin to go in little flocks of six or seven by the end of July or beginning of August. On August 2nd, 1867, I saw in Surrey a flock of six Cuckoos in the plumage of the first year, and later in the day a second group of four, also in the plumage of the first year. They arrive in April in flights of twenty or thirty birds. The Cuckoo has a long, plaintive, somewhat wailing note, very soft and musical. It has also a rattling note, not altogether unlike that of a Landrail. Cuckoos vary much in colour, some young birds being dark ash-coloured, or cinereous; others dark rufous, resembling the colour of a Kestrel; while some are intermediate and tinged with both colours.

## XIX.

## THE BIRDS OF NIDDERDALE,

*(Continued,)*

*With a Digression on the name of " Gabble-Ratchet."*

The Evejar occurs in the District.   On May 8th I started one in Jonas Wood, near Farnley Hall, Wharedale, and I have also seen and heard them in the woods under Guy's Cliff, Nidderdale.   They begin to migrate early in August, when they appear on the coast of Sussex.   This bird is locally called the " Gabble-ratchet."   Beside the jarring noise or " churr," it has a piercing, distressed note, which sounds from several different places.   Like the Grasshopper Warbler, the Nightjar seems gifted with ventriloquial powers.

Mr. Atkinson, in his Cleveland Glossary, enumerates four different superstitions associated with the name of Gabble-ratchet.

1.—A yelping sound heard at night, and taken as an omen of approaching death.

2.—A mysterious bird with *(a) large glowing eyes, (b) hooked beak*, and an *(d) awful shriek*, which appears to, accompanies, or is *(e) heard by the death-doomed.*

With which compare—

O. Dan.—HEL-RAKKE, a bird with a large head, *(a) staring eyes, (b) crooked beak*, sharp claws, *(c) used to fly abroad by night*, and *(d) shriek aloud*, and *(e) foreboded great mortality.*

3.—In Leeds, Scotland, and Devonshire " Gable-Ratchet "

S

is held to be "the souls of unbaptized infants, which are doomed restlessly to wander about in the air."

4.—In Cleveland a tradition exists that a gentleman who had been very fond of hunting, when on his death-bed ordered all his hounds to be killed and buried with him, that no one else should enjoy the sport with them when he was cut off from it.

Now as regards No. 1, the full explanation of that single point is in itself a large matter. The following extract from an article by F. W. J., Bolton Percy, in the *Leeds Mercury Weekly Supplement*, Saturday, February 28th, 1880, will show that it is part of a well-known superstition also known under the names of *Padfoot* and *Barguest*, as well as other names :—

"At the outset understand that I do not speak from personal experience, or from actual knowledge of this fear-inspiring bogie. I never foregathered with this "boggart." I have frequently had it described to me as being a large four-footed creature, something in the shape of a dog, with "saucer eyes," and carrying a portion of a chain which it rattled now and again. In this neighbourhood (*i-e.* near Tadcaster) what is spoken of as the "Barguest" seems to have been identical with the "Padfoot" of Wakefield, Brighouse, and Halifax, and the vicinities of those places. I am told by an old resident at the village of Colton that fifty years ago, if it were heard (as he averred it had been) under the window of the room where a sick person was lying, it forboded certain death. We can imagine what a terrible power the belief by the people in general in such a creature might be in the hands of a less credulous, unfeeling, and unprincipled man.

"Camden, the celebrated antiquary, speaking of a certain stone that had been found in York near what was known as the "multangular tower," and which had the words "Genio loci feliciter" inscribed on it, seems to think that it had some reference to the "Barguest of York." Another writer has the following :—" As the heathens had their good genii, so likewise their evil ones are traditionally handed down to us by those many idle stories of local ghosts, which the common people do still believe haunt cities, towns, and family seats, famous for their antiquities and decays. Of this sort are the Apparitions at Verulam, Gilchester, Reculver, and Rochester, the Demon of Tedworth, the Black Dog of Winchester, the Padfoot of Ponfrete, and the Barguest of York.

" Anent this subject there is a very pretty ballad in Hone's " Table Book," entitled,

## THE LEGEND OF THE TROLLER'S GILL.

On the steep fell's height shone the fair moonlight,
    And its beams illum'd the dale,
And a silvery sheen cloth'd the forest green,
    Which sighed to the moaning gale.

From Burnsall's tower the midnight hour
    Had toll'd, and its echo was still,
And the elfin band from faërie land,
    Was upon Elboton hill.

'Twas silent all, save the waters' fall,
    That, with never-ceasing din,
Roar and rush, and foam and gush,
    In Loupscar's troubled linn.

From his cot he stept, while the household slept,
    And he carolled with boisterous glee,
And he ne hied to the green hill's side,
    The faërie train to see.

He went not to roam with his own dear maid,
    Along by a pine-clad scar,
Nor sing a lay to his ladye-love,
    'Neath the light of the polar star.

The Troller, I ween, was a fearless wight,
    And, as legends tell, could hear
The night winds rave, in the knave-knoll cave,
    Withouten a sign of fear.

And whither now are his footsteps bent ?
   And where is the Troller bound ?
To the horrid gill of the limestone hill,
   To call on the Spectre Hound !

And on did he pass, o'er the dew-bent grass,
   While the sweetest perfumes fell,
From the blossoming of the trees which spring
   In the depth of that lonely dell.

Now before his eyes did the dark gill rise,
   No moon-ray pierced its gloom,
And his steps around did the waters sound
   Like a voice from a haunted tomb.

And there as he stept, a shuddering crept
   O'er his frame, scarce known to fear,
For he once did dream, that the sprite of the stream
   Had loudly call'd—FORBEAR !

An aged yew in the rough cliffs grew,
   And under its sombre shade
Did the Troller rest, and with charms unblest
   A magic circle made.

Then thrice did he turn where the streamers burn,*
   And thrice did he kiss the ground,
And with solemn tone, in that gill so lone,
   He call'd on the Spectre Hound !

And a burning wand he clasp'd in his hand,
   And he nam'd a potent spell,
That, for a Christian ear it were a sin to hear,
   And a sin for a bard to tell.+

And a whirlwind swept by, and stormy grew the sky,
   And the torrent louder roar'd
While a hellish flame , o'er the Troller's stalwart frame,
   From each cleft of the gill was pour'd.

And a dreadful thing from the cliff did spring,
   And its wild bark thrill'd around—

* The Northern Lights, very frequently and vividly seen in Yorkshire.

+ These two lines are from a German Ballad.

Its eyes had the glow of the fires below,
   'Twas the form of the Spectre Hound !

When on Rylstone's height glow'd the morning light,
   And, borne on the mountain air,
The Priorie* bell did the peasants tell
   'Twas the chanting of matin prayer.

By peasant men, where the horrid glen
   Doth its rugged jaws expand,
A corse was found, where a dark yew frown'd,
And marks were imprest on the dead man's breast—
   But they seem'd not by mortal hand.

In the evening calm a funeral psalm
   Slowly stole o'er the woodland scene—
The harebells wave on a new-made grave
   In " Burnsall's " churchyard green.

That funeral psalm in the evening calm,
   Which echo'd the dell around,
Was his, o'er whose grave blue harebells wave,
   Who called on the Spectre Hound !

" The above ballad is founded on a tradition very common among the mountains of Craven. The spectre hound is *Bargest*. Of this mysterious personage I am able to give a very particular account, having only a few days ago seen Billy B——y, who had once a full view of it.

## BILLY B——'S ADVENTURE.

" You see, sir, as how I'd been a clock-dressing at Gerston (Grassington), an' I'd staid rather lat, an' may be gitten a lile sup o' spirit, but I war far from bein' drunk, an' knaw'd everything 'at pass'd. It war abowt eleven o'clock when I left, an' it war at back end o' t' year ; an' it war a grand neet. T' mooin war varra breet, an' I nivver seed Rylston Fell plainer i' a' my life. Now, yo' see, sir, I war passin' down t' mill loin, an' I heerd summut cum past me, brush, brush, brush, wi' chains

* Bolton Abbey.

rattlin a' t' while ; but I seed nowt ; an', thowt I to mysel', now, this is a most mortal queer thing.   An' I then stuid still, an' luik'd abowt me, but I seed nowt at a', nobbut t' two stane wa's on each side o' t' mill loine.   Then I heerd again this brush, brush, brush, wi' t' chains ; for yo' see, when I stuid still it stopp'd ; an' then, thowt I, this mun be a Bargest, 'at sae mitch is said abowt : and I hurried on towards t' wood brig, for they say as how this Bargest cannot cross a watter ; but lord, sir, when I gat o'er t' brig, I heeard this same thing again ; so it wud either hev cross'd t' watter, *or gane round by t' spring heed!* (About thirty miles.)   An' then I becom a valliant man, for I war a bit freeten'd afore ; an' thinks I, I'll turn an' hev a peep at this thing ; so I went up Greet Bank towards Linton, an' heerd this brush, brush, brush, wi' t' chains a' t' way, but I seed nowt ; then it stopp'd a' of a sudden.   So I turned back to gan hame, but I'd hardly reach'd t' door, when I heerd again this brush, brush, brush, an' t' chains going down towards t' Holin House, an' I follow'd it, an' t' mooin then shone verra breet, an' *I seed it tail!*   Then, thowt I, thou owd thing! I can say I've seen the' now, so I'll away hame.   When I gat to t' door, there war a girt thing like a sheep, but it war bigger, liggin across t' threshold o' t' door, an' it war woolly like ; an', says I, 'Git up,' an' it wouldn't git up ; then says I, 'Stir thysel,' an' it wouldn't stir itsel' !   An' I grew valliant, an' rais'd t' stick to baste it wi', an' then it luik'd at me, an' sich oies ! (eyes) they did glower, an' war as big as saucers, an' like a cruell'd ball ; first there war a red ring, then a blue one, then a white one ; an' these rings grew less an' less, *till they cum to a dot!*   Now, I war nane feer'd on it, tho' it girn'd at me fearfully ; an' I kept on sayin' 'Git up an' stir thysel ;' an' t' wife heerd as how I war at t' door, an' she cum to oppen it, an' then this thing gat up an' walk'd off, *for it war mare fear'd o' t' wife than it war o' me!*   An' I tell'd t' wife, an' she said it war t' Bargest, but ah've nivver seed it since ; and that's a true story."

Mr. T. F. Thiselton Dyer, in an interesting article on " The Dog and its Folk-Lore," *(The Gentleman's Magazine,* Vol. 246, p. 489, April, 1880,) has the following remarks upon this part of the subject :—" In Lancashire this spectre dog bears the name of " Trash " or " Striker," *(Notes and Queries,* First Series, ii., 51.) In Cambridgeshire it is known by the name of " Shuck," and in the Isle of Man it is called the ' Mauthe Doog.'" At Norwich Castle there is also a " Mauthe Dog." Sir Walter Scott in the " Lay of the Last Minstrel," sings :—

> " For he was speechless, ghastly, wan,
> Like him of whom the story ran,
> Who spoke the Spectre Hound in man."

See for further instances the *Book of Days,* ii., 443.

Touching superstition No. 2. The O. Dan. version (taken from Atkinson) proves that it is of Danish introduction. The description contained in points (*a*) and (*b*), seem to be nothing but exaggerated notions formed upon the features of the Goatsucker, the point (*c*) is true of that bird, and (*d*), another exaggeration of some debateable sound. Anent these points, I would observe that (1), the Nightjar or Gabble-ratchet is a very *local* bird. (2), that, in consequence, very few people know it at all. (3), That the few who use the name Gabble-ratchet,—in the Otley District—mean the Nightjar, and some of these *do not know that bird by any other name.* (4), that the habits and voice of the bird, are well calculated to develop superstition, and afford a living stock on which to graft the creations of the imagination.

As regards No. 3,—infant baptism—it is a matter of history that Christianity found a slack acceptance with the body of the English people. Notwithstanding this, it was evidently not deemed expedient to use any legal force, for it was not till a century after Augustine came that Wihtræd, King of Kent, (A.D. 691-725,) at the instigation of Archbishop Birhtwald, imposed a punishment for the worship of heathen gods.—*Laws of Wihtræd, Clause 16.*

"GIF THEOW DEOFLUM GELDATH, VI SCILL. GEBETE,
If   a thew   to devils pay (honour), 6   shillings, he pays
OTHTHE HIS HYD."

or   his hide-gild, (i.e., money paid to escape flogging).

At the same time we find Ine, King of the West Saxons, 688-728, led by Bishops Hedde and Eorkenwolde, to make the first law respecting *infant baptism*—the subject of the superstition No. 3, attached to the name of GABBLE-RATCHET. "CILD
Child

BINNAN THRYTTIGUM NIHTA SY GEFULWAD GIF HIT SWA NE SY XXX
within   thirty   nights let be baptised if   it   so   not be 30
SCILLINGES GEBETE.       GIF HIT THONNE SY DEAD BUTAN
shillings let (the parent) pay.   If   it however be dead without
FULLUHTE, GEBETE  HE HIT MID EALLUM THÆM  THE HE AGE."
baptism, let him pay for it with   all   the goods that he owns.

For two centuries from this time we hear no more of the subject, when the influx of the Danes brought a fresh race of heathens into the country.

In the Treaty of Edward (the first King of all England) and Guthrun, A. D., 906, we read, "THÆT IS ÆRES THÆT HI
This is first   that they
GECWÆDON THÆT HI ÆNNE GOD LUFIAN WOLDON & ÆLCNE
command   that they one   God   love   would   &   each
HÆTHENDOM       GEORNE AWEORPAN." (*Clause 2*, preamble).
heathenish practise diligently cast aside.
And again, C. 3, " GIF MÆSSE PREOST TO     RIHT ANDAGAN
If a mass priest to the   right   day
CRISMAM     NE   FÆCCE   OTHTHE       FULLUHTES
the chrism   do not   fetch   or   give previous notice
FORWYRNE  THÆM THE THÆS THEARF SY,   GILD WITE
of the baptism to them that have need of it, let him pay his 'wite'

MID ENGLUM Æ MID DÆNUM LAH SLITE, THAT IS TWELF
with the English and with the Danes 'Laweslight,' that is twelve
ORAN.
oras.

This is the first punishment for neglect of baptism attached
to the priest, who is thus made to have a personal interest in
seeing it properly carried out.

The particular offences indicated, are, neglecting to provide
the holy oil, and the white garments in which children were clad
after baptism, and neglecting to give notice of the day on which
the baptism would be held. In explanation of this, I may
observe, that formerly, baptism was not performed except at
stated times, that is, Easter and Pentecost, nor anywhere but
in public, except illness required it. Next in the section of the
Canons, temp. Edgar, 959-675, on " The Modes of punishment," we read c. 44, " GIF UNTRUM CILD HÆTHEN GEWITE
      If a sick child die heathen
& HIT ON PREOST GELANG SY THOLIGE HIS HADES &
& it be 'lang o' the priest* let him lose his order &
BETE HIT GEORNE, & GIF HIT THURH FREONDE
do penance for it diligently, & if it be through its friends'
GIMELISTE WURTHE, FÆLTE III GEAR, AN ON HLAFE & ON
carelessness, let them fast 3 years, one on bread and
WÆTERE, & THA TWA GEAR III DAGAS ON WUCE, & BEREOWSIAN HIT
water, and then two years 3 days a week, & rue it
ÆFRE."
for ever.

The priest has here a heavy personal interest at stake,
if infant baptism be not performed. Next in the Laws of the
Northumbrian Priests made at York about the same date,
we find, Sec. 8, " GIF PREOST FULLUHTES OTHTHE SCRIFTES
      If a Priest deny baptism or confession,
FORWYRNE, GEBETE THÆT MID XII OR, & HURU WITH GOD
let him pay for that with 12 oras, and especially diligently

* i.e. the fault of the priest.

            T

THINGIGE GEORNE." C. 10, " ÆGHWILC CILD SY WEL
ask forgiveness with God.        Let each child be properly
RATH GEFULLOD BINNON NIGON NIHTON, BE WITE        VI
    baptized    within nine nights, [on pain] of 'wite,' i.e. vi
OR & GIF HÆTHEN CILD BINNON IX NIHTON THURH GIMELISTE
oras, & if a heathen child within 2 nights through carelessness
FORFAREN SY,  BETAN FOR GODE        BUTON        WORLDWITE
    dead be, ask forgiveness of God without the 'wite' of this world
& GIF HIT OFER NIGAN NIHT GEWURTHE BETAN FOR GODE, &
and if it be over nine months old let them pray  to  God, and
GILDE XII OR FOR THARE HEORDE THE HE WÆS HÆTHEN SWA
    pay xii oras to the  Parish in which he  was  heathen  so
LANGE."
long.

The struggle did not end here.  Heathen worship was still
practised in A.D. 1008, as appears from a passage in the Liber
Constitutionum drawn up at that date.  " EALLE WE SCYLAN
                        All  we  must
ÆNNE GOD LUFIAN & WEORTHIAN & ÆLCNE  HÆTHENDOM
one  God love & worship  &  each  heathen practise
MID EALLE AWEORPAN."
altogether cast away.

Clause 33, again repeated in slightly stronger words in
clause 52 of the Code of A.D. 1013.

From a chapter in the Laws of Canute, 1017-1035, we infer
that heathen worship was still rife in the land.  C. 5, *De
Gentilium Superstitionibus abolendis.*  " & WE FORBEODATH
                        And we    forbid
EORNOSTLICE ÆLCNE HÆTHENSCYPE.  HÆTHENSCYPE BITH, THÆT
earnestly  each  heathenship.  Heathenship is,  that
MAN IDOLA WEORTHIGE, THÆT IS, THÆT MAN WEORTHIGE HÆTHENE
man idols worships, that is, that man worships heathen
GODAS, & SUNNAN OTHTHE MONAN, FYRE OTHTHE FLODWÆTER,
Gods and the Sun or  Moon, fire,  or  rivers,

WYLLAS OTHTHE STANAS, OTHTHE ÆNIGES CYNNES WUDU TREOWA
Wells    or    Stones,    or      wood trees of any kind
OTHTHE WICCAN CRÆFT LUFIGE, OTHTHE MORTHWEORC GEFREMME
or   loves witch-craft,      or     murder   commit
ON ÆNIGE WYSAN, OTHTHE ON BLOTE, OTHTHE ON FYRTE, OTHTHE ON
on any wise,    either by lot    or    by torch,   or   dree
SWYLCRA GEDRYMERA ÆNIG THING DREOGE."
anything by means of such phantasms.

    This is a remarkable and valuable passage and serves to dispel
our common, but erroneous notions as to the rapid and universal
hold that Christianity took upon this country. Next in the
Liber Canonum Ecclesiasticorum about A.D. 1052, canon 27,
we find the infant baptism question,

"& GIF   UNGEFULLOD CILD FÆRLICE BITH GEBROHT TO THAM
and   if an unbaptised   child   be suddenly     brought   to   the
MÆSSEPREOSTE         THÆT HE HIT MOT FULLIAN SONA MID
Mass priest, (we command) that he must   baptise it soon   with
OFSTE THÆT HIT    NE SWELTE HÆTHEN."
haste that it do not    die heathen.

    In the Book of Ecclesiastical Law, commonly called the
"*Capitula incertæ Editionis*," c. 17, we find GIF MAN HWYLC
                                   If   any   man
METRUM CILD TO MÆSSEPREOSTE BRINGE SY OF SWYLCRE MÆSSE-
a sick child  to the Mass-priest bring, be it of    what   parish
PREOST SCYRE SWYLCE HYT SY THONNE FULLIE HE HIT    SONA &
             soever   it may,   then baptise he it   soon   and
FOR NÆNIGUM UNÆMTAN   NE FORLÆTE   HE HIT NE FULLIE, SY
for    no     hindrance let him neglect    to baptise it,   be it
THONON THE HIT SY.    GIF HE HIT THONNE FOR ÆNIGUM THINGE
whence that it may.   If   he  it however for     any     thing
FORÆT, & HIT BUTAN FULLUHTE   GEWIT,   THONNE   WITE   HE
neglect  and it die,      without baptism,   then let him know

THÆT HE SCEAL ON DOMES DÆGE FOR THA SAWLE RIHT AGYLDAN
that ho shall at Domesday account for    that    soul    to
GODE."
God.

From these passages we learn that for a period of three
hundred and fifty years after the first attempt at legislation on
the subject of infant baptism, and four and a half centuries after
the coming of Augustine, the difficulty was apparently as great
as ever it was.    What they failed to do by compulsion, the
priests, who had a personal interest at stake, therefore endeav-
oured in self defence, to bring about by superstitious means.
In other words, the superstition of the Gabriel-ratchet being
the souls of unbaptised infants flitting about in the air, probably
originates with the priests, sometime during the Anglo-Saxon
period.    Its very nature proves it to be of Christian growth
therefore it is useless to look back to Pagan times for any earlier
traces of it in this particular form.

Superstition No. 4 is part and parcel of the Wild Huntsman
Legend, as remarked by Mr. Atkinson, and, like No. 2, a mere
graft onto the name of Gabble-ratchet.

M. Thiselton Dyer, in the above cited paper, says (p. 404)
that in Lancashire, these spectre hounds are locally termed
' Gabriel-Ratchet,' (Roby, *Traditions of Lancashire ;* Harland
and Wilkinson, *Lancashire Folk-Lore* 89, 167).    Kennit (M.S.
Lansd., 1033) says " At Wednesbury in Staffordshire the colliers
going to their pits early in the morning, hear the noise of a pack
of hounds in the air, to which they give the name of Gabriel's
Hounds, though the more sober and judicious take them only to
be Wild Geese making this noise in their flight."    We have here,
continues Mr. Dyer, " the solution of this popular superstition,
for it is a well-ascertained fact that these spectre hounds are no
other than numerous flocks of Wild Geese, or other large
migratory birds."    I cannot accept this ' solution,' which seems
to be only another ' superstition ' instead of a ' well-ascertained

fact' Mr. Dyer claims it to be. Even the authority of Yarrell, (*Notice and Queries*, 1st series, v. 596) that Kennet's 'geese' are of the species *Anser Segetum* is unconvincing. It may be that the judgement of the ' sober and judicious' is still *sub-judice* " Reverting, however, once more," continues Mr. Dyer, " to the Gabriels Hounds :—In Northamptonshire they go by the name of ' Hell Hounds.' In Devonshire ' Yeth Hounds,' or ' Heath-hounds,' ' Yeth ' being the dialect form of ' Heath.' In Wales *Cwn Annwyn* or ' Hell Hounds.'

Wordsworth alludes to this Superstition :—

> " For overhead are sweeping Gabriel's hounds
> Doomed with their impious lord the flying hart
> To chase for ever on aërial ground."

Mr. Robert Ingleby, of Pateley Bridge, informs me that he has always heard the name of Gabriel-Ratchet applied to the Nightjar, and has known it as the common name of that bird from his boyhood.

## XX.

# THE BIRDS OF NIDDERDALE,

*( Continued ).*

The Swift frequents some of the higher ground. August 5th, 1867,—Examined and measured five dead Swifts, and a dead Martin.

| | SWIFT. | MARTIN. |
|---|---|---|
| | Inches. | Inches. |
| Length from tip to tip of wings, extended... | 16 | 11 |
| Tip of beak to tip of tail ...    ...    ... | 7 | 5¼ |
| Length of leg when straightened ...    ... | 1½ to 2 | 1¼ |
| Length of wing    ...    ...    (average) | 7¼ | 4 |
| Length of tail    ...    ...    ...    ... | 8 | 2¼ |

The shortness of the leg of a Swift is a remarkable feature. The arrangements in the mouth of a Swift are admirably adapted both for catching and for retaining flies when caught. The gape of the mouth is exceedingly large, and the sides are provided with skin walls. The roof of the mouth is provided with a triangular plate divided into two, and whose apex is at the beak. This plate is studded all over with short spines and edged at the base, and on the inner margins of each half with stronger spines. All these spines point towards the throat. The tongue is of two portions, one in the throat, and one in the mouth, consisting of a sagittate plate, the hinder parts of the barbs sharply serrated. The lower portion at the entrance of the throat is also sagittate, but broader, and the teeth upon it are weaker. The bird has the power of elevating these spines, at least all those of the tongue, to hold or impale the flies when caught. Behind the roof-plate, and lower in the throat, is another plate, also armed with spines pointing downwards.

The tongue of a Martin is on the same type as that of a Swift, the mouth plate being sagittate and barbed with several points, but the lower plate is deeper in the throat. The roof of the mouth is also covered with spines, but far fewer and smaller than those of a Swift. There is much more of the mandible exposed in a Martin than in a Swift. The plates in the roof of the mouth are not nearly so distinct as they are in a Swift. The flies I found in the Swifts were in the mouth, those in the Martin were in the throat.

Swifts do not associate with Martins, and they are never seen in the same air together. When Swifts fly high, Martins may be seen nearer the ground ; but when Swifts are low there are no Martins. Martins ascend to the Dale Head.

The House Martin seems to be one of those creatures whose fortunes to a certain extent follow those of man. I fancy that the Celt on coming to these islands must have found very few Martins, and those few only in localities where there were limestones cliffs for them to build against. Nor is it at all probable that the Romans found many more. The Martin could not have become the very generally distributed and common bird it now is for centuries after the construction of stone houses with mortared walls afforded it a site for its marvellous nest.

Among the very few natural nesting places of the common Martin is Kilnsey Crag, Wharfedale, a magnificent beetling cliff of limestone that rises abruptly from the level of the river to a height of about 165 feet. The horizontal extent of the projection of the upper part of the cliff beyond its base must be considerable, probably some 40 feet. Under the shelter thus formed many birds—but more especially the

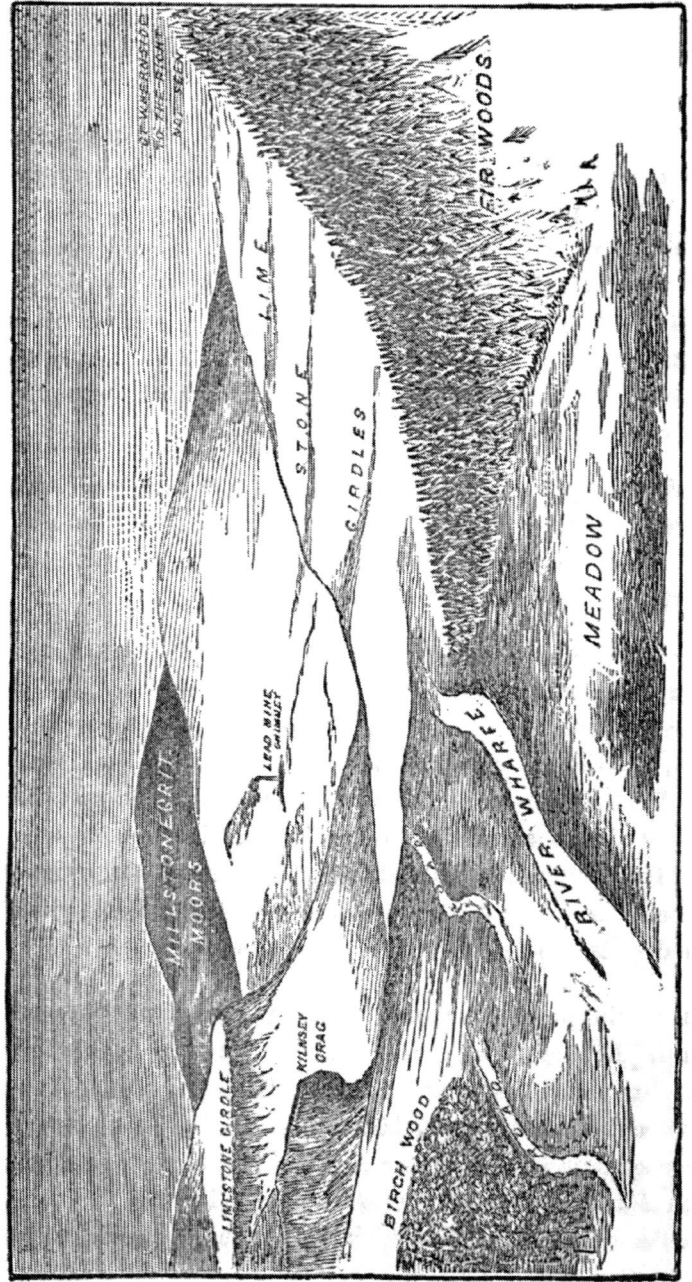

VIEW UP WHARFEDALE FROM NEAR NETHERSIDE.

Martins—build their nests, which, in the breeding season, may be counted by thousands. The air about the cliff seems alive with Martins, and the face of the cliff literally swarms with their nests. Kilnsey Crag is nearly a quarter of a mile long, and forms a most striking object from any point of view, but it looks especially grand and imposing from the flanks of Great Whernside, on the descent towards Kettlewell. The full face of the cliff is there seen, either white in the morning sun, or black when he has sunk behind the mountains to the west, when it looks double its size. The most characteristic view is however from the slopes near Netherside, from which point in company with Mr. J. R. Dakyns, west of the river, the above sketch was taken. On the left, Kilnsey Crag is distant two and a half miles, beyond which the river Skirfare flows from the exquisitely sweet Littondale to join the Wharfe. The bold bluff beyond that is " Knipe," (W. CNAP ; O. N. KNAPPR ; Dan. KNOP ; A. S. CNÆP, a *top. Knop*, etc.,) three and a half to four miles distant ; a name occuring at Kniphill, near Leatherhead in Surrey, and commonly. In the dale beyond this lies Kettlewell respecting which we may add to the remarks on page 95, "spelt ' Ketylwell ' in the *Compotus* of Christopher Lofthouse, Prior of Bolton, A.D. 1471, [12 Ed. iv.] " The lead-mine chimney is distinctly seen five miles off ; at seven miles we see ' Tor Mere Top ' on Starbotn Moor, and at eight and a half miles, ' Buckden Pike,' 2302 feet above sea level. To the right the limestone girdles forms part of Langliffe, an obvious corruption of Langcliff, some three to four miles distant, while on the right, in the immediate foreground is ' Grass Wood.'

The picture would lose none of its beauty if we could show the magnificent Heron that rose from the Wharfe as we sat admiring the beauty of the evening.

U

## XXI.

# THE BIRDS OF NIDDERDALE,

*( Continued ).*

Sand Martins are very scarce, or rather very local in the district.    I noticed them twice at Apperley Bridge, Airedale, (about 200 feet) where they build in the sandy river bank ; and on the Ure below Tanfield.    In a gravel pit here (150 feet) there was one lenticular bed of sand, one foot long, by six inches thick in the middle, and in this I found a Sand Martin's nest with eggs, on June 12th, 1870.    Until the last few years, however, they used to build in the bank of the Nidd, below the weir, at Pateley Mill.    But they never build there now, on account of the floods having taken away the bank, as I am informed by Mr. Robert Ingleby.    " Sand Martins " writes Mr. Thorpe, " are certainly plentiful on the Nidd in the Season.    I have myself known them build a little below Lofthouse, near ' Sykes' and various other places on the banks of the Nidd both above and below Pateley Bridge.    I should think they are to be found in the season above Lofthouse.    They have had their nests in the banks of the Nidd, ever since I can remember."    On the Wharfe, near Otley, they are to be seen by hundreds, as I am informed by Mr. Yorke's present gamekeeper.    He was formerly keeper at Farnley Hall, and when fishing in the Wharfe, he has taken the birds and their nests.    This bird does not seem to ascend above five or six hundred feet.

The highest elevation at which I found a Pied Wagtail's nest was 1050 feet, near the Dale Head.    This was on the face of a limestone scar, in a tuft of moss covered with long slender grass, six feet above the waters of the Nidd ; young birds, May 21st, 1871. The hole was bored into the clump of moss from low down in the side ; nest made of grass. Pied Wagtails arrive in parties of forty or fifty, early in April. On March 11th, 1868, I saw a pair of Grey-headed Wagtails beside the canal near Manningham. Striking points are the head being a much lighter grey than the back, and the small size of the bird.

The Titlark, here called " Lingtit," breeds on the moors, especially on the grassy moors or bents. I give the descriptions of three nests, taken down from nature in 1871 :—

No. 1. Near Carlton, Coverdale, N.W., 1000 feet May 19.— Open grassy moorside bank above little running stream. Bent-grass nest, round; five eggs. Internal diameter, 2¼ inches. Length of eggs, ·75 in. ; breadth, ·6 in. ; ochreous ground, thickly covered with dark brown stains, blotchings, and markings —darker at larger end ; still darker lines and streaks at larger end.

No. 2. Near Lodge, Nidderdale, S.W., 1600 feet, May 22.— Open grassy moor, nest with three young birds in a tuft of ling and bents. Young birds covered with long grey down.

No. 3. Angram Pasture, Nidderdale, S., 1350 feet, May 23rd.—Found a Titlark's nest with eggs. Instead of being all dark, they were dark only at upper end, with usual darker markings and stripes. The lower halves were very pale greyish ochre, almost white. The bird was distinctly striped down the breast.

The Redpoll breeds in Nidderdale. On May 19th, 1869, I found a nest in an alder bush on the bank of the Nidd, (about 390 feet), just above the weir at Pateley Bridge. The nest was in a fork a few feet from the ground, composed externally of roots and twigs. Four eggs ; small, pale bluish green, spotted and streaked at larger end with brown.

On February 22nd, 1868, I saw an immense flock of Chaffinches, which must have numbered some thousands. They were in beautiful bright feather, apparently all cocks. A strong west wind was blowing, with hail and rain, and they took shelter in the low hedges. The place was a steep hillside, two miles east of Shipley, Airedale, facing north-west, in the teeth of the wind.

Mr. Dakyns writes, "The Chaffinch is called "Bull-Spink"." (W. YSPINCYN, a *finch*, also called PINC. *Yspinc*, that is *smart* or *trim*, (Ow.) Other Welsh forms are ' *Gwinc* ' and ' *Winc*, ' which rather suggest the sharp note of the finch tribe. The double application of the name ' Bull,' probably evidences a confusion between the two.

I noticed the Bullfinch on four occasions only, as follows :— November 9th, 1870. Hedges near Rasp Wood, three miles S.W. of Bedale, sheltered situation (375 feet) ; Nov. 29, 1870. Ellington Firth, in valley in large wood, sheltered (500 feet) ; Dec. 6th, 1870. Roadside hedges between Azerley and Kirkby Malzeard (375 feet) ; June 13th, 1871. Follifoot Ridge, western exposure, summit of ridge (400 feet).

The only Crossbills I have ever seen wild, stayed for some time in the autumn of 1874 at Sandsend, near Whitby.

Starlings go right up to the Dale Head, but I do not remember seeing them on the moors. They begin to flock in June, as I observed near Bewerley, June 17th, and again early in August, 1869. In February, the Starling sits upon a twig and sings three notes ; one as if his beak were chattering with cold, another like in sound to the Corn Crake's, but far less loud, and a third like the clucking of violin-strings with the finger. It utters also a fourth note—a long sweet cadence gradually dying away and descending the scale at the same time.

The Dipper I did not observe in the Aire below Shipley, doubtless on account of the polluted state of the river ; nor in the Wharfe below Otley ; nor have I noted it in Nidderdale below

Pateley Bridge ; nor in Washburndale below Blubberhouse. In the Ure, however, I have seen it as low as Ripon (90 feet). It follows almost every beck right up on to the moors. They are generally seen singly, sometimes in pairs. On May 9th, 1869, I watched two Dippers in the afternoon flying about over some shallows near Ramsgill. They kept chasing each other at a great pace, flying close above the water. In order to escape its pursuer, the pursued now and then followed through the water, entering and leaving it without any apparent check. I was astonished at the freedom with which they could transfer them-selves from the air to the water or the water to the air. Even a duck seems to rise out of the water with difficulty. They rested frequently on snags, stones, and roots of trees, and kept up an incessant " chip, chip," quickly repeated. The Dipper's nest is sometimes so placed that the bird would have to fly through the water every time it entered or left the nest. They frequently build under waterfalls.

I observed the first and last flocks of Fieldfares as follows :— Stainburn Moor (800 feet), October 15th, 1868 ; Crag Wood, near Brimham Rocks (500 feet), June 1st, 1869 ; Appletreewick, Wharfedale, October 17th, 1869 ; Hardgap, near Stean, Nidder-dale (1200 feet), on border of moor, September 2nd, 1870.

The Fieldfare in Craven and Westmorland, and in the East Riding is called " Fell-for " or " Fell-fare." A. S. FEALA-FOR, the *many goers*, because they always go in flocks. (In Nidderdale they are called " Chuckers," but the Dan. and Germ. names are different, being respectively Dan. *Kramsfugl*, Germ. *Krammets-vogel*. In O. N. *Kramsi* is poetic for a Raven).

This raises an interesting question as to the original meaning of our word " field." The English " FIELD " is A. S. FEALD, FELD, FÆLD, FILD—and " many " is A. S. FEALA, FELA, FÆLA. Again " field " is Germ. FELD, (but Dan. MARK. Felt is a mili-tary term, and the Dan. for many is "*mange*,") and the Germ. for many is *viels*. Now the Dan. for a common is FŒLLED, Schleswig

Holstein "Fielled, so called," says my friend, Lieut. Rasmussen, of the Danish Navy, "because it is the right of *many* owners to run cattle on it—because it is held by or belongs to many." Now the passage in the Laws of Ine, cited at length on page 62, brings out so strikingly the connection between a "common" and a "field" as to leave little room to doubt the correctness of this explanation. "If farmers have a *grazing field* in common." Safety and economy were the motives, no doubt, for adopting this custom. Of course the origin of the word is farther back than Anglo-Saxon times, but it is remarkable that TÚN and not FELD is the word used in the passage in question.

| Gothic. | Filu, | *many,* | A. S., Fild, *field* |
| A. S. | Feala, | ,, | A. S., Feald, ,, |
| O. H. G. | Filo, Filu | ,, | Feld, Longbard, O. Sax. and A. S., Féld. |
| M. H. G. | Vil, | ,, | Völt, *field,* Netherland, Veld. |
| Germ. | Viel, | ,, | Feld. ,, |
| Frisian. | | ,, | Field, Fäld, *field*: Dan. Fielled, a common. |
| Gr. | Polus, | ,, | Polis, (a city). |
| O. N. | | ,, | Fold, a field; A. S. Folde a fold. |

So also—like 'Field' from Filu,—we have 'Fold' from Fol.

From the same root come :—

| Gr. | oi polloi, | *the many,* | Folk, which means "the many." |
| Gothic. | Fulls, | *full,* | |
| O. H. G. | Fol, | ,, | Fulk, Folc, | *Folk.* |
| M. H. G. | Vol, | ,, | Volc, | ,, |
| Germ. | Voll, | ,, | Volk, | ,, |
| O. Sax. | | ,, | Volc, | ,, |
| Icel. | Fullr, | ,, | Folk, | ,, |
| New Fris. | | ,, | Folck, | ,, |
| Gr. | Pleos | ,, | Plethos, (a crowd) | ,, |

As *Turba* a crowd gives *Thorpe* a village; so *Polloi* the many gives *Polis* a city; and *Folk* gives *Fylki* a county. All these meanings date from the ancient Village Community, but before leaving "Field" I may remark in parenthesis that Land or Lond means "*lent,*" or *that which is lent, loaned,* and dates from that epoch in the history of the Village Community in which certain plots were "loaned" to certain persons to revert to common property at the expiration of stated periods.

# XXII.

# THE BIRDS OF NIDDERDALE,

*( Continued.)*

The Thrush and Blackbird go up to the Dale Head, at least as high as 1200 feet, where there voices lend to the wild beauty of the scene.

> " Et Merulus modulans sat pulchris *tinnitat* odis,
> Nocte ruente tamen cantica nulla canit."

" Lodge, May 21st, 1877. The chorus of birds on this still calm, sunny evening, 6-30 P.M., consists of the notes of the Curlew, (of which a pair, wheeling about, has gone to the Nidd to drink), the Ring Ouzel, the Cuckoo, the Snipe high in air, and the Chaffinch, with his sharp, ' wit, twit, twit,' while Starlings are busy with their young in the neighbouring barn-roofs.

> ' Tunc Turdus *truculat*, Sturnus tunc *pusitat* ore.'

7 P.M. The Thrush has only just begun to sing, and now, save for the distant Curlew, he has it all to himself. 7-30 P.M. Curlews all around making a sweet melodious chorus; Swallows gone; Martins flying about; Starlings gone; the last warm, soft, rose-coloured tint fading and darkening on the opposite cliffs. Four distinct Thrushes singing; Partridge noisy in the dale below the house.

> ' *Cacoabat* hinc Perdix, hinc, *graccitat* improbus Anser.'

A troop of clouds that came over this afternoon have all gone, but there is a haze forming." Partridges W. Y PETRUS lit. *the starters*; PETRUSEN, *A Partridge*, (Ow.)

The Ring Ouzel has a sweet song, not unlike part of a Thrush's. It has a beautiful note, which it repeats thrice,— not inaptly represently by the words " tree, tree, tree,"—smart, but extremely melodious. The Ring Ouzel does not ascend to the very highest hills, nor does it go below the heathery moors, and even on these is not to be seen everywhere. Its favourite haunts are broad shallow valleys with numerous running " sikes," and having on each side a flat ridge. There the ling grows long, and its nest may be found near to some running stream. I give descriptions of four of these from nature :—

No. 1. May 13th, 1869. Brimham Rocks (900 feet), in an east and west sike, on the northern side, under a tuft of heather.—Composed of sticks of heather and pieces of dry strong grass, rather loosely compacted, but strongly built, and lined with finer grass. The nest contained four eggs; light bluish green ground, mottled with dirty brown spots.

No. 2. May 14th. 1869. Pateley Moor (1000 feet),—constructed like No. 1, and exposed to the east. Three eggs.

No. 3. May 11th, 1871. Moors near Kettlewell, (1440 feet), in a cleft in limestone.—Made of grass, &c., lined with fine grass; internal diameter, ♥ inches; outside, 7 inches. Four eggs; pale blue ground, faint blotches, pale purple and brown, thicker at upper end; length, 1·2 in.; breadth, ·9 in.

No. 4. May 22nd, 1871. Lodge (1075 feet), under a tuft of wood-sage in a vertical bank on a bed of sandstone.—Made of wiry roots and stems of bracken, pieces of moss and coarse grass, lined with fine grass; internal diameter, 4 inches, round. Four eggs; pale green ground, irregularly but somewhat thickly speckled with umber blotches of a pale tint, and less distinctly with pale purple, especially about the larger end; a few dark lines and dots at larger end ; length, 1·25 in. ; breadth, ·9 in. Nest three inches deep ; seven feet above stream.

The Ring Ouzel is somewhat uncertain in its appearance upon the South Downs ; sometimes it will not appear for years together. 'The first flock seen for years came to West Tarring, 15th October, 1862,' as I learned from the notes of my late venerable friend, The Rev. J. W. Warter, Vicar. On January 29th, 1879, I observed a small flock amongst some furze bushes on the downs about a mile above Michelgrove, in Sussex.

The Dunnock (Hedge Sparrow), is so called from its dun colour, as the Robin is called Ruddock (Welsh RHWDAWG, A. S. RUDDUC,) from his red breast. Let me record my tribute of admiration for the gentle bird, whose rich little canzonet may be heard on the silvery mornings of those rare bright days when an atmosphere, clear as crystal and of alpine purity and freshness, descends to invigorate the less favoured regions of the plain in bleak November.

The Redstart is quite as characteristic of the larger woods as the Grouse, Golden Plover and Ring Ouzel of the moors. It abounds in the district, and ascends to 1000 feet, perhaps higher. I have noticed it in Airedale, Wharfedale (as high as Starbotn), Nidderdale, Colsterdale, and Coverdale. The Willow Wren, Redstart, and Chaffinch have a note in common—most delicately modulated and drawn out by the Willow Wren, rather more quickly repeated by the Redstart, and somewhat more coarsely by the Chaffinch, which seems to mock the Willow Wren.

There are no Stonechats in Nidderdale. On July 6th, 1869, I saw the only Stonechat I remember to have seen anywhere in the neighbourhood ; that was on Constable Ridge, near Haverah Park (750 feet). The place abounds with low stunted furze-bushes.

The Whinchat is extremely common, and ascends to 900 feet ; in Airedale, east of Shipley, there is not a field without

V

several.  It has a favourite note, " tooee, tuck, tuck,"—the
" tooee " drawn out beautifully modulated, the " tuck, tuck "
rather reedy in sound, somewhat like picking the end of a thin
piece of wood with the finger.   The whinchat and Wheatear have
this note in common ; so great is the similarity that I question
whether the most practised ear could tell by the sound alone
which bird uttered the often-repeated and slightly varied " twee,
chuck, chuck,"   They also have the same habit of flying before
one along the road—a trick common to the Whitethroats, Flycatchers, and many others.   Whinchats swarm along the railway
between Pateley Bridge and Dacre Banks.   Wheatears are
common on the higher ground.   They abound on Greenhowhill,
1400 feet, with its grass fields and stone walls, in the flat green
fields of Cracoe (700 feet), near Linton in Wharfedale, where
there are stone walls or iron railings, and no hedges, with a few
scattered thorns.   They evidently consider, with Colonel
Lovelace, that—

> " Stone walls do not a prison make,
>    Nor iron bars a cage."

A few were still to be seen at Greenhowhill, September 6, 1881.
The young Wheatears arrive at the south coast early in August,
where they flock during the autumn.

 I have not seen the Grasshopper Warbler in the whole
district, except once, about June 15th, 1869, at Garth Crook
(1000 feet), on the border of the high moors of Barden Fell,
between the Wharfe at Bolton and the Washburn, an exposed
situation, with an easterly aspect.   I have observed it farther
south, near Huddersfield.

   Notwithstanding the efforts of a local author to disprove the
existence of the Nightingale in this district, I venture to record
two localities in which I have seen these birds,—Esholt Woods,
in Airedale, in the summer of 1868, and on May 8th, in Jonas
Wood, near Farnley Hall, Wharfedale.   Nightingales usually
reach the south coast the first week in August.   On July 27th,

1867, I saw the first at Heene.   On the 15th one was for some time on a geranium, in front of a window where I was writing, pecking the underside of the leaves.   On looking to see what it could get, I found numbers of cobwebs stretched in various directions to catch the flies that might shelter there from the rain that had fallen lightly all the morning.   On August 16th I saw a beautiful cock bird in the asparagus bed, of which dense forest it seems particularly fond.   It runs nimbly up the perpendicular stalks, now and anon pecking on its way.   It flew to a tree about thirty yards off—a straight slightly undulating flight.

I used frequently to hear the Blackcap singing through the night, in company with the Corn Crake, at Apperley Bridge and at other places in the district.

The Whitethroat occurs in Nidderdale, where its "ee tschuk" may be heard, but not plentifully.

The Lesser Whitethroat is by far the commonest bird in the whole district, from the vale of York up to the borders of the moors, where its place in this respect is taken up by the Titlark. It ascends Nidderdale to Angram (1200 feet), at the Dale Head. The inclined plateaux, peculiar to the eastern slopes of the mill-stone-grit range, with their small clusters of *Acer pseudo-platanus*, and frequent small ponds, afford just the conditions that suit this bird.   No table land is too exposed or too elevated; provided there is a cluster of two or three trees and a pond, there will be Lesser Whitethroats.   This lively bird has a loud attractive song, consisting of four notes quickly repeated, then another four a shade lower, then a third and a four, thus :—

After the last four the song dies away in a beautiful little trill. It has also a note like the Whinchat's, softened and modified. The Lesser Whitethroat's note has ceased by the beginning of July, when the pretty and frequently repeated trill is much missed.   This bird may often be seen inspecting the intruder from the leafy cover of its favourite tree, *Acer pseudo-platanus*.

The Wood Wren is somewhat more local, but in suitable situations is sure to be heard. Tall trees and thick underwood, firs and *Acer pseudo-platanus*, deep sheltered " gills " with wooded sides, and large woods, are the favourite haunts of this bird ; where these prevail it ascends to 1000 feet, and to the borders of the moors.

The Willow Wren ascends the dale to Angram (1200 feet) ; but I have no special notes about it, from which I conclude that the bird is rare here.

The Chiffchaff ranges up to little above 700 feet. The steep wooded sides of the valleys and extensive woods, with tall firs and beeches, or any tall trees, are the favourite haunts of this bird. It is not so common as the Lesser Whitethroat, but considerably more common than the Wood Wren.

The Common Wren ascends to 1000 feet, perhaps higher.

The Woodpigeon is called " Cowshot," the *shot* seems to be from the Welsh YSGUTHAN, lit. " the scudder," a name of the Woodpigeon.

The Rock Dove breeds at Guy's Cliff, and at Brimham Rocks. On May 13th, 1869, one flew out of a hole bored for more than a yard into the peat on the top of a crag amongst the Hare Head rocks. A yard from the nest I picked up two eggs, one broken, the other addled ; these may have been turned out by a Cuckoo, but I had no opportunity of proving this point. The Rock Dove only lays two eggs.

On August 12th, 1871, Mr. Ormerod shot a Grey Hen on Cockley Hill, (1300 feet), on the moors east of Lofthouse.

The Grouse vary much in colour. Some 12 or 14 years ago there was a family with sandy and whitish feathers on the moors near Nursa Knott. Mr. Newbould has all three stuffed at the " Moor Cock Inn," Dry Gill.—(1881.)

Mr. Reason has stuffed at Wath, 1881, a light brown coloured Grey Hen, a very pale bird, shot on Sigsworth moor, by Mr; Tennant, of Low Green, in 1879.

The Grouse is a capricious bird in its choice of residence. The fact that they do not abound everywhere on the moors is doubtless not without its influence on the leases of moors. They are most plentiful in the zone between 1000 and 1500 feet, and do not go much above 1700. Spots where bilberries ripen, kept moist by springs, and with a southerly exposure, attract them in autumn, though they lie under a northern " edge " in the spring. For their nests they like broad shallow hollows with springs at the edges, and a flat ridge, at least on one side, on to which they adjourn to crow and sun themselves. " Cocklakes " is the name of one of these " Riggs " on the moors, west of the River Washburn. What a flood of beauty is shed upon the word when we learn that it means the "playing-ground"* of the moor-cock! They build also in the peat in deep-stream courses. Here is a description of two nests :—

No. 1. May 10th, 1871. A light nest, beside a deep stream-course in sandstone. Made of round rushes, a few feathers mixed ; 7½ inches across. Seven eggs ; pale grey, irregularly speckled and blotched.

No. 2. Same date. Deep-stream course, in peat under tuft of grass; exposure N., sheltered. Made of grass; 7 inches across. Ten eggs.

Many young Grouse are hatched before this; and it is astonishing how fast they grow, how soon they are able to fly, and how strong they are on the wing.

It has been my good fortune to spend nine successive years, —spring, summer, autumn and winter—on and around the moors, and to have sat among the long heather, in the fresh spring evenings, listening to the melodious clamour of the piping birds. Here I will fall back upon first impressions, lest the picture should suffer from the rude touch of familiarity :—May 22nd, 1869. On Masham Moor, a glorious expanse of heather,

* Goth. LAIKAN, O. N. LEIKA, *to play;* LEIKR, a game, or play.

lying to the north of Nidderdale, 1500 feet above the level of the
sea, from 6 to 8 P.M. Air resplendently clear and transparent,
not a cloud to be seen ; the sun lighting up the moor. Grouse
calling all around, with Curlews wheeling in the air, and Golden
Plovers swiftly skimming the ground ; the Ring Ouzel suddenly
rising on to some spray of heather, and uttering his melodious
" tree, tree, tree "; the Snipe wildly flying high in air, with his
peculiar knocking noise and startled whistle—hundreds on every
side, all together in full chorus. The charm of the place, with
its wildness, the incessant harmonious clamour of the piping
birds, and the complete novelty of the scene, inspired me deeply.
The Golden Plover has a single sweet mellow pipe, which is
answered by his mate a semitone lower ; also a note which he
frequently repeats, ⸺⸳⸳⸳⸳-⸳⸳⸳⸳⸳, like the ' Hallelujah ' of the
' Hallelujah Chorus,'—and who knows but that this refrain may
not have been thus suggested to the great composer !—while
with some of his single pipes there is a beautiful and inimitable
little roll. The Curlew keeps up an incessant ' toor-r-lui,
toor-r-lui,' in a flute-like, melodious, piping tone, while the
Grouse utters a peculiar guttural call as he flies off, in the time
of what is generally understood as a ' double knock,' the syllable
repeated being ' coc.' All these together form a chorus to be
heard nowhere else but in these moorlands."

The Woodcock sometimes appears on the moors. On the
31st of October, 1871, I saw one near Greenhowhill, (1325
feet).

The Peewit,—called " Tewfit," ' Tewit,' and ' Tee-wit,' (cp.
Dan. Tyvit,) is generally distributed and very plentiful, ranging
to at least an equal height. Young birds begin to call imperfectly
in July. They come down to the Wharfe to drink just as it is
getting dark, and continue crying " peewit " as late as a quarter
past nine.

The Corn Crake is found in the larger dales, but does not
ascend to their upper parts.

The Heron pays periodical and solitary visits to the dales. One was hanging about the Washburn from September 14th till October 31st, 1868, and doubtless much later. One came to the waterfall in Wath Wood, Nidderdale, on August 2nd, 1869; but with the exception of one or two occasions in the upper part of Wharfedale, I have not noted them elsewhere.

I have been much struck with the tactical methods of the Snipe. On July 30th, 1868, I put up four of these birds in a stream among the broad meadows between Otley and Burley, in Wharfedale. They divided, each in its own course flying head-long at a great pace for about two hundred yards up stream. On being a second time roused they rose, each in its own course, to a great height, and flew right away. 'Jack Snipe' seems a reduplication, for GIAÇ is the Welsh for a Snipe.

The Common Sandpiper is found along the streams in the dales throughout the spring. I have no note of its occurrence above 900 feet.

The following summary will give an idea of the distribution of some of the birds observed by me in the district, and will show the various elevations at which they were respectively met with :—

*SUMMARY OF THE ORNITHOLOGY OF THE DISTRICT.*

Elevation.      H I G H    M O O R S.

2000 ft. Raven.

1500 ,, Titlark, Buzzards, Snipe, Grouse, Golden Plover, Merlin, Ring Ouzel, Curlew. Cuckoo, Fieldfare, Peewit.

D A L E S.

UPPER.                        LOWER.

1200 ft. Dipper.

 900 ,, Sandpiper.

 700 ,, Heron, Whinchat - - - - Redstart, Chiffchaff.

 800 ,, - - - - - - - - Red-backed Shrike.

 600 ,, Redpoll - - - - - Nightjar, Nuthatch.

 500 ,, Pied Flycatcher - - - - Jackdaw, Jay.

## LOWLAND.

400 ft. - · - · - · - - - Corn Crake.
800 ,, Sandpiper - - - · · - · Kingfisher.
200 ,, - · - · - · - · · - Sand Martin.
100 ,, Dipper.

### EASTERLEY SLOPING PLATEAUX.

| BARE. | WOODED. |
|---|---|
| 1200 ft. Peewit, Swift. | |
| 1100 ,, Gulls. | |
| 1000 ,, Fieldfare · - - · - · · - | Lesser Whitethroat. |
| 700 ,, Stonechat, Wheatear. | |
| 600 ,, - · - · - · - · - - | Wood Wren. |
| 500 ,, - · - · - · - · - - | Bullfinch. |

---

## SUMMARY OF LOCALITIES.

PIED FLYCATCHER, *Muscicapa atricapilla.*

Bolton Woods, Wharfedale, 400 ft., May 20th, 1869. Deep
wooded gorge, sheltered. Breeds.

Harefield Woods, Nidderdale, W., 500 ft., May 14th, 1869.
Wood on east side of dale. Breeds.

Bewerley, E., 400 ft., July 25th, 1869. Wooded. Breeds:

Hackfall, Ure, 200—500 ft., June 23rd, 1869. Deep wooded
gorge, sheltered. Breeds.

REDSTART, *Ruticilla phœnicurus.*

River cover. above Carlton, 700 ft., June 5th, 1871. With
Lesser Whitethroat ; noisy.

Deep Gill, N.E., 800 ft. Deep narrow gill, wooded sides,
near Jervaulx.

Starbotn, 800 ft., May 9th, 1871. In the upper part of
Wharfedale.

Litton, 600 ft., May 7th, 1871. More open country to W.

Ilkley, Wharfedale. Saw first April 26th, 1870.

Riffa Wood, S., 225 ft., April 30, 1870. Sloping fields, hedges.

Arnagill Tower, 1000 ft. Deep wooded cleft, in moors, falling to N.

Bridge Banks, Laver Bottom, 800 ft., 1870. Wooded sides to valley.

Swetton, E., 725 ft., 1870. Exposed easterly-sloping plateau.

Wetshod Lane, N.W., 700 ft. Exposed, hedgerow trees.

Bramley Fall, N., 200 ft., April 30th, 1868. Airedale, west of Leeds ; extensive woods, sheltered, low in valley.

LESSER WHITETHROAT, *Sylvia curruca.*

Middleham, Wensleydale, N., 400 ft. Broad valley, E. and W.

Carlton, Coverdale, E., 900 ft. Few trees ; hillside, 800 ft. above river.

Angram, Nidderdale, 1200 ft. At bottom of dale, last trees near Dale Head.

Lodge, Nidderdale, S., 1200 ft. In *A. pseudo-platanus*, 200 ft. above river.

High Woodale, Nidderdale, N. and S., 1000 ft. Dale side, steep, few trees.

Black Hill Ho., Kex Beck, S. 825 ft. Exposed, on ridge ; in garden.

Biggin Grange     ,,      E., 575 ft. In avenue, protected ; valley slope.

Sker Beck     ,,      325 ft.

Spring Hall     ,,      S., 425 ft. On ridge.

Owster Hill     ,,      E., 450 ft. Wood cresting hill ; several small ponds near.

Kendale Wood, Kex Beck, 350 ft. Sheltered.

Bridge Banks     ,,      800 ft.

A small wood     ,,      E., 350 ft. S. of road, small stream, sheltered.

N. of Upper Holborn Bridge, Laver, 500 ft., exposed.

Drift Lane, Laver, 450 ft.   Sheltered; near foot-bridge; small woods.

Belford Lane, Laver, 600 ft.   Exposed; with Wood Wren.

Wetshod Lane   ,,     700 ft.   In company with Redstart.

River Nidd, 490 ft.   Trees by River above Pateley Bridge; broad meadows.

Oxmires Plantation, Washburndale, 800 ft.

Swinden Hall, Wharfedale, 200 ft.   A few trees; in valley, E. and W.

Newall Hall, S., 175 ft.   Cluster of trees N. of Otley; on level of Wharfe; close to river.

Riffa Pasture, 150 ft.   Banks of Wharfe; on alluvium.

York Gate Plantation, 825 ft.   On summit of Chevin ridge.

Black Horse Inn, Airedale, S., 650 ft.   Gently sloping to S. from Chevin; a belt of trees, N.E. and S.W.

Kereby Town End, Wharfedale, S., 280 ft.   On ridge; avenue.

Owl Head Wood        ,,     S., 150 ft,   Steep wood, to alluvium; with Chiffchaff.

Near West Plantation, Wharfedale, 825 ft.   Cluster of trees in fields.

Belt near Halfway House, 575 ft., May 1st, 1871.

Little Plains Wood, 350 ft.   On table land S. of Aire, near Calverley.

Hollin's Wood, N.E., 800 ft.   Lies low, steep bank to Aire.

WOOD WREN.   *Phylloscopus sibilatrix.*

Long Side, Birk Gill, 850 ft., May 19th, 1871.   A deep cleft in moors, with native forest.

How Gill, N., 850 ft.   Narrow wooded gill in steep hillside, above Jervaulx.

Arnagill Tower, 1000 ft., June 14th, 1870.   A deep cleft, N. and S., in moors; wooded sides.

Burntroots Plantation, 800 ft., June 1st, 1870.   Sheltered; wooded sides of Thieves Gill, N. and S.

Carter Sike, Laverton, N., 300 ft., 1870.   Exposed, groups of trees; hedges.

Belford Lane, 600 ft., 1870. Exposed ; with Lesser Whitethroat.

Picking Gill, Sawley, 625 ft., 1869. Deep gill, sheltered ; wooded sides.

Moseley Wood, 525 ft., May 1st, 1869.

CHIFFCHAFF, *Phylloscopus collybita.*

Kirkby Malzeard, 425 ft., May 20th, 1870. Protected ; Park Wood, sides of narrow valley.

Wood near E. Tanfield, W., 125 ft., September 21st, 1870. Small wood in steep bank above Ure ; heard.

Steadbars Wood, S.W., 200 ft., June 1st, 1870. Near Lightwater, moderately protected from E.

Winksley Bridge, N., 300 ft. Wooded sides of Laver. Valley, N.E. and S.W.

Winksley Banks, W., 400 ft., August 27th, 1870. ,, N. and S.

Low Ray Carr, 500 ft. N.E. and S.W. ,,

North Wood, N. 325 ft. E. and W. ,,

Eavestone Lakes, N.E., 600 ft., May 27th, 1869. Deep gill with steep wooded sides, lake at bottom.

Low Wood, S.E., 650 ft., May 24th, 1869. Valley, wooded sides ; stream, S.E.

Warsill Pasture, E., 720 ft., 1869. High table-land ; wood on edge of moor.

Oakshaw, Clark's Carr, and Hag Pits, E., 400 to 600 ft., 1869. West side of Nidd ; extensive woods.

Shepherd Wood, S., 225 to 375 ft., July 21st, 1869. Steep wood to alluvium of Nidd.

Cockbur Bank, 700 ft. Washburndale. Steep wooded sides ; valley 800 feet deep.

Swinden Wood, 300 ft., June 1871. Lies low ; N. side of wood ; no other woods near ; singing 3 P.M.

Rudding Park, 260 ft., June, 1871. Tall trees ; considerable wood ; singing 1 P.M.

Kirskill Wood, N., 350 ft., June, 1871. On S. side of Wharfe ; steep hillside ; singing 11 A.M.

Whin Covert, N., 375 ft., June, 1871. Steep bank close to Arthington tunnel ; chiefly tall firs and beeches ; singing 12, noon.

Hunter's Wood, N. slope, 250 ft., June 7th, 1871. In narrow valley ; small wood ; singing 4-15 P.M.

Keswick Oxclose Wood, N.W., 150 ft., June 7th, 1871. Steep bank above Wharfe ; Singing 4-15 P.M.

Owl Head Wood, S., 250 ft. Steep wood to alluvium of Wharfe ; singing 3-40 P.M.

West Plantation, S., 275 ft. On table-land ; large wood.

Longridge Plantation, N., 325 ft., July 3rd, 1871. Harewood Park, protected ; singing 5-30 P.M.

GROUSE'S NEST.—Great Blowing Gill Beck, N., 1820 ft. ; in gentle hollow on moor S. of Great Whernside.

SANDPIPER, *Tringa hypoleucos.*

Pott Beck, River Burn, 500 ft., 1871. Deep valley with narrow alluvium, wooded N. and S.

Pateley Bridge, Nidderdale, 390 ft., May 10, 1869. One in Nidd, on shallows ; broad meadows.

Lofthouse, Nidderdale. S., 430 ft., 1869. Nest with four eggs, bank of Nidd ; broad meadows.

Ramsgill, Nidderdale, 460 ft., May 9, 1869. One in Nidd, on shallows ; broad meadows.

Stean Beck, Nidderdale, 875 ft., 1869. Deep gorge, very narrow, rocky shallows, wooded sides.

Trows Beck, Nidderdale, S.E., 1300 ft., 1871. Lodge Pasture ; sloping open moorside ; in dale.

Tanfield Mill, Ure, S.E., 125 ft., June 12, 1871. Limestone shallows ; rocky ledges, in river.

Above Winksley Bridge, River Laver, 300 ft., 1870. Wooded sides ; narrow meadows.

Galphay Wood, 250 ft., 1870. Steep woods, to river on E. side.

Apperley Bridge, N., about 800 ft. Stream in wood, overgrown with trees.

SNIPE, *Scolopax gallinago*.

Angram Pasture, S., 1550 ft., May 23, 1871. Caught young Snipe ; attracted by old bird feigning lameness.

Dale Head, 1350 ft., May 22, 1869. Breeds ; and on Masham Moor.

Coal Dike, N., 750 ft. Very small stream on high ground.

Galphay Moor, N., 525 ft., May 26, 1870. Saw five, 5 P.M. ; flattish boggy land, slightly exposed.

Jackhole Head, W., 1250 ft. Saw seven, High Moors, W. of Greenhowhill ; wet, exposed.

Stainburn Moor, S., 800 ft., Oct. 22, 1868.

Burley, in Wharfedale, N., 200 ft., July 30, 1868. Stream in alluvium of Wharfedale ; saw four.

DIPPER, *Cinclus aquacticus*.

Sowden Beck, N.E., 1075 ft., September 14, 1871. Stream on open moor.

Spruce Gill Beck, N.E., 900 ft., 1871. Deep valley in moors.
    ,,       ,,    N.E., 1075 ft. Valley in moors.

Trows Beck, S.E., 1300 ft., May 24, 1871. Flew against a stone and killed itself. I have this bird stuffed.

Bain Grain Beck, E., 1600 ft., May 11. Near watershed ridge between Wharfe and Nidd ; High Moors.

River Nidd, Ramsgill, 460 ft., May 9th, 1869. Meadows, a pair ; nest near.

River Ure, near Ripon, S.E., 90 ft., 1870. Broad meadows, stony shallows.

Spinksburn Beck, S.E., 550 ft. Meadows, shallow stream in slight hollow in table-land.

North Gill Beck, 850 ft. Deep gill, wooded sides, sheltered.

————:o:————

# THE CLIFFORD FRAGMENTS.

*Being studies from nature to illustrate the story of*
## THE SHEPHERD LORD.

———◆———

## INTRODUCTORY NOTE.

———◆———

The subject of the following fragments of the story of a really noble character, is well told by Miss Julia Corner, in her story of The Shepherd Lord. *

Lord De Clifford, who was killed in a skirmish after the battle of Towton, 1460, left a son about seven years of age at the time. His title and estates being forfeited, he lived as a shepherd's son for about ten years at Londesborough, but for sixteen years after that as a shepherd on the estates of Sir Lancelot Threlkeld—whom his mother had married—among the mountains of Cumberland, near the borders of Scotland. Towards the end of this period, or when he was about 32 years of age, " a gentlemen of noble family and good estate, Sir John St. John of Bletso, in Bedfordshire, came on a visit to Threlkeld, with his daughter Anne, a fair girl in the bloom of youth and beauty." The Shepherd Lord, " who had seen her riding out over the hills with her father and Sir Lancelot," fell in love with her. " She had seen him too, and had observed how far superior he was in appearance to other rustic swains," and being no doubt secretly informed or influenced by Lady Margaret Threlkeld, De Clifford's mother, reciprocated his affection while he was yet a shepherd. " It chanced one day as he watched his flocks feeding on the mountains, he saw the damsel on her white

* Magnet Stories, Groombridge P. 134.

palfrey, attended by a single page, riding direct towards him"...she stopped her horse and said in the sweetest tones imaginable, " Good day, shepherd Henry, I came to ask a service of you...in riding over the hills this morning I have lost a golden clasp with three diamonds, that fastened my gorget, and I would ask you, should you meet with such a bauble in your ramblings to carry it to the Lady Margaret of Threlkeld, who will see that it is returned to me."  " Lady I will not fail to do thy bidding. Few persons traverse these hills, and I doubt not the jewel may be recovered."  " Thanks, gentle shepherd : we leave Threlkeld this day, so farewell, and be assured your courtesy will not be forgotten by Anne of Bletso."  That night by moonlight he wandered over the hills in search of the lost treasure, and for many hours he sought in vain ; but at length, oh joyful sight ! he saw the diamonds glittering in the moonbeams.  Lord De Clifford was restored to his title and estates on the accession of Henry VII, 1486, when he married Anne St. John, and lived to a good old age at Barden Tower, which he built for himself.

# THE CLIFFORD FRAGMENTS.

## CANTO I.

### SUNRISE IN EARLY SPRING.

**1.**

The winter-trees had dropped their chips ;
And shivering dews, by lent winds shaken,
Fell from their skeleton finger-tips.

**2.**

When the last melted icicle drips
In the silver mists of morning,
After the weeks of winter-night,
Oriens, all the earth adorning,
Flashed like a new Apocalypse.

**3.**

Glad songs of spring the wet boughs waken,
As scandent Phœbus, with his streams
Of mingled light that quivering held
The golden fogs whose vapours hung
Over the dripping woods, dispelled
Their morning mildews in his beams.

**4.**

Loudly the early song thrush sung,
And, echoing in the pendulous beech,
Again was heard the jay's harsh screech.
The squirrel had begun his tricks,
The rooks were busy collecting sticks,
While, in the mists of morning grey,
There might be seen the lambs at play.

### 5.

Algeria's olives all forsaken,
Frail little wings, that o'er the ocean
Wondrously sustain their motion,
Flit alike from palm and citron.
Songsters that had refuge taken
In the carob and pistácho—
      Not the loveliest glade
Amidst the chestnut groves of Spain,
      Nor the leafy vine
That doth with loving tendrils twine,
      Nor the cool fig-tree's shade,
      Can tempt them to remain ;
But, northward with the lengthening light,
The blithe birds winging their vernal flight
      Make the green woods of England ring
      In the early days of spring.

---

## CANTO II.

### EARLY MORNING AMONG THE MOUNTAINS.

### 1.

By Eden's Vale at this sweet hour,
A shepherd, striding up the steep,
Mounts to the moors to lait his sheep,
A-feeding on the Mosscrops flower,
And, swift to hem the stragglers in,
Glan* and Roy† behind him rin.

* 'Glan' is Gaelic *Glan*, pure, Welsh *Glân*, pure, fair, beautiful.

† 'Roy' is Gaelic, red, russet.

X

## 2.

When the steep ascent was done,
He turned to rest and see the sun—
Glorious, ever glorious sight,
It was rising utmost bright.
In the still morning seen afar,
Rose a pale blue line of smoke,
      Rising perpendicular.
Not a sound the silence broke,
Save the Blackcock from the bent
To the Birks for shelter went,
Or the Ouzel's wild note uttered
As from rock to rock it fluttered.

## 3.

The great mountains to the west,
Always lovely, look their best
When the early morning ray
Lights their cliffs and corries grey.

## 4.

The shepherd in his frock of serge
Stood standing on the craggy verge
That fringed about a lofty scar
Whence he could scan the dales afar.

## 5.

Beneath him, in the coombe there lay
A vestige of the forest spare
That flourished once on fell and dale—
The mountain-elm, the rich-leaved plane,
The red scotch-fir, the hollin grey,
The rowan-tree rooted in the shale ;

And silvery willows here and there,
The which perennial springs maintain—
While straggling birk and eller trees
Were thinly scattered on the screes.

6.

And, wonderful no less than these,
He marked the lesser plants that sprung—
The shimmering moss, the lichens pale,
All in a wondrous verdure hung.
Fast upon the steep rock-wall,
It sprouts from every little ledge—
No shelf so strait, no clint so small,
But there upon the utter edge
Its little fronds and flowerets fall.

7.

A scornful goat with her nimble kids,
        Was feeding in unconcern,
Over the edge of a little ledge
        That left no room to turn—
And while he watched, the Rock Dove blue
Forth from her craggy fastness flew.

8.

Perched on a pinnacle of the rocks,
        There sate a valiant Peregrine.
He viewed her deviating line,
And like a bolt from heaven amain
In a swoop that made the quarry swerve,
        He passed her in mid air ;
        And then with bold repair
        Described a wondrous curve
        Up to his post again.

Beneath him in the waving pine
The Raven croaks, and the Woodpecker knocks ;
He sees the Wild Duck flying in line,
He watches the Starling drilling his flocks ;
The Roe bounds over the twisted roots ;
And, heavily rising once in his swing,
The Blackcock like a rocket shoots
        Along the purple ling.
As many an unrecorded thing
        The silent falcon notes,
Above him on majestic wing
        A Golden Eagle floats.

### 9.

The shepherd was o'erjoyed with joy,
The blithesome morning made him gay—
" Hey Glannie lad, far yaud ! Hey Roy ! "
And they to the moors were off and away.

---

## CANTO III.

### THE SHEPHERD ON THE MOORS.

### 1.

A swelling ridge doth crown the moorland bogs.
Perched on its summit is a boulder laid—
In early morning when the dew distils
Its cup of raindrops from the larch's blade,
A startled beam, aimed at Italian hills,
Had missed his mark, and through more northern fogs
Struck the old stone.   All day the spent beam played
On his grey granite.   There the red-deer crops
His morning lichens, and, in slumbers laid,
Sleeps through the frosts of night beneath its fervent shade.

### 2.

There's many an old unnoted stone,
There's many a monumental crag,
Stands up upon the moor alone—
But this from those discern you can,
For all men call it ' Jonaman.' *

### 3.

The shepherd came with Roy and Glan.
At their approach the grand old stag,
Startled, Iwis, sprang from his lair,
Threw up his noble head in air,
Stamped his fore foot and shook his horn,
Then, snorting at the dogs in scorn,
Set quickly off at a stately trot.

### 4.

Sayes, while he was yet within arrow shot—
" Live, graceful creature, in thy glen.
" Live, freest, noblest denizen.
" Had I been born like other men,
" What angel could have saved thee then ! "
Then, sniffing towards the new laid slot,
The trusty Roy and faithful Glan
Crouched by the shepherd on Jonaman.

## CANTO IV.

### THE PASSIONATE SHEPHERD TO HIS LOVE.†

### 1.

Ere the earliest grouse-cock had shaken his feather,
    And called up his mate from her bed,    [heather
Ere the first morning sunbeam had touched the dark
    And tinged the black moorland with red,

---

* Jonaman '=John-stone.   Wel. *Maen* a stone.
† The title of Christopher Marlow's beautiful little ballad.

A damsel fair of tender age
Came riding out through Threlkeld gate,
Attended by a single page.

### 2.

They struck off through the woods in a wavering line,
For a while by the side of the stream ;
Then up through a forest of scented pine,
Till at last they saw the white precipice shine
In the light of the sun's first beam.

### 8.

Before them, under the birky bræ,
The shepherd's cote in shelter lay.
" Prithee, gude wife, an by your grace
I would desire to rest a space
Under the cover of these trees,
And break my fast in this sweet place."

### 4.

" Ay marry, hooney,* if ye please.
All that I have to give
Is at your service laid.
'Tis nobbut plain we live—
Besides some oaten cake,
I have this morning made
A rye-bread loaf, and there is a goat's milk-cheese.

### 5.

" As luck will have it, I fear
There is no sweet milk to day,
For at this time of year
My goats wander off to the fells,
And my cows go to feed on the bræ ;
And now, as I cannot hear their bells,
I fear they are far away."

* *Hooney*=' you there,' (see Gloss.)

### 6.

" Indeed I count this sumptuous fare—
The thick sour-milk, this mountain cake
That only the stean ewn can bake
With fagrant fuel of Juniper,
The scented Ling, or sweet Scotch Fir—
Indeed I count this sumptuous fare.

### 7.

When the light repast was o'er,
As it by chance, a noble fell
And rolled across the sanded floor.
Then, giving them no time to thank,
The maiden bade the folk farewell,
And whipped her palfrey up the bank.

### 8:

A little later, on the moor
Full loud she heard the shepherd sing ;
In tones full clear, and accents pure
The notes came floating o'er the ling :—

*Ruth-a-riding.* *

#### i.

" Of all the roads that bridges bear
        " O'er waters shining in the heat,
" Or bow-necked steeds, in summer, wear
        " To flying dust with bright-shod feet,
" The dearest winds through Ryal's† glades,
" Where o'er the knaps in elm-tree shades,
" The air-blown primrose blooms and fades,
        " And Ruth comes out a-riding.

* Taken from Barnes's Philological Grammar, 1854, p. 800,—with two
verbal alterations, 'longsome' to 'langsome,' in V. 2; and 'Her' for 'A'
in V. 3, line 1.  I do not know where the original is to be found, or who
is the author.

† Ryal is in Northumberland.

ii.

" And I would fain, with early feet,
        " Arise ere morning dew is dry,
" And wend through dust of mid-day heat
        " To bluest hills of all the sky,
" If there, at last, ere dusk of day,
" The evening sunlight would but pay
" The langsome labours of my way
            " With sight of Ruth a-riding.

iii.

" Her feathered cap with bending brims,
        " O'er shades her warmly-blooming face,
" Her trim-set waist and slender limbs
        " Or rest or bend with winsome grace ;
" And as her skirt o'er-spreadeth wide
" With flowing folds the horse's side,
" He flings his head and snorts with pride
            " To carry Ruth a-riding.

iv.

" While bright below her sable cap
        " Her sparkling eyes look down the lanes,
" And, loosely bending o'er her lap,
        " Her slender hands hold up her reins,
" The gateman fain would open wide
" His gate, and smiling, stand aside,
" Foregoing all his toll with pride
            " To look on Ruth a-riding."

9.

As the last clear note dies away,
The damsel on her palfrey grey,
And a page upon a galloway,
        Come riding o'er the moor :—

" Good shepherd, tis a maiden's task
Of thee a service now to ask,
Yestreen, in riding o'er the Flask
    I lost a brooch of gold.
In it there is a diamond set,
Round it is written '𝔇𝔢 𝔟𝔬𝔫 𝔠𝔬𝔯,'
    And in the marge '𝔓𝔢𝔫𝔠𝔂 𝔞 𝔪𝔬𝔂.'*
Now should the bauble's brilliant glance
Happen to catch thine eye by chance
    As thou rakest thy sheep to the fold,
Wilt thou convey it for my sake
Back to the Lady Margaret
    Who will in safety hold—
Trust me, though more I dare not break,
    Thy kindness I will ne'er forget."

10.

With mute delight the shepherd hears,
Her voice like music filled his ears
    As he drank her accents in.
And ere, with eager utterance strung,
The loosened bridle of his tongue
    Had courage to begin,
A lile bird wewtaled on the bræ.

11.

Perched upon the topmost spray
Of a lonely juniper-thorn,
A Finch as dusky as the ling
Sprake † its sprightly twittering—

---

* " De bon cor," and " Pency a moy." " Be of good heart," and " think of me." From a massive gold ring figured in Aubrey's History of Surrey.

† *Sprake*, A. S. *Spræc*, p. of *sprècan*, to speak.

Y

Sweet wild notes that seemed to sing
　　" Hail ! smiling morn
　　" That opes the buds of May "—
And then it flapped its little wing,
Nor could ye reckon its wither-away.

### 12.

Sayes, " What pretty bryd * is this so gay ? "

### 13.

" Oh, that is a little bunting bird
That flits in early spring.
In March, as I have heard,
Despite its slender wing,
A gaumless flight it takes
Along the northern path,
Towards the silver hills and little lakes
Where the old Reindeer bells in noble wrath,
On fields on ice when Artic morning wakes.

### 14.

Then hither again in dark October nights,
Tinged by the northern snows, he flitteth, white. "

### 15.

Once loosed, his speech began to flow.
He marked the maiden's loveliness,
And she, to see his ardour grow,
Divining that the shepherd's dress
Was but a veil that none might know
The wearer's native birth and breed,
Suffered the shepherd to proceed.

* Bryd, young bird. Bunting bird.  The Snow bunting.  I here recount an experience in Unst, the most northerly of the Shetland Isles, in June, 1874.

## 16.

" There be few that gan these gates, Iwis,
Ay, marry ! but I can tell thee this,
I'se warrant, save my dogs and me
There's not a carl in all the land,
That, from the spot whereon we stand,
Could look around and rightly tell
The name of every dale and fell."

## 17.

" Now I will scour the mountains ower,
        First I will try the Flask,
Then double back along Foulcauseway Slack,
        And count full light the task.
Nor yet content, upon the Bent
        I will wander round and round ;
I give thee my pledge, I'll search the Edge,
Nor will I pause, but through the Shaws,
And all the Fleak, alone I'll seek
        Until the gem be found.

## 18.

She essayed to speak.   Her tongue refused.
And as the mantling blush suffused
The maiden's face, the shepherd read
The one shy glance, the half-averted head,
And seizing the happy moment's chance,
With frank and fearless confidence he said :

## 19.

" There rankleth that within my brain
        I could wish thy spirit to hear.
Shall it with brazen chafing smart,
Till, by its fiery weight amain,
        Like molten lead through cere,
        It burn its way down to my heart ? "

### 20.

" Hard were the kyst as amethyst
Could feel the inner senses prank
With untold love, its prongs grown rank,
Could feel their courage and resist !"

### 21.

" Though I do keenly, keenly feel,
That, trodden in the underdust
Beneath new Education's heel,
Love, that vain old sentiment,
Hath disappeared, and must."

### 22.

" Aloft on high advancement's wing
We clutch at every shooting star.
On the great struggle of fame intent,
We shake off each retaining thing
That tends to keep us where we are."

### 23.

" While yet the golden early day
Lights down on thine unclouded brow,
While yet those fleckless beams array
The dimpled smiles that fade and grow,
Thou shalt not lack the multitude
To whom thy very words are food,
Who, could they clasp thee as their prize,
Would 'sign their claim to Paradise."

[*The maiden draws her rein, as though to retire.*]

### 24.

" I yet thy mute attention claim
      For one short moment only,
Ere the world's pleasures have grown tame,
      And life feels cold and lonely."

## 25.

" When Death hath in his work begun,
  And doth thine home dismember,
Thy friends, departing one by one,
Shall leave thee like the lessening sun
  That yields to chill December."

## 26.

" If ever, Annot, in thy need
Alone thou wendest all the earth,
If ever thou hast cause indeed
To curse the day that gave thee birth—
If ever on that hated road
The stones have made thy poor feet bleed,
Then, wanderer, next thy God"......

## 27.

" Thou weepest—then, ere quite debarred,
Lend me once more thy dear regard.
And mark thee—if 'twas I that marred,
If jaded slavish word, ill starred,
Fleet in its uninstructed path,
Hath stricken chord of thine so hard
As wring out notes of grief or wrath,
My conscience, 'midst its general stain,
Burns smartly that I gave thee pain,
And rather would I with the slain
Lie dead upon the battle plain
Than live to say the same again."

## CANTO V.

### MOONLIGHT AMONG THE MOUNTAINS.

#### 1.

All day through the shepherd true
    Had followed the loved behest,
Till the black pall of dark night-fall
    Constrained enforced rest,
But he rose as soon as the clear full moon
    Gave light to renew the quest.

#### 2.

The quiet mountains slept
In the dream of their midnight swoon,
The tips of their loftiest pinnacles lit
    By the light of a frosty moon,
Or wrapped in a shroud of fleecy cloud,
    Like a moth in its soft cocoon.

#### 8.

At last as he sought—now left, now right—
In the stillness of the alpine night
Broken only by murmuring streams—
Just as a falling meteorite
Startled the stars from their dreams—
The diamond, sparkling at his feet;
Flashed in the white moonbeams.

#### 4.

The hardy shepherd well-nigh wept for joy,
And when his spirits had ta'en a moment's grace,
He clapped* his faithful Glan, and huggled the noble Roy,

---

* *Clapped*, i.e. patted ; O. Norsk, *Klappa*, to pat, stroke gently.

Then framed for heäm* and in a little space
Had reached the summit of the grassy knowl
That rises near the lile Blow Tarn † sae lonely—
The stillness of its waters broken only
      By the plash of the startled wild-fowl.
            5.

In the weird moonlight night among the mountains
      He sate him down to rest on those wild shores,
The silence only broken by the torrent
That bears the waters of a thousand fountains,
      Together rolled in one ambiguous surge,
Down through the wooded cliff with stark pines horrent,
    And over the force that leaps its craggy verge.

           6.

Fed by the scene, his wild imagination,
Bound in the spell of moments all too fleeting,
Fast yielded to the heavenly fascination
While far off on the fells the wild sheep bleating
Back to the herder's voice sent distant greeting,
As from his innermost heart he uttered the burning invocation.

## CANTO VI.

### THE INVOCATION.

#### 1.

    " Sibyl, at thy Campanian shrine,
        If thou cans't Fate unveil,
        Betray the lurking tale
         And tell me mine."

* *Framed for heäm*, made for home—O. N. *Fremja*; A. S. *Fremman*, to make, etc. Heäm—Norweg. and Dan., *Hjem*. The parallel northern form ' hame ' is O. Norsk. *Heim*, acc. of *Heimr* home.

† *Blow Tarn*, i.e., Blue Tarn. O. N., *Blár*, lead coloured, blue ; in compos. *Blá*. As *Blá-ber*, Blæberry, *Blá-mær*, blue moor, so *Blá-Tjörn*, Blow Tarn. There are several small lakes so called.

2.

" For, Annot, me thought with meteor flashed unguided,
The sharp knife Separation struck our star.
I felt thine anguish, heard thy cry ' Divided,'
But ere I claimed thee, lo, thou wast afar."

8.

" Thine orb shines pale at midnight now, beloved,
Whilst I from out the most unfathomed Hell
            Look on thy glory.
Distance, the long-rayed, peering down his beams,
            Of all the firmamental field
            Marks thee the veriest far."

4.

" How have I longed for thy return !
Day chaseth day, while yet the sand
Runs swiftly on at Time's demand.
The hours are eager in the chase.
As each one passes in his turn,
Up steps the next to take his place."

5.

" Forgive my ravings, for the wandering light
That floats before me roaming through the night,
Hath led me from thee, led me far astray,
Far from the usual, plainly painted way,
Painted upon a sign-post with a hand
To show where men should follow—
And now the very ground whereon I stand,
Shaken and cracked with earthquakes, trembles hollow."

6.

" ' Tis night, and past the hour of eventide !
While morn was young I watched thee, bathed in pride,

That thou wast happy.  But while thus so proud
To watch thine eye, a little sailing cloud
Passed over it.  Sadly thy sweet face bowed,
Sudden of all its brightness disillumed,
And thou didst weep.   What did those barbéd poigns
Those ranks of thunder, demon prongs that fumed
In Hell their crackling furnaces, conjoin
To lunge thy lovely heart because on mine
Their lightnings burned and baffled, unconsumed !

. . . . . . . . . . . . . . . .

. . . . . . . . . . Annot, farewell.
That most extremest distance, bridged by the beams
That fled towards me when from thy dear eyes
Too gracious thou hast deigned regarding me,
And now do perish glistening on my tears,
Doth stand most unsurpassed, dissundering us.
One word from thee, and snapt the slender shaft
That points me from thee, hostile though I viewed
Thy lanced guardian, when his lightnings flamed
Their ruddy hatred lest the pretty word
Should 'scape thy lips, and with a rosy smile
Light up the shadows of my sorrowing heart.
Banned in love's darkest deepest catacombs,
The stringéd thoughts, vibrating in my brain,
Draw tensely that my native strength doth fail
To raise my lowly level to thine own."

# CANTO VII.

## THE SHEEPSCORING.

### 1.

The shepherd and his dogs, the twain,
Were early agate and on the moors
Bound for the scoring.   Many a swain
Comes with his brace of curs.*
And as he lightly strode along,
They heard the careless shepherd's song.

### 2.

" I'd as lief be a carl on these mountains of ours
As heir to a peerage with paralysed powers.
Let me drink the pure air on my bonnie wild fells,
And I'll leave them to live in their lordly castells.
While sheep run on mountains, and cattle on plain,
And there's strength in this arm, I'll not spend it in vain."

### 3.

" Hey Glannie, lad, fa' yaud, fa' yaud ! "
Twenty flocks are mixed together.
Wildly waving arms and shouting,
Twenty shepherds, nothing doubting,
Send their dogs across the heather.

### 4.

Bute, Craft, Corby, Cort, †
Crab, Fleet, Flora, Gade,
Gess, Glan, Houve, Jock,
Each knows his proper flock.
Donald Bayne and Anty Horner
Wave their hands to Rake and Morna.

* ' Cur ' is the general name for Sheepdogs.   Lapp. and Fin. 'Coira,' a Dog.

† Sheep dogs names—see p. 13.

Rap, Ring, Roy, Rock,
Jos, Laddie, Lassie, Luce,
Shep, Spot, Swift, Sweep,
Single out their proper sheep.
Tip, Trip, Tossel, Turk,
Watch, Watch'em, Wenny, Wench,
Whip, Wily, Sprat, and Yarrow —
Each does his proper work.

5.

While all the shepherds shout
' Drive him in,' or ' Fetch him out,'
Soon the contrived to sever
Flock from flock, with dogs so clever.
Then the scoring work began,
And this is how the numbers ran.

6. *

" Yahn, Tayhn, Tether, Mether, Mimph,
Hither, Lither, Anver, Danver, Dick,
Yahn-dic, Tayhndic, Tethordic, Methordic, Mimphit,
Yahn-a-mimphit, Tayhn-a-mimphit, Tether-a-mimphit,
                [Mether-a-mimphit, Jigit.''

7.

Shepherds from their different dales,
Told the same with varied tales.
But when all the sheep were scored—
Here we leave the Shepherd Lord.

——————

* Sheepscoring Numerals, p. 11, and 35. This should be read very
fast, as the shepherds run throught it.

## CANTO VIII.

### REST.

### 1.

The battle had been lost and won ! *
Into Barden Tower there ride
Lord De Clifford and his bride.†

### 2.

Sayes, " Now the race is over
Let the good steed eat his clover."

### 3.

" Brightly, bravely, heroine,
I have seen thy virtues shine.
Bravely, brightly, all enduring,
Thou hast ended in securing
Heaven's favour, wife of mine."

### 4.

" When the rough tempest struck thy fragile form,
Stedfast thou stoodest in thy meek defence.
Though veterans quavered, thou wert undismayed.
I marked thy seasoned mind, thy sober sense,
The stern occasion kindled thy quick resource.
Thine even temper and thy passive force,
With meek retirement of thyself, displayed
That mental sovereignty that makes, the modest maid,
The faithful wife, the gentle mother, the prudent dame."

[*End of the story of Henry De Clifford, the Shepherd Lord.*]

* *Bosworth Field.*   Fought August 22nd, 1485.   Immediately after his accession to the throne, Henry VII restored to their titles and estates all those Nobles who had been deprived of them by Edward IV. in 1461.

† *His bride.*—Lord De Clifford had married Anne St. John of Bletso. Their son was the 1st Earl of Cumberland, and the hero of the ' Nut-brown Maid.'

## XXV.

# WEATHER AND FLOODS.

### 1. YOREDALE.

The 'Great Flood' in the Ure, at Masham, happened Feb. 2nd, 1822. There had not been such a flood since February 2nd, 1782 or 3, when the 'tymbar' bridge at Masham, mentioned by Leland, and Tanfield bridge, were washed away. This was the greatest flood known in the memory of men then living. (Fisher, *Mashamshire*, 1865).

### 2. NIDDERDALE.

The following notes have been contributed by Mr. R. Ingleby.

*Pateley Bridge,,* 1881. RESPECTING OUR FLOODS. The door check of our old mill, which we have this year covered up, has a many floods marked on it. Previous to covering it up we took the levels, and had some of them engraved on the new door-jamb of our present old mill. 'The Great Flood' which was talked of as the largest flood in the memory of man by our fathers was the 6th May, 1825. It was quite local, all the rain falling in a very short space of time, between Pateley Bridge and Ramsgill, principally on the east side of the valley, but more especially on the lower end of the township of Fountains Earth, and on High Bishopside, a large amount of damage being caused in Pateley Bridge, none falling further up the valley. It was severe and destructive, owing partly to the suddenness of the water coming down. The February 1st, 1868, flood was the largest ever known in this neighbourhood. It was up for several hours, and was a foot higher than the 6th May Flood. It was 3ft. 6in. deep on the mill threshold. All the ground floors of our buildings were under water.   The pigs, over 20, we got into the houses, but in the bottom floor they would have been drowned.   Therefore we had to take them up into the bedrooms ; and our two cows we took into the house also.   We lost no stock.

Heights above mill threshold :—

| | | |
|---|---|---|
| February 1st, 1868, | 3. | 6 |
| May 6th, 1825, | 2. | 6 |
| September 29th, 1852, | 2. | 0 |
| July 4th, 1777, | 1. | 7 |
| July 6th, 1881, | 0. | 6 |
| November 28th, 1881, | 0. | 9 |

Between July 6th, and November 28th, 1881, a series of seven floods occurred, the largest of which was on November 28th.   On July 6th, nearly the whole of the Holme meadow land was under water, and after the grass was cut, other floods occurred which swept away entire fields of hay, thereby causing a great amount of damage to the farmers.   It is a noticeable fact, that no two floods in Nidderdale are alike in effect, which is locally accounted for by saying, " that the rain falls in planets."*   A great many floods have occured between 1777 and 1881, but those we have recorded were the highest.   I myself witnessed the extraordinary amount of destruction of property caused by the Floods of 1868, and July 6th, 1881.

### 3. WHARFEDALE

Mr. John Leyland, of Kettlewell, from whom in 1871 I derived much information respecting the working of the reins, (p. 60 et. seq.) kindly allowed me in 1881 to copy the following notes from his note book, on the subject of Floods and Weather.

*May 28th*, 1860.   A great snowstorm on the Monday morning. Wm. Wrathall had about 30 ewes and lambs overblown in the

* Halliwell (*Archaic and Provincial words*) has this word : as has Forby, (*Vocab. of East Anglia*) 1830-58, but neither explains its origin, (*see* Gloss.)   It means locally, and in sheets.

snow on Langliffe [part of which is shown , marked ' LIMESTONE GIRDLES ' on p. 160, see also p. 161] Pasture. The fences in several places quite covered.

*February 9th,* 1861. Great Snowstorm. I had two horses overblown and died on Haytongue Pasture. Two men lost at Cray same time.

1868. A very hot summer, no rain from the last of May, to 5th of August. The 4th day of August was the hottest day. The hottest summer in the memory of anyone living. [In this never-to-be-forgotten summer, I was engaged in working out the geology, and constructing the map of that fine range of pasture land to the north and south of the Wharfe, E. of Otley. The whole country was burnt up so that the soil of the pasture fields was everywhere exposed. Not a blade of grass remained green, but curled up dry and brown as the soil itself, and to all appearance the roots were dead. Towards the end of the drought, an Indian officer, a friend, happened to return to England. On my remarking to him that the grass was killed, he replied 'In three weeks after the rain falls the grass will be as green as ever,' a prediction which was borne out by the result].

*Kettlewell, December* 18th, 1869. The largest flood on the Saturday night that has ever occurred since I came to live at Kettlewell, *viz.* :—10 years. We had to dam it out at both doors in the cellar. It reached the top of the gantry. It was 8 in. higher than the flood in February last, in the same year.

*June* 18th, 1872. A large flood or thunderstorm on Coniston Moor [hidden by Grass Wood on p. 160] and Whernside, doing a great deal of damage on the east side of Wharfedale: [This happened while I was at Harrogate shortly after leaving the Lodge near the Dale Head, Nidderdale. In the *Transac.* Institution of Surveyors, *Vol. IX.* p. 146, reference is made to this event. " Mr J. Lucas (visitor) said that he remembered a waterspout (he believed in July 1872) which burst on Great Whernside, one of the Yorkshire hills, and swept away a vast amount of property in Coverdale, demolishing among other things a semi-circular bridge in Nidderdale, which had withstood the floods of 200 or 300 years." [It was on this occasion that the then newly erected stone bridge over the Nidd near Lodge, which had cost £500 to build, was swept away].

*October* 21*st*, 1874.   On the Wednesday night at 9 o'clock, one of the greatest floods that has occurred since I came here, viz.: for 16 years.   The water came through the bar on a stream.   I had to dam it out of both the front and back doors. 8 inches deep in the cellar.   It was 4 inches above the taps on the gantry.

1878-9.   A very severe winter.   Snow fell on the 8th ·November, and continued until March 1st.   The frost very severe.   A deal of snow till the 20th of March.   Never clear of snow from the 8th November till May 13th.   A very late spring.

*November* 8*th*, 1878.   A very severe snowstorm.   William Coates had 30 sheep overblown on Gillside Pasture, and several more in other places on the Friday.   Saturday a fine day.

1880.—*October* 27*th*, 28*th*, *and* 29*th*.   A very severe snow-storm, accompanied with a very strong wind.   A great many sheep overblown, and several dead.   4 large trees blown down at Whitehouses, and 1 at Throstle Nest on the Thursday Afternoon.

*January* 22*nd*, 1881.   The waterfall at Hardraw Scarr, near Hawes, supposed to be about 110 feet high, was frozen to one solid icicle from top to bottom, supposed to be 80 feet in circumference.   [Photographs of the frozen fall were taken at the time].

*January* 26*th*, 1881.   A very severe frost.   Had the milk frozen on my can handle during the time I was milking the cow at 7 A.M.

*March 3rd*, 1881. A very severe storm. Snow continued to fall without intermission from March 3rd to Sunday March 6th. The Mail did not arrive at Kettlewell at all on the Friday, March 4th. Came on the Saturday, March 5th, at 4-30 P.M., with the Friday's Mail. Badger's carts left on Cassa Moss, near Cray, same time. Going from Kettlewell market.

*March 4th*, 1881. The mail bags had to be conveyed on foot from near Craven Heifer to near Catch Hall. Conveyances overblown in several places on the road from Skipton.

*June 8th*, 1881. Great Whernside quite covered with snow at 8 o'clock in the morning.

*July 5th*, 1881. A very severe thunderstorm on the Tuesday night. Very severe lightning until 8 in the morning. This was followed by a very severe flood on July 6th, in Nidderdale.

JOHN LEYLAND.

### 4. THE IRWELL.

The ' Great Flood ' on the Irwell at Salford, happened November 16th, 1866. (Jacob, *Proc. Inst.* C.E., 1882).

A 2

## XXVI.

## ANTIQUITIES, Etc.

STONE CELTS. Mr. George Metcalfe has a stone celt of the ordinary shape, 6 ins. long, by 3 ins. wide at larger end, of which I have seen a drawing only. It was found on Pateley Moor. Mr. Metcalfe has also sent me drawings of two PERFORATED STONE HAMMER HEADS, which are *comparatively* modern. Both are flat, but otherwise differ in shape. One is long-shaped, wide at one end, and pointed at the other. It is 2¼ ins. thick, by 3½ ins. wide at widest, with a circular hole of 1¾ ins. in diameter. It was found near How Stean by Old Willie Beckwith, about 40 years ago, (1882). Along with it was found a bronze spear-head, which has been lost. The other hammer-head is circular, reminding one strongly of a stone-breaker's hammer formed by fastening a thick iron ring on to the end of a stick. It was found up dale, somewhere near Lofthouse, where it was lying for some time in John Kirkbright's house, and was used as a plaything by his children. Mr. Robert Ingleby has two stone celts, one of *Greenstone*, 5¾ inches long by 2¾ inches wide at the broadest part. It is studded with minute black crystals, apparently hexagonal, and star-shaped with six points. The other is *Whinstone*. It was picked up in a farm yard at Calf Haugh, in 1879, by Mr. Robert Ingleby. Interior, slate colour, rough texture. Exterior, worn smooth, dirty brown. Length 6¾ inches. Width at broadest part 2¼ inches. I have drawings of both these celts.

FLINT ARROW-HEAD. A very perfect flint arrow-head was picked up on Mr. Tennant's allotment on Pateley Moor, April 29th, 1881. Its length is 1.19-32 *inch*, and width 1.8-32 *inch*. It is symmetrical, sharp pointed, and beautifully barbed.

Two CANNON-BALLS have been found—one near Middlesmoor about 12 years ago, 13 ins. in circumference, weight 8¼lbs, in the possession of Mr. F. W. Theaker, of Pateley Bridge—the other 7lbs. 9oz., found near How Stean, in March, 1874; in the possession of Mr. Metalfe, of Castlestead, who has also a very curious old BRONZE KAIL POT, (see p. 19), which was found on Greenhowhill. The body is globular in shape, 7 ins. diameter with a projecting rim or neck at the top, measuring from the bottom of the pot to the top of the neck 5½ ins.; this rim is 6 inches external diameter. A straight handle projects from the neck, having a curved support fastened to the middle of the globular portion, which was once supported upon three legs, about 4 ins. high, making the total height 9½ inches Mr. Metcalfe has also two WOODEN SPADES found in Cockhill mine, near Greenhowhill,—one with a shaft 2 ft, and blade 6 ins.; the other with a shaft 17 ins., and blade 5 ins. Mr. Newbould has another, 2 ft long, found in the ' old man ' (i.e. old mine or old workings) of the Yorkshire mine about 13 years ago, Mr. Metcalfe has an IRON AXE-HEAD found buried 3 feet deep on Coldstones, by Thomas Blackah, the Greenhowhill Poet and Miner, June 19th, 1873. The shaft portion is 3 ins. deep by 1¾ ins. wide, blade and shaft, 4½ ins. across. The peculiarity of the shape is, that the neck is not opposite the medial line of the blade, but towards its upper edge. I have seen a drawing of this axe only.

A fragment of a POLITICAL MEDAL was taken out of a loose stone wall on April 1st, 1874, in Nidderdale, above Pateley Bridge, on one side preserving the letters THE GENERO......... GYLE round the margin, and at the foot NO PENTIONER, with a full length portrait of the duke, (all but the head) having behind him guns, swords, and flags. On the other side MAKE ROOM FOR SI......BERT round the margin, and a full length portrait, (all but one foot) of a gentleman in the dress of George I. time, but with a rope round his neck, by which he is led by Old Nick with horns and tail and goat's legs, and a four pronged fork, towards the open mouth of a Dragon representing Hell. The lower part of this side is broken off. A perfect example in the Brit Mus. shows on one side " MAKE ROOM FOR SIR ROBERT " and at the foot 'No EXCISE,' and on the other ' THE GENEROUSE DUKE OF ARGYLE,' and at the foot 'NO PENTIONER.' It is wrongly classed in the Brit. Mus. under date 1739, as will be seen from Keightley's History of England, 1839, V. 3, p. 376. Sir Robt. Walpole formed a grand scheme for abolishing the Land Tax, preventing fraud, increasing the revenue, simplifying the taxes, and collecting them at the least possible expense. This was what was called the Excise scheme. Walpole's plan, which he introduced March 1st, 1733, was confined to the article of tobacco. It was what is now called the warehousing and bonding system. The word Excise was odious in the ears of the people....Riots ensued. The Bill was abandoned ; rejoicings and illuminations took place all over the Kingdom ; the Ministers were burnt in effigy, cockades were worn inscribed with ' Liberty, Property, and No Excise,' and medals were struck, of which the present is an example. On other medals Sir Robert is associated with other characters. The medals are a very fine brass-like bronze, and in all probability of German manufacture. As works of art they rank high, the design and execution being masterly and bold, and the minutest details of the dress faithfully expressed. The medals are lens-shaped, with a raised rim all round. The fragment belongs to Mr F. W. Theaker, of Pateley Bridge, who has also in his possession three medals (two bronze and one brass) struck in honour of Admiral Vernon, who took Porto Bello with only six ships, November 22, 1739. They were found about 15 years ago, in the neighbourhood of Lofthouse. One is brass (?) double-concave with raised rim ; another brass (?) double-convex, with thin edges ; and the third is bronze, double-concave, having *Obv.*—Figures of Admiral Vernon and Commodore Brown, with Cannon on one side.

Inscrip.— " ADMIRAL VERNON AND COMMORDORE BROWN. " *Rev.*, View of Porto Bello, Harbour, Forts, Six British Men of War, and Two Guardacòstas, with Merchant Ships behind Forts. Inscrip.—Took Porto Bello with six ships only, November, 22nd, 1739.

————:o:————

## COINS AND MEDALS.

Mr. R. Ingleby has a considerable collection of old English Coins which have been found in various parts of Nidderdale. Amongst others a guinea which was ploughed up in a field at " Red Brae," in the Township of Bewerley. A large number of Gold *Spanish Coins*, 1750, Josephus, J. D. G., were found at Woodale, in the wall of an old house when being pulled down, one of which the above-named gentleman has in his possession. Philip V. was King of Spain at this date.

A small Silver Coin of Elizabeth was found by Mr. Peter Green on a by-road near Gowthwaite Hall, June, 1881, having been washed bare by the rain. It is now in the possession of Mr. H. Verity, Bewerley.

Mr. Metcalfe, of Castlestead, has in his possession four Silver Coins,—James I., Charles I., and Elizabeth,—which were found in the wall of an old house at Whitehouses, near Pateley Bridge, by a person named Jackson.

————:o:————

## MR. JAMES INGLEBY'S COLLECTION.

Mr. James Ingleby, of Brimhouse Farm, Eavestone, has kindly contributed the following note. He has in his possession the following objects found in or near his farm, which lies out of the dale, some four miles east of Pateley Bridge. " Two Greenstone Celts ; five barbed flint arrow heads ; two leafed

ditto ; one diamond ditto ; one other (which has been broken) ;
five flint spear heads ; two flint saws ; a large number of flint
scrapers.

A hollow dish was found near Skellgill covered over with a
*flat stone*, the whole being buried in the ground.  It contained
burnt human bones and several peculiar small stones."  [A full
account of similar cases will be found in the works of Tylor,
Lubbock, and others, but it may be as well to mention that the
Rev. W. C. Lukis, Rector of Wath, will give a description of
this particular find in a forthcoming work.]  "Mr. J. Ingleby
has a large collection of other flints and coins, one a silver coin
of Charles I., found on the high road near Pateley Bridge.  He
has also a valuable collection of birds and their eggs.  Nearly
all have been 'collected' by him during the last 15 or 20 years.
In a field behind his house he shows a cremation ground in
which a number of burnt human bones have been ploughed up,
in company with several bronze articles."

I understand from Mr. Thorpe that he has visited Brimhouse
Farm, and was shown the above-named articles.

———— :o: ————

## WHEELED CONVEYANCES.

Wheeled conveyances are of very recent introduction in the
upper part of the dale.  During my stay at The Lodge, an
account was related to me (if my memory be correct) by Anty
Horner, of the first pair of wheels that were seen above Lofthouse
or Middlesmoor.  They were all in one piece, and quite solid,
being cut out of a single piece of wood.  This would be some 50
or 60 years ago.  Mr. Thorpe states that about two years ago
he saw a conveyance of this description in a cart shed belonging
to Mr. Matthew Teal, at the Tenement House, Wath, near
Pateley Bridge.  The wheels were wood, all in one piece, very
thick and strong, and without tier ; when in motion the axle

went round with the wheels. The body of the conveyance had low sides, strong-made, and was so constructed that it could be lifted off the axletrees and wheels and then used as a coop cart. All the work was done, and much is still done as has been related, with the sled. My amiable landlady at Apperley Bridge, used to tell a good story of the year 1828, illustrating the inconvenience arising from bad roads and defective conveyances. "It was before hearses were used in this part of the country, when the vehicle used for the conveyance of the dead, was a kind of litter drawn by two horses, one before and one behind. My grandfather had gone to Manchester, and while there, had the misfortune to break his leg. My grandmother was at home at the time, [at Apperley Bridge]. Being anxious to get him home, she went to Manchester with a litter, as, owing to the bad state of the roads in those days, that was the easiest way for him to travel. My grandmother had to walk all the way. They had got as far as Keighley on their way back, when the litter broke down, and my grandfather was thrown on to the road. My grandmother ran straight into the nearest cottage, seized a chair, and without stopping to explain, ran out with it. A minute afterwards, the woman of the house being anxious about her chair came out to see what had become of it. The sight that presented itself to her astonished gaze, was the broken litter, my grandfather like a ghost, sitting in his night-dress on her chair. As soon as she was able to speak, she called out to the other inmates of her cottage, "Come, quick, here's a dead man come to life again." "

## XXVII.

# THE DIALECTS OF NIDDERDALE.

### PART I:—

## Dicky and Micky Date.

### By THOMAS THORPE.

I what ear Dicky Date wer born he said he cuddant tell, an he diddant think onnybody livin cud.   Dicky had an only son call'd Micky.   When seen togither it wer hard ta tell whether Dicky er Micky wer t' oader.   They baith dress'd alike fra top ta ta'ah they wok'd alike, an they tok'd alike.   Wat taine did tother did ! Were yan went tother went, in fact they wer as Ruth an Naomi— they cuddant ner wuddant be'y parted.   They had an ass call'd Jerry as oade as Micky, if nut oader.   They all three liv'd tagether in a oade thakt buildin i t' loanside, leadin up ta some farm-hooses at t'hill top, at Herefild.*   Dicky an Micky occupied t' maist o' t' buildin, Jerry hevvin a corner tav hissen i yah end. I summer, Jerry preferr'd ta hev his aboad, wen nut otherwise ingag'd, i t' loanside i cumpany wi' t' pigs an coafs belanging t' neeberin farmers.   That part o' t' buildin occupied be'y t' fad-ther an son wer divided inta twea rooms—t' livin end an t' par-ler end as they call'd 'em.   T' livin end wer ther aboad baith day an neet, for ther bed steead i' yah corner.   T' parler end wer occupied entirely wi' t' oade leam, at which Dicky had sat thraw-in t' shuttal weavin harden fer monny a lang ear.   Micky wad noo an then tak his turn wi' t' warp an weft an rattle away—

* Heathfield, near Pateley Bridge.

clickity clackity, flickity flackity—wal his fadther com again ta
tak his turn. Oade Dicky hoose wer a faverhite plaise fer all t'
young chaps roond ta gan sittan o' t' neets. They yuse ta git sat
roond t' oade fireplaise—t' fadther at yah side an son at tother—
tellin all soarts o' tales, baith possible an impossible, er else
coontin stars hoot o' t' chimler top fer a wager as they sat, fer
it wer yan o' thease oade fashun'd chimlers at's rarely ta be'y
seen noo-days. Ye cud see hoot o' t' top ont fra onny part o'
t' harstan. Doon chimler hang a gert chean fra t' rannel-boak
at which they yuse ta hing t' poddish pan, t' fryin pan, t' kettle,
er howt else at wanted ayther boilin er fryin.

I ther business ramals monny a act o' kindness wer shown
Dicky an Micky wer knawn be'y baith oade an young fer miles
roond aboot, fer they went fra yah plaise tav anither hawkin harden o' ther awn manifackter. Sometimes Jerry went wi' 'em,
pertiklerly if they had a lang journey. At other times they yuse
ta carry it thersens i ther turns. They baith lik'd a bit o' bacco
bud they nobbut carrid yah pipe, an when they did smeak yan
had a few puffs an then t' pipe wer handid ta tother.

I ther business ramals monny a act o' kindness wer shown
tul 'em which they certainly desarv'd, fer they wer twea as honist,
harmless mortals as ivver wok'd this earth ; an tho' ther lot wer
a hard yan, they seem'd happy an contentid, an thank'd ther
Creator fer His manifold blessins bestow'd upon them—which
blessins seem'd nowt bud poverty, hunger, an starvation. It
seems strange an unreasonable at foaks sud be'y thankful fer
bein pinch'd an punish'd efter toilin ommast day an neet, an sa'ah
monny aboot em i luxery an er thankful fer nowt. It is na'ah
wonder then at some foak sud git t' noashun at tharr's yah God
fer t' ritch, an anither fer t' pooer. Well ; let me remain ta t'
end o' my days—like oade Dicky an his son—honist, an contentid if ivver sa pooer, an still thankful to that Great Supreme Bein
'at rules all things, even t' sparros. Dicky an Micky warrant o'
the hypocrite stamp, ner Jerry nayther—jackass as he war—fer

B 2

it diddant matter ta him whether it wer prince, squire, er begger at pass'd him at t' loanside, he maaid na'ah distinction, he wad cock his lugs at taine as seeane as tother, an if ayther on 'em touch'd him wear he cuddant bide it he gav 'em his reet hinder leg quick, accompanied wi' his perculiar scream, fer he, like t' rest ov his tribe, gat marr kelks an thumps ner corn.

Dicky an Micky com in fer ther sharr o' teazin an varra oft abuse be'y a lot o' mischeevous young fellos i t' neeberhud. All soarts o' pranks wer play'd wi' em ; they had been subject ta this soart o' thing all ther lives. Sometimes when they wer sittin quiatly of a neet at t' fireside, wi' ther elbows o' ther knees an ther heeades i t' fireplaise nearly, a cat wad drop doon t' chimler, set up a yowl an cut intav a corner, er off thro' a brokkan square i t' winder terrified, an t' two oade fonk wad be as freetan'd as t' cat, an jump up an run ta t' far side o' t' hoose thinkin at t' varra divil hissel had landid, or some evil sperit had cum an wer boon ta dew some harm i t' neeberhud, fer they, like maist o' foak i t' locality, i ther day, possess'd a gert amoont o' superstition.

Yah neet a lot o' mischeevous young scamps fer miles roond had arrang'd ta hev wat they call'd a lark. They gat ther faises black'd, an dress'd thersens i all soarts ov queer fashuns. Two on 'em wer comin ta t' plaise o' meetin, an they wer just passin a lair, when a sarvant lass wer comin hoot wi' twea canfuls o' milk, an when shey'd just turn'd t' corner she'y spied thease two black ens. She'y threw t' cans doon, spillin all t' milk. Ower t' wall she'y went, an off as fast as ivver her legs cud carry her, an nivver stopp'd wal she'y gat inta t' hoose, screamin' like somebody terrified. T' mis'ess wer sat darnin stockins ; she'y threw 'em doon as seean as ivver she'y saw t' lass an seazed a pailful o' watter at wer standin a back o' t' deer, beside t' peat creel, an threw it reet i t' lass faise an nearly droondid her. T' mis'ess wer sewer t' lass wer ayther in a fit er else gon mad. T' two young *taistrills* wer sewer t' lass wad dee wi' freet, sa'ah they went efter her ta t' farmheose, an' wen they gat tharr, t' lass wer comin roon a bit, an wer tellin t' mis'ess wat she'y had seen ; but as seean as she'y clapt een on 'em cumin inta t' hoose she'y flang her arms up, gav a gert scream, an fell agane t' oade 'ooman on t' top o' t' laugsettle. Yan o' t' chaps sed—" Its nobbut us." T' oade wooman set her een on 'em, an thinkin it wer " Oade Nick " at had cum fer t' lass cos she'yd laid lang i t' mornin an haddant had time ta say her prayers, she'y doon on her knees an sed—" Tak me, maister, tak me Mr. Nick, fer t' pooer lass is ower young ta gan yet." T' chaps begin ta be'y flaid the'y freetan'd baith t' mis'ess an t' sarvant hoot o' ther wits, an at the'yd git hang'd. Hooiver, i t' end—wi' a gud deal o' coaxin an declarin at it wer nowt bud thersens wi black faises an queer dresses, they gat 'em baith roond, an yan o' t' chaps maaide it all reet wi' t' lass we'y a few kisses an leavin a black mark ov her faise. " Giv ower, noo ; gan awa wi' ye'y, ye'y nasty gudfernowts, ah's tell hooer Bin when he cums heeame." Wen Bin heeard t' tayle he ommast crack'd his sides wi' laffin, an sed it wer worth two canfuls o' milk ta hev freetan'd his oade wooman, fer he cud nivver dew it.

Efter they'd maaide all reet wi' t' oade wooman an t' lass, they set off as fast as they cud ta meet t' other chaps, an they fand 'em all waitin ; sa'ah they tell'd 'em o' ther spree they had wi' oade Mally an her sarvant lass, which wer rare fun fer all t' lot.

T' next job wer ta plague pooer Dicky an his son. Yan o' t' chaps had a pistil i his pocket charg'd wi' pooder, an another had a squirt fill'd wi' watther colour'd wi' bleead. They all gat roond t' hoose, an leakin throo t' winder they saw Micky cleanin t' poddish pan hoot fer his supper. Yan o' t' fellas had a turnip an he threw it throo a brokkan square i t' winder an just miss'd pooer oade Dick heeade.

" Seesta, fadther," sed Micky, " that turnip's cum'd through t' solid wall."

" Nay nivver," sed t' oade man ; " thoo can mak me beleeve howt ommast, but nut that, Micky my lad. Its cum'd throo t' winder. Ah beleeve its that young scamp o' Jonas's but ah'le see.''

Up Dicky jump'd an oppen'd t' deer, an just as he put his heeade by t' deer-cheek a pistil wer fired off—tother fellow squirted t' watter reet inta t' oade man's neckhoal. Dicky sprang reet back, an fell ower t' creelful o' peats, an bit wi' t' back ov his heeade agean a deer, an tharr he laid deeade fer howt he knew. Micky gat him intav his chair i t' corner, an when he saw t' colour o' blud aboot his neck he fetch'd a deep sigh, an said— " Thoo's dun for this time, fadther. If they'd nobbut hittan me an all, ah waddant hev carr'd sa mitch ; but if ta dees, fadther, thoo sal be'y laid be'y side o' me'y muther, an ah sa'ant be lang efter the'. Ah'le put t' harden mezzer an the' Garman silver specticles inta t' coffin, an ah'le fetch oade Susy Barker an Pally Spence ta lig the' hoot. Can ta' speeak fadther ? "

" Oh I," sed Dicky, " ah izzant geean yet, bud pretha tak that bullet hoot o' me'y neck, fer it does hurt.''

Wen t' pooer fellow—efter t' pistil had gon off—fell agane t' deer, he gat a spell of it run intav his nek, which he wer certain wer a bullet.

Micky tewk t' cannal an tried ta fin'd t' bullet, but he cud see nowt but bleead, sa'ah he clapt t' cannal doon an said he'd fetch t' docter.

" Nay, nivver bother, Micky, fer he'll charge me'y three-an-sixpence, an happen winnat dew me'y a fardin's worth o' gud. If ah dee, ah dee ! the Lord's will be'y dun.''

Just as Dicky had finis'd his prayer, in bounc'd a gert rough farmers' lad call'd Tom Merrifield, but he wer awlas call'd " Yallo Bullock," becos hede a carroty toppin. He ass'd wat wer up. Micky tell'd him all t' concarn fra t' *threead ta t' needle.*

" Why," Tom sed, " hev ye'y sattal'd yer worldly affairs, Dicky, fer ah see na'ah chance o' ye'y livin wal mornin ?"

T' tears ran doon t' oade mon's faise, as he glaspt his 'ands, shut his een, and then began—

"Few an eval hez me'y days been he'er belo, bud ah've a gud hoap o' tother side o' t' greeave. Eh Tom, ah beleeve Providence hez sent ye'y i' t' nick o' time ; sa'ah ye'y mun sit ye'h doon an write me'y will."

Tom gat a pen an ink, a lump o' tea paper, an put oade Dicky specticles on. T' oade fello sat up i t' chair an began—

"I, Richard Date, o' t' oade loanside, i t' toonship o' Steanbeck Up an Doon, i t' Parish o' Kirkby Malzeard, an i t' Coonty o' York, bein o' soond mind, wind, limb, an eeseet (howt bud hevvin a bullet i me'y neckhoal), beleevin i t' Lord's prayer an t' ten cummandmense, an nut expectin ta ivver see dayleet again, I he'erby mak me'y last will an testament. Ah leeave ta my son Micky all my personal property—t' oade harden leam, sowlin can, an' t' windin wheel amang t' rest ; I further order all my just debts ta be'y paid hoot o' me'y bit o' lowse brass—t' main bulk al be'y fun i a oade coffee-pot widoot a spoot, felt up i t' thak aboon hooer Micky bed an mine.

T' first—ah owe oade Tommy Kidd fer hoaf-a-laaid o' hav- vermeeale, an oade John Weatherhead a foarpenny bit at ah borrow'd on him fer thare charity sarmons at Gowthit. Jinny Varty wants pay fer twelve ounce o' garn, an she'y can ayther hev t' brass er t' garn back, fer ah've nivver had time ta knit it yet. Oade Jim Covert wants pay fer t' last sheep heart he sent, bud tell him ah said afoar ah deed at heetpence wer plenty for't. An now ha mak me'y deein declaration an ah've geean a faithful statement o' me'y warldly consarns, an ah put Tom Merrifield an his bruther-i-law (at wed his oadest sister Liza) in as me'y exeketers."

All wer as still as a mouse wal Tom read t' will hower, an when he'de finish'd t' last words, tears began a rowlin doon t' oade mon's cheeks an he tewk hod o' Tom hand an sed—

"Eh Tom, it feels hard ta hev ta leeave this warld an this lad o' mine wi' sitch a lile bit o' warnin. Ah could hev lik'd ta hev liv'd other two er three ears fer Micky saaike.  We've been varra cumfertable tho' we've sumtimes been pinch'd; bud still we've had nowt ta grummal at bud thease gudfernowt chaps at's kill'd me, bud ah fergiv 'em all, Tom, an' wen ah's geean thoo can tell 'em sa'ah."

Tom tewk up his hat an bid t' oade fellow farrweel, an' just as he oppen'd t' deer two chaps went by wi Jerry.  Dicky saw it wer him, an fergittin he wer o' t' point o' deeath, he sprang hoot o' t' chair an ran ta t' deer, shootin, "bring t' wokin stick, Micky, bring t' wokin stick, ther runnin awa wi' t' ass."

Doon t' loan they went—by t' oade steane troff—wi' Dicky an Micky behint 'em shootin—"Jerry, Jerry, doant leeave us!" Yan o' t' young scamps wer astride o' Jerry, wi' his feeace ta t' tail, singin at top ov his voice.

Just when hede finish'd singin, doon com Jerry his full len'th, an his rider flew like a *scopperdil* reet hower his heeade; his mates thowt he wer kill'd.  They gat him up an he went limpin on as weal as he cud ta get hoot o' t' road o' t' fadther an son, wa'ah wer cloise at ther heels.  When Dicky an Micky saw it wer na'ah yuse ta run after 'em onny farther, they turn'd back ta leak efter Jerry.  They fand him quiatly grazin o' t' roadside as if nowt warr.  When they gat up tul him Dicky sed—"Pooer Jerry."  Ta witch Jerry replied wi' a roat at wad hev alarm'd onnybody bud his maister an Micky.

When they gat heeame Micky sed—"Ah think, fadther, ye'll git better noo."

Why'a, thoo sees, Micky, fer all ah'se sa'ah oade an sa'ah near me'y end, ah cannot bide ta see pooer Jerry abus'd, heze been sa lang i t' family.  If ah wer droin away, ah beleeve ah sud git up if onnybody wer dewin howt at him.  If ah sud dee afoar thee—an thoo sud liv langer ner him—thoo mun giv him a reet berrin.  Mak him a reet greeave doon t' loanside, under t' gert plane-tree, aside Jinny Lellan coaf garth."

" That's his faverhite plaise, fadther ; he awlas liggs tharr, an hez dun ivver sin ah knew him."

" I, I, that's wat ah meean ; an ah think his banes 'al rest tharr t' best ov onnywear."

Dicky, Micky, an Jerry, haz gone t' way o' all flesh. T' oade hoose i' which they lived an struggl'd, hez been pull'd doon, its foondation *rip'd* up, an it is noo grown ower wi' gers. Not a vestige is left ta mark t' plaise warr it stead. It may be'y truly said o' them an ther habitation, that the place which kent 'em yanco will ken 'em agean na marr.

XXVII, *(continued)*.

# THE DIALECTS OF NIDDERDALE.

## PART 2:—

## THE GLOSSARY.

### By *JOSEPH LUCAS*.

# XXVIII.

## THE DIALECTS OF NIDDERDALE.

William of Malmesbury, who wrote in the 12th century, says, in the "Gesta Pontificum Anglorum":—

" Sane tota lingua Nordanimbrorum, et maxime in Eboraco, ita inconditum stridet ut nichil nos Australes intelligere possimus. Quod propter vicinium barbararum gentium, et propter remotionem regum quondam Anglorum, modo Normannorum, contigit, qui magis ad Austrum quam ad Aquilonem diversati noscuntur."

Truly the whole language of the Northumbrians, and especially in Yorkshire, sounds so confused that we Southerners cannot understand it at all. This is because the district is that of the barbarian races, and on account of the overthrow of the former English kings by the Normans, who sojourn more in the South than in the North.

*Prologus, Libri III.*
*(Chronicles and Memorials of Great Britain and Ireland,* 1870. P. 209.)

*a*

# A GLOSSARY

## OF SOME OF THE WORDS USED IN

## THE DIALECTS OF NIDDERDALE,

### CHIEFLY FROM WORDS COLLECTED BETWEEN THE YEARS 1868 AND 1872.

### By JOSEPH LUCAS.

---

**ABEAR,** *A. S.* **Aberan,** *bear, suffer, endure.* 'Abere se borh thæt he aberan sculde.' 'Let the surety bear that which he ought to bear.'—*Laws of Edgar*, c. 6.

**ABOON,** *above, A.S.* **Abufan** (*Sax. Chron.*, Anno 1090). That is the full form, the simplest being 'ufa'=over. There also occur ufan, ufane, ufenc, ufenan, ufon; be-ufan, b-ufan, b-ufon. 'At-be-ufa-n' contracted to a-b-ufa-n = abufan; but *Goth.* ufar, ufaro. 'Swà we her *beufan* cwædon.' 'As we herein above ordained.'—*Laws of Æthelstan*, Pt. 2, c. 2. 'Thære rode the stode *bufon* tham weofode.' 'The rood that stood *above* the altar.'—*Sax. Chron.* A.D. 1083. In the ballad of *The King of Almaigne*, A.D. 1264, temp. Ed. II., we have 'By God that is **aboven** us;' and in the *Ancient Ballad of Chevy Chase*, probably about 1400, we find the contracted form, 'In Cbyviat the hyllys **aboun**,' Fit. 2, l. 102. In Nidderdale now common, as 'Tharr's nut **aboon** three on 'em,' *colloq. Dan.* oven, *Dut.* boven, *Gr.* huper, *Lat.* s-uper. In a transition state, *O. E.* **abowyne** (*Barbour's Bruce* in *Wedg*) and **abowen**; also abowne, abouene, abouen (Atk), 'That from abone shall fall.'—*Townley Myst.*, p. 23.

**ABOOT,** *about, A. S.* **Abutan, abuton**; *a* stands for *on*, as appears from the passage 'Lagon onbúton tham weofode,' 'Lay about the altar' (*Sax. Chron.*, 1083), which gives on-búton, on-b-úton, on-b-út-on or on-be-út-an, which after removing prefixes and suffix leaves *út*, out. There also occur út-an, but-an (be-út-an). Unlike 'aboon,' this word is not necessarily a contraction of the full form. I suspect that in the phrase 'I don't care a button,' we are really using the full form without knowing it—'I don't care **abutan**,'—which, when the word was forgotten and the real meaning of 'a button' with it, was corrupted into the present shape—reduplicated in the sentence 'I don't care a button about it.' *Buton* is the commonest form, 'Gif dynt sweart sie búton wædum.' 'If a black bruize be left *outside* the clothes'—*Leges Æthelberti*, 59, —*i.e.*, on the face, hands or neck. 'C buton áthe.' 'An hundred withont oath.'—

*a* 2

*Laws of Lothair*, 10. Abúton was a very uncommon form in *A.S.* It occurs only twice in the Laws. 'Abúton ende on écnesse. Amen.' 'Without end for ever. Amen.'—Art. 10, '*Confession*,' 'Canons,' temp. Eadgar. 'Abúton stan.'—*Laws of the Northumbrian Priests*, c. 54, temp. Eadgar.

**ACORA**, '*Acora Scar*.' *O. N.* **Akr**, *Goth.* (*Ulf.*) Akrs, *A. S.* Æcer, *Ger.* Acker, *Gr.* agros, *Lat.* ager, arable land.

**ACOORA EARTH**, *green arable earth* (*Grose*). 'Acoora earth,' *O. N.* **akra-gerthi**, a *field garth*, ploughed field. In c. 42, of the *Laws of Ine*, cited at length on pp. 62-3, we find 'æceres oththe gærs,' 'ploughed land or grass;' 'æcere gemete,' 'the boundary of his *piece*,' where several parties cultivated a tract of common land; each having allotted to him a certain small 'division,' not fenced off, but marked by a strip of unploughed turf, and therein called his '*æcre*.' These are the senses of 'Hæge' and '*aceres*' in the proverb cited below. Here we have the rudiments of the modern meaning. Again, in c. 67 of the same *Laws* we find the word *æcra*, in the *gen.* plural, meaning the ploughed part of a small farm, 'and thólige thæra *æcra*' but in the Rochester MSS. (*Roffensis, i.e.*, of *Hrófesceastre, gen.* of *Hrófe-ceaster*, Rochester) 'thólige his *acera*.' c. 67. '*Be gýrde landes*.—Gifmon gethingath gýrde landes, oththe mære, to ræde gafol, & ge-eræth [ereth, MS. *Roff.*], gif se hláford him wille thæt land aræran to weorce & to gafole, ne thearf he him onfón, gif he him nan bótle ne sýld [slíhd MS. *Roff*. "built" suits the sense], & thólige thæra *æcra*.' '*Of a virgate of land*.—If a man rent a virgate of land, or more, at a fixed rent, and plough [ear] it, if the lord determine to raise that land in work and in rent, (there is) no need that he take it if he has not built any house thereon, and let him lose those acres.' In the *Laws of Alfred*, 26. 'Gif hwá gewerde othres monnes wingeard oththe his *æceras*.' 'If a man damage another man's vineyard or his *field*.'—From *Exod*. xxii. 5. 'iii Æcera-bræde.'—*Laws of Æthelstan* (A.D. 924-940), Pt. 2, c. 2—implies a recognised standard measure, under a furlong, as appears from the context. In a charter of Edred, King of Great Britain (A.D. 948), we find '26 *acras* prati, 50 *acras* silvæ, et 70 *acras* de Brushe.' The first Statute General defining the value of an acre was 31 Edward I., 'Bis octogies perticam continens.'—Containing 160 perticas (sq. meas.)—*Spelm.* It appears from the *Hist. of Foundn. of Abbey de Bello*, a pertica = 16 sq. ft. (perch). Another was issued, 12 Edward II., No. 18, York. '*Decem acræ faciunt ferlingatam, quatuor ferlingatæ faciunt virgatam, et quatuor virgatæ faciunt hidam, quinque hidæ faciunt feodum militis*.'—*Du Cange*. This is, apparently, the same edict as that quoted from the *Lib. Rub*. under the word *Farden*—which, it is to be remarked commences with the *Magnum Feodum Militis* and ends with *decem acris*. This would suggest that the Danes still had the privilege, conceded in the Laws of Eadgar, of 'observing the General Statutes according to the best form of laws which they could choose.'—Leg. Eadgari, *Supplement*, Par. II. Thus we see that 'acre' originally meant '*ploughed* land;' then, *a measure of land*. The word occurs in the sense of arable land in the Saxon *Chron*. A.D. 1130.

| 'Hæge sitteth | 'The hedge abideth |
| Tha *aceres* dæleth.' | That *acres* divideth.' |

The Latin had the word *ager* in the same sense, but later adopted the new forms *acra* and *acrum* from the German, meaning a measure of land, before A.D. 948, as shown above. Brachet quotes from Du Cange 'Ego Starchrius do S. Florentino octo *acra* de terra.'—'Give to S. Florentinus eight *acres* of land.'—*Chartul. de S. Flor*. A.D. 1050. Now, the word *terra*, used simply in this form, denotes *arable land* as distinct from wood, meadow and pasture. (*Domesd., Surrey*, Vacher's Extension, 1862, p. 3, Note K). In Domesday Book, 'acra' is used instead of acrum, 'una *acra* prati.' 'One *acre* of meadow.'—*Domesd., Surrey*, Vacher's Extension, p. 8, l. 5. 'xx *acræ* prati,' &c. The Domesday acre contained 160 perches, but the perch had not the same value in all counties. In Domesday

Book the amount of arable land is given not in acres, like the woods and meadows, but in 'ploughs.' 'Terra est vi. carucarum.'—'The arable land is for six ploughs.' But we have seen that *acre* means '*plough*' in the same sense. This explains the transition of meaning from 'ploughed land' to our sense of 'acre.' The rough or primitive 'acre' was *as much as one plough and the beasts belonging to it could cultivate in one year*—the quantity varying with the soil, mode of tillage, &c. Lord Macaulay well expresses the primitive notion of an acre not as an *absolute* measure, but as *a* measure of quantity, in the lines—

> ' They gave him of the *corn land*,
>   That was of public right,
>   *As much as two strong oxen*
>   *Could plough from morn till night.*—Lay of Horatius, v. lxv.

Du Cange gives one instance of *ager* being used in the sense of *acre*, ' Terra unius hidæ, et terra 28 *agrorum.*'—*Lib. Rames.*, § 245. ' Acair,' the *Gælic* form looks like the sister of our 'acre,' which is not found in Skinner, *Lex. Ang.*, 1671.

**ADDLE**, *to earn*; *O. N.* Odal, *property*, seems like 'boun' to have been made into a verb, *to earn*; *A. S.* eadan, *to produce*; eadgian, *to make prosperous* or *happy*; *O. N.* audga, *to enrich*; *Goth.* (*Ulf.*) authagjan, *to bless*; *O. N.* audr, *wealth*; *A. S.* eåd; *Hel.* od; *O. N.* odal, *property*; *Goth.* auds, *blessed*; *Gr.* ousia, *property*, and onos, *a price, value, payment, articles of traffic*; *Lat.* vas, *surety*; *Sans.* vasnas, *price* (as *O. N.* audr. *empty*; *Lat.* vastus; and *O. N.* and, *Gr.* aisia, *Lat.* fas, *Gr.* ousia, onos *as* aisia, ainos). Brockett has '*Sax.* edlean, recompense or requital,' but this cannot be the source of 'addle.' Of a horse, ' when he'd **addled** his shun,' *earned his shoes.*—*Bla.*, p. 13. 'I aidle my keep.'—*Grose.* 'Gather,' hence 'addled,' *corrupt.*

**ADOOT**, *without.* 'He did it **adoot** a grummal.'—*Nid. Al.*, 1880.

**AFOOR, AFORE**, *before*; *A. S.* Æt-foran. ' Æt-foran wiofode,' *before* the altar.—*Laws of Wihtræd*, A.D. 695. ' Æt-foran eagum,' *before* his eyes.—*Canons*, Eadgar, 32. A rare form in *A. S.*

**AGAIN, AGANE**, *against*; *A. S.* Agen, *against*.

**AGEAN, AGEN**, *again*; *A. S.* Agean, agen, *again.* See ANENT.

**AGATE**, *lit.* ' on the way,' *about*; **A-gate** for 'On-gate'; *A. S.* geat, *road, way.* ' Thou art early **agate**'—early *about* this morning—(*Atk. Cl. Gl.*) '**Agate** cleanin.'—*Colloq.* '**Agate** a new cart'—*engaged upon*—(Wilbraham *Chesh. Gloss.*)

**AGG**, *lit. to goad, to provoke,* ' egg on,' *to quarrel*; *O. N.* agg, *brawl, strife*; frequent in Mod. Icel. (*Cleas*); *Swed.* agg, *a goad, secret hate*; agg, *root form Gæl.* Ag, *doubt, to doubt,* hesitate, refuse; *Gr.* AK in ake, akis, &c.; *Sans.* AC. in Acan, *dart*; acus, *swift*; *Lat.* acus, acuo, acer, &c. (*Cur.* 2).

**AGGING**, *quarrelling.*

**AGGLING**, *quarrelling (Pateley).* '*Aggling*' is more probably 'Haggling' than a form of 'Agging.'

**AGWORM**, see HAGWORM, but the orthog. being doubtful the deriv. is also.

**AH**, *I, ego.*

**AHS', AHS'LL**, *I shall.* 'Ahs git me noase ta t'tree if ah doant maind.' ' Run against the tree.'—(*Nid. Al.*, 1880). ' I'se warrant,'='I'll warrant.'

**AN**, *and.*

**ANENST**, *against, opposite to, over against, in face of, as regards.* ' Anens the cherche.'—M.S. *Bible* in Halliwell.

**ANENT**, *against, about, concerning, over against.* ' *A. S.* Nean, nearly, nigh, almost' (Huntley) cannot be right; nor can *Sax.* Anan, *to give* (Brockett). Anenst and Anent have a common origin with *A. S.* Ongean, on and geon, *against, opposite*; in *compos.* Foreanent and Thereanent:—'And swince thar-ongean,' 'and labour thereanent' (Canons, Eadgar *Be Bétan*, 16).

Wedgwood correctly observes, 'The word **anent** does not seem to come directly from the *A. S.* **ongean**. It shows a northern influence from the *Isl.* giegnt, *Sw.* gent, *opposite*.' They are all collateral and imperfect forms. In the *A. S.* Laws **ongean** first appears in the sentence 'Thurh thæt he **ongean** Godes rihte.' 'Through that he *against* God's law.' The simplest *A. S.* form is **gen**, ongen, but *on* is frequently represented by *a*, whence *agen*. The *n* and *g* have not been able to survive together in English. While some dialects have selected the *n* for elision, others have dropped the *g*, giving anen, anent, anenst. The 'st' is in the nature of a superlative termination, as in 'whilst' from 'while,' 'alongst' from 'along,' 'amongst' from 'among.' '**Anentis** men it is impossible, but not **anentis** God, for all things ben possible **anentis** God.'—(Wicliff's *Bible* in Wedg.) *Ger.* entgegen, *Gael.* an aghaidh. It is evident that the full form is lost, and that it might be built up out of the materials supplied by these various fragments.

**ANTERS, ANANTERS, ENANTERS,** *in case, lest, it may be.* Two very opposite derivations have been proposed for this word. Brockett goes to *Dut.* **Anders**, which involves *Ger.* anders, *otherwise*; *A.S.* other; *Goth.* anthar; *Mod. Gr.* enantiōs, *otherwise, on the other hand*; *Anc. Gr.* antios, enantios (*adj.*), enantion, enantia (*adv.*), *against*; *Sans.* antara. Here the passage of meanings is, *opposite, on the other hand, otherwise, in the alternative, in case.* The likeness between the Sanscrit, Greek, Gothic and dialect forms is striking, and the explanation simple. Atkinson (*Cl. Gl.*) brings forward a formidable rival in *Nor. Fr.* **aventure**; *Chauc.* **auntre**, which derives great support from Chaucer's 'auntrous,' *adventurous* (Sir Topas), and from 'anters,' still meaning *adventures* in the North. But that will only explain **anters**, and not **ananters**. The prefixed *an* either means *on*, or, as Brockett suggests, *if*. Now, while neither 'on-adventure' nor 'if-adventure' could mean 'per-adventure,' which is the nearest we can get to the sense of our word, it seems also the highest improbability that the *A. S.* 'an' should be prefixed to the *Nor. Fr.* auntre, to make up a word already existing in the Greek in the sense of opposition, and in the *Sans.* anta, *end, limit, boundary*; *nearness, proximity, presence*; antar, *within, between, amongst* (*Zend*, antarĕ; *Lat.* inter; *Goth.* undar); **antara**, *within, among, between, by the way, in the meantime*; an-anta, *endless, boundless*; an-antara, *continuous, contiguous, immediately after,* &c.; words already ripe to form the modern *alternative sense* of **anters, ananters**. The word is too deeply rooted and widely spread in the North of England to be a *Nor. Fr.* word, I think. '**Ananters** he come.'—*Grose.* '*In case* he should come.'

**ARF,** *afraid.* Brock. has also **ARFETH** and **AIRTH**, *afraid*; Hal., **ARFE**, *afraid, backward, reluctant.* We find *A. S.* **earfoth**, *difficult*; **yrth**, *fear, cowardice*; and *Pers.* khauf, *fear.* Curtius (398) finds *Sans.* arabh, *to do anything actively or with vigour, to work hard*; *Ger.* arbeiten, *to labour*; *Goth.* arbaiths, *Ger.* arbeit, *work*; *Lat.* labor. Work produces *gain, profit*, whence *Gr.* alphēma, *the price of work, the cost of labour, a contract price*; *Sans.* argha, *worth, value, price*; alphanō, *to bring in, to yield.* But work also implies *difficulty*, whence *A.S.* **earfoth**, *difficult*, whence *reluctance, fear.* 'I'se **arf** to do it'— because it is difficult; whence *A. S.* **yrth**, *fear*, &c. I intend to trace the passage of meanings, not the passage of forms. 'Mither I'se **arf**, I'se **arf**,' or **arfish**, which seems a mere corruption of **earfoth**. Brachet (*Et. Fr. Dict.*, 1873) finds *O. H. G.* eiver *contr.* to eiv'r, whence *O. Fr.* **afre**, *fright*, introduced into Gaul either previous to the invasion of the Germanic races by barbarians serving under the Romans, or in the invasion of the Franks, Goths and Burgundians (*Ib. Introd.* § 20, p. 22.) *Fr.* **affre**, *fright*, used as late as 17th Century by Bossuet, and in the 18th Century by S. Simon, 'Les **affres** de la mort'— the *terrors* of death. Atk. (*Cl. Gl.*) correctly identifies *O. N.* argr, *O. Sw.* arg, *a coward*; *A. S.* earg, earh, *timid, slow*; *Scot.* arch, argh, airgh, ergh, *afraid*; and Cleas. (*Icel. Dict.*) *Ger.* arg, *Gr.* argos, and *Mod. Eng.* arch, archness; and finds (*Paul Diac.*, 6, 24) a Latinised form, arga. We have also *O. Ger.* arg, ark, or arag, arak, *miserly, wicked, impious*; *Ger.* arg, ärgern; *Sans.* argh, *to be worthy, to cost.*

**ARR**, *a scar*; *O. N.* Arr, örr; *O. Swed.* œrr; *Dan.* ar, *a scar.* The first scar or *ar* was that caused by the plough. *Gael.* and *Wel.* ar, *ploughed land*, probably the root word; *Sans.* arus—which also gives

**EAR**, *to plough*, also *ore* and *earth* (*see* ACCORA); *Lat.* aro, *Gr.* aroō, *to plough*; *Eng.* harrow; *Mid. Lat.* caruca, *Hind.* (Dakhnī) har, *a plough.*

**ARM'D CHAIR**, *arm chair.*

**ARRAN**, *spider*; *O. Fr.* Araigne, *Lat.* aranea, *Gr.* arachnē, *Span.* arana, *Ital.* aragno, *Mod. Fr.* araignée—*Patois* aragne. In *O. Fr.* araignée was *a spider's web.* Araigne does not appear in classical Fr. later than La Fontaine, but survives in the *Patois* aragne. Araignée drove out araigne in the 17th century.—*Bra.*

**ART**, *a quarter*, point of the compass. Mr. Dakyns sent me this word from Wharfedale. 'The wind is in a cold **art**.'—*Colloq.*

**AS**, *than*. 'I'd onny time rather be hittan **as** droondid.'—*Al.*, 1880. 'I'd rather break steeans by t'rooad **as** dew that' (be a gentleman's servant), *Colloq.*

**AS**, *as*. To express a superlative degree **as** is often used as follows:—'**As** heait **as** heait'='as hot as hot' [can be]—*very hot.*

**ASK, ASKERD, ESK**, *lizard*; *Gael.* Aso, *snake, adder*; *Gr.* askalabos, askalabōtēs, *lizard*. Askerd seems a contrac. of askalabōtes; *r* and *l* being interchangeable. Hence, probably, *O. N.* askr, *a spear*, and so the **ash-tree**; *A. S.* æsc, *Ger.* esche. 'An' lile bonny **askerds** wad squirt amang t'ling.'—*Bla.*, p. 38.

**ASK-WIND**, a sharp, cutting wind, a hard, dry, *biting wind*; *W.* **Asgell-wynt**, *side wind*—connected with the last word (*see* p. 72).

**ASS**, *to ask*; *A. S.* Ahsian, *to ask*. 'Ah thowt o' **assin** them.'

**ASSED**, *asked*; *A. S.* Ahsode, *p.* of Ahsian. 'He **ass'd** what were up.'—*Al.* 1880. 'They **ass'd** him what his assets were.'—*Al.*, 1880.

**ASTEEAD**, *instead.*

**AT**, *prep., to*; *Welsh, A. S., O. N.* and *Dan.* At, *to, towards.* 'Listen **at** it.' 'A gert chean . . . **at** which they yuse ta hing,' &c. 'A great chain **onto** which they used to hang,' &c.—*Al.*, 1880.

**AT**, *conj.*, *that*; *O. N.* **At**. 'Ah wish fra me heart **at** ah yet wor a lad.'—*Bla.*, p. 37. *Swed.* At, *Dan.* at, *Goth.* thatei, *A. S.* thæt, *Ger.* dass, *Ormul.* at.

**AT**, *rel. pron.*, *that, what, which*; *O. N.* **At**. 'He tried ta due t'best **at** he cud.'—*Bla.*, p. 12. 'An them **at** they diddant keep locked.'—*Bla.*, p. 12. The two latter (*conj.* and *rel. pron.*) are, both in *O. N.* and *English*, contractions. In *O. N.* the full form was T̄had, T̄hat. With the initial 'Thorn' (T̄h) dropped, it became **at**. In *A. S.*, on the other hand, the **at** was dropped in abbreviating, and 'Thorn' (T̄h) used to represent the whole word. At is also a contraction of *A. S.* hwæt, *what*, acc. plu. of hwá, *who, which*. as in Ex. 2, under *rel. pron.* above.

**A GOOD FEW**, *a good many.* 'How many of them were there?' 'Wal, there was *a good few*.'

**ATAFTER**, *afterwards.*

**AWLUS**, *always.*

**AWN**, *own, property of*; *A.S.* Agan, agen, *own*; originally *p.p.* agen, *of* agan, *to have, possess, own*, with auxiliary *to be*, that which is agen, *had* or *possessed* by a man is his **agen**, *own*. The form 'ain' is *Dan.* egen, from a verb lost in *Dan.*; the *O. N.* eiga, *to own.*

**AX**, *to ask*, *A. S.* Acsian, axian, *to ask.*

**AXED**, *asked*; *A. S.* Acsode, axode, *p.* of acsian, axian. 'He **acsode** hi,'—he *axed* them.—(*Laws of Edward*, c. 4.) 'Acsa hine,'—*ax* him.—*Canons* temp. Eadgar, *De Confessione*, 2.

**AYTHER**, *either*; *A.S.* Ægther. 'Buton wite **ægther** ge hý sýlfe ge heora hýndas.' 'Without punishment **ayther** or themselves or their shepherds.'—(*Laws of Eadgar*, par. 18.) In the A. S. Laws **ægther** is followed by ge . . . ge; **athor, ather** by oththe . . . oththe, and is used to indicate the dilemma, ' either, or this or that,' as we now say ' either this or that.' ' **Athor** oththe feo oththe feore.' ' Either or property or life,'—*Laws of Eadgar*, c. 4.) ' **Ather** deth, oththe tha Godes wanath . . . oththe waccor,' &c.— (*Ib. Suppl.*, par. 8.) ' He thowt had **ayther** been caught,' &c.—*Al.*, 1880.

# B.

*Grimm.* { III. *Gothic* (*Eng.*) B commonly = *Lat.* F, *Gr.* Φ, *Sans.* Bh, *O. H. G.* P.
{ IX.   „      F, B   „   =  „ P „ P  „  P   „  F, B, V.

**BACK-CAN**, *a milk-can*, flat on one side and having tight-fitting lid, made of tin and strapped on the back knapsack fashion; for the steep dale sides. Also called ' Budget,' which *see*, also, p. 31..

**BACKEND**, *autumn.* ' And oft i' t' **backend** '—(*Blackah*, p. 38)—' in *autumn*,' but also of other periods. ' I'll try and get at it t'**backend** o' next week.'—*Colloq.*

**BAD.** A somewhat stronger term than ' Awk'ard.' ' Peats ' are ' awk'ard ta reet' when they won't stand up, but coal is ' **bad ta git** ' when the roof is dangerous, or from any other cause in the workings. A cheat, sharper, or bad-tempered man is ' **bad ta dew wi'**.'

**BADJER**, *a pedlar.* A travelling, originally walking, grocer and butter-man, licensed victualler. *Lat.* **bajulus** (*Brock.*); *Gr.* badizō, *to walk*; *Lat.* bājulŭs, *foot carrier, porter.* Bra. finds *Wel.* baiç, *a burden, load; Gael.* bag, whence *Fr.* bague, *bundles, parcels*, bagage, *luggage*; we find also *O. N.* baggi, *a burden, a packsaddle*; *O. Swed.* bagge. I suspect a connection between all the above. I cannot follow *Fr.* bagagier (*Gent. Mag.*, Aug., 1829), or bladier (*Wedg.*) Though **badger** originally meant a walking merchant, we now talk of ' **badgers**'' carts (*see* p. 208). **Badjer** is probably a Latin word.

**BAIN**, *near*; *O. N.* Beinn, *straight*; *Gr.* pelas (IX.), *near* (*Cur.*); *Lat.* fere ferme (III.) ' **Bain** Grain Beck ' = ' *near* Branch Beck ' (p. 92).

**BAINEST**, *nearest.* The ' **bainest** way ' is exactly *O. N.* or *Icel.* ' beinstr vegr,' *the shortest way.*

**BAITH**, *both*; *O. N.* Bœthi. ' **Baith** his sen and a' his band '—' himself and all his company.'

**BAK**, *to bake*; *O. N.* Baka, *to bake*; *A. S.* bacan; *Ger.* backen; *Gr.* phōgein (*Cur.*); *Hind.* pakānā, *to bake*; *O. H. G.* bahhu, *bake*; *Sans.* bhaktas, *baked, cooked* (*Cur.* 164); *Lat.* coctus; *Gael.* fuin, *to bake.*

**BAKSTON**, *bakestone.* Gives the name ' Bakstone Gill ' to several narrow glens in which the flaggy sandstone from which they were, and still are, made, occurs (but *see* pp. 16-18).

**BAND**, *string, &c.* Hal. gives ' a space of ground containing 20 yards square.'—*North.* (*See* also p. 82.)

**BANG**, *a blow*; *O. N.* Bang, *hammering*; **banga**, *to hammer.*

**BANK**, *a steep hill*; *O. N.* Bakki, *Norweg.* and *Dan.* bakke, *A. S.* banc, *Wel.* bant, *a height.* ' Tir Bant,' *upland* (*Owen Wel. Dic.*). Gives the name to ' Owster Bank ' (p. 90) and to ' Dacre Banks.' Oft has the weary tourist thought himself at the end of the endless succession of hills on the hilly Norwegian roads, and been saluted with the information ' Stor bakke til ! ' ' *A big hill yet*,'—and so in life it is ' Stor bakke til ! '

**BANKY**, *hilly.* ''Tis *banky* i this coontrie.'—*Colloq.* ' Bank Top ' = ' hill top,' as the name of a farm, &c. (*see* p. 32, l. 22); *see* also Armstrong (*Gael. Dict.*), baenn.

**BARN**, *a child*, also *a man*; *O. N.* Barn, *Dan.* barn, *Goth.* barn, *A. S.* bearn, *Scot.* bairn; *Gr.* pais, paidion, *a child, boy*; pherō, *I bear.*—*Cur. Gael.*

paisde, paisdean; *Lat.* puer. **Barn**=*'born.'*—"A bolder **barne** was never born.'—*Chevy Chase.* 'We like to see wer **barns** at neet.'—*Bla.* 'T' lile **barns** start a beggin'.'—p. 44, above. The Scotch 'bairn' seems to be *A. S.*— 'Gif heo cwic*bearn* gebyreth.—*Laws of Æthelb.* 77—'if she living bairn bear.' 'Wife and *bearne.'—Laws of Hlothær* 6.

**BARGUEST.** For one view of the **Bargest**, *see* pp. 149-50 ; for another, Ritson (*Fairy Tales*, p. 58). *Hal.* 'a frightful goblin armed with teeth and claws, a suppositious object of terror in the North.' In Nidderdale, a word used to frighten children into obedience, 'also an imaginary hobgoblin, sometimes applied to a worthless, ragged, and ill-mannered fellow.'—*Grose.* *O. N.* **bar.** in compos., and **gestr.**, *a stranger.* Grose finds 'bar' and 'gheist' from an erroneous sense of *bar.*—Drake (Eboracum, p. 7, app.) has 'Sax. burh, *a town*, and gast, *ghost.'*— Brock. '*Dut.* berg, *a hill*; geest, *ghost*: or *Ger.* Bahr-gheist, *spirit of the bier.'* Atk. supports Bahr-gheist. I find in Reg. Scot. (*Disc. upon Devils and Spirits*, 1665, Bk. I., c. xxxiii, § 4), a list of the seven good and the seven evil Demons known to the Black Art. No. 7 of the latter is '**Barman**, who most commonly possesseth the souls of those who are joyned unto him.' I think the same '**bar**' entered into *Icel.* bar-axladr, *high-shouldered*, bar-átta, *a fight* (átta, *on all sides*), bardagi, lit. *battle-day*, metaph. *a calamity, scourge.* Bar-efli, *a club*, (eflir, *helper*); bar lómr, *a wailing*, (lómr, *the loon*). **Gestr**, *a stranger*; so, like *Lat.* hostis, *an enemy.*

**BEAK**, *a toothed crane* above the kitchen fireplace; *Wel.* beçyn, *a little hook*, dim. of 'baç' (*see* p. 20); *Gael.* bacan.

**BEEAK**, *bake* (see BAK). The *ē* runs through *Russ.* peche, peku, *to bake*; *Pol.* piec, *a stove*; piec, *to bake*: *Bohem.* pec, *heat*; pec, *an oven*; pecu, pecý, *to bake.* 'Ah've a potfull o' floor yet to **beeake**.'—*Blackah*, p. 29.

**BEAST**, *cow*; *Gael.* **Biast**, *Dut.* **beest**, *Dan.* **bœst**, *Gr.* boskēma, *a cow*; *Lat.* bestia, *a wild* beast ; *O. Fr.* beste, *Fr.* bête, but *Lat.* bestialia, *cattle*, whence *Fr.* bestiaux, bêtail, *cattle.* **Beast**, now the general name of a cow (beasts, *cattle*) in the Dialect, is neither *O. N.* nor *A. S.* It is only represented in this sense by ‖*Wel.* 'biw,' *cattle.* In *Lat.* it is evidently a borrowed Teutonic word. In Nidd. it may really be a Celtic word, for we find *A. S.* beost, býst, *beestings*, there in use; but, as we have seen, beost does not appear in *A. S.* meaning a cow. Its connections are with *Lat.* pascere; *Gr.* boskein, *to feed*; pateomai, *to eat.* Also phagein, *to eat*; *Sans.* pitas; *Goth.* fodeins, *food*; fodgan, *to feed*; *A. S.* feoh, *cattle*; *O. N.* Fé. **Beast** comes under Grimm IX. for pascere, pastus; under Grimm III., for phagein (phadgein), whence, perhaps, *Goth. fodgan*: but, as might be expected, many of the forms being names of *food* and *eating* handed about from one nation to another, defy all laws, *see* also BEWCE and BOKE, BAK and BEEAK, for other connections. In Surrey's ballad of *Harpalus*, 1557,

> 'His **beastes** he kept upon the hill
> And he sate in the dale.—V. 41.

**BEAST-STANG** (*see* p. 31 and *s.v.* STANG), *a short stick* to thrust through the legs of calves to hang them up by.

**BECK**, *a stream*; *O. N.* **Bekkr**, *Dan.* bœk, *Swed.* bäck, *Ger.* bach, *Dut.* beek, *A. S.* Becc (from the *O. N.*), *O. Swed.* bækker, *O. H. G.* pah. *a beck*; *Gr.* pēgē, *Lat.* fons, *a spring.* **Bekkr** means both *bank* and *beck*, which are variations of one word. As *Lat.* 'ripa' and 'rivus,' *O. Sw.* 'bænker' and 'bœkker,' *O. H. G.* 'Panh' and 'Pah,' (*see* also p. 28). 'Tooting Beck,' in Surrey, takes its name from the Abbey of Bech, in Normandy (to which it was given), which was called by the *O. N.* name (see BANK, BINK).

**BEEAT**, *bit*; *O. N.* biti, 3rd pers. plur. of pret. of **Bita** ; *Goth.* (*Ulf.*) beitan, *A. S.* bitan, *Ger.* beitzen. 'T'lile midgies they **beeat** seea we hardly cud bide.'— *Bla.*, p. 30.

**BEEATH**, *both*; *O. Sax.* **Betthia**, *bede*; *Goth.* ba, bajoths; *O. N.* báthir, *gen.* beggja, *neut.* bæthi; *Ger.* beide; *A. S.* bútu, bútwu, bá (*f. n.* of begen), bá-twá, bégen (*gen.* bégra); *Sans.* ubhau, *Gr.* ampho, *Lat.* ambo, *Lith.* abbu, abbu-du; *Lettish,* abbi, abbi-diwi; *Slav.* aba, o-ba-dwa (*Dief., Cleas., Wedg.*); *Norweg.* begge, ' begge to,' *both.*—*Colloq.*

**BEEFCASE,** *a ladder-shaped frame,* hung horizontally under the ceiling near the fire. Beef was formerly hung on it to dry (*see* Frontispiece).

**BEER TUL'T,** *beer to it;* used so much like one word, and actually written 'tea tult,' '**beer-tult.**' *Dan.* til, *to,* which see. ' Ah had a glass o' t' best **beer-tult,** and it's maaide me'y feel sa pooerly.'—*Nid. Al.,* 1880.

**BEFOOAR,** *before.*

**BEHINT,** *behind;* compares with *Ger.* Hint-an, hint-en (*adv.*), *behind;* hint-er (*prep.*) *behind.* ' Wi' a tail hung **behint** at sweeps t' street like a brush.'—*Blackah,* in *Al.,* 1880.

**BEILD** (1), *the handle of a '* skeel*;' Wel.* Beiliad, *a projection.* The handle is formed by leaving one of the staves projecting above the others (*see* p. 31, and SKEEL).

**BEILD** (2), *a shelter; O. N.* Byli, *an abode,* is closely allied; also ' bæla,' *to pen sheep* during the night. On the high moors a shelter of loose stone walls, generally in one of the two forms ⊤ or ∩. **Beild** is properly something **bylled,** or *built* from *O. E.* **bylle,** *to build; A. S.* byld-an. In the *Creed of Piers Plowman,* about A.D. 1390, we find—

'Swich a **bild** bold
**Y-buld** upon erthe heighte.'—Lines 311-12.

**BE'Y,** *be; A. S.* Beo. ' Ic **beo,**' *1st pers. fut., I shall be,* and the *1st pers. subj., I may be,* of **beon,** *to be.* This is a genuine survival of the *A. S.* inflection, as it is not always used by the same writer or speaker, even in the same sentence. In the sentence ' tell em thoo'll **be'y** cumin bye and bye,' (*Blackah,* p. 15) it probably represents the *2nd pers. plu.* of the *subj.* **beoth,** as it is an indefinite promise.

**BELONED,** *or improp.*

**BELLONED,** *poisoned* by the fumes of lead, but it has no doubt had a wider meaning; *A. S.* Belene, belone, belune, *the henbane,* a very poisonous plant (*Hyoscyamus Niger*); *Wel.* bela ; *Dan.* bulmeurt, *henbane.* Watson (*Cybele Brittan. Compend.,* p. 251) 'Native, Europe all. Low grounds. Humber to 100 yds.' Pateley Bridge is 500 ft. *Lat.* fel, *bitterness of poison; A. S.* bealo, bealu, *bale, evil; O. N.* böl; *Russ.* boli, *pain; Pers.* bala, *misfortune.* This may also explain *bar* in *bargest. W.* bele ('*bale*'), *a marten, or fomard; Gr.* galeē, galē; *Lat.* feles ('the *fell* one '), from its death-carrying qualities. *W.* bela, *henbane,* is connected by Owen with Bel, *war, havoc;* Bel = Mars. Owen mentions a ' Romano-British' altar found in the North of England, having the script ' Bel y duw Cadyr,' 'Mars, the puissant god.' ' Bel' appears as 'bane' in ' henbane '; *Pers.* bang, *Arab.* banj, *henbane; O. N.* bani, *death; A. S.* bana, *killer, death, &c.; O. H. G.* bano; *O. N.* bana-mathr' = ' bane-man,' *i.e. slayer* = ' Barman,' ' Bargest,' *q.v.* (*see* also BEWT).

**BEND,** *band, flock, company; A. S.* Bend (beand), *a band; O. N.* bendi, *a cord;* whence *Mid. Lat.* benda, *a band* (*Du Cange*). 'Mid **bende**'—'with bands '—(*Laws of Ælfred,* c. 2). I was told that a **bend** of black swans came down the dale, and that several were shot near Pateley. They must have strayed from some ornamental water. Grose also has ' Bend, the border of a woman's cap.—*North.*' Bosworth (*A. S. Dict.,* 1860) has 'Bend, a band, bond, ribbon; a chaplet, crown, ornament.'

**BENSEL,** *to beat; O. N.* Benzl, *a bent bow* (from benda, *to bend,* in its turn from band, bendi, *a band*), applied probably to any curved stick used for beating. *Dan.* bengel; *Ger.* bengel, *a cudgel.* Brock. has ' Teut. benghelen,' *to '* band,' to beat with *band.* Connected with this is *O. N.* ben, *a wound.* ' I'll gie thee a good **benselling,**' said J. A. to his son, at Lodge.

**BENT,** *coarse grass on the moors;* the *grassy moor itself,* as opposed to the heathery or ling-covered moors; *O. E.* **Bent.** Sir J. Hooker (*Stud. Flora,* 1870, p. 431) says 'an old Greek name,' without authority or explanation, apparently without foundation. *Wel.* banad, *broom; Sans.* and *Hind.* **bhend,** *a kind of reed;* **bāns,** *a reed;* binna, bunna, *to twist, to mat; Gr.* sphingion, *a band;* sphingo, *to bind together; Lat.* fingo. '*Gr.* phimos, *a muzzle; Lat.* figo' (*Cur.*) *O. H. G.* pinoz, pinuz (*Wedg.*); *Ger.* binse, *a rush bent.* A general name for the coarse grass or the grassy moors, in place names, 'Blayshaw **bents**' in fields, as in p. 32, l. 25; certainly not confined to genus agrostis.

'Bomen bickarte upon the **bent.**'—*Chevy Chase.*

' A Skottyshe knyghte hoved upon the **bent.**'—*Otterburn,* l. 77.

'Then a lightsome bugle heard he blowe
Over the **bent** soe browne.' —*Sir Cauline,* l. 83.

**BERRIN,** *burying, funeral.*

**BESOM,** *broom, A. S.,* **Besom, beam,** *Dut.* and *Ger.* **besem,** possibly a *Dut.* form. *B-s-m* a failure to pronounce *b-r-m.*

'Here's the **beesom** of the Reformation
Which should have made clean the floor,
But it swept the wealth out of the nation.'—
*Rebellious Household Stuff* (*Pepy's Collect.*)

**BETTERLY FOLK,** gentry, or thereabout —'They're *betterly* folk, Mr. N—'s *well up*' (*q.v.*).

**BETWENGED,** cattle are said to be **Betwenged** when suffering from a disease which causes them to swell up about the eyes and tail (*see* p. 4), from which it would appear to mean *stung,* '**be-stinged.**' *But* (?) The disease is said to be caused by eating something in the hedges, and '**betwenged**' to mean ' bewitched.' I strongly incline to connect it with *A. S.* **thwæng,** *a thong, a phylactery,* **thwungen,** *forced, constrained, compelled* (pp. of Thwingan), by the votaries of the Black Art. An obscure word (*see* p. 4).

**BETWIXT,** *A.S.* **Betwyx,** very commonly used. '**Betwixt** you and me,' in confidence. 'The **betwyx** us sylfum syndon,' which are *betwixt* us.—*Laws of Eadmund* c. 6. 'Swá swá lamb **betwux** wulfas,' 'as sheep among wolves.'— *S. Luke,* x. 3. 'The **betweox** preostan sy.'—*Canons* temp. Edgar, 7.

**BEWCE, COW-BEWCE,** *boose, cowshed; Wel.* Buçes, *a fold to which cows are brought for milking* (Ow.), whence *A. S.* bós, *a stall, manger; O. N.* báss, whence *Fr.* bauge, *a boose; Ger.* banse; *Wel.* buçes, from buç, *cattle;* bu, *a living being, kine,* whence *Ital.* bú, *an ox; Gr.* phuō, *to bring forth;* phus, *a son; Sans.* bhù, *earth;* 'Bhu, bhavàmi,' *I come into existence,* &c.; *Lat.* fui, futurus, &c.; *A. S.* Beón, *to be, exist, become; O. H. G.* bim, *Ger.* bin, *am; Goth.* Bauan [Bauains, *dwelling,* Mar. 5, 3, whence also *Bavaria*], *Ger.* bau, *house;* bauen, *to build; Slav.* byti, *to be; Lith.* buvu, *I am,* (Cur. 417, c. 564), *see* also BYRE—and for **bewce,** p. 31.

**TO BEWT, TO BUTE,** *to boot; A.S.* to Bóte, to bót; from bétan, *to better, to improve.* **Bote,** therefore, meant *that makes good, an emendation, compensation.* Thus in the Laws, 'xxx sceatta to bót' (*Æthelb.,* 71); 'twybóte,' *double amends* (*Ib.,* 35); 'to bóte' (*Ælf.,* 2, 40); 'twybót' (*Ælf.,* 36); 'twi-feald bóte'; and in later *Sax.* bótleas, *inexpiable;* as 'housebreaking and arson, and open robbery, murder in public, and treachery to one's lord.'—*Canute,* A.D. 1017-35, pt. 2, 61. **Boot** or **bute,** in the Ballads, was used in opposition to *bale*—

' For now this day thou art my bale,
My **boote** when thou shold bee.'
—*Rob. Hood and Guy of Gisborne,* l. 72.

'Sen God he sendis **bute** for bale.'—*Robin and Makine,* l. 37 (A.D. 1568).

Blackah uses ' **to bewt**'—*Poems in the Nidderdale Dialect,* p. 34.

**BIDE,** *to remain, dwell, endure, wait; A.S.* **Bidan,** *O.N.* bída. 'Whar dosta **bide**?' 'In London.' 'I Loondon!' (*Colloq.*) 'We hardly cud **bide**,' *endure* them.—*Bla.*, p. 38.

**BIGG,** *to build; O.N.* **Byggja,** *Dan.* bygge, *Swed.* bygga, *A.S.* byggan, *Gr.* pēgnumi, pēguo, *Lat.* Fīgo, *to build; Goth.* búan, *Gr.* oikein, *A. S.* búan, *Hel.* búan, *to inhabit; Ger.* bauen, *Swed.* and *Dan.* bo, *O.N.* búa, *to dwell; Gr.* phuō. *See* **Bewoe** for *Sans.* bhū, bhavāmi; *Lat.* fui.

**BIGGIN,** *building; O.N.* **Bygging,** *Nor.* **byggen** (*Fritzner*), *Dan.* Bygning, *Gr.* oikos, *Lat.* vicus, and (from *Gr.* pēguō) pagus, whence pagensis; *Ital.* paëse, *Fr.* pays; *Lat.* paganus, *Eng.* pagan; *Sans.* paç, paçayami, *to bind; Lat.* pax, *peace;* pango, *to fasten, fix,* &c. (*Cur.*, 343); *Eng.* pitch, pack, peg (*Lid. e Sc.*). Vigfusson, in Cleasby, does not connect pēgnumi. The *Dan.* bygning follows this form, as **bygging** follows pēguō. '**Biggin** Grange,' and freq. as a place name, also occurs as a man's name.

**BINK** or **BINCH,** *a flagstone, a stone seat.* A large flagstone leant against a wall, and used to bray sand upon; also improperly called '**Bukker**,' (which see). *O. N.* Bekkr, *Dan.* Bænk, *A. S.* Benc, *Eng.* bench, *Wallach.* bénca or bicasu, *flint; Hung.* béka; *see also* **Bank.** *O. N.* Bingr, *a bolster, bed, heap of corn! Swed.* binge, *a heap; Dan.* banke, *a bank, hillock; see* **Bunch.** In place names, '**Binks** Wood' and '**Jenny Binks** Moss'=Jenny's *Binks* Moss—places where they were dug (*see* p. 28, also **Beck**).

**BIRK,** *the birch; O. N.* **Bjork,** *Dan.* birk, *Ger.* birke, birken (*Schellem*, 1727); *A. S.* beorc, *Eng.* birch. 'Birch' is not understood by many, or is thought to mean 'beech,' to which, as well as to *O. N.* börkr, *Eng.* bark, it is nearly related; all having furnished food. That bread was made from birch-bark, *see* Ray, *Hist.*, 3, p. 12. Linnæus (*Flora Lapponica*, 1737), says, of the birch, 'Cortex nunquam editur a Lapponibus' (p. 264), 'the bark is never eaten by the Lapps,' which implies that it is, or was, eaten by others. He gives, however (p. 276), a curious account of the mode of making 'bark broed,' *bark bread*, from the Scotch fir (*pinus Sylvestris*), which is called by the Lapps 'Betze.' 'Betze *Lapponibus* bietze aliis' (p. 274), that is, I doubt not, 'the food tree,' betze—from *Russ.* péshche, *food;* found equally in *Eng.* 'beech,' *Gr.* phēgos—for which *see* **Boke**—and *Ger.* fichten (*Dan.* fyr, *Swed.* (Scania) fur, *O. N.* fura, *Nor.* (Trondhjem) furu, *O. H. G.* foraha, *Ger.* föhre, *E.* fir; *Swed.* tall). The *Lat.* is betula; 'betulla,' Plin. (Lib. 16, c. 18); according to Camden, from an old Celtic name, bedu, but Vossius laughs at this; *O. Fr.* boule, boulay.—*Cot.* The existence of 'föhre' and 'fichten' in *Ger.* as names of the same tree is suggestive (the former from the 'spines' or 'pines' (leaves), *Lat.* pinus or 'firs'; in Surrey reduplicated 'far-pins'), the latter from its *food*-giving qualities—seemingly a borrowed word, probably from the Greek. An identity is thus established between **birk**, bark and beech, as food, which goes a long way towards proving their identity as words. Nowhere is the birk more beautiful than in those majestically pathetic verses of Hamilton (who died 1754) on *The Braes of Yarrow*, where

> 'Sweet smells the birk, green grows, green grows the grass,
>    Yellow on Yarrow's bank the gowan.'—Ll. 50, 51.

**BIT,** *beat.*

**BLAKE,** *yellowish-white, bright yellow; O.N.* **Bleikr,** *yellow; Dan.* bleg, *pale, &c.; Swed.* blek; *Ger.* bleich and blass, *pale; Russ.* byelieÿ, byelé, *white,* (zhÿlteig, *yellow); Gr.* palleukos, *white;* but *O. H. G.* plak, *black.* If the *Gr.* palleukos be really for pan-leukos, *all white* (*Lid.* and *Scott.*), the 'b' in **blake**, and the 'byé' in *Russ.* byélieÿ, represent an old word meaning *all.* 'Gode **blake** bollys.'—*Tourn. of Tottenham.* 'As **blake** as a marygold.'—*Colloq. Nidd.*

**BLAY,** *bleak, A. S.* **Blæd,** *a blowing,* looks tempting, but this very northern word must be accounted *O. N.*, an adj. connected with *Icel.* blasa [*Eng.* blaze]; of places, in the phrase '*blasa* vith' *to lie full and open* before the eye, said by

Cleasby to be modern. Perhaps, explains 'Blazefield,' certainly 'Blayshaw,' 'Blaywith,' &c. 'It's a **blay** poor place, fit to flay yan.'—*Colloq.* Middlesmoor. This word is no doubt connected with *O. N.* blása; *Goth.* (Ulf.) blêsan, *Swed.* blasa, *A. S.* bláwan, blæwan, *Ger.* blasen, *Eng.* blow, *Lat.* flare.

**BLEA,** *lead-coloured*, also *blue*; *O. N.* **Bly,** *lead*; *A. S.* bleo, *a colour, hue, blee; blue* (Bos.) *O. N.* blár, *lead-coloured*, whence *Wel.* **blawr,** *grey, iron-grey; Scot.* bla, *livid; Gr.* molybdos, *lead; Lat.* plumbum, *lead*, lividus, *lead-coloured*, closely allied to *Gr.* leukos, *Lat.* flavus, *yellow, golden-coloured*, as blea to BLAKE, *q. v., Gr.* 'leukoi konisalō'ᵥwith *grey* dust (Il. 5, 503). 'Lead' stands for 'blead,' as 'lividus' for 'flividus,' and 'leukos' for 'fleukos.' *O. N.* blý, *lead; Ger.* blei, *O. H. G.* pli, *lead. O. H. G.* 'blei-faro' became *Fr.* blafard, *wan, pallid* (*Bra.*), cf. also *Eng.* 'lake' and 'flake,' *Russ.* golyboe, *sky-blue* (*Riola*) ; *Swed.* blå, *blue; Dan.* bla, *Ger.* blau; *O. H. G.* blao, whence *Fr.* bleu, *blue* (*Bra.*). Probably the metal took its name from the colour, '**blee**' is common in the ballads.

'All wan and pale of **blee**.'—*Sir Cauline, Fit.* 2, l. 80.

'That bride so bright of **blee**.'—*Sir Aldingar,* v. 52.

'She threw down the mantle that was bright of **blee**.'
—*Anc. Metric. Romances,* '*Boy and Mantle*,' l. 50.

The *Russ.* Blyednie, *pale*, forms a link between this and the following word.

**BLEEAD,** *blood;* from its colour, as with *Gypsy,* ratte, ret, *blood; Hind.* rakt, *blood and red.*

**BLEEAM,** *blame.*

**BLINDERS,** *blinkers,* of a horse.

**BLOWSEY,** *blouse.*

**BODUM,** *bottom; Dut.* **Bodem,** *Ger.* boden.

**BOGGART, BOGLE.** 1. *A hobgoblin, a sprite*₁ properly a spectre, phantom; *Wel.* **Bwg,** *a hobgoblin, scarecrow,* **bwgan,** *a bugbear, scarer; Gr.* phasma, *a spectre, ghost, &c.;* phaō, *to shine, to appear,* phainō, *to bring to light, &c.; Ger.* gespenst, *a spectre; Lat.* spectrum, *a form or image*, real or imaginary, from spectare *freq.* of specio, *to look at; O. N.* spá; *Scot.* spac, *to look at; Fr.* spectre, *Eng.* spectre, *Swed.* spöke, *Dan.* **spogelse,** which comes so near to **boggle** as to make it almost certain that it is the parent form, modified in its initial by the *Wel.* **bwg,** which has lost an 's.' There is an apparent dilemma in connection with this word. *Lat.* specio, specto has the sense of *Gr.* skeptomai, wherefore they are admitted to be akin, but if this, therefore skeptomai is also akin to phaō, phainō (sphaō, sphainō). 'Skep,' by metathesis for 'spec' (*Grimm* IX.), with the aspirate 'sphec' (*Grimm* III.), brings them to a common point, spha, sphe. 2. *To waver, to shy* of a horse. 'To take **boggart**, said of a horse that starts at any object in the hedge or road. *North.*'—(*Grose*). *Wel.* **bogelu,** *to terrify, to hide from fear.* 'Arthur n'm **bogela**.' Arthur will not frighten me.—*Trystan a Gwalçmai in Ow.*

**BOKE,** *book; O. N.* **Bok,** *Swed.* bok, *Dan.* bog, *Goth.* bóka (*Ulf.*), bóca; *A. S.* bóc, *Ger.* buch, *M. H. G.* Büeche, *O. H. G.* puochi, *book; Gr.* phēgos, *Lat.* fagus, *Goth.* bóka, *A. S.* bóc, béce; *O. N.* bók, *Dan.* bŏg, bog; *Swed.* bok, *Ger.* buche, *M. H. G.* buoche, *O. H. G.* puocha, puochǎ, puohha, *beech* (*Grimm, Curtius, Cleasby*); *O. N.* bæki, beyki, *beech-wood*, on slabs of which the 'runes' were engraved—bók-rúnar (Sdm. 19, *Cleas.*). The name of the tree also used for the 'mast,' from *M. H. G.* we find *Swiss* buech, *beech-mast* (*Stalder,* I., 237); buchen, *beech-mast* (Simpliciss. herausg., *A. Keller,* 1854). The 'mast' gave the name to the tree, not *vice versâ.* For *Gr.* phēgos meant *oak.* Theophrastus (*Hist. Plant.* III. VII., 2), B.C. 322, is clear upon this point, as are Dioscorides (*Hist. Plant.* I., 145), 2nd Century, and Pausanias (*Descr. of Greece,* VIII., 12, I.), A.D. 170. In *Mod. Gr.*, however, phēgos certainly means *beech.*—Kontopoulos (*Mod. Gr. & Eng. Lex.,* 1868). Phegous, *beech-nuts*—Plato (*Rep.* 372, c.)—'Roast myrtle berries and *phegous* at the fire.' Phakos, *pulse, beans, &c.;* phasēlos, *kidney-bean;* all from phagein, *to eat,* whence phegos was derived by Eustathius (*Comment.* A.D. 1160, 594, 33, *et seq.* on *Il.* 5, 693). *Gr.* phagein, *Sans.* bhaks, *to eat,* whence Bopp derives bacca, *a berry; Goth.* basi; veina-basga, *grapes* (*Ulf. Matt.* vii. 16, *Luke,* vi. 44); *Russ.* pêshcha, *food,* comes very near beech and buech, *beech mast.* Much attractive learning has been bestowed upon the meaning of phegos from Theophrastus to Max Müller. Among the modern essays *see* Conrad Gesner, 1541 (p. 107); Curt. Symporian. 1560 (*Hort.* XXVI. 19); Isidorus (*Deriv. and Etym.* XVII. 7), 1585; Mitford (*Hist. of Greece,* VI. pp. 9-11), 1818 ; Carl Fraas (*Klima und Pflanzenwelt,* p. 119), 1847; Curtius (*Grundzüge,* p. 156), 1858; Pott (I. 112); Grimm (*Gesch.,* 398); also (*Deut. Wörtub. s. v.* buche); Kuhn (IV. 84); H. Merivale (*Hist. Stud. 'Anc. Ital.'*), 1865; Max Müller (*Lect.* 2nd Ser. pp. 216, *et. seq.*), 1864; also Meyen (*Geog. of Plants,* Ray Soc., 1846, p. 347) for species; *Quercus Ægilops,* also probably *Q. Ballota.*

> ' Theyr **bokes** thou burnest in flaming fire,
> Cursing with **boke,** bell, and candell.'
> —*A Ballad about Luther, the Pope, &c.,* temp. Ed. VI.

**BOKE** for **BALK,** *a beam.* ' Ah jumped off t' **boke** onta t' hay mew.' For ' Rannel-boak,' *see* pp. 21-22. *O. N.* bálkr, *a beam.*

**BOOT,** *a turn, fit.* ' Thoo had sike bad **boots** now an then.'—*Al.,* 1880.

**BOUN (BOON),** *gone, going, on the way, off to ; O. N.* Búinn, *past part.* of búa, *to make ready, prepare.* A very favourite word in the Ballads. *O. E.* bone, boon or boun, *ready;* later corrupted into ' bound,' from which the Ballad writers formed a fresh verb ' to **boun** ' (*Cleas.*), of which these examples —

> ' Busk ye, **boun** ye, my merry men all.'—*R. Hood and Guy of Gisb.,* v. 21.

> ' He **bowynd** him over Solway.'—*Otterb.,* l. 6.

Of its proper use the following are examples from the Ballads—

> ' To battle that were not **bowyn.**'—*Otter.,* l. 16.

> ' To battle make you **bowen.**'—L. 110.

> ' Our kynge was **bowne** to dine.'—*Sir Cauline,* l. 22.

Chaucer also, ' As she was **boun** to go the way forthright.'—*Cant. Tales,* 11807.

In Nidderdale, ' Where is t' **barn?**' (*Colloq.*) ; and in a local rhyme—

> ' Ye mud really hae thowt it warr **boune** to drownd Craaven.'

**BOWT,** *a turn, fit.* ' Thoo's browt this badly **bowt** on wi' the own carrlessness.'—*Ib.*

**BOWT,** *bought.*

**BRANDERI,** *a moveable framework of iron bars to put over the fire.* For a view of same *see* p. 19. *Dan.* Brænderi, *O. N.* brandreith.

**BRANG,** *brought; A. S.* Brang, *p.* of bringan, *to bring.*

**BRUNG,** *brought; A. S.* Brungon, 1st pers. *p.* of bringan; *p.p.* **brungen,** *brought.*

**BRANT** (1), *steep; Swed.* Brant, *A. S.* brant, bront; *O. N.* brattr, *steep; Nor.* bratt-bjerg, *a precipice, cliff* (*Colloq.*); *Lat.* frons, frontis, *forehead; Eng.* front (*Grimm* III.); *Gr.* prōtos, prōteros, *in front; Sans.* pratamah (*G.* IX.) Also probably *Gr.* phrēn, *midriff,* because it is in front, whence phrontis, *thought, care, heed, &c.* (*G.* III.) "Tis a varra **brant** hill.'—*Colloq.* (2) *Forward;* ' T'lile thing wer as **brant** as cud be.' (3) *Proud, stiff;* ' She war as **brant** as **brant.**'—*Colloq.*

**BRASHWOOD,** *brushwood; O. N.* Breyskr, *weak, brashy, hair-like;* applied,

I suppose, to the straggling runners and shoots that are trimmed off a hedge; variously used (*see Atk. Cl. Gl.*) Spelman cites ' 50 acras sylvoe, et 70 acras de brushe.'—*Chart. Edred.*, A.D. 948. Skinner derives brushwood from *Teut.* bürsle, *a hair, a bristle,* whence *Ital.* bruccioli, brucciare; *Fr.* brosser, bresse, broisse, brosse, to which we may add *Gr.* prason, *a leek,* which is bristle-shaped, phríx, phríssō; *Lat.* frigeo.

**BRASS,** *money, pron.* brăss; *A. S.* Bræs (*Somner*); from *O. Ger.* bras, *the fire;* *Ger.* bras, *that which is cooked on the fire, food;* *O. N.* brasa, *to braze, harden in the fire;* bras, *that which was brazed, solder (Cleas.);* *A. S.* bræsa, *brass,* from being used in the *brazing* or soldering of iron (*Wedg.*) From *O. Ger.* bras, *fire,* come also *Span.* brasas, *Port.* braza, *Ital.* bráce, brácia, brágia; *Fr.* braise *embers;* braiser, *a brazier.*

The Heir of Linne   ' Had never a penny left in his purse,
>     Never a penny left but three,
>     And one was **brass,** another was lead,
>     And another it was white money.'—Ll. 61-64.

' I don't care a **brass** farden,' is a common expression in Nidderdale (*see* FARDEN), and Blackah ' For wer **brass** 'll nut gan a girt geeat,' ' Our money will not go far' (p. 20). ' Bronze' is a twin word, from *Goth.* Brann, *O. N.* brandr, *the hearth.*

**BRAT,** *apron;* *Gael.* Brat, *an apron, mantle;* *Wel.* brat, *a clout, piece* or *rag;* (*Ow.*); *A. S.* bratt, *a cloak* (*Somn.*); brat (*Wedg.*). ' We're gaeing ta bring thee a new **brat.**'—*Bla.*, p. 18. *Gr.* phâros, pháros, *a cloak;* phársos, *a piece torn off;* *Lat.* pars, *a part.*

**BRAY,** *to pound sand;* *Fr.* Brayer (*Skinner*); *Wel.* breuanu, *to bray* (*Ow.*); brau, *brittle;* breuan, *a quern, mill;* breuanu, *to grind* or *bray;* *Fr.* broyer, *to grind, crush, bray;* *Goth.* brikan, *to break,* whence *Lat.* bricare; *A. S.* bracan, breacan, brecan, *to break, bruise;* *O. N.* braka, *to creak;* *Ger.* brechen, *to break;* *A. S.* breotan, *to bruise, break;* *O. N.* brjóta, *to break down;* *Lat.* and *Span.* britare, which Cleasby thinks 'came into Spain with the Goths;' *Span.* bregar, *to knead;* *Gr.* 'rēgnumi, *to break.* **Bray** may be direct from *Fr.* **brayer,** but this is certainly not from *Lat.* bricare, as Brachet thinks, but from the Celtic. For method of braying sand (*see* p. 28), also BREAH, BREEA.

**BRAWN,** *the place at which the branches begin in a tree;* *Wel.* brawn, *abounding with growth;* or, perhaps, **baren,** *a branch.* A tree which stood on the edge of a landslip at High Scar, above Lofthouse, was said to have been ' roven up to the *grain*' or **brawn** (*see* p. 108).

**BRAZZANDLY,** *in a brazen-faced manner;* *A. S.* Bræsen, *made of brass, strong, powerful.* ' And fair befooare t'winder he **brazzandly** stood.'—*Bla.*, p. 18.

**BREAH,** *the broken bank of a river* (*Grainge*); *A. S.* Breah, *Eng.* and *Scot.* brae.

**BREEA, BREAR,** *briar;* *A. S.* Brær. ' Before "Turner Carr" (on the Ord. Map, "Turnacar") was riped, it was all **brears** and chewps,' *see* CHEWPS. The Heir of Linne found

> ' The little window, dim and dark,
>     Was hung with ivy, **brere** and yewe.'—Pt. 2, l. 10.

*Span.* abrojo, *Gr.* 'rachos, proves correctness of Skinner's suggestion that **brear** is contr. from **breaoer,** *breaker,* so called from its tearing propensities.

**BREAD,** *bread;* *A. S.* Breod, *bread*—the *A. S.* pron. well preserved.

**BREET,** *bright;* *A. S.* Beorht, *bright;* breahtm, breahtem, *a shining;* which suggests a form [breaht] repres. by pres. word. ' And t' fire burns as **breet** as can be.'—*Bla.*, 26.

**BREK,** *to break;* *A. S.* Brecan.

**BROKKAN,** *broken; see* BRAY. This a piece of pleasantry anent a lazy man : 'Ah wish t'storm wad brek sa'ah as ah cud git ta me'y wark.' ' They say he dozzant knaw yet at its brokkan.'—*Nid. Al.,* 1880.

**BROWN-LEEMING-NUT,** *hazel nut; A. S.* Leome, *a bough, branch, limb.* 'Brown leemers' or 'brown shuilers' (*Hall*). Is 'brown-leemin' the *hazel tree,* from the colour of its bark (?)

**BROO,** *brow; A. S.* Brew, brœw, *brow,* the common pron; *Gr.* ophrûs; *Ion.* ophruē; *Sans.* bhru, bhruwa; *O. H. G.* brâwa (*Cur.* 405).

**BRUSH-SHANK,** *a small brush* used for working wheaten flour through a tiffany (*sieve*) for making ' tiffany cakes '; *prop.* ' brush-handle ' (*see* p. 15).

**BUD,** *but; as A. S.* abbud, abbudisse, for *abbot, abbotess* (abbat, abbatissa).

**BUDGET,** *a backcan; O. Fr.* Bougette, 'a little coffer or trunke of wood covered with leather, wherewith the women of old time carried their jewelles, attires and trinkets at their saddle-bowes when they rid into the country; now . . . any such trunke,' &c.—Cotgrave, *Fr. Dict.,* 1650. *Dim.* of bouge, a *budget, wallet, great pouch,* male, or case of leather serving to carry things in behind a man on horseback.' *Gr.* molgos, *skin; Lat.* bulga, *a hide, a skin, a bag.* According to Festus of Gaulish origin. 'Bulgas Galli saculos scorteos vocant.' The Gauls call their leather bags bulgœ (in *Du Cange*). Bulgia same as bulga, from *Ital.* bolgia; *Late Gr.* boulgion. *Will.* of Malmesbury writes 'bulgias et manticas coram efferri et expilari jussit.'—Gest. Pontif, Lib. I. (*Spelman*). 'Bulga = hýdig-fæt,' *a leather vessel.*—Gloss. Sax. Ælfric. 'Bulgœ et manticœ reseratoe sunt '—*budgets* and *saddle-bags.*—*Eadmer,* Life of Anselm, 2, 27. Du Cange said 'bolgan' was a Welsh word in his time, and that the Armoricans (Brittany) call it boulchet (*see* p. 31 and BACKCAN).

**BUKKER,** or more properly Booker, *Swed.* bokare, *breaker;* boka, *to bray sand;* whence *Fr.* bocarder. The original booker was *a beech stump, Goth.* bóka, from its hardness. Brockett describes an improved form of this, ' Bucker, an iron instrument with a wooden handle, used in the country to bray sand with.' A similar instrument used for ramming asphalte pavements near London is called a punner, *i.e.* pounder. For búkker see also p. 28, and BOKE.

**BULLACE,** *the bullace, a wild sour plum; Wel.* bwlas (*Wedg.*), from bwl, *a ball,* whence *Fr.* boule, bulle, *a ball; Lat.* bulla. From bwlas come *Ital.* bullos, bulloi, *sloes; Eng.* bollis (*Skin.*), *Bret.* bolas or polos; *O. Fr.* bellocier, *a bullace tree.* 'As heet as a bullace.'—*Colloq. Nidd.*

**BUMMEL-KITE,** *blackberry.* 'Bumble-kites' (*Halliwell*), *i.e.* bumble-belly, from the effect of eating too many. Brockett says ' I have often been admonished by the "good old folks" never to eat these berries after Michaelmas Day, because the Arch fiend was sure to pass his cloven foot over them at that time.' Atk. (*Cl. Gl.*) gives a similar explanation. The name is used in Hampshire (*Warner,* Hist. of Hampshire). *It.* bombare, *Lat.* bombilare, *Gr.* bombos; *Late Gr.* bomboin, bombulē, bombulios, &c. (*Skin.* Et. Ang.)

**BUNCH,** *kick; O. N.* Bunki, *a heap, pile; O. Sw.* bunke. *a heap; O. N.* bunga. *elevation; O. Sw.* bunga, *to beat; Dut.* bunzen, bumsen, *to knock;* bons, *a knock.* (*Wedg.* and *Cleas.*) 'bunch.' *Lat.* pungere, pugnus; *Bel.* boken, boocken, whence *Fr.* buquer (*Skin.* Et. Ang., 1671).

> 'Or mebbe thoo'll be bunched aboot
> Wi' t' barns across o' t' fleur.'—*Bla.* p. 33.

**BURN,** *stream; A. S.* Burn, burna, burne, byrne, from *Goth.* brunna, *a spring,* whence *O. N.* brunnr, *Swe.* brunn, *Dan.* brönd, *O. H. G.* brunno, *Ger.* brunnen, born; *S. Eng.* bourne, *Gr.* phear (*Cur. Skeat.*) Only occurs in the name of the River Burn, Colsterdale. 'Burn Gill,' Gouthwaite = ' Burn's Gill,' after a farmer who lived up there. The Greek equivalent, phrounos, *a toad,* seems to have baffled etymologists. Grimm's Fairy Tales, however, will explain this. It is connected with fish, reptile, and water worship. 'Beck' is a parallel case.

*Sans.* bhekka, *a frog;* also ' fish,' which means *water* as well. *Gael.* Tasg, *a fish,* gen. Éisg, *Gael.* Uisc, *Eng.* Esk, *Siber.* Wiska, *water; Dan.* fisk, *fish;* so also *Nor.* lax, *salmon; Lat.* lacus, &c. Probably **Burn**, *a stream,* should be classed as *Gael.* bùrn, *water.*

**BUSK**, *a bush; Icel.* **Buskr** (*Wedg.*, neither Fritz. nor Cleasby give this); *Dan.* busk, *Swe.* buske, whence *Med. Lat.* busca, busketus, busquetus, buscagium, &c. in *Du Cange* who derives them from 'hoscus.' I should not like to separate ' bush' and ' brush' however, *thin, weak wood,* and for other reasons, in part given on pp. 103-104, ' bush' cannot derive from 'boscus' (*see* BRASHWOOD).

**BUSK**, *the front bone of women's stays; Fr.* **Busc**, busq, also buc, buste, ' *a busks;* plated body or other quilted thing worne to make or keep the body straight' (*Cot.*): a corrup. of *Ital.* busto, from *Lat.* bustum (*Skin.*) ; originally the busk, *Fr.* bu, bust, buste, meant the body ; or busk, the long small (or sharp-pointed) and hard quilted belly of a doublet.—*Cot.* Busk in this sense occurs in the Ballad of *Edom o' Gordon,* 105. Compare *Eng. Gypsy* troopias, *women's stays; Wallach.* trupu, *the body.*

**BUTTERFLEE**, *butterfly; A. S.* **Buter-flege** (*Somner*); *Teut.* **butter-fliege;** *Bel.* boter-vliege.

**BUTTER SHAG**, *a slice of bread and butter,* Bla.—*Gael.* **Sliseag,** *a slice.*

# C.

*Grimm.* {
IV. *Eng.* C, *Goth.* K, *Sans., Gr., Lat., Celt.,* G; *Slav.* G, Z; *O.H.G.* Ch.
VII. *Goth.* h.g.(f); *Sans.* K, h; *Gr.* K, *Lat.* c, qw; *Celt.* c, ch; *Slav.* K, *O.H.G.* h.(g.k).
}

**CABIN**, *Gael.* and *W.* **Caban**, dim. of cab. *a cot, booth,* &c.; used by the lead miners at Greenhow Hill, of the huts or shelters they erect. *It.* capanna, *Fr.* cabane. 'Tugurium parva casa est quam faciunt sibi custodes vinearum ad tegimen sui. Hoc rustici **capannam** vocant.'—*Isidore of Seville.* The Welsh **cab** was 'in the form of a cone made with rods set in the ground and tyed at the top.'—*Ow.* The charcoal burners in the forests of the Brocken make these cabins of firpoles tied at the top, as I have seen.

**CADGER**, 'a miller's man who goes from house to house collecting corn to grind, and returning it in meal.'—*Grainge.* O. F. [Achateur] **acheteur**, *Gr.* chaō, kaō, kapō, *to take in, comprehend;* chandanō (chadein, chadeein), *to take in, comprise; O. N.* kæja, *decoy, allure* (?); *Lat.* capio, capto—adcapto, accapto. *Fr.* acater, 11th century; achater, 12th century; acheter, 13th century.—*Bra.* From achater, *to buy,* comes achat, *a purchase* (accaptum); similarly, from achater [achateur] acheteur, *purchaser.* If the *ad* be dropped throughout (in its later form *a*), we have [chateur] cheteur for acheteur, which, I suspect, is our word ' cadger'=*caterer,* from cater. In the Rouchi dialect, or the patois of the Hainault, we find acater for acheter; *O. Fr.* achepter, *to buy; It.* accatare, *to acquire; Provence* acapta, acapte, *acquisition of an estate. Neapolitan* accattan, *to buy* (*Diez*) ; hence *Old Eng.* acates, cates, *victuals, provisions purchased.* The catery was the *store room,* whence to cater, *to purchase provisions* (*Wedg.*).

**CAIKE**, *cake.*

**CAIME**, *comb.*

**CAM**, *a fence; O. N.* **Kambr**, *a ridge, a fence* on the moors, formed by digging two ditches and throwing up a ridge between them; *W.* **camlas**, *a trench* or *ditch*, in this district as a place name ' **Camless Dyke**' on the moors; *O. N.* **kambr**, *a comb; Dan.* and *Swed.* **kam**, *comb; A. S.* camb, *O. H. G.* champ, *Ger.* kamm, *Eng.* comb. **Kambr** first meant *a ridge,* afterwards *a comb,* from its shape; *Gr.* kamptĕr, *a bend, angle; the point at which a line turns;* kamō, kamptō, *to bend, to turn round a point or angle; W.* camu, *to bend, bow,* or *curve; Gael.* cam, *crooked;* cam, *to bend.* Connected with next word.

**CAMBRIL,** *a curved wooden frame* to lay sheep or pigs on. **Pig-cambril,** another name for the sheep-cratch, for which *see* pp. 9 and 31, also CRATCH, below; (?) direct from *O. Fr.* Cambré *crooked; Gr.* kampulē, *a crooked stick;* kamptŏ, *to bend;* kampulos; *Lat.* camŭrus: *Wel.* cam, camawg, *bent, crooked; M. Lat.* camerare; *Fr.* cambrer, *to bend;* cambré, *crooked; Span.* combar. *to bend; O. H. G.* or *Goth.* (?) whence *Lat.* hamus, hamulus, *a hook; A. S.* hamere, *a crooked stick* used for steering a boat; *Gr.* kampsa, *a wicker basket; Russ.* korobe; *Eng.* hamper; *O. Wel.* cwrwgyl, *a coracle; Russ.* korable, *a ship,* whence *O. N.* kobl, *Eng.* koble, *a boat,* on the Yorkshire coast; *Lat.* curvus; *Gr.* kampē *a caterpillar; Sans.* kapanā, kampanā (*Cur.* 31, b). 'Taureaux aux pieds cambrés.' C. Carapanos (*Dodone et ses Ruines,* p. 149), 1878. **Cambrel,** generally *pron.* 'Cam'ril,' but in view of the *Gr.* and *A. S.* forms the dialect word may be independent of the *Fr.—Gael.* cam-luirg, camlorg, *a crooked stick.*

**CANNAL,** *candle; A. S.* Candel, from *Lat.* candēla, *a candle,* from candeo, *to shine;* whence also *Fr.* chandelle. The dropping of the *d* is a Danish characteristic, as 'mand,' 'man'; 'vand,' 'van,' &c. Of monastic origin.

**CAP,** *to beat* as a difficulty. Capped, *beaten,* in argument or otherwise, *outdone, surprised, astonished; O. N.* **kapp,** *contest, zeal, &c.* 'It caps me wer he gits it fra.'—*Colloq.* 'Ah wor **capped,**' 'That **capped** me.'—*Colloq.* 'Ye'd been **capt** to have seen.'—*Bla.*

**CHAIMED,** *combed.*

**CHAPMAN,** a small travelling *merchant; A. S.* **Ceapmann,** *Dan.* kjöbmand, *Swed.* köpman, *O. N.* kaup-mathr, *Ger.* kaufmann, *Russ.* kypets, *a merchant—prop.* the *striker* of a bargain, COWP, which *see.* If we cannot now readily picture the importance of the effete 'chapman' to this country in times past, there are not wanting materials to aid our perceptions. The A. S. Laws are full of special enactments respecting them; thus, in Kent, a man who '"farmeth" a "comer" three nights in his own house, **cepeman** or other traveller,' is made responsible for his conduct.—*Laws of Hlothær,* 15 (A.D. 675-685). The Laws of Ine, King of the West Saxons (688-728) have a special chapter 'on the journeys of chapmen up country.' 'Be **cypmanna** fóre up on lande.' 'Gif **cypeman** up on Folc ceapige.' 'If a chapman (ceapige) 'chop' with folk [let him] do that before witnesses. If a man receive stolen property—(thýfe feoh) '"æt **cypmen**" (*dative*)—from a chapman, and he has not bought it before good witnesses, let him prove that he neither knew it, nor was the thief, or he must pay his "wite" 36 shill.'—*Ine,* 25. In the Laws of Ælfred (872-901) there is a chapter 'Be **cypmannum.**' 'On chapmen.' 'Also it is ordained (ceapmannum) for *chapmen* that they bring the men whom they take up [coun'ry] with them before the King's sheriff at "Folc gemóte" [the general assembly of the people on May 1st] and show how many there are of them, and that they take those [same] men with them, whom they must afterwards bring back, according to law, to Folc gemóte. And when it is necessary for them to take more men up with them on their journey, let them declare it every time as oft as may be necessary for them, to the King's sheriff before the Gemóte.'—*Ælf.,* c. 30. The Folc gemóte could be assembled any time by ringing the Moot Bell. The necessity of having proper witnesses to every bargain is still more strongly insisted upon in the Laws of Eadgar (959-975). The passage is too long to quote, a great many cases, with penalties, being instanced (*Eadg.,* Suppt., Parags. 13 to 20). Chapmen had to be particular as to the quality of their purchases, which made old Tusser remark 'For that every **chapman** they seem not to please.'—(500 *Points,* 1557, 'Tillage,' v. 27.) The pleasant Dr. Plot tells us that if wheat 'stand too long, much will shatter out of the hand in reaping, the worst only remaining, which will be Pale in the hand, an unpardonable fault where the baker is the **chapman.**'—*Nat. Hist. of Oxfordsh.,* 1705, c. 9, § 99.

**CHEAN,** *chain; Fr.* chaine, *Lat.* catena, *Gael.* ceangal.

**CHEWPS,** *rose bushes, red seeds of wild rose; O. N.* kjúpa, *seeds of the rose.*

Neither Fritzner nor Cleasby give this word as *O. N.*, but the fact that **kjupa**, **hjupa** is used in Norway in the same sense with the *Swed.* **hjupon** indicates the source, while its presence in Nidderdale proves its antiquity. Wedgwood, who gives the Norsk forms, adds *Dan.* hybe, *A. S.* hiope, heope; *Eng.* hip. 'When Turner Carr was riped some years ago, a many **chewps** were taken away.'— *Colloq.*—where it means rose bushes.

**CHIMLER-HOAL**, *chimney* of the old open kind (*see* p. 20, *et seq.*).

**CHINCE**, *tabby.* A ' **chince** tom-cat.'

**CHIPPED**, *chapped.* ' **Chipped** hands.' *O. N.* **kipra**, *to wrinkle*; kippa, *to quiver*; *Dut.* kippen.

**CHOOAK**, *choke*; *O. N.* **Quok**, *the throat*; kjökr, *a choking voice*; kjökra, *to speak with a choking voice.* Of a horse ' He'd hommast ha drawn whal he **chooaked**.'—*Bla.* p. 13, l. 12.

**CHOOKERS, CHUKKERS**, *fieldfares.*

**CLAG**, *to hang on*; *O. N.* **Klakkr**, *a peg on a packsaddle* on which the packs were hung (*Cleas.*) Of a horse, ' **Clagged** on fra his tail tuv his heead.'—*Bla.* p. 12, l. 12.

**CLAISE**, *clothes*, and

**CLEEASE**, *clothes*; contr. from *A. S.* **Clæthas** (*pl.* of clæth), *garments*, as 'cloze' from ' clothes '; *O. N.* klæthi; *Dan.*, *Swe.* and *Nor.* klæder, *pron.* (in Norway), klehur; *Dut.* kleed, *O. H. G.* chleit; *Ger.* kleit, kleid; *Eng.* cloth (*see* also CLOOT and CLEET, below).

**CLAISE-CORD**, *clothes-line.*

**CLAP**, *a pat* with the hand; *O. N.* **Klapp**, *a pat.*

**CLAP**, *to pat* a dog; *O. N.* **Klappa**, *to pat*, whence Klappe-bröd.

**CLAP-CAKE**, *a baked oaten cake*, originally ' **clapped**,' or beaten out thin, with the hand. *Dan.* Klappe-bröd (*see* pp. 15 and 18).

**CLAP.** Other usages, ' **Clap** cannal doon,' ' set the candle down ; ' ' To **clap** een on '=*to see.*

**CLAVER**, *clover*; *Dut.* **Claver**; *Dan.* klever, klöver; *Swe.* klöfver, *Ger.* klee, *Gr.* chloē, chloa, *clover*; *Ion.* chloiē, *the tender shoots* of plants in spring (*L.* and *S.*); the *blade* of young corn or grass; chloeros, *clover colour, green*, contr. chlōros; *Eng. Gypsy*, chor, *green clover*; *Hind.* khur, *clover.*

**CLEET**, *coltsfoot* (tussilago farfara); *A. S.* Cleot, *a little cloth.* As burdock and butter-bur compare with cloth-bur, and blanket-plant with blanket— from the woolly leaves (*see* also CLAISE and CLOOT).

**CLEET-WINE.** ' The beverage made from it,' writes the Rev. S. R. Anderson, Vicar of Otley, ' is called **Cleet-wine**,' (MS. letter). ' Hooer Liza had maaide some **cleet-wine**, a kind of yerb.'—*Nid. Al.*, 1880.

**CLETCH**, *a brood*, whence *O. N.* **Klekja**, *Dan.* klœkke, *Swe.* kläcka, *to hatch*; *Sans.* kilĭ, kilĭ, *a key*; *Hind.* kila, *fort*; *Arab.* kala; *Gr.* kleis, *a key*; *Lat.* clavis; *Gr.* kleiō, *Lat.* claudo, *to shut*; *Mid. Lat.* claia, cleia, cleta, clida; *Fr.* claye=*A. S.* hirdel, *a hurdle*, whence a fold. Clida, *a cage for prisoners* (Leg. Ripuar, 77). (*Williams, Sans.; Shakspear, Hind.; Spelman;* and *Wilkins Gloss.* to *A. S. Laws*); *see* also CLUTHER, CLOOASE.

**CLINKER.** ' That's a **Clinker** '—exceedingly good one.—*Colloq.*

**CLINKING.** ' He's a **Clinkin** good walker.'—*Colloq.*, Middlesmoor.

**CLINT** (1), name of a place near Hampsthwaite; *Dan.* and *Swe.* **Klint**, *brow of a hill, promontory.* Clint is situated upon the jutting spur of a hill. (2) *Flint, chert.* At and above Lofthouse and Middlesmoor the chert beds at the junction of the Yoredale and Millstone grit beds are so called. (3) ' Crevices among bare limestone rocks ' (*Brockett*), so used in Wharfedale. *Ger.* **klinze**, klinse, *cleft, slit, gap* (*Grimm* Dict., *s. v.* **klinse**, 3, a); *Swe.* glänt; *Wel.* glyn, *Gael.* Gleann, *a glen*; *pl.* glinn.

**CLOG**, *a log, a wooden shoe*; *Wel.* **Clog**, clwg, *a large stone* (*Ow.*), with the sense of the following : *O. N.* klot, *Swe.* klot, *Dan.* klods; *Ger.* klotz, kloben, a *log; Russ.* gleiba, *a clod; comp. Eng.* glebe, *Mid. Lat.* gleba. 'T'ool-clog,' or 'T'yule-clog,' (*see* p. 42) ; *Gael.* cloch, *a stone.*

**CLOISE,** *close.* 'Cloise at ther heels,' (*Al.*, 1880), and in a frng. of a local rhyme—

        ' Then up there sprung a little breeze
          Anent the larchy cloise.' ·

**CLOOASE,** *close* (Greenhow Hill); *Lat.* **Clusum,** *an enclosed place;* clusum, clausum, whence *Fr.* clos, *close; A. S.* clýsan; *Franco-Gallic,* clorre (*Skinner*), *Gr.* klision, *Ger.* schloss (*see* also CLETCH and CLUTHER) ; *Gael.* clos, clobhsa.

**CLOOT,** *a kerchief; Gael.* Clùt, clùit, clùd, clùid, *a rag; Wel.* Clwt, *a piece* = *A. S.* clút, *a clout, little cloth* (*see* CLAISE, CLEET). *Pers.* kālū, *silk cloths;* kāla, *cloth; Russ.* cholste.

**CLUTHER** (*n.*), *a-cluster, group; Wel.* Cluder, *a heap* of anything carried (*Ow.*) Of a horse, 'Sike cluthers ah've seen on his back ' (*Bla.*, p. 12). (*v.*) *To collect, to flock; Wel.* cludeiriaw, *to heap together.* ' An t' sheep cluther on t' t' hill-end,' (*Bla.* p. 21). This word cluder explains the names of Great Clowder and Little Clowder, a part of the Craven Fells, where there are cluders of limestone rocks; also our beautiful English word 'cloud,' which Minshew (*cit.* by *Skinner*) acutely connected with *Lat.* claudo, Somner with 'clod' and 'clodded' (*see* also CLETCH and CLOOASE) ; *Gael.* cludair, *clouts, rags, patches.*

**COA UP,** *come up.* 'Coa up, coa up, oade meeare, ooa up, den,' an affectionate call to a horse (mare).—*Al.*, 1880.

**CONEY,** *rabbit; O. N.* **Koni** (of doubtful signif.), *Dan.* kanin, *Swed.* kanin, *Dut.* konijn, whence *Ger.* kaninchen, kanin ; *Icel.* kanína, kúnína ; and *O. Fr.* connil, *Eng.* cony, *Gael.* coinein, coinean; *Span.* conejo, *Port.* coelho, *Ital.* coniglio, *Lat.* cuniculus, *Gr.* kouniklos, kuniklos, kounikoulos (*Grimm*); *Mod. Gr.* kouneli (*Contopoulos*).

**COOL,** *coal; A. S.* Cól, *Dan.* kul. In the Aire Valley, near Bradford, called 'coil.' The *Ord. Eng.* pron. 'coal,' follows *O. N.* kól, *Swed.* kol, and *O. H. G.* and *Mod. Gr.* kohlen, *Russ.* ygole, *Sans.* ko'eta, *charcoal—perhaps* from its colour, kālū (pr. kawlo), *black.* Cool above Middlesmoor. 'Colsterdale'='Coalstrathdale,' however, is called 'Cowsterdil.'

**COOP-BARROW,** *a wheel-barrow; W.* cwb, *a cup, kennel,* &c.; *O. N.* kupa, *a cup, bowl; Dut.* kuip, *coop* (*Ogil.*); *Ger.* kufe. Affords another example of the name of the older article being transferred to the new and improved one.

**CORF,** *calf; O. N.* **Kálfr,** *Swed.* kalf, *Dan.* kalv. For the ord. pron. *A S.* cealf, *Goth.* kalbo, *O. H. G.* chalbâ, *Ger.* kalb.

**COW-BOW, COO-BOW,** a large horseshoe-shaped *wooden-collar,* generally of ash, to fasten cows up by in the ' bewce.' Used principally above Lofthouse. The two ends hang downwards, and are joined by a cross-piece designed to catch, and remain fastened by the elasticity of the bow. In place of this cross-piece, or wooden key, a loop of birch was formerly, and is still sometimes, employed (*see* also p. 31). Birch boughs are very extensively used for tying purposes of all kinds in Norway. The name, as well as the article, is genuine Scandinavian. *O. N.* Kú, *cow;* bogi, *a bow.*

**COWL,** 1. *a bruize,* esp. on the head; *O. N.* **Kúla,** *a ball, knob; Swed.* kula, *a ball, bump;* 2. *v. to bruize;* 3. *to hoard* money, *to collect.*

**COWP,** *to exchange, to chop, swap; O. N.* **Kaupa,** *to barter, bargain, buy;* kaup, *a bargain; Goth.* kaupon, *to negotiate, bargain;* kaupatjan (*Ulf.*), *to strike* in the face (Grimm, *Dict.* V. 5, p. 323, col. 2). For part of the evidence for this *see* under CHAPMAN. First of all, when two persons wanted the same thing they fought for it. Hence, long after barter was in use in the presence of witnesses, the parties struck one another, latterly shook hands to cement the bargain. Hence the phrase, ' to strike a bargain,' that is *lit.* to cowp, kaupa. Chop, the twin word, is *A. S.* ceap, which came to mean *cattle,* because they were the principal subject of barter. **Ceape** first appears in the A. S. Laws in the sense of cattle in the *L. Ine,* c. 40. **Cheape,** in the sense of a bargain, occurs in the *Heir of Linne*—

> 'Thou shalt have it back again better **ceape**
> By a hundred markes than I had it of thee.'—LL 99, 100.

*i.e.,* a better *bargain, chop.* Hence also *Russ.* kýpetz, *a merchant.*

**COWSHOT,** *a wood pigeon,* cushat; *A.S.* **Cu-sceote,** of which the second half is probably from the Welsh name of the wood pigeon, **ysguthan,** *the scudder* (*see* p. 172); *Gael.* **Smudan.**

**CRANE,** *a revolving arm* above kitchen fire, usually called 'swape' at and above **LOFTHOUSE**; and **BEAK** (*see* pp. 17, 18). *A. S.* **Cræn,** crán, cráno.

**CRATCH,** *a curved frame* to lay sheep on, &c. (*see* **CAMBRIL,** also pp. 9 and 31). *O. N.* **Kraki;** *Dan.* krage, *a looped and branched stem* used as a staircase, still so used in Norway. Stiles are often so made, as in Tusser.

> 'Save step for a stile of the crotch of the bough.'—(*April Husb.,* v. 10.)

Skinner derives **cratch** from *Lat.* **cratica,** craticula, crates, *a hurdle* (*Lex.*); in *Gr.* trasiá, tarsia; *Mod. Gr.* tarros. From the *Lat.* crates comes *A. S.* crata, cratu, cræt; *Eng.* cart and cradle; and cratitius, *a hurdle, lattice, sheep-pen, fold,* *Ital.* craticia, whence *O. Fr.* creiche, creicche, cresche, 'a cratch, rack, oxe-stall, or crib' (*Cot.*); *Fr.* créche, *a crib.* 'And she baar her first borun sone and wlappide him in clothes and layde him in a **cracche**.'—*Wicliff* (cit. in *Wedg.*) I suppose **crech** means a wooden hurdle as opposed to a wattled hurdle in the following humourous northern satire—

> 'Sum on dores, and some on hech,
> Sum on hyrdyllys, and som on **crech,**
> And sum on whele-barows.'—*Tourn. of Tottenham,* l. 205.

**CREEL,** *a hazel* or *willow basket,* commonly used for holding peats, the **peat-creel;** *a fishing-basket. O. N.* **Krili,** *a basket;* 'krila,' *to weave, plait.* Atk. (*Cl. Gl.*) has *Gael.* criol, *a chest* or *coffer. Irish,* kril or crilin, *a basket,* but the former is manifestly an after sense, and the *Irish* creel is probably a Scandinavian word. From kríli comes *Fr.* creil (*Wedg.*), which Roquefort would connect with 'craticia'; in *Russ.,* **kreilo** is *a wing;* **kreilatie,** *winged;* but the **creel** has another name. 'We can put all wer rubbin steeans into my **creel**.'—*Bla.,* p. 17.

**CROFT,** *a home field; A S.* **Croft,** from *Græco-Lat.* **Crypta,** *a closed* field (*Spel.*). In the same sense, in *Piers Plowman*—

> 'Til Lammesse time
> And by that I hope to have
> Hervest in my **croft**.—*Vis.* ll. 4386-2.

[The *Russ.* is 'ogorod,' *i.e.,* 'garth,' for which *see* pp. 51, 54.] *A. S.* **Croft,** cruft; *Belg.* **krufte, crofte,** is, like 'close,' another word denoting 'enclosure,' of *Latin,* i. e., *Monastic* origin. *Lat.* **crypta,** from *Gr.* krūpto; croft was again Latinized into croftus, croftum, cruftum (*Spel.*).

**CROOANIES,** *cronies,* old friends; *Gael.* **Crò,** *O. N.* **Krò,** a small *pen* or *fold;* **króinn,** penned in a **kró,** in Iceland the pen in which lambs when weaned are put during the night—cronies '*fellows of one fold.*' 2. In the same way *Scot.* **cronies,** *boon companions,* from *Dan.* **kro,** *a beer-house.* Skinner unworthily goes to *Gr.* chronos, *time,* or to *Lat.* congerro. 'Bud t' best of all **crooanies** mun part.'—*Bla.,* p. 14.

**CUBBERT,** *cupboard.*

**CUD,** *could; A.S.* **Cude,** *p.* and **cud,** *pp.* of cunnan, *to be able.* The survival of the *A. S.* spelling is not less remarkable than that of the pronunciation of many words.

**OUR**, *a sheep dog*; *Lapp.* and *Finn.* coira, *a dog*.

**OUSS**, *to kiss*, pr. like puss; *Anc. Wel.* Ousanu, *Franco-Teut.* cussan, *A. S.* cyssan, *O. N.* kyssa, *Dan.* kysse, *Swed.* kyssa, *Goth.* (*Ulf.*) kukjan, *Belg.* kussen, *O. H. G.* chussian, chussan; *M. H. G.* küssen, *Ger.* küssen, *to kiss*; *Anc. Wel.* cus, cusan; *A. S.* coss, *O. N.* koss, *Belg.* kus, *Teut.* kuss, *a kiss*; *Hind.* (*Sans.*) chūman, chūmnā, *to kiss*; chūmā, chummā, *a kiss*.

**CUTTHROATS**, the genus *eriophorum*, *cotton-grass*, otherwise called 'moss-crops and cutthroats,' and 'moor silk.'

# D.

$$\text{Grimm.} \begin{cases} \text{II. } \textit{Goth.} \text{ D, } \textit{Lat.}, \textit{Celt.}, \textit{Slav.} \text{ D; } \textit{Lat.} \text{ B; } \textit{O.H.G.} \text{ T; } \textit{Gr.} \text{ Th, Ph;} \\ \textit{Sans.} \text{ Dh, } \textit{Lat.} \text{ F.} \\ \text{VIII. } \textit{Goth.} \text{ Th and D, } \textit{Lat.}, \textit{Celt.}, \textit{Slav.} \text{ T; } \textit{Lat.} \text{ B; } \textit{O.H.G.} \text{ D; } \textit{Gr.} \text{ T;} \\ \textit{Sans.} \text{ T.} \end{cases}$$

Eng. D commonly = *Lat.* F, *Gr.* Th.

**DAD**, *father*. Almost as universally spread as baba or papa (*Wedg.*), which forms the subject of a very able and exhaustive excursus by Sir John Lubbock (*The Origin of Civilisation, &c.*, pp. 323-8, 1870), in which he gives the name for father in 124 languages other than those derived from *Sans.*, and 16 American tongues. Dad appears in *Wel.* tad, *Bohem.* tata, *Gr.* tata and tetta (*Cur.* 243), *Gael.* daidean, *Lapp.* dadda, and several others.

**DAVERED**, *daft, muddled*; *O. N.* **Dapr**, *downcast, weak, &c.*; deyfa, *to cleave, stupefy*; *Swe.* döfva, *Dan.* döve, *Goth.* ga-daubjan, *Ger.* betauben (*Cleas.*); *Gr.* tuphō, *to raise a smoke* (*Cur.* 251); tuphoō, *to wrap in smoke*; tuphos, *smoke*, that which *darkens* or *clouds* a man's intellect (*L. and S.*); tuphlos, *blind*; *Goth.* daubs, *blind*; *O. N.* daufr, *Swed.* döf, *Dan.* döv, *A. S.* deáf, *Eng.* deaf, duffer, dupe; *Sans.* dhûp, dhûpayâmi, *to smoke*; *Gr.* thuō, *to offer burnt offerings*; thumos; *Æol.* phumos; *Lat.* fumus, *smoke*; *Ger.* dimpfen, *damp, steam, fume*.

**DAYLEET**, *daylight*.

**DAZZIN**, *lazy*; *O. N.* **Dasinn**, *lazy*; dasask, *to become weary*; *Swed.* dasa; dasadr, *exhausted, weary*; *Eng.* dazed with sleep.

**DEACENT**, *decent*.

**DEAR, DEER**, *door*, at Ramsgill, Pateley, &c.; *A. S.* [Dyru?] gen. **Dyre** *of a door*; duru, dör; *Lat.* fores, *Gr.* thura, *Sans.* dvār, *Gael.* dorus.

**DEER-CHEEK**, *doorpost*; *A.S.* Ceaca, céca, ceóce, chéce.

**DEE**, *die*; *O. N.* **Deyja**, *to die*; *Goth.* (*Ulf.*) dauthus, *death*; dauths, *dead*; *Gr.* thnēskein, thanein, *to die*; thanatos, *death.* Wedgwood, who misses the Greek, but gives several other forms, finds it (*s. v.* DEAD) 'impossible to draw a distinct line of separation either in form or meaning between *dead* and *deaf*' (*Dic.*, 1859). Die is a Norsk word (*see* SFETTLE). 'If ah dee, ah dee' (*Al.*, 1880).

**DEEA, DEAH**, *do*; *Gael.* Dean, *A. S.* [dión, an obsolete form, whence 'did']. An interesting relic of antiquity. *Russ.* dyalate, *to do*.

**DEEADE**, *dead*.

**DEEATH**, *death*.

**DEFT**, *neat, nice, pretty*; *A. S*, **Daefte**, *convenient, mild* (Benson, *Voc. Ang.-Sax.*, 1701); defre, *timely, seasonable*; 'dæft' = 'de-æft' and 'dcfre' = 'de-efre'; 'De' freq. occurs in the A. S. Laws for 'the' conj. than, whether, either, *in proportion as*—so 'de-æft,' *as after, conveniently to*, deftly, *conveniently*. 'We've had a gay deft bit o' sno.'—*Bla.*, p. 21.

**DEM**, *a dam*, from the verb existing there must have been a noun; *A. S.* Dem.

**DEM**, *to dam*; *A. S.* Demman, *to dam, stop water*.

**DEMMED**, *damned; A.S.* **Demde**, *p.*, and **demed**, *pp.* of déman, *to condemn; Lat.* damnare. Part of an interesting conversation overheard one winter night in the inn at Lofthouse, which we know to be a Danish settlement, —'He says we're Saxons, an it's a demmed lee.'

**DEW**, *do; A.S.* [Dión obsolete form], *see* DEEA.

**DIKE**, *a stream; A.S.* **díc**, *a ditch; O.N.* **dík**, **díke**, *Dan.* dige, *Swed.* dike, *Ger.* teich, *Gr.* teichos (*Curt.*). Often applied to small streams running off the moors or down the dale sides, but it originally meant *a ditch.* For instances, *see* p. 104. Synonymous with SIKE, *q.v.* In Shetland, 'dic' means a 'fence,' even a wire fence is called a 'dic.' This illustrates two principles—*First,* 'dic' meant the *place dug* and the *stuff dug*, which was ranged in a long heap beside the trench, so 'dic' came to mean *fence*'; *Second,* the transference of the name of the old article to the new and improved one, which has frequently to be borne in mind (*see* DOOF).

**DILL**, *to lull* to sleep ; *O.N.* **Dilla**, *to lull.*

**DON ON**, *to put on; A.S.* **Don**, *to put on*;on, on. 'So don on thee bonnet, we'll beeath gan togither.'—*Bla.*, p. 17. 'Don,' *to put on,* is well known to be 'do on,' as 'doff' is 'do off'; but 'do,' in *A.S.*, is 'dón,' *imperat.* 'do.' **Don on** may be only an ignorant reduplication, but the many old forms found in this vocabulary should place us on our guard against pronouncing any peculiar words or phrases to be either the result of ignorance, or incorrect. 'Do off,' which proves **Do on**, is prettily introduced in the Ballads, thus:—

'Robin *did off* his gown of green.'—*Rob. Hood and Guy of Gisb.*, l. 177.

'And lyghtly *dyd off* his hode.'—*Adam Bell and W. of C.*, l. 40.

**DOOANT**, *do not*, not quite so much contracted as 'don't.'

**DOOF**, *dough*, dialect form; a variation of *A.S.* **dág**, **dáh**, *Swed.* deg, *Dan.* dei, *O.N.* deig, *Dut.* deig, *Goth.* daigs, *Ger.* teig, *Eng.* dough, duff, doof, also dig, dike, ditch; *A.S.* hlæf-dige, *Eng.* lady, 'the loaf-maker.' 'The fundamental notion,' says Cleasby, 'is plasticity—*O.N.* deigr, *moist*; digna, *to become moist*,' &c., which fully explains all the above, and *Goth.* deigan, *to mould. Goth.* daigs, *Lat.* fingo, *Gr.* thinganō (thigganō).—*Cur.*, 145. Also *Lat.* tango, tetigi; *Eng.* touch. Also *Fr.* diner, *Eng.* dine, dinner, that is, 'dough,' or food moulded with the fingers, from *Goth.* digans, *moulded*; deigan, to 'dine,' mould.

**DOOT**, *think, believe, doubt*; *O.Fr.* doubter, *Fr.* doute, douter; *Catalon.* dubtar, *Lat.* dubitare, *to doubt.* French pron. well preserved.

'Ah doot it'll rain afore neet.'—*Colloq.*

'Neea doot bud he thowt it wur reet.'—*Bla.*, p. 12.

**DOWLY**, *lonely, dull; O.N.* **Daufligr**, 'deaf-like,' *lonely, dull.* Brock. suggests *Gr.* Doulion, *Lat.* dolor, *Fr.* deuil, douleur. Though the origin of *Gr.* doulos, *a slave*, is unknown, Brock. must be regarded as wild. **Dowly** is connected with *Goth.* daubs, *see* DAVERED.

'Bud t'hoose leaks **dowly** all t'week lang.'—*Bla.*, p. 16.

'Ah feel sa **dowly** an sa pooerly.'—*Al.*, 1880.

**DOWTER** (pron. like 'doubter'), *daughter; Goth.* **Dauhtar**. Fabian, who by the way served as Sheriff of London, and refused the office of Lord Mayor, 1493, repeatedly uses the word, *e.g.*, 'That his xxx **doughters** should slee theyr xxx husbands' (*Chron.*, c. i.)—'Constantius . . . Senator of Rome . . . married Helen the **doughter** of Cœlus last King of Britain . . . which Constantius was after made Sesar' (cap. lxvii.). A survival of a *Gothic* form.

**DAHTAR**, *daughter*—another variety; *Dan.* **Datter**, with *Swed.* dotter, *O.N.* **dóttir**, and *A.S.* **dóhtor**, **dóhter**, allied to *Goth.* dauhtar; *O.H.G.* tohtar,

*Ger.* tochter, *Dut.* togter, *Lith.* dukter, duktere; *Gael.* dear, *Bohem.* dcera, *Russ.* dshchere [with which compare *Copt.* scere, *a son,* and other allied forms, for which see my *History of the Gypsies.* Rutherford. Kelso, 1882]. *Finn.* tüttär, *Lapp.* daktar, *Slav.* dushti, dusti, *Armen.* dustr, *A.* and *M. Gr.* thugatēr, *Sans.* duhitri duhitâ—'the milkmaid of the family'—*Zend.* dughdhar (*Williams*).

**DRAB'D,** *covered with mud or dirt;* *Gael.* Drab, *a spot, stain;* *A.S.* drabbe, *lees, dregs, drab.* 'Drab'd up to t'knees.'—*Bla.,* p. 36. 'Drab,' the colour, therefore means *mud colour* or *dirt colour.*

**DREE,** *tedious;* *O.N.* Drjúgr, *lasting, slow but sure;* *Swed.* dryg, *Dan.* dröj, *Gael.* draghalach, *tedious.* Many of the meanings in *Swed.* dryg, great, strong, long, voluminous, large-limbed, glutting, nourishing, dear, proud, stiff, disdainful, haughty, &c., correspond with *Gr.* thrasus, bold, spirited, audacious, impudent—all implying *endurance* or *last.* *Gr.* thrasos, tharsos, *courage, confidence;* *Sans.* drishtas, *daring;* drish, drishnomi (*I dare*), *Goth.* gadaursan, *O.H.G.* gidar, *Lith.* drasus (dreist) (*Cur.* 315), *Gael.* dragh, *trouble, vexation, annoyance.*

**DREE,** *to endure;* *O.N.* Drygja, *to make or keep longer, to lengthen;* *A.S.* Dreogan, *to endure.* Cleasby gives *N. Eng.* 'to dree one's weird '—to abide one's fate. Common in the Ballads.

     'Heawing on yche othar whyll the might dre.'—*Chevy Chase,* 2, 93.

       'That all this dill I drye.'—*Sir Cauline,* l. 43.

     'Some other dule ye drie, o'.'—*Edward, Edward,* l. 20.

     'And quhatten penance will ye drie for that?'—Ib., l. 27.

       'And if ye brenn my ain dear babes
         My lord shall make ye drie.'—*Edom O'Gordon,* 52.

**DRAW AWAY,** *to die.*

       'Her oade fadther drew away
         Sat in that oade arm chair.'—*Bla.,* p. 41.

**DROIN AWAY**=drawing away, *dying.* 'If ah wer droin away.'—*Al.,* 1880.

**DRIVE,** *sleet,* &c.; *O.N.* Dríf, *driven snow;* drífa, *sleet;* *Scot.* 'Stoor and drive,' *dusty snow wind-blown.* 'Vethr var drífanda,' it was driving weather, *i.e., sleeting* or *snowing.*

**DUB,** *a puddle or small pond;* *O.N.* dapi, *a pool;* *Gael.* dubadh, *a pond;* dub, *to dip;* *Fris.* dobbe, *a puddle;* *Wel.* dwb, *mortar, cement,* originally mud or clay walls.

**DUDS,** *clothes;* *Gael.* Dud, *a rag;* dudag; *Icel.* dudi, *swaddling clothes* (*Cleas.*); duda, *to swathe in clothes.*

     'The gay their gaudy duds display.'—*Bla.,* p. 1.

**DEW or DUE,** *to do;* *A.S.* dión, *a lost form* (*see* DEEA); cf. *Icel.* gjöra and göra, *to do;* and *Dan.* gjöre, *Swed.* göra, *to do,* with *A.S.* dión and dón.

**DURST,** *dare;* *A.S.* Durste, dyrste, or dorste, *pret.* of dear, *to dare,* but commonly used in other tenses, as 'I durstn't do this or that,' I dare not. 'For tham ic ne dorste,' for that I durstn't.—*Laws of Ælfred, Introd.* 'Ne dorsten ná út gan,' durstn't gan oòt.—*Sax. Chron.,* A.D. 1083. 'Little John Nobody that durst not speak.'—*Reformation Ballad,* 'Lit. John Nobody,' l. 16. *Gr.* tharseō; *New Attic.* tharreō, *to dare.*

# E.

**EA or YAH,** *one;* *A.S.* Ean, *one.* *See* also pp. 37-40.

**EAR,** *year;* *Goth.* Jér, *O.N.* ár, *Swed.* ar, *Dan.* aar, *Dut.* jaar, *Germ.* jahr. *A.S.* gear, *Gr.* & *Lat.* hora.

**EASINGS,** *eaves;* *A.S.* Efesan, *eaves.*

EEN, *eyes; A.S.* Eagan, *eyes.* .

EEBREES, *eyebrows.*

EFTER, *after; Dan., Swed.* and *A.S.* Efter. 'The hyrefter gægeth,' which hereafter goeth.—*Laws of Hlothær,* A.D. 675-685. 'Tha geworhte he hi efter to leode,' then wrought he it efter into verse.—*Pref.* to *Ælfred's Transl. of Boethius.*

'Nut varra lang efter laid deead i't' Sack Syke.'—*Bla.,* p. 39.

ELDING, *fuel; O.N.* Elding, *fuel;* eldr, *fire.*

ELLER, *alder; O.N.* Elri (*Fritz.*), *Dan.* eller. Common in place names, as 'Eller-beck,' 'Eller-carr'; and *Colloq.* freq. as 'birk an eller.'

AT T'END ON'T, *at last, after all.*

ENEAF, *enough.* 'It's reet eneaf' is frequently used ironically, meaning it is *not.*

ER, *are.* 'Whar is t' bahn?' 'To Gt. Whernside.' 'Ye er, er ye. We'll see aboot that, hooiver!'—*Colloq.*

EWER, *a jug; A.S.* Ewe, *water*—therefore properly *a water jug.*

# F.

Grimm, IX. $\Big\{$ *Eng.* F, *Goth.* F and B; *Sans., Gr., Lat., Celt., Slav.* P; *O.H.G.* F and V.

---

FADTHER, *father; O.N.* Fathir. It is not possible to write the pron. of this word other than by the letters *dth* run into one soft sound. *Goth.* Fadar, *A.S.* fæder, *O.H.G.* fater, *Ger.* vater, *Lat.* pater, *Gr.* patēr, *Zend.* patar, *Sans.* pitâ, pitri.

FAIN, *glad; A.S.* Fægn, *O.N.* Feginn, *Hel.* fagin. Most common in the Ballads, *e.g.:*—

'Thes worthy freckys for to fyght,
   Thereto the wear full fayne.'—*Chevy Chase,* 2, 30.

'Sent George the bryght, ower ladies knyght
   To name they were full fayne.'—*Otterburne,* 2, 78.

'The Percy and the Dowglass metto
   That ether of other was fayne.'—*Ib.,* 86.

'Soe fayne of fighte.'—*King Estmere,* 157.

'I'll make yond fellow that flyes so fast
   To stopp he shall be fayne.'—*Rob. Hood & Guy of Gisborne,* 64.

Ah's fain, lad, to see thee come in.'—*Bla,* p. 21.

FAIR, *altogether, very; Gael.* Fior, *very; Dan. dialects,* fœr. Fœr (*adj.* and *adv.*) *greatly, in a high degree, remarkably* (*Molbech* in *Atk.*). 'They wer fare capt wi' gittan lost in a wood like that.'—*Al.,* 1880.

FAND, *found; O.N.* Fann, 2nd pers. fannt, pret. of finna, *to find.*

FAR PASTURE, a common name of *upland moorside pastures,* is, I doubt not, like so many other double names, a reduplication—*Gael.* Feur, *pasture*—as with feur-ach, feur-achadh, wherein 'ach,' 'achadh,' also mean *pasture.* Before finding the *Gael.* feur, *pasture,* I was for fourteen years baffled by this word. It is curious that 'aire' und 'ray,' both meaning *pasture,* are also *Gaelic. Dan.* fœr, *grass; Lat.* fœnum, *fodder.* (*Armstr.,* who also allies *Lat.* ver, *spring.*) *See* p. 31.

FARDEN, *farthing; A.S.* Feording, feorthung (for feorthling), *i.e. a fourth part of a coin*—Shilling, *Ger.* schilling. According to Ihre. from *Swed.*

skilja, *to divide.* The name originally of pieces of money stamped with an indented cross and broken into four, a quarter of which, schilling, was called in *A. S.* **feorthlyng,** or ferlyng, but not styca, *a bit, piece,* as Wedgwood suggests. Lye gives the full A. S. form, **feorthling,** ' the uttermost farthing.'—*Matt.* v. 26. ' **Feorthling** and feorthan dæl thinges,' the fourth part of a thing. ' Twegen **feorthlingas,**' ' two mites.'—*Luke* xxi. 2. **Feorthung,** *farthing.* ' Twegen sticas thæt is **feorthung** peninges,' ' two mites which make a farthing.'—*Mar.* xii. 32. This passage proves the value of a *stica.* Lye has ' sticce, stycca, a kind of brass money among the A. S., so called because it was the smallest of all moneys, being worth only half a farthing.' But **feorthling,** meaning a fourth of anything, was not confined to A. S. In *Icel.* fjórthungr means generally *the fourth part* of anything; also a small coin, a liquid measure (ten pots), a weight (ten pounds), a fourth share of a tíund (tithe). In Norway countries were divided into fjórthungr, *quarters;* thridjungar, ' *ridings,*' or *third parts, &c.* Again, in *Icel.* the whole land was politically divided into fjórthungar, *farthings;* ferlyngs, or *quarters* in A.D. 964, and these still exist (*Cleas.*). The following note in the *Liber Rubus* in the Exchequer proves that it was also a measure of land in this country : ' Sciendum quod magnum feodum militis constat ex quatuor hidis, et una hida ex quatuor virgatis, et una virgata ex quatuor **ferlingis,** et una **ferlinga** ex decem acris (cit. p. 5, *Gloss.* to *Domesd. Bk.,* V. II., *Warner's Hist. of Hampshire*). Ogilvie (*Eng. Dict.*) has ' **Farthing,** a division of land equal to thirty acres. Obsolete;' but gives no authority for the value, which is three times that given in the *Lib. Rub.* There is a curious agreement between the ' ten pots,' ' ten pounds' of *Icel.* and the ' ten acres' of *Lib. Rub.,* which suggests that **farthing** as a land measure was like ' Riding' of Scandinavian origin in this island. ' I don't care a **brass farden,**' in Nidderdale a common colloquialism, not only conveys a tradition of the brass money of our A. S. forefathers, but suggests the necessity of distinguishing one farthing from another at a time when the word had such widely different meanings.

**FASH,** *to trouble;* O. Fr. **Fascher,** *Mod.* fâcher, which Brachet ingeniously traces through *Provence* ' fastigar,' whence ' fast′gar,' ' fas′gar,' then ' fascher.' Fastigar, from fastig, *ennui;* *Lat.* fastidium.

**FAST,** *stuck, in a fix;* O. N. **Fastr,** *stuck fast;* *Swed.* and *Dan.* **fast,** *A. S.* fæst, O. H. G. fasti, *Ger.* fest. ' I′m not **fast** for a pound or two.' *cf.* O. N. **fasti,** *a fix.*

**FASTENED,** ' **Fastened** ta t′sod '=' rooted to the soil.'

**FEEL,** *to hide.* At and above Middlemoor and Lofthouse. ' Feeling and lating'=' hide and seek.' Thus, ' That ′ud be a rare place to get **felt** o′anyone, if one was laking at feeling and lating.'—*Colloq.* at Lodge, 1871. Mr. Thorpe, however, gives for Pateley Bridge, ' **felt,**' *to hide.* ' Felting and lating,' hide and seek. O. N. **Fela,** *Dan.* fjœle, *to hide;* *Gael.* falaich, folaich, *to hide.*

**FATTY-CAIKE,** *short-cake.* ' Ah felt pooerly . . . sa′ah ah maaide a **fatty-caike.**'—*Al.,* 1880.

**FELL** (1), *mountain;* O. N. **Fjall,** *Nor.* fjœld, fjeld ; *Swed.* fjäll, *pl.* fiellen. Said by Cleasby to be a Scandinavian word. In Norway, however, it means *rock* as well as *mountain,* and thus corresponds with O. H. G. felisa, *a rock,* whence O. Fr. falize, faloise; *Mod. Fr.* falaise, *a cliff;* *Gr.* phellos, *a rock, stone;* phelleōn, phellion, phellis, Phelleus, *stony ground,* the last being the name of a rocky district in Attica. Pausanias (*Descrip. Grec. Lib.* VIII., c. 12, § 1), speaking of the cork-tree, tells us that some of the Ionians,′as does Hermesianax, the poet, call the bark of this tree ' phellos,' *i.e. rocky.* For place names *see* p. 92, but it is uncertain whether they severally refer to this or the following word. Meantime the *Mœso-Goth.* fera, *a country;* and *Lapp.* vari, *fells,* bear a strong likeness to pres. word.

**FELL** (2), *a moor,* or *open waste ground (Halli.).* ' Properly the *unenclosed* mountain land; if enclosed it is so and so′s " pasture "' (*Dakyns M S.*). That this word is *Dan.* fielled, *a common, the property of many, see* pp. 165, 166, and add thereto *Gr.* polus, *many; Russ.* pole, *a field* (whence 'Poland'); polya, *fields; Gr.* polis, *a city.* Brocket (*Gloss.*, 1846) has '**Falls**, the divisions of a large arable field attached to a village, annually cultivated in a fixed rotation of crops.' The Old German also explains the origin of our word 'village,' by the same transitions of meaning as turba, thorpe; polloi, pole, polis; folk, fylki; so vil, vëlt, village.

**FELLFOR,** *fieldfare; A. S.* **Fealafor,** *the many goers,* because they go in flocks, *see* p. 165.

**FEOWER,** *four; A. S.* **Feower.** ' Æt tham **feower** tóthum fýrestum,' the *four* front teeth.—*Laws of Æthelb.*, 52. '**Feower** sceáp' with ánum,' *four* sheep for one.—*Laws of Ælf.*, 24, from *Exod.* xxii. 1. But with these exceptions for a full account of this word *see* Stratmann, *O. E. Dict.*

**FER,** *for.* ' Ah's **fer** off,' I am just going.

**FERGIT,** *forget.*

**FETTLE,** *n., condition, preparation; O. N.* **Fetill,** *a strap or belt; O. H. G.* fezel, *Ger.* fessel, *A. S.* fetel, *a chain, belt;* fetels, *a belt, bag; Gr.* pedílon, *a sandal;* pedē, *a fetter; Lat.* pedica. ' In good **fettle**,' *condition.*

**FETTLE,** *v., to harness, to prepare; A. S.* **Fetelsian,** *to put on a belt, to harness; Gr.* pedaō, *to fetter.* Freq. in the Ballads.

> ' Then John bent up his long bende bow,
>   And **fetteled** him to shoote.'—*Robin Hood and Guy of Gisb.*, 66.

> ' When the Sheriffe saw Little John bend his bow
>   He **fettled** him to be gone.'—Ib., l. 225.

> ' Ah've **fettled** ivvery button hoal.'—*Bla.*, p. 16.

For further remarks on ' Fettle ' *see* Atk. *Cl. Gl.*

**FEWT,** *foot,* points to a lost A. S. form (feót), whence ' feet.' ' Feót ' is to ' fót ' as ' feower ' to ' fower,' *four,* and is preserved in feotere, *a fetter.*

**FIND** (pron. finnd), *to find; A. S.* **Findan,** *O. N.* finna, *Swed.* finna, *Dan.* finde, *Goth.* (*Ulf.*) findan, *Ger.* finden, *Dut.* vinden.

**FIT** (1), *ready, &c.* ' They're jest aboot **fit**,' *ready, in proper condition.* ' It's **fit** to flay yan,' *cold enough* to.

**FLAID,** *afraid.*

**FLAIN,** *a ghost,* ' something that **flaits** one ' (*Dakyns, MS.*).

**FLAY,** *to frighten; O. N.* **Flæja** flœja, made by Fritz. and Cleas. to = flýja, *to flee.* Atk., *Cl. Gl.*, however, finds in Egilss. *to put to flight, to frighten,* which is clearly the sense here. Dakyns gives ' **FLAIT,** *to frighten.*—Wharfedale.'

**FLAY-CROW,** *scare-crow.*

**FLANG,** *flung; O. N.* flengja, *to whip; O. E.* **Flang.** Alisaunder, 2749, in Stratmann.

**FLAT,** *a lead vein lying in the plane of the bedding; Dan.* flöts, *a bed, layer in mines.* **FLOUTS,** *a slice of turf,* p. 119, also explained by *Dan.* flöts.

**FLAY** (of the wind), *to cut off the skin; A. S.* flean, *O. N.* flá, *Dan.* flaae, *to flay, pull off the skin; O. N.* flagna, *Dut.* vlaegen, vlaen, *to flay,* but espec. of a cold wind; *Swed.* flaga, vind-flaga, *a flaw* of wind. Of a cold wind, ' Fit to **flay** yan.'

**FLEÄING-SPADE,** '*flaying-spade: O. N.* **Flaga,** *to cut thin turfs; Dan.* lag, *a flag* or 'flout' of turf.

**FLEAK,** *a rack* hung under ceiling to hang oatcake on to dry; *O. N.* flaki, fleki, *a hurdle.* A *fleak* is a *wattled* hurdle, as being made of 'flakes' of wood. *Gael.* cliath, *a hurdle.* Small houses or cottages were formerly built of ' fleaks ' covered with mud or clay, which gives the names of ' fleak,' ' flack,' to villages. Such an one may still be seen near Farnham, Surrey (1879). Percy remarks, in a footnote on the line ' To milk kye at a **fleyke** ' (' *Reform*,' *Ballad,*

Lit. John Nobody, l. 14), that cows are frequently milked in hovels made of fleyks.—*Gloss.* to *Reliq.*).

**FLEE,** *a fly;* *A. S.* **Flege,** *a fly;* fleoge, *fly;* *O. H. G.* fliuga, *O. Dut.* vlieghe, for many *O. E.* forms and passages *see* Stratmann, *O. E. Dict.*, 1878.

**FLEAR, FLEUR,** *floor;* *A. S.* flór, *O. N.* flórr, *O. Dut.* vloer, *M. H. G.* Vluor, which last our word most resembles,

**FLIPPER** (*Middlesmoor*), **FLEPPIN** (*Pateley Bridge*), *to cry;* *O. N.* Fleipra or fleipa, *to bubble, prattle;* fleipr, *babble, prattle.* Children are said to 'flipper and winge,' when crying, &c., *see* WINGE. cf. *Russ.* lepetate, *to prattle;* lepetanie, *prattle.*

**FLIT,** *to remove* from one place to another; *O. N.* Flytja, *Dan.* flytte.

**FLITE,** *to scold, quarrel;* *A. S.* Flítan, *O. H. G.* flízan, for *O. E. see* Stratmann. 'Ænig flít ne beo betweox mannum,' 'that there be no *quarrelling* amongst men.' —*Canons, temp.* Eadgar, 23.

**FLOUT,** *see* FLAT.

**FLUZZ,** *to blunt, to bruise;* *O. N.* Flosna, *to wither.* 'Flosna upp,' *to break up* a household.

**FOG,** *aftergrass, autumn grass;* *Gael.* Foghar, *lit.* a spoiling the fields of their crops, harvest, autumn. Foghar na said, *the hay harvest.*—(*Armstrong*); *Wel.* **Fwg,** *long dry grass,* hay.—(*Ow.*); *O. N.* fok, *hay.* The **fog** in Nidderdale is the young grass that springs up after a field has been mowed, the *after-math.*

**FOMUD,** *the pine marten* (Martes Sylvatica), for some speculations on the name 'Fomard' *see* Study XVI. pp. 130-5.

**FOND,** *foolish, soft;* *O. N.* Fáni, *a fool;* *Swed.* fáne, *a fool;* '*Gael.* faoin, *Ir.* faon, *foolish, fond;* *Lat.* Vanus, *Arm.* vean, vaen; *Eng.* vain.—(*Armstr.*) 'Ah's naaine sa fond as ye think ah is.'

**FOOAL,** *foal,* *A. S.* Fóla, *O. N.* fóli, *Swed.* fále, *Dan.* fole, *O. H. G.* folo, *Ger.* füllen, fohlen; *Goth.* fula, *Gael.* foilid, *Wel.* ebol, *Gr.* pólos, *Lat.* pullus—for *O. E.* examples *see* Stratm. 'Follifoot'='Fólafoten,' a *Norw.* place name, imported.

**FOR,** *before;* *A. S.* For, fore; '**for** Gode and **for** worolde,' *Concil.* Ænham. about A.D. 1010. 'T' birds sing . . . . their carols **for** clooasing the day.'—*Bla.* p. 25.

**FORCE,** *waterfall;* *O. N.* Fors, *Swed.* & *Dan.* foss. As a place name in Nidderdale, 'Park Force,' How Stean Beck.

**FORELDERS,** *forefathers;* *O. N.* Foreldri, forellri; *Dan.* forældre, *Ger.* Vorältern; *A. S.* forealdian, *to grow old, O. H. G.* faralten.

'**FOURTH FROM THE CROWN**'=of high rank. I heard this curious expression more than once at Middleham, Wensleydale, but lack evidence to explain it properly. I suppose it means in the 'fourth *rank*,' &c.

**FOARCED,** *forced.*

**FORNENST,** *over against, opposite;* *A. S.* Fore ongean, *A. S.* & *O. E.* fornean (*Stratm.*), *see* ANENST.

**FOWER,** *four;* *A. S.* Fower, *see* FEOWER.

**FRA,** *from;* *O. N.* Frá, *Dan.* fra, *A. S.* fra, common in the *A. S.* Laws. 'Clagg'd on **fra** his tail tuv his heead.'—*Bla.*, p. 12.

**FRAME,** *to prepare, to do anything;* *O. N.* Frama, *to further, to advance;* fremja, *A. S.* fremman, *to make,* &c. (*see* p. 199).

> 'Fer t'weather's been pashy this spring,
> Bud ah fancy it's **framing** ta mend.'—*Bla.*, p. 21.

**FRATCHIN,**' *falling out;* *Gael.* Fraoch, *wrath, fury;* *O. E.* fracchin. *Prompt. parv.*, 1440.

**FREEAT,** *to fret;* *A. S.* Fretan, *to fret.*

**FREET,** *fright.*

**FRIDGE,** *to rub against;* *A. S.* Freothan, *to rub,* as a stocking **fridges** the heel with an ill-fitting boot; *Gael.* frid, fride, *a pimple* (*see* also Atk. *Cl. Gl.*)

**FROMATY**, *O. Fr.* Fromentée, *sodden wheat; Ital.* frumento, *wheat; Lat.* frumentum, *O. E.* frumentee, *see* p. 42.

**FUIT**, *foot* (*see* FᴋᴡT).

**FULL OFT**, *very often; A.S.* **Ful oft**. 'For thon hi ablændath **ful oft** wisna manna gethoht,' for that they blind **ful oft** wise men's thoughts.— *Laws of Ælfred*, Introd. 46, from *Ex.* xxiii. 8.

**FUNT**, *found; O. N.* **Funnit,** *found;* finna, *to find; pret. plu.* fundu, *part.* fundinn, *sup.* fundit. Cleasby says 'The forms "funnu" and "funnit" may be found in MSS., but were probably never so pronounced.' This Nidderdale word would appear to cast doubt upon the correctness of this suggestion.

> 'Ah, barn ! noo we sud ha **fun**'t oot
> If breead haddunt kept doon seea lo.'—*Bla.*, p. 21.

# G.

|  | I. *Goth.* G; *Lat.* gᴠ, g, ᴠ; *Celt.* g; *Slav.* g, ᴢ; *O.H.G.* K; *Gr.* Ch; *Sans.* gh, h; *Lat.* h, f. |
|---|---|
| *Grimm.* | VII. *Goth.* h, g, f; *Lat.* c, qu; *O. Irish*, c, ch; *Slav.* K; *O. H. G.* h (g, k); *Gr.* K; *Sans.* h, K. |

*Eng.* G commonly = *Gr.* Ch.

**GAEING**, *going* (Greenhow Hill); *O.N. 1st pers. sing.* **Geng**, and *plu.* göngum, *pres.* of ganga, *to go; Sans.* kank, *Lith.* kankù, *to go.* 'We're **gaeing** ta bring thee a new brat.'—*Bla.*, p. 19.

**GAN**, *to go; A. S.* **Gan.** *to go.* 'Wilta **gan** wi' me?'—*Bla.*, p. 17.

**GANNING**, *going.* 'They're **ganning** for scooring steeans.'—*Ib.*, p. 18.

**GAINE**, *gone.*

**GAIN**, *near; O.N.* **Gegn**, *short; Dan.* gjen, gjen vei, gjensti, *short cut* (Worsaae); *Gael.* gann, *near, parsimonious.*

**GAINEST**, *nearest; O.N.* 'Hinn **gegnsta** veg,' the **gainest** way.— *Maríu Saga*, 545, in Cleas. *Gael.* 'is **gainne**,' or 'ni's **gainne**,' *nearest* (*Armstr.*).

**GALLOWA**, the general name for *a horse* in Nidd.; *Wallach.* calu, *a horse;* càlàu, *a large horse; Ger.* gaul, *a horse; M.H.G.* gul, *Dut.* gúl, guil; *Hind.* (*Sans.*) ghorä, *a horse;* ghorí, *a mare; Sans.* ghota, *a horse;* ghotaka, *a horse; Gael.* gearran, *a galloway, horse.*

**GAP**, *gate; O. N.* **Gap**, *a gap; A.S.* geáp, *Gael.* cab.

**GAPSTEAD**, *gateway.*

**GARN**, *yarn; O.N.* **Garn**, *A. S.* gearn. 'Oade Mally Mawson at used to spin **garn**.'—*Bla.*, p. 42. *O. N.* 'Spinna **garn**,' to spin **garn** (Eb. 92 in *Cleas.*). 'Lin ok **garn**,' 'line (flax) and **garn**' (Is. 78 in *Cleas.*) as used in Nidd. *Gael.* calanas, *yarn.*

**GARTH**, *a field near a house* (see *Study* VI., pp. 51-4, to which add *Gael.* gàradh, *a yard; Russ.* ogorod, a **garth** (p. 52), and to ortgeard, p. 51. 'Orcheyardes and erberes' (*Creed of Piers Plowman*, l. 329), and 'Byland Abbey. *Item,* There is a grownde called the Ortyarde adjoynyng the late Abbat Chambre,' containing 8 acres pasture (*Paper Survey*, Hen. VIII., Augmentn. Office).

**GAT**, *got; O. N.* **Gat**, *got; pret.* of geta, *to get.*

**GATE**, *a road, path, way; O. N.* **Gata**, *Swed.* gata, *Dan.* gade, *a way;* *Goth.* (*Ulf.*) gatva, gatwo, *a street; A. S.* geath, *a street; Gael.* geata, *a gate;* 'With them that **gate** come.'—*Ormulum.* 'The **gates** he knoweth eche one.' —*Rob. Hood and Guy of Gisb.*, v. 52. See GEᴇᴀᴛ and p. 9. *O. H. G.* gaza, gazza ; *Ger.* gasse.

**GAY**, *very; Gael.* **Ceart**, *Dan.* **sehr;** *Fr.* **tres.** Very common colloquialism. 'We've had a **gay** deft bit o' sno.'—*Bla.*, p. 21.

**GEEAN**, *gone* (*Bla.* p. 11), *see* GAINE.

**GEARN, GERN**, *yearn; A. S.* **Giernan, girnan, gyrnan,** *to yearn; O. N.* **Girna**, *Goth.* (*Ulf.*) Gairnjan, *to yearn.* 'Gif death scyldig man scrift spræce gyrne,' 'if a death-doomed man desire confession.'—*Treaty. Ed. Gath,* c. 5. 'I real doon gud **gernin** hearnist.'—*Al.*, 1880.

**GEARS**, *grass; A. S.* **Gears.**

**GERS**, *grass; A. S.* **Gers, gærs.** At Lofthouse and Greenhow Hill. 'Æceres otthe **gærs**.'—*Laws of Ine*, c. 42. 'Nepping bits o' yung **gerse** o' t'rooad-sides.—*Bla.*, p. 11.

**GERSIN' FIELD**, *a grazing field.* 'Grassington' is called 'Gerston' and 'Gers'n.'

**GEEAT**, *a way; A. S.* **Geát**, *Gael.* **geata**, *see* p, 63, l. 3, where 'that have "gates"' should read 'that own that gate,' *i.e., gap* or breach in the fence, the portion unbuilt. 'For wer brass 'll nut gan a girt **geeat**,' 'our money will not go a great way.'—*Bla.*, p. 20. In this sense from *O. N.* **gata** (*see* GATE).

**GETTEN**, *got; A. S.* **Geten**, *pp.* of gitan, *to get;* also *O. N.* getinn, *part.* of geta, *to get.* In places where a bed of coal is worked out, it is said to be all **getten.**

**GIE**, *give; Norw.* **Give**, is pron. 'gee.'

**GIEN**, *given, if.* This, taken with *A. S.* 'gif,' *if,* suggests that 'gif,' 'if,' 'gien,' 'gin,' all meaning, 'if,' are all contracted from gifen, *given.*

**GIE OWER**, *stop, cease, leave off.* 'Give over.'

**GIMMER**, *ewe lamb; O. N.* **Lamb-gymbr**, *a gimmer.* An ewe that has not lambed (*Cleas.*). *Dan.* **gimmer-lamb**, *ewe lamb.*

**GINE**, *going* (*Pateley*).

**GIRD**, *churchyard, see* GARTH, and pp. 52 and 54. This word, one of the most interesting in the Dialect, seems to be *Danish*, and to complete 'the transition from the thing enclosing to the thing enclosed,' mentioned in para. 3, p. 54: for *Icel.* kirku-gardr is *churchyard*, wherefore I incline to refer present word to *Dan.* **Gjerde**, *a fence, hedge.* 'Ah've thowt mesen thoo mud gan i yan o'the **girds** sum o' these days.'—*Al.*, 1880.

**GIRN**, *yearn; O. N.* **Girna** (*see* GERN).

**GIRT, GERT**, *great.* Like gers, grass; cart, crate; bird, brid, &c.

**GISS**, *goose.* A *sing.* to which *plu.* geese belongs, comes nearest to the *Polish* ges, *a goose; Sloven.* and *A. S.* gós, *pl.* gés or gees; *O. Russ.* gnsi, *Russ.* gus, *O. N.* gás, *pl.* gæss, *Dan.* gaas, *pl.* gœs, gjœs; *O. H. G.* ganzo, *Germ.* ganz, *pl.* gänze; *Lat.* anser, *Gael.* geadh, *Gr.* chēn, *Bohem.* hus, *Hind.* (*Sans.*) hāns, hans.

**GIT**, *get; A. S.* **Gitan**, *to get.* 'Ah've summat to tell the' barn when we **git** thither.'—*Bla.*, p. 17.

**GITTEN**, *got; plu-perf.* **geten**, *got.*

**GITHER**, *gather.*

**GLASP**, *clasp.* 'He **glaspt** his hands.'—*Al.* 1880. *Gael.* glac, *to clasp;* clasb, *a clasp.*

**GLEEAM**, *gleam.*

**GOB**, *mouth; Dan.* **Gab**, *mouth; Guel.* cab, *mouth; O. N.* gabb, *mockery;* gabba, *to mock; A. S.* gabban, *to scoff;* gabbung, *a scoffing; Russ.* goboru, *I speak.*

**GRADELY**, *adj., orderly, friendly, agreed.* Of a horse, 'Fer he awlus wer **gradely** wey me.'—*Bla.*, p. 12. Hal has '**Gradely**, decently, orderly, moderately. Also an adjective.—*North.*'

**GRAIN**, *branch; O. N.* **Grein**, *Swed.* gren, *Dan.* green. 'Not found in Ger., Sax. nor English.'—*Cleas.* This last is an error (*see* pp. 92 and 108).

**GREASY**, *muddy.* In a particular state of the mud, in which it is very slippery, the salutation is sure to be 'Tis *greasy.' Russ.* **gryazi**, *mud.* In *Russ.*

only does **grease** mean *mud.* Thus *Nor.* griis is *a pig, Dan.* gris, *pig; Gael.* créis, *grease;* creiseach, *greasy.*

**GREEAVE,** *a grave.* 'Mak him a nice **greeave** doon t' loan side.'—*Al.,* 1880.

**GREEAVE,** *to grave, dig; O. N.* grafa, *Dan.* grave, *A. S.* grafan, *Gael.* grabh, **sgriobh;** *O. H. G.* and *Goth.* graban, *Ger.* graben, *Dut.* graven. 'They're agate **graavin** peäts.'

**GREET,** *to weep; Goth.* **Gretan,** *A. S.* **greetan,** *to weep; Gr.* chalaza (*Cur., Skeat's Handlist*); *O. N.* gráta. For a long list of O. E. passages *see* Stratm.

> 'I'll fill the air with heavy sighs
> And **greet** till I am blind.'—*Gil Morrice,* l. 188.

**GRIP,** *a narrow, open drain; A. S.* **Grep,** *a furrow.* 'Grépe,' in the 'Originals and analogues of some of Chaucer's *Cant. Tales,*' 1875, p. 214, which Stratm. cannot explain, is perhaps cleared up by this word.

**GROOVE,** *the line of workings on the* '*back*' *of a lode,* being marked by a ditch, is so called. *e.g.* As a place name, 'Stony **Grooves.**' It means simply a 'dug' place. *Dut.* **Groeve,** *O. N.* Gröf, gröftr, gróf; *Ger.* and *Dan.* grube; *Goth.* groba, *a hole, dug place; O. H. G.* gruoba, *Mid. Low. Ger.* gröve, which, I take it, is the source of our word *O. E.* gröfe (*Romance of Alexander,* Stev. 5395 in Strat.). 'Grough,' 'gruft,' a word meaning the hollows cut by stream courses in the peat, which I heard on the Marsden Moors west of Huddersfield (*O. N.* gröf, gröftr), is quite unknown on all the moors around Nidderdale, but appears no doubt as a place name at 'Griff,' in Coverdale, as noted on p. 94.

**GRUMMAL,** *grumble.* 'He did it adoot a **grummal,**' without a grumble. *Comp.* 'hummal' and 'humble.'

**GRUND,** *ground; O. N.* **Grund,** grunn; *Dan,* grund; *Goth.* grundus (*Skeat*); *Dut.* grond; *Ger.* grund, 'whence the Dan. and Swed.' (*Cleas*).

**GUD,** *good; Goth.* góths, góds; *Dut.* goed, *Ger.* gut, *A. S., O. L. G., O. Fris.* gód; *O. N.* gódr, *O. H. G.* quoter. *O. E.* **Gud** is written by Laurence Minet in his poems, 1352, and for other places *see* Stratm.

**GULL,** *porridge; Wel.* **Gwl,** *damp, moist; Gael.* goile, *the throat; O. Fr.* goule, *throat;* goulée, goulette, *a mouthful;* goulu, *a glutton; Lat.* gula, *the throat; Dut.* gullen, *to swallow; Pers.* gulū, *the throat; Sans.* gal, *to drip, to eat, swallow;* gala, *the throat,* whence *Hind.* gal, galā, gala, *the throat.* Compare *Hind.* gulgulā, *fried flour dumplings,* and gulgulē, *swollen rice mixed with molasses formed into balls.* **Gull** is always spoken of in the *plu.* as 'them,' and is often called 'hasty pudding.'

**GULL-THIVEL,** *a flat stick* for stirring 'gull' (*see* THYVEL).

**GULLY-KNIFE,** *carving knife;* also called 'whittle;' perh. goulée. Brock. supposes originally a butcher's knife, for the gullet.

# H.

|  |  |
|---|---|
| *Grimm,* VII. | K. *Sans.* K, *Gr.* K, *Lat.* c, qu; *O. Ir.* C, CH; *Slav.* K. |
|  | K H. *Goth.* H, q, f; *Sans.* H. |
|  | G. *O. H. G.* H (G, K). |

*Eng.* H commonly $=$ *Lat.* C $=$ *Gr.* K.

**HADE,** *heed.* 'Nivver **hade** yer feet,' the boots being muddy (*Colloq.*). *O. E.* hede, *O. Fris.* hóde, *O. H. G.* huota, *Ger.* achten, *heed; Lat.* cura, custodia (*Stratm.*); *Gael.* cùram, *heed; O. N.* **Heidra,** *Dan.* **hædre,** *to honour; O. N.* **heidr,** *honour; Dan.* **hœder,** *honour.*

**HAGWORM**, *adder*; *O. N.* **Höggorm**, *Swed.* and *Dan.* huggorm, hugorm; *lit.* 'the biting worm,' from *O. N.* höggva, *to bite*, of snakes (*Cleas.*).

**HAINING.** (1.) In the name 'Heäning Top,' mentioned on p. 81, it may be more probable that we have *O. N.* **Hegninn**, *fenced*; and not *A. S.* hean, *high*; ing, *field.* As a matter of fact, it *is* a 'high field,' being some 600 feet above the bottom of the dale, and the highest field on the farm. Moreover, 'Highfield' is a common enough name. Furthermore, 'Heenc,' in Sussex, stands on a ridge, a low ridge truly, but still the highest for miles round, wherefore it was referred by the late Rev. J. W. Warter to *A. S.* heán, *high.* The *Domes.* 'Hene' throws no light. But against this we have the necessary concession in the '**Heaning**,' a flat meadow by the Ure. *O. N.* **hegninn**, *fenced, enclosed* (p. 81); also the phrases cited in Cleasby, *e.g.*, 'At **hegna** lönd sín' (*Fornaldar Sögur*, l. 376), to **hain** or *protect* his land, which falls in with '**haining** land,' a phrase in Brock. *O. N.* **hegna**, *to fence, to protect*; *Dan.* **hegne**, *Swe.* hägna in; *Ger.* hegen, *A. S.* hegjan, *Dut.* heggen, *to hedge, enclose*, so to *protect, save, preserve.* 'A **haining** day,' in Scot. means a time for *saving*, putting away money against a 'rainy day.' 'Grete hertes in the **haynes**, *parks, enclosures* —MS. *Lincoln*, in *Hal.* 'Faiere parkes in with **hainus**.—*Sir Degrevant*, 70, in *Stratm.* In James I. (Scot.), c. 10, 'All destroyaris of grene-wod—and sic like of all new **haningis**.'—*Jamieson.* Also *Helenore*, p. 14—

> 'As **haining** watered with the morning dew.'—*Ross* in *Jam.*

**HAINING** (2), *cold, drizzly*, or *rainy and blowing*, but do not expect to meet one person in the district who knows the word. By chance in 1871 I was just enabled to rescue the word from oblivion, during the oft-mentioned visit to Lodge. Mrs. Allen then told me that her grandparents used it, but she had long forgotten it, and it only came to her memory as we were talking about words. Since then I have made further inquiries, but have not found anyone who knows it. The answer to my inquiry at Middlesmoor was that I was 'right in the meaning, but wrong in the spelling. It should be "hazy."' (!) Hal., however, has '**Hainish**, *unpleasant*, Essex,' which may be this, or connected with *A. S.* hean, *poor*; honth, *poverty*; *Goth.* hauns, *humble, poor*; *Gr.* hohn, *scorn*, &c.; *Dut.* hoon, *O. Fr.* honnir; but whether or no, our word is clearly *Gael.* **ainbhidh**, *rainy weather* (*Armst.*), from ain, *water.*

**HAN'CLOOT**, *towel*; *O. N.* **Handklæthi**, *a towel*; *Dan.* **haandklæde**; *A. S.* clút, cleót, *a little cloth, clout* (see CLEET).

> 'Git t' wallet fra oot o' low drawer
> An' leuk fer t' clean **han'cloot** and all.'—*Bla.*, p. 20

**HANDSEL**, *to use for the first time*; *O. N.* **Handselja**, lit. *to give the hand, so to stipulate, bargain*; handsala, *to make over by* 'handsel;' **handsal**; *Dan.* **handsel**, *the transference of a right*; *Wel.* honsel, *handsel*; *Gael.* sainnseal (from the O. N.), *a handsel, a New Year's gift.* (*Dut.* handgift, *Ger.* handgeld, handkauf.) **Handsel** is a purely Danish word. In the A. S. Laws we find first:—Ine. c. 53 (A.D. 688-728). 'If a man receives from another a stolen man and sy seó **hand** othcwolen the hine **sealde** and the hand be dead (quelled) which gave him,' [*i.e.* if he who **handselled** him be dead] 'let him who has him declare upon the grave thæt seó deade **hand** hine him **sealde** that the ded hand him to him gave.' Again, c. 56, 'If a man buy anything and find within thirty days any fault with it, thonne weorpe he thone ceáp to **hand** tham **syllende**,' then let him give back the purchase to the handseller. Again, *Laws of Ælfred* (872-901), c. 38, 'Gif he wille on **hand** gan, and his wæpnu **syllan**,' if he will submit and give up (**handsel**) his weapons, *i. e.* 'wæpnu on **hand syllan**.' Next in *Laws of Eadmund* (940-946), c. 7, 'If a man kill a man thonne syththan gebyreth thæt man sýlle thœs slagan forspræcan **on hand**, then afterwards it behoves that one *give* for the murderer surety *into hand* that the murderer shall surrender peacefully.' Next in the *Lib. Constit.* (A.D. 1008), temp. Æthelred, ' [the breach of] that [peace] be inexpiable thæt he mid his agenre **hand sýld**,' which he with his own *hand gave*. Again, 'The him man on **hand sýld**,' that the man *gave it into his hand*; and a little further on, 'The heom man on **hand sylle**,' that which to them the man *gives into their hand*. Wedg. observes ' The formation of the word has been commonly misunderstood as if it signified *delivery of possession, giving a thing into the hand of another*,' which is clearly the meaning in all the above A. S. passages. The fact is that we should never have had the word from the A. S. We find nothing but possible rudiments of such a word, which, had they matured, would have given a *different* sense from our word **handsel**. The word cannot, therefore, possibly be derived from the A. S., as Atk. (*Cl. Gl.*) would have it, but only from the O. N.

**HANG**, *hung, pret.* from a *pres.* HING. *q.v.*, ' Doon t'chimler **hang** a gert chean . . . o' witch they yuse ta **hing** t'poddish pan,' p. 21.

**HANNAL**, *pron.* of *handle*, as ' cannal' of ' candle.' The dropping of the *d* is *Dan.*

**HAPPEN**, *adv., perhaps; O. N.* **Heppinn**, *lucky;* heppni, *good luck.* Heppnast, *to have good luck.*

**HAPSE, HAPS**, *latch; A.S.* **Hæps**, a *haps*, hasp; from *Gr.* 'apsos, *a fastening, haps.* These are very generally used in place of locks, for all inner doors, except in very modern houses. A Greek name imported by early Gypsy metal workers. *See my Yetholm Hist. of the Gypsies.*

**HARDEN**, *hemp, hemp-fabric; A.S.* **Heordan**, *tow refuse* (*Bos.*); *Goth.* hazds, *O.N.* háddr, *Dan.* and *Dut.* haar, *Swed.* hár, *hair; O.N.* and *Dan.* hörr, *flax, linen;* ' Sat thrawin' t'shuttle weavin **harden** for monny a lang ear' . . . ' hawkin **harden** o'ther awn manafakter.'—*Al.*, 1880.

**HARSTAN**, *hearthstone.*

**HASTY-PUDDING**, *gull, gulls,* or *oatmeal porridge,* or *poddish,* in this neighbourhood Scot. oatmeal ground over again, boiled in milk, and then mixed with more milk till it obtains that consistency from which it takes its name. The ' hasty pudding' of the south is *diff.*

**HAVE**, *behave.* ' häve yersel.'

**HAVER**, *oats; O.N. plu.* **Hafar**, *oats; Dan.* & *Dut.* **haver**, *Swed.* havre, *Ger.* hafer, *Russ. plu.* ovese, *oats; Lat.* avena, *oat.*

**HEEAD**, *head; A.S.* Heáfod (*gen.* heáfdes) heáfd, hæfd; *O.N.* höfud, *Swed.* hufwud, *Dan.* hoved, *head,* höved, *head of cattle; Dut.* hoofd, *head; O. Fris.* háved, *Russ.* golova, glava, golovka; *Goth.* haubith, *Ger.* haupt.

**HEEAM**, *home; Nor.* **Hjem**, *Dan.* **hiem**, *A.S.* hæm, *Ger.* heim. ' Hame' is *O. N.* ' heimr'; ' Home,' *A.S.* ' hám.'

**HEEARIN**, *herring; A.S.* Hæring, *Dut.* háring, *Ger.* häring, *Fr.* hareng, *O. Fr.* harenc, from *O. H. G.* harinc.

**HEEARIN**, *heron. See* HEERINSEW.

**HECK**, a swinging *fence* where a wall crosses a beck, as far as I know the only sense in which this old word is preserved, except in the name following. *Dan.* **Hekke**, *O. N.* heggr, *Swed.* hägg, *Dan.* hegn, *A. S.* hæge, hege, *a hedge; A. S.* hæca, *a bar of a door;* hæcce, *a shepherd's crook.* ' Sum on dores and sum on **heck**.'—*Tourn. of Tottenham,* l. 205. In Surrey, 'Hatch,' *a wicket gate.*

**HECK-BERRY**, *bird-cherry* (*Prunus Padus*); *Dan.* **Hœkke-bœr**, *the bird-cherry.*

**HEETEEN**, *eighteen.*

**HEIGH, HEE**, *high; A. S.* **Heah**, high.

**HEFTIN**, ' gert *heftin* shignons.' *Bla.* in *Al.*, 1880. *O.N.* **Heptinn**, *part. of* ' hepta' or ' hefta,' *to bind.* ' Heftin' above means ' sham,' 'artificial' from their being *tied on.*

**HELD-ON CAKE**, *a kind of oat-cake* (*see* p. 15).

**HELL**. In place names common, as ' Hell Hole,' ' Hell Beck.' I believe all the 'Hell' holes or becks that have come under my observation have been deep, narrow, wooded (but that is not essential), gills, with spring at the bottom. I gave it in evidence before a Committee of the House of Commons that 'Hill Farm,' in the parish of Buckland, Surrey, is built over a spring, the source of the 'Shag Brook,' and that this spring is called the 'Held.' I have been tempted to explain this by *A. S.* keld, *O. N.* **Kelda**, *a spring; Swed.* källa, *Dan.* kilde, *Ger.* quelle, *M.H.G.* qual, quil, *Eng.* well; *Gr.* helos, *a marsh; Lat.* vallis (*Cur.*, 530); and to regard 'hill' as a corruption of the same word, in the same way as the three place names on p. 92. 'Hell Hole' might thus mean '*spring hole.*' But the ear and inclination suggest that 'Hell Hole' is like 'How Hill,' a reduplication, in favour of which view we have *O. N.* **hellir**, *a cave in rocks,* but in most 'hell holes' there is no cave. Except that there is no religious meaning or application in the word, I have formed no more definite conclusion respecting it than the above (*see* WELL).

**HELM, HELLAM,** *straw, thatch, a shed, barn; O. N.* Hálmr, helma, *straw;* hjálmr, *a barn; Dan.* and *Ger.* halm, *straw,* haulm; *A.S.* healm, hælm, *straw, stubble;* haulm, *a thatched shed; Gr.* kalamos; *Lat.* calamus, culmus; *Sans.* kalama, *rice, a reed; Arab.* kalam, *a reed* (see also Study VII., pp. 55-9).

**HEM,** *to draw in; O. N.* **Hemja,** *Dan.* hemme, *to stop, stay, limit;* hemme sig, *check, restrain.* 'The days **hems** in short, sir' (*Middlesmoor*) reminds one of the beautiful opening line of *Little John Nobody:*—

'In December, when the days draw to be short.'

**HENNOT,** *have not.*

**HEPN, HEPEN,** or *improp.* epn, *able, well; O. N.* **Heppinn,** *lucky.* 'ord **heppinn,**' *ready-tongued.*

**HE'RE,** *contr. fr.* 'he war'=he was (*see* WAR).

**HEERINSEW,** *heron; O. Fr.* heronçeau (*Tyrwhitt*), sometimes called 'beearin.'

'Nor of their swannes, ne their **heronsewes.**' —Chauc. *Cant. Tales,* v. 10,382.

'Heronshaw'='handsaw,' in the *Prov.*, not to know a hawk from a *handsaw.* The second half, 'shaw' or 'sew,' is *Gael.* corr, corra, *a heron, crane,* or *stork; Russ.* tzaplya, *a heron;* so that heron-çeau is a reduplication. I perceive that several dicts. make heronshaw=heronry. *O. E.* hairon, from *O. Fr.* hairon, *a heron* (*Stratm.*), which is probably from *Goth.* hairus, *a sword,* from the beak.

**HERSEN,** *herself* (*see* SEN).

**HET,** *heated; O. N.* Hèt, *pret. sing.* of heita, *to heat.* In an early 17th century ballad, 'Limping Vulcan **het** an iron barr.'—*Tom of Bedlam,* l. 31.

**HEV,** *have*
**HEVVANT,** *haven't* } *A. S.* hæbban, hæbbe, are related to hev as habbe
**HEVVIN,** *having* } to have.

**HEYTHER,** *either* (*see* AYTHER).

**HEZ,** *has; A.S.* 'hæfth' is to 'hez' as 'hafth' to 'has'. 'At **hez** him near two hands in height,' *exceeds.*—(*Bla.*).

**HIF,** *if; A. S.* gif (*see* GIEN).

**HIND,** *a man put in to occupy a farm house* where a farmer has more than one; *A. S.* hína, híne, *a servant;* hína-mann, *a farmer; O.N.* hjón, hjún or hjú, *one of the persons belonging to the household* (*Fritz.*).

**HINDER,** *hind, back, behind; A. S.* Hinder, *Goth.* hindar, *O. N.* hindri, *O. H. G.* hintar, *Ger.* hinter. **Hinder** leg=hind leg of a horse.

**HING,** *to hang.* An original form, lost except in these Dialects. Like *A. S.* bringan, brang, brungen; *Eng.* bring, brang, brung; *A.S.* swingan, swang, swungen; *Eng.* swing, swang, swung; sling, slang, slung; sting, stang, stung—so **hing, hang, hung,** as actually used in this Dialect, *see* HANG for *Ex.* Considerable vagaries are noticeable in the forms of this word, thus *Dut.* hing, *hung, is imperf.* of 'hangen,' *to hang.* In *O. N.* hanga, *pret.* hekk, *part.* hanginn; and *A. S.* hangian, hón, *part.* heng, hangen; the *pret.* and *part.* point to an original *infin.* hinga and hingan. *O. H. G.* hahan, *Ger.* hangen, *Dut.* hangen, henghen. 'Hinge'. that on which a door ' hings.'

> ' Gae bring a robe of your cliding,
> That **hings** upon the pin.'—*Gil Morice*, l. 98.

**HIPPINGS**, *stepping stones*, over the Nidd, as at ' Haxby Hippings'; *Wel.* hypynt, *a sudden effort*; hwp, *a sudden effort*; hwb, *a push forward, an effort*; *Eng.* hop.

**HIPPINGS**, *a baby's napkins*; *A. S.* **Hip**, hípe; **hyp**, **hype**, *fem.* **hype**, hypan, *the hip*; *O. N.* huppr, *the hip*, which in the North and Scot. means the buttocks.

**HISHER**, *higher.* In the *sh* we have a very remarkable relic of the guttural running through *Goth.* hauhs, *A. S.* heáh, *Eng.* high, *O. N.* hár, *Swed.* hög, *Dut.* hoog, *Dan.* höi, *O. H. G.* hoh, *Ger.* hoch. ' Are you going to Ramsgill?' ' Nay, were fer a lile bit **hisher** up t'daal.'—*Colloq.*

**HISSEN**, *himself* (*see* SEN). 'Jerry hevvin a corner tav **hissen** i yah end.' —*Dicky and Micky Dale.*

**HIT**, *eat.*

**HITTIN**, *eating*; *A. S.* **Hitath**, *to eat*; *Goth.* **itan**.

> ' It's a job ta git summat ta **hit**.'—*Bla.*, p. 23.
> ' And gave ower **hittin** just then.'—*Ib.*, p. 14.

' Eat' is *A. S.* etan, *Dut.* eten, *Ger.* essen, *Lat.* edere.

**HOAFE, HOFE**, *adj., half*; *O. N.* hálfr; *Dan.* halv, *Goth.* halbs, *Ger.* halb, *Dut.*, *Swed.* and *Eng.* half, *Russ.* polovenneië, poly.

**'T'HOASTIK CARLES.'** ' Foaks hez lang toked aboot " t'hoastik carles ".an ther wallin t' cuckoo in, an sike like.'—*Al.*, 1880. The **carls** here referred to are no doubt spirits of .the woods, the idea springing from the echo in Hoastik Wood in the little story, 'Lost in the Wood,' *Al.*, 1880. **Carl** is a word long lost, but formerly existing in this district in a more material sense, and still preserved in one or two place names, *e.g.*, **Carleside, Carle Fell, Carlton**, in Coverdale, &c. *O. H. G.*, *O. N.*, *Dan.* and *Swed.* **karl**, *Dut.* karel, *O. H. G.* charl, *A. S.* ceorl, *a man, a rustic*; *O. E.*, mentioned several times in *Stratm.* as a name; *Lat.* Carolus, *Eng.* Charles. As above instanced, the meaning of the word being forgotten, a superstitious sense has attached to it. The names of gypsies offer many parallels.

**HOD**, *hold.*

**HOG**, *a lamb a year old*; *Gael.* 'Og, *young, youthful*; òg, òig, *a youth, young child*; ogan, *dim.* of og, *a young man, twig, seedling*; *Wel.* hogen, *a girl nearly full grown*; hogyn, *a young man.* Hawg, *pl.* hogion, *completeness, fulness, perfection.* **Hog** therefore means the same as *Lat.* pubes. Hence also *prob. Mod. Midland Eng.* hoggerel, hogget; *Nor. Fr.* hogetz, *a year old sheep.* **Hog-colt**, *a colt a year old* (*Devonsh.*).

**HOLLIN**, *holly*; *A. S.* **Holegn**, holen; *Gael.* cuileann, crann, cuilinn. Holly is never used colloquially. **Hollin** is also freq. in place names (*see* p. 117).

**HOLM**, *low, flat land by rivers*; *O. N.* Hólmr, *meadows beside rivers* with ditches at the back, which exactly describes the sense here. *Dan.* **holm**, *low, flat land, &c.*; *Swed.* holme, *an islet*; *A. S.* holm, *a river island, &c.*

**HOLM**, *a tree.* In answer to many inquiries I was positively assured that it was not the ' holm' oak, and as far as I could determine it was the ' witch,' or mountain elm, that was so called. This seems probable, as the *O. N.* for elm is almr, álmr; *Lat.* ulmus, *Ger.* ulme, *Walach.* ulmu, &c.

**HOMMAST,** *almost,* seems to be a parallel form with 'almost'—corrupt. from 'whole-most.' *A. S.* Hál, mæst, as 'almost,' from *eal* or *al* and *mæst,* most, as a dropped or added *h* is a most exceptional thing here, though so common in the South.

**HOONEY,** a familiar word, used in addressing another, ludicrously connected with 'honey' and 'sweetness,' by popular misconception. It simply means 'you there,' or 'you,' and is connected with *Wel.* **Hwn,** this here, this masc. one present; **hwna,** that there, that one present; **hwnacw,** that one yonder; **hwnw,** that one absent; **hwnyma, hwnyman,** this one here; **hwnyna,** that one there. Hòn, this fem. here; hòna that fem. here; **honyma, honyman,** this fem. here, &c. It is either **hwn,** fem. hòn; or **hwna,** fem. hòna, according as it is addressed to a man or a woman.

**HOO,** *how; A. S.* **Hwu.** The ord. pron. 'how' is *A. S.* hú.

**HOOALE,** *hole; Goth.* **Huls** (*adj.*), *hollow; Ger.* hohl, *Dut., O. N.,* and *Swed.* hol, *a hole.*

**HOODEND,** 'that side of the fire opposite to the oven where there is no boiler.'—(*Mr. Thorpe,* of Pateley Bridge) *see* p. 21.

**HOOIN,** *to punish, trouble; O. E.* Hûnen (*Stratm.*), *Goth.* **haunjan,** *to humiliate.* 'From "hean," hins (*hoin*) (*Stratm.*); from hauns, *humble* (*Skeat*); *A. S.* hýnan, hénan; *O. Fris.* héna, *O. E.* henen, *O. Dut.* and *O. H. G.* hónen, *O. Fr.* honnir, *to humiliate; Goth.* hauns, *A. S.* heán, *humble; Dut.* **hoon,** *a scoff, taunt, affront, disgrace, contempt, &c.,* which may be the immediate parent word; *Goth.* hunths, *captivity; A. S.* honth, *penury, poverty.* An old woman says to her 'owd man,' 'Ah cannot abide to **hooin** thee.'—*Bla.,* p. 28.

**HOOKABACK,** *huckaback,* tablecloths, &c.

**HOOP,** *hope.*

**HOOR,** *hour; Dut.* uur, *Ger.* uhr, *Swed. & Dan.* ur, *Mod. Gr.* hora, *Gyps.* hora, *a watch, clock; Lat.* hora, *Fr.* heure, *Gael.* uair.

**HOOSE,** *house; Goth.* **Hus,** *O. N.* hús, *Swed.* **hus,** *Dan.* **huus,** hus; *Dut.* huis, *O. H. G.* hûs, *Ger.* haus, *A. S.* hús, give ord. pron. 'house.'

**HOOT, OOT,** *out.* 'Fer heeame hoot o' this as sean as ah can.'—*Al.,* 1880. *Dut.* **Uit,** 'uit het huis,' 'oot of the hoose.' The prefixed *h* is of the more corrupt *Dial.* of Pateley Bridge.

**HOOIVER,** *however.* 'Ah thowt ta me'y sen "thoo's a feal" **hooiver.**'—*Al.,* 1880. Frequently terminates a sentence.

**HOPERTH,** *ha'p'orth.*

**HOPPEN,** *open* (*Bla.*)

**HOUST, WHOOST,** *to cough; Ger.* **Husten,** *M. H. G.* huosten, *O. H. G.* huostôn, *A. S.* hwóstan. 'I can't bear to hear ye **houstin'** like that.' *O. N.* hosta, *Swed.* hosta, *Dan.* hoste, *Gael.* casd, *Hind.* khānsnā, khāsnā, from *Sans.*

**HOW,** *hill; O. N.* Haugr, *a tumulus; A. S.* **how,** *a hill; Dan.* hö, *hill.* In place names only, as 'How Hill,' 'Greenhow Hill,' and as names of tumuli. 'The Three Howes' occur over and over again on the Yorkshire moors, being generally three tumuli ranged in a straight line on some prominent ridge.

**HOWD,** *hold.*

**HOWT,** *ought, anything* (Pateley) for 'owt,' which see, 'How's yersel?' 'Warse, if **howt.**'

**HUG,** *to carry, to fetch and carry,* as a dog game. 'Ah thowt ah wad **hug** fadther across t' watter.'—*Colloq* 'Noo come let me **hug** the' the' cooate,' *fetch thee thy coat.*—*Bla.,* p. 28. *O. N.* **huga,** *to attend to, look after; Goth.* (*Ulf.*) hugjan, *to think; A. S.* hugian; *O. N.* hyggja, *to think, take thought for, attend to.*

**HUGGIN' STICKS,** *carrying-poles* on which a coffin is carried to the grave.

**HULLOT,** *owlet; O. Fr.* hulotte, *dim.* of huëtte, *owl; Lat.* ûlula (*Cot. Bra.*).

**HUMMALED,** *hornless;* as 'a **hummaled** stot,' *hornless ox. Gael.* umhall, *humble; A. S.* homola, homela, *a man who has had his head shaved* (for pillory), 'Gif he hine on bismor to **homelan** bescyre,' if he to his disgrace shave his head as though he were going to the pillory.—*Laws of Ælfred* (872-901), c. 31. Atk. (*Cl. Gl.*) collates *O. N.* **hamla**, *to maim, mutilate*; *Swed. dial.* hammla, *to make pollard* a tree; *O. Swed.* hambla, *to lop off* the limbs; and with *O. N.* **hamla** Cleas. collates *A. S.* hámelan, *the private parts which were cut off* for several offences; *O. N.* hamal-stut, *locus supplicii, place of punishment*; *Ger.* hammel, *a wether*, with which Grimm *Ger.* hamalstat, *M. H. G.* hamelstat, pihamalôn, *truncare, to mutilate*; *A. S.* hamelian, *Eng.* hamble; *M. H. G.* hamel, *a castrated ram.* Holtrop gives *Dut.* hámel, *a wether*. In Oldenburg **hummel** is *hornless cattle.* Flügel gives 'Hummel (provincial), a bull kept for breeding.' *Lat.* humilis, *Eng.* humble, &c.

**HUMMER.** I suppose corrup. of Hanover in the sentence 'Ah wish all ther sticks wer at **Hummer**.'—*Al.*, 1880.

**HUT**, *to set up peats on the moor*, as described on p. 119; *O. Fr.* **Huter**, *to build, to set up* (*Cot.*); *O. Ger.* **hütten**, *to build huts*, from *O. H. G.* hutta, *Ger.* hütte, *Dut.* hutte, *Dan.* hytte, *a hut.*

# I.

**INTA**, *into.*

**INTUL**, *into*; *O. N.* Intill, *Dan.* indtill, *into.*

**IS**, *are.* 'These **is**;' commonly used in N.E. and Scot. It is a survival of an older form than 'are.'

**IVIN**, *ivy.* The place name 'Ivin Waite' = 'Ivy Thwaite.' *Gael.* Eitheann, *O. Dut.* ieven, ivin; *O. E.* 'ivenléf,' *ivy leaf.*—*Seven Sages* (Ed. Wright, 1845, p. 181, in Stratm.). 'Ivy,' *A. S.* ifig, *O. H. G.* ebah, *Ger.* ephew.

# J.

**JOWL**, '*puffin away "cheek by Jowl."*'—*Al.*, 1880. *Gael.* **Gial**, *Ir.* giall, *Wel.* kill, *Eng.* gill, *A. S.* ceole, *the jaw*; *Fr.* gueule, *throat*; *O. E.* jol (*Prompt.* 264)=*O. E.* chavel, *A. S.* ceafl, *O. N.* kafel(?) *M. L. G.* kavel, *O. E.* chavel, chavil, chewil, choule, *a jaw*; *Var. Dial.* chon, *to chew.*—(*Stratm., Hal., Amstr.*), *see* GULL.

# K.

*Grimm IV. Goth.* K, *Celt., Gr., Lat.* G; *Sans.* G, *Slav.* g, z.; *O. H. G.* Ch.

---

**KAIL**, *soup*; *Gael.* Càil, càl, *kail, colewort*, a name for all sorts of cabbage; *Scotch-broth*, of which **kail** is a principal ingredient (*Armstr.*). *A. S.* cawl, *O. N.* kál, *Dan.* kaal, *Swed.* kal, *Russ.* zelenaya, *Dut.* kool, *Ger.* kohl, *O. H. G.* kol, *Fr.* chou, *O. Fr.* chol, *Lat.* caulis, *a cabbage*; *Mod. Gr.*, kaulos, kauli, *a stalk.*

**KAIL POT**, pot in which soup, &c., was cooked (*see* pp. 19 and 211).

**KARKIE**, *cake*; *O. N.* Kaka, *Swed.* kaka, *Dan.* kage, *Dut.* koek, *cake*; *Scot.* cookie, *Gael.* caraiceag, *a kind of pancake.*

**KAY**, *key*; *A. S.* Cæg.

**KELD**, *a spring*; *O. N.* Kelda, *A. S.* keld. Gives the name 'Kelds' to the dale side N. of Thwaite House (*see* HELL).

**KELK**, *a kick*; *O. N.* in compos. 'Thrá-kelkinn,' *obstinate* (in Cleas.), indicates a form kelk; *Russ.* tolchoke nogore, *a kick*; tolkate nogore, *to kick.*

**KEN**, *know*; *O. N.* and *O. Fris.* Kenna, *Swed.* känna, *Dan.* kjende, *Ger.* and *Dut.* kennen, *Fris* kenna, *A. S.* cennan, *M. H. G.* kennen, *Goth.* kunnan, *A. S.* cunnan, *to know*; *Eng.* cunning, *Russ.* znate, *to know*; *Gael.* vainich, *token.*

The passage, 'Gif he thonne oenth,' in the *Suppt.* to the *Laws of Eadgar* is transl. by Wilkins (wrongly, as I think), 'Si autem notum sit . . . illis.' It should read, ' But if he *can prove*—from *A. S.* cennan, to *produce evidence.* *Gr.* gignōscō, *Lat.* gnosco, *Sans.* gànâmi (*Cur.* 135).

**KERN,** *a churn*; now a revolving tub on a horizontal axis, but, till a few years ago, an upright tub, in shape 'ike a truncated sugar-loaf; none of these are now seen. *O. N.* **Kirna,** *Swed.* **kerna,** *Dut.* **kern, karn.** 'Churn,' *Dan.* kjerne (*see* p. 28).

**KERN,** *to churn*; *A. S.* **Cernan,** *to churn*; *Ger.* and *Dut.* **kernen,** *Swed.* **kerna** smör (*to churn butter*); *Dan.* kjerne, *Dut.* karnen.

**KERSAMAS,** *Christmas, i.e.,* **Chirs'imas,** sometimes **Chris'imas;** *Dut.* **Kersmis;** all for Christi-mæss.

**KI,** *cows*; *A. S.* **Cý, cí,** *nom.* and *acc. plu.* of cú. Used at Lodge and thereabout, where I have shown (pp. 80, 104, 106), by several independent tests, proofs of an Anglian settlement preponderate.

> ' More meet it were for them to milk **kye** at a fleyke.'
> —*Lit. John Nobody,* l. 14.   Reformn. Ballad, temp. Ed. VI.

**KINK,** *a bend, a twist*; *Swed.* kink, *Dut.* and *Dan.* kink, *O. N.* kengr, *a horseshoe*; keng-boginn, ' bend-bowed,' *crooked*.

**KINK,** *hysterics.* Atk. (*Cl. Gl.*) has 'kink-cough,' *whooping-cough*.

**KINK,** *to cough*; *O. N.* **Kinka,** *to nod the head*; kingja, *to wallow*; *Dut.* kinken, *Dan.* staa kinker, *to kink*; *Swed.* kikna, *to choke*; *Hind.* (Telugu) kakwān, *whooping-cough* (Dakhnī, *Harris*). ' That bai'ns **kinkin,** hit it ower t'back.'— *Colloq.* (Pateley). *Swed.* ' **kikna** af skratt,' ' to die of laughter,' *i.e., to double up.* ' I laghe that I kinke.'—*Towneley Mysteries,* 309 (Yorks, about 1450).

**KITE,** *belly*; *Goth.* (*Ulf.*) **Qithus,** *A. S.* cwith, *Swed.* qwed, *O. H. G.* quiti, *the womb*; *Russ.* zhēvote, *the belly*.

**KITTLE,** *to tickle*; *O. N.* **Kitla,** *Swed.* **kittla,** *Dut.* **kittelen,** *A. S.* citelan, *Ger.* kitzeln; *Gael.* cigeall, gigeall, giogall ; *Russ.* shchekotate, *to tickle*.

**KITLING,** *kitten*; *O. N.* **Kitlingr.**

**KIST, KYST,** *chest*; *Gael.* **Ciste,** *Wel.* cìst, *A. S.* cist, cyst; *O. N.* and *Swed.* **kista,** *Dan.* kiste, *Ger.* kisti, evidenced by their identity to be all from *Lat.* cista (*Cleas.*). ' & hyre cýste.'—*Laws of Canute,* c. 74.

> ' Some ran to coffer and some to **kist,**
> But nought was stown that could be mist.'
> —James V. of Scotland.   *The Gaberlunzie Man,* l. 37.

**KNAW,** *to know*; *A. S.* **Cnáwan.**

**KNEP,** *to browse* as a horse; *O. N.* [**kneppa**], *Dan.* knibe, *to nip*; *O. N.* knapper, *Dan.* knap, *scanty*; *Dut.* afknabbelen. *to browse*; *Russ.* shchēpate travy, ' *to nip grass,*' *to browse*; shchēpoke, *to nip*; *Ger.* kneipen, *to nip*; *Russ.* shchèptzei, *O. N.* kneif, *nippers or pincers*; *O. N.* knífr, *Swed.* knif, *Dan.* kniv, *Eng.* knife. Of a horse, ' **Nepping** bits o yung gerse o' t' rooadsides.'—*Bla.,* p. 11.

**KONK,** *nose* (properly *cheek*); *O. N.* kjálki, *cheek*; **Kjánka,** *to make grimaces*; from which I infer a *noun* [kjánki], *cheek*; *Russ.* shchēka, *Dut.* koon, *Swed.* and *Dan.* kind (*Dut.* wang, *Ger.* wange), *cheek.*

# L.

**LAAIDE,** *a load.* ' A **laaide** o' sticks.' *O. N.* Hlad, *A. S.* lad, hlad; *Gael.* luchd, lòd, *a load*; *Dan.* lade, *to load, lade*; *Gael.* lòd, *Dut.* láden, beláden, belasten; last, *a load*; *Ger.* laden; *Goth.* hlathan, *to lade.*

**LAD,** *a man*; *Goth.* **Lauds,** *a lad*; *W.* llawd, *a lad*; *Dan.* lad, *idle, lazy.*

**LAIR,** *a cowshed, &c.*; *Swed.* läge, *Dan.* lage; *Goth.* ligrs, *a bed*, from ligan, *to lie*; *Russ.* logovĕahche, *a lair*; but this Northern word is *O. N.* leir, *cluy* (*see* p. 80).

**LAITH, LATHE,** *shed*; *O. N.* Hlatha, *Swed.* lada; *Dan.* lade, *a barn*; *Ger.* and *Dut.* láde, *a box.*

**LAIK, LAKE,** *to play*; *Goth.* Laikan; *O. N.* leika, *to play*; *Swed.* leka; *Dan.* lege; *M. H. G.* leicha, *to laik, play*; *A. S.* lǽcan, lácan, *to 'lark,' play*; *O. N.* leikr, *a game*; *A. S.* lác, *a 'lark,' game.*

'And live in lust in lechery to leyke.'—*Lit. John Nobody*, l. 22.

'He lakes up an doon amang t' bogs.'—*Bla.*, p. 22.

**LAIT, LATE,** *to seek*; *Goth.* (*Ulf.*) Wlaiton, *to look round about* (*Mark* v. 32); wleitan, *to look*; *A. S.* wlitan; *Goth.* leyta (*Cleas.*); *O. N.* leita; *Dan.* lede, *to seek*; *Gr.* lēthō, *to escape notice*; laō, *to see, look at.*

**LAND,** *to arrive anywhere*; *Dan.* Lande, *to land.* A person lands on reaching the end of his journey. 'Then ye've landid,' or 'So ye're landid,' is a freq. salutation. 'Thinkin at t' varra divil hissel had landid.'—*Al.*, 1880. This expression may well have arisen among the islands and isthmuses of Denmark, where there would be much boat traveliing, and so become generalised.

**'LANG O',** *owing to, through* ('ALL ALONG ON'); *A. S.* Gelang on. '& hit on preost gelang sý,' and if it be lang o' the priest, *i.e., the priest's fault.*—*Canons, Eadg., On Punishments*, c. 44. 'On wisum scrifte bith eac swithe forthgelang wíslíc deadbót,' a wise-like punishment is forthgelang on, *the property of*, a wise priest.—*Ib.*, 9. 'He sed summat aboot it bein' lang o' that gert parlement man we had sike bad weather.'—*Al.*, 1880.

**LANG,** *adj., long*; *O. N.* Langr, *Dan.* lang, *A. S.* lang, *Dut.* lang, *Goth.* laggs, *Swed.* long. The pron. is A. S. probably.

**LANGEST,** *longest.* 'An' t' langest of days hez an end.'—*Bla.*, p. 14.

**LANG-SETTLE,** *settle, seat by kitchen fire* (see p. 25).

**LANGSOME,** *slow, tedious*; *A. S.* Langsum. 'Hú langsum wæs,' &c. —*Alfred's Boet*, 18, 4. 'The langsome labours of my way.'—*Ruth-a-riding*, p. 192. *O. N.* [langsamr], langsamlega, 'langsomely,' *incessantly*; *Swed.* longsam.

**LANG-STREAKED,** *stretched at full length*; *Dan.* Lang-strakt. Of a horse, 'Ligging lang-streaked upo' t' green.'—*Bla.*, p. 11. 'Long-stretched,' from *Dan.* strœkke, *to stretch.*

**LANT,** *to delay*; *O. N.* lata, *Goth.* latjan, *A. S.* latian, *to be slow, delay.* The word is evidently Dut., for we find *Dut.* lanter-fanten, *to loiter, lounge*; lanter-fant, *a lounger*; lunderen, *to loiter*; *Low Ger.* luddern. Atk. (*Cl. Gl.*) advances for 'lantered' that it='lated' with the nasal added, as described by Wedgwood under 'loiter,' 'lounge.' 'If he's ony notion of anither takkin me plaise, ah'll lant him.'—*Al.*, 1880. 'I'll *keep him waiting, disappoint* him.'

**LANTED,** *disappointed.* 'Ah's lanted this time.'

**LASTY,** *lasting*; *Dut.* Lastig, *troublesome, burdensome, inconvenient.* 'Een lastig werk,' a troublesome business.—*Holtrop.* 'It's been ower lasty by hoafe,' has *lasted* much too long.—*Bla.*, p. 19.

**LEE, LEA,** *scythe*; *O. N.* Ljár, lé, *Dan.* lee, *Swed.* lia, *a large heavy scythe* which has the blade in the same plane as the handle (*see* p. 33 for descrip. and mode of using). Comp. *Chin.* lei, *a plough.*

**LEAD,** *to fetch in a cart*; *A. S.* Lǽdan, *O. N.* leida. 'Whar's Tom?' 'He's leadin peäts off t' moor.' 'Leadin cooals fra Pateley.'

**LEEAK,** *look*; 'Leeak, muther, here's a gentleman on horseback.'

**LEE,** *lie*; *A. S.* Leah, *a lie*; leeas, *false.* '& thæt leeas bith,' and that is *false.*—*Laws of Eadg., Suppt.* *Goth.* liugn, *a lie.*

'Ye leid, ye leid, ye filthy nurse,
Sae loud I heird ye lee.'—*Gill Morice*, ll. 87-8.

STUDIES IN NIDDERDALE.—*Lucas.*

Can a tradition of Celtic hatred have come down to modern times? *e.g.* (at Loft-house), ' He says we're Saxons, an it's a demmed **lee**.'

**LEEARN**, *learn*; *A S.* **Loernan**, (*Cleas.*)(?) from *Ger.* lernen, lehren; *Dut.* leeren; *Swed.* lära, *Dan.* lœra, *O. N.* læra, all from *Goth.* leisan, *to learn*; laisjan, *to teach.*

**LEEAM**, *loom*; *A. S.* **Leome**, *a bough, branch.*

**LEEAT**, *late.*

**LEEAVE**, *leave*; *Goth.* **Leiban.**

**LEET**, *light*; *A. S.* **Leoht.**

**LENGER**, *longer*; *Dan.* **Loengere**, *A. S.* **lengra**, *longer.*

> ' No **lenger** wold I lye.'—*Sir Cauline*, l. 46.

' No **lenger** make delay.'—*The Nut-browne Mayd*, l. 104, about 1520.

**LET**, *leave off, give up*; *Dan.* **Lette**, *to free, discharge*; *Goth.* letan, *A. S.* lœtan, *let go, release.* ' Ah've **let** thinkin' 'f it,'—*given up* thinking of it.—*Al.*, 1880. *Dut.* laten, *Ger.* lassen.

**LET ON**, *give up* a secret. ' Gif thœt he ne mæge, læte on.' If he cannot do that, *give it up.*—*Laws of Hlothœr*, 7. ' Mind you don't **let on**,'—*tell* anyone. Mr. Thorpe supplies the following word:—

**LET ON**, *to succeed.* ' Hoo hez ta cum on, lass?' ' Oh ah've **let on** rarely, ah've gitten all ah wantid.'

**LEUK, LEWK**, *look.*

**LICK**, *beat*; *Gael.* leac, *to flay, destroy*; *Wel.* **Llac, Llyad**, *a slap, lick, blow.*

I **LICKER**='in liquor,' *drunk.*

**LIG**, *to lie*; *O. N.* **Liggja**, *Dan.* **ligge**, *Swed.* ljuga, *Goth.* (*Ulf.*) **ligan**, *A. S.* **licgan, liggan**, *Dut.* **liggen.**

> ' Two yonge knightes **ligging** by and by.'—*Chauc. Cant. Tales*, v. 1013.

> ' What houndës **liggen** on the floor adown.'—*Ib.*, v. 2207.

**LIG**, *to lay*; *O. N.* **Leggja**; *Dan.* **loegge**; *A. S.* **lecgan**, *to lay*; *Dut.* **leggen**, *Ger.* legen. ' To **lig** a body oot.' ' To **lig** a rate.'

**LIKER**, *more like, more likely*; *A. S.* gelíc, *like*; gelícost, *most like*; requires a compar. supplied by pres. word.

**LILE**, *little*; *Wel.* **Llai**, *little*; lleiach, *smaller.*

**LIMMERS**, *shafts*; *O. N.* **Limir**, *pl.* of limr; *A. S.* limu, *pl.* of lim, *a limb.*

**LĬN**, *flax*; *O. N.* **Lín**, *Wel.* **llin**, *Gael.* lion, *Dut.* lijn, *Eng.* linen, *Gr.* linon.

**LĪNE**, *flax*; *A. S.* **Lín**, *Goth.* and *Ger.* lein, *Lat.* linum. From the noun comes the verb to ' line.'

**LIS'NERS**, *ears.* A cant word.

**LITE**, *to wait, to expect*; *O. N.* **Líta**, *to look for*; *Dan.* **lide**, *to rely.* ' To **lite** o' yan,' *to wait on* (*i.e.*, for) anybody.

**LITHER**, *lazy*; *O. N.* **Lithugr**, *yielding*; *Dan.* ledig, *lad*; *A. S.* lítha, *lithe.* From *soft* we pass to *pliable*, yielding, weak idle. *Russ.* lyentyac, *lazy-bones.*

> ' " My ladde he is so **lither**," he said,
> " He will doe nought that's mete." '—*King Estmere*, l. 203.

Means *lithe* in the following passage—

> ' But up then rose that **lither** ladd!
> And hose and shoone did on.'—*Glasgerion*, l. 33.

**T' LIVIN' END**, *inner room*, where there are only two. ' T' livin' end an t' parler end.' *Scot.* ben=*the inner room*; but, *the outer*; in ' But and ben '= ' be-out and be-in.'

**LOAN**, *lane*; *Prov. Dan.* **Laane**, *lane, an open place* (*Wedg.*); *W.* **llán**, *a clear space, small enclosure* (*Ow.*); *Fris.* **laan, lona**, *a lane or narrow passage.* 'An oade thakt buildin i t' loanside.'—p. 216.  'Doon t' loan they went, by t' oade steane troff.'—p. 222.

**LOANING**, *lane*; *Gael.* **Loininn, lonaig.**

**LONESOME.**  Many are the places that are truly such as here described:—

> 'Thus he hath sold his land soe broad,
>  Both hill and holt and moore and fenne,
>  All but a poor and **lonesome** lodge,
>  That stood far off in a lonely glenne.'
>  —*The Heir of Linne*, v. 11.

**LOFFER**, *lower*; *Dan.* **Lavere**, compar. of lav. *low.*  'Hisher and **loffer**.'

**LOSS**, *to lose.*  Apparently a noun used as a verb, but an *infin.* and *pres.* are wanting, from which the *pret.* and *part.* 'lost,' has been formed 'lossed' itself, unless preserved in pres. word.

> 'Hoo badly off wad wimin be
>  If they sud **loss** all t' men.'—*Bla.*, p. 16.

*Goth.* Liusan; *A. S.* losian, *to lose*; *Dut.* verliezen; *Ger.* verlieren.

**LOWE**, *a flame*; *O. N.* **Log, logi**; *Dan.* **lue**; *Swed.* **låga**, *A. S.* lig, *a flame*; *Gr.* luchnos (*Cur. Sk.*).

**LOWE**, *to burn, flame*; *O. N.* **Loga**; *Swed.* **låga**, *to burn with a flame*; *Swed.* 'Elden begynner **laga** up,' the fire begins to *flame* (*Serenius*), or as would be said in the same words on the Pennine Hills, 'The Eldin begins to **lowe** up.'

**LOWN, LOWND**, *calm*; *O. N.* **Laun**, *hidden, secret*; 'laun stígr,' *a secret path*; 'laun vagr,' *sheltered creek*; laun contr. for laugn; **logn**, *calm, tranquil*; *Swed.* lugn; *Dan.* luun, lune.  **Lownd** places, *sheltered, low lying.*

**LOWSE**, *to loosen*; *O. N.* lausn, *release*, and lausnari, *a releaser*, indicate a verb [**lausna**] *to release.*  To **lowse** a horse out of a cart.

**LOWSE**, *loose*; *O. N.* **Lauss**, *loose.*

**LU'WARM**, *lukewarm.*

**LUGS**, *ears* of a dog, horse, &c. ; *O. N.* **Lögg**, a ledge, rim, margin; a small square piece *cut out of the ears* of sheep to mark them.  Atk. *Cl. Gl.* gives '*Pot-lugs*, the *perforated ears* of metal rising above the edge or brim of the pot, and receiving the ends of the movable bow or kelps.'  Cleas., however, makes lög mark = a *lawful* mark on sheep.  It is, however, open to question, whether lög-mark does not = löggmark, not '*law-mark*' but '*ear-mark*,' for we find *Russ.* **slyche** (pron. slooche), *an ear*, which is probably the parent word.

# M.

**MAD**, *angry.*  'Ah was **mad**.'  I was angry.—*Colloq.*

**MAAIDE**, *made.*

**MADDLED**, *confused*; *A. S.* **Madelod**, *pp.* of madelian, *to discourse*, and so 'to get confused.'

**MADDLE**, *v., gabble, prate*; *A. S.* **Madelian**, *to speak, talk, prate, gabble* (*see* MAWNED).

**MAIN**, *n., the greater part*; *A. S.* **Mægen, mægn**, *main, body.*  'T'main of t'day.'  The greater part of the day.—*Bla.*

**MAINLY**, *for the most part.*  'We **mainly** taks wer tea aboot this tahm.' —*Colloq.*

**MAIR**, *more*; *O. N.* **Meiri**, *Dan.* **meer, mere**, *more.*  From Lofthouse upwards, but at Pateley 'marr.'  Thus on p. 73, I took down from the mouth of the narrator, ' I'll *wark* na **mair**; but Mr. Thorpe gave it in its Pateley form, ' Ah'll *work* na marr,'—' wark ' is pron. like ' bark.'

**MAISTER,** *husband, master*; *O.Fr.* **Maistre,** *Wel.* **meistr,** from *Lat.* magister. Many years ago, the late Mr. Bury, having been promised the living of Burnsall on its becoming vacant, thought in the meantime he would like to see the place. On reaching the garden gate, he saw an old woman at work among the pea sticks, and enquired, ' Is your master at home?' She, not at all offended, replied that he was; for she was used to hearing her husband called her 'maister.' This story I had from the late Vicar, in 1869.

**MAK,** *make*; *O. N.* **Maka,** *A. S.* macian, *to make.*

' In joye yt **maks** our mirthe abounde.'
—*To the Lute in Music,* l. 7, temp. Hen. VIII.

**MALLY,** *Molly.*

**MANDERS, MANTHERS,** *manners*; *O.Fr.* **Maniere;** *th,* pron. soft, like *th* in ' this,' and *d* are a corruption of the *ni* sound. A blundering attempt to pronounce the liquid. ' Sin then ah've been donned in all **manders** o' things.'— *Bla.,* p. 25. ' It's sported all **manthers** o' cullers bud blue.'—*Ib.* p. 43.

**MANISH,** *manage*; comp. ' poddish' *porridge*; ' hish,' *high.* ' Ah felt as if ah cud **manish** a taaiste o' sum soart.'—*Al.,* 1880.

**MAR, MARR,** *more.*

**MARRY,** *indeed, forsooth*; *O.Fr.* **Marie**—an expression belonging to Roman Catholic times. ' Noa, nut I, **marry!**'—*Colloq.*

**MASALGIN,** *a mixture* of rye and wheat; *O.Fr.* **Mestillon,** from *Lat.* miscellanea; but in this *Dial.* word the *Lat.* form is better preserved than it is in the *Fr.* mestillon, mesteil, *Mod.* mêteil, *muslin* (*Bra.*); metail, measling or masslin (*Cot.,* 1650); *Guel.* maslaim, maislean. ' If the land be of that sort which they call maumy, it is commonly sown with all sorts of wheat, miscellan, barley,' &c. (*Plot, Nat. Hist. of Oxfordshire,* c. 9, p. 245). ' Beans, wheat, miscellan, barley and pease in their order.'—*Ib.,* § 61. Wanting in *Ital.,* but ' mescolato' is *mixed,* and in *Span.* mesolado = maslin. *Fr.* metail = *Eng.* ' metal.'

**MAWN,** *A. S.* **Mánian,** *to exhort, remind, &c.,* see MADDLED.

' He **mawned** and maddled all aboot
His daddy cumin heame.'—*Bla.,* p. 16.

*i.e.,* he kept on *reminding,* or *mentioning* and chattering about, &c. *A. S.* mánian, *to remind,* passes into mænan, *to have in the mind, to remember, to remind,* and that into mænan, *to moan, complain*; *Swab.* maunen, *to speak* with the mouth nearly shut; maunzen, *to speak* in a whining tone.

**ME,** *my*; *O. N.* **Minn,** mín, mit, *my*; *Dan.* min neut. mit, *my.*

**MEEAD,** *made.*

**MEEAN,** *mane*; *O. N.* **Mön,** *Wel.* mwng, *mane*; mwn, *the neck*; *Gael.* muing, muidh, muinnidh, *mane.*

**MEEAR,** *mare*; *A. S.* **Mearh,** mearg, mear, *a horse, steed* (*Bos.*); *O. N.* marr; *O. H. G.* marah, *a horse*; *O. N.* merr, *a mare.*

**MEBBE,** *may be.*

**MENSE,** *decency*; *O. N.* **Mennskr,** *human*; *Swed.* menniska, *Dan.* menneske, *A. S.* **mennisc,** *O. H. G.* mennesco, mennisk; *M. H. G.* mannisk, *Ger.* mensch, *Netherl.* minsk. Of a cradle, ' My mother she charged me to clean it for **mense.**'—*Bla.,* p. 43. Of a drunkard, ' He's lost baith sense an' **mense.**'

**MESEL,** *myself*; *Dan.* **Mig,** *me, myself*; mig-selv.

' I'll fetch yond pedlars back **mysell.**'—*Sir Andrew Barton,* pt. 2, l. 44.

**MESEN,** *myself* (*see* SEN).

**MEZZER,** *measure*; *O.Fr.* **Mesure,** from *Lat.* mensura; *A. S.* mæth.

'Be his mæthe.'—*A. S. Laws*, freq.   O. Fr. pron. distinctly preserved, though somewhat mutilated.

**ME'Y**, *my*.  'Me'y fewt, an me'y noose, an me'y mooth.'—*Bla.*, p. 34.

**ME'Y**, *me*; *Dan.* **Mig**, *me*.  'It winnat dew me'y a farden's worth o' gud.'

**MICH**, *much* (see MITCH).

**MICKLE**, *much, great*; *O. N.* **Mykill, mikill**; *A. S.* **mycel, micel**, *great*; *Gr.* megas.  'Gif seó micele tá bith ofaslagen,' if the *big* toe be cut off.—*Laws of Ælfred*, c. 40.  'On tham miclan synod,' at the *great* synod.'—*Laws of Æthelstan*, c. 26.  'That did Sir Andrew mickle scare.'—*Sir And. Barton*, pt. 2, l. 54.

**MINCH**, *mince*; *O. Fr.* **Mince, mynsser**, *to mince*, prob. from *Russ.* smyagchate, *to mince*, with 'cockney' *Russ.* koochnya, *kitchen*, and several other words relating to cookery.

**MIND**, *to remember*; *A. S.* **Mynan**, *to remember*.  'Ah maind this or that.'—*Colloq.*

**MISTAL**, *pigsty or cowshed*; *O. N.* **Myki.** *dung*; **stallr**, *stall*; *Dan.* **mög**, *muck*; **stald**, *stall, stable*; *Ger.* **mist**, *dung* (see also p. 80).

**MITCH**, *much*.

**MON**, *man*; *A. S.* **Mon**, *man*.  'Gif mon othrum steow asette,' if *one* trespass on another's place.—*Laws of Hlothær*, 12.  'Thonne mon monnan betýhth,' when mon indicteth mon.'—*Laws of Ine*, 46.

**MONNY**, *many*.

**MOORGAM**, *moor-game, grouse*.

**MOORPOOTS**, *peewits*.  Poot = poult, Fr. poulet (*Brock.*), but (?).  The common peewit is called **pew-it**, which contracts into **pewt, poot**.

**MOOTH**, *mouth*.

**MOSSCROPS**, *cotton grass* (see p. 10), called 'mosscrops and cut-throats,' or 'moorsilk' (*Eriophorum*).  It is this which figures so gracefully in Macpherson's *Ossian. Cathlota*, Duan. 2 :—
'If on the heath she moved her breast was whiter than the down of Cana.'

**MOUD, MOWD**, *mould*.

**MOUDHILLS**, *molehills*.

**MOUDYWARP**, *mole*; *Icel.* **Mold-varpa**; *A. S.* **molde-wyrp**, *the mould caster*; *O. N* verpa, varpa; *A. S.* weorpan, *to cast up*; *Goth.* (*Ulf.*) wairpan, *Dut.* werpen, *O. H. G.* werfan, *Ger.* werfen, *to cast*.

**MUCK**, *dirt, mud*; *O. N.* **Myki**, *Dan.* mög.  ''Tis mookie,' is said of any muddy road or place.

**MUD**, *might*; *A. S.* **Mót**, *can, may, might*; comp. 'bud' for 'but,' &c.  'Bud let me come heame seun or late as ah mud,'—*Bla.*, p. 36.

**MUG**, *a Leicester tup or ram*; *A. S.* **Muga**, *a ball, heap*, as they are called 'tup' from *O. N.* tupt or tuft (see TUP, also p. 7).

**MUN**, *must*; *O. N.* **Man**, *pres.* mun, *imperf.* of munu, *must, will, shall.*

'I ween but thou mun die.'—*Sir Cauline*, l. 93.

And in the beautiful lines in Hamilton's *Braes of Zanors*:—

> 'Lang maun she weep, lang maun she, maun she, weep,
>    Lang maun she weep with dule and sorrow,
> And lang maun I nae mair weil be seen
>    Puing birks on the Braes of Yarrow.'

**MURN**, *mourn*; *A. S.* **Murnan**; murnende, *mourning* (*Boet.*, 3).

**MURNING**, *mourning*; *A. S.* **Murnung**.

**MYSEL**, *myself*; *Dan.* **Mig**, **selv** (see MESEL).

'Yes, I may tell, and fret mysell.'—*The Auld Good Man*, l. 33.

# N.

**NA,** *no*; *Wel.* **Na.**

**NAAINE,** *none, not.* 'Ah's **naaine** mitch up on her cummin here.'—
*Al.*, 1880.

**NAANINE,** *none, not*; *A. S.* **Nænigne,** contr. from *ne ænigne, not any.*
' & mon **nænigne** mon on thæt ne sýlle.'—*Laws of Ælfred,* c. 10, also c. 18.
'She's **naanine** ower honist.'—*Al.*, 1880.

**NANGIN,** *gnawing*; *Gael.* **Cnamh,** *to gnaw.*

> ' T' biggest pleasure, lang endurin,
>     Wad becum a **nangin** pain.'—*Bla.*, in *Al.*, 1880.

**NANPIE,** *magpie*; *Wel.* **Piog, pia, pi**; pioden, *a piannet, magpie*; *Gael.*
pigheid. 'Mag' and 'nan,' prefixed to the Celtic name, give magpie and nanpie.

**NAR,** *near*; *O. N.* **Ná,** *Dan.* nœr, *Swed.* när. '**Nar** Sleet,' the name of a
field below Middlesmoor.

**NATTERIN,** *peevish, cross, &c.*; *Dan.* **Gnaddre,** *Swed.* **gnata,** *to grumble*;
*Dan. Dial.* **gnaddrig,** *fretful, peevish*; *Swed. Dial.* gnataktig, gnatiger, gnatuger,
gnetuger, gnatu, *peevish*; gnater, gneter, *a natterer* (*Atk. Cl. Gl.*); *Gr.* knaō,
knaiō, *to scrape or grate*; knēthō, *to scratch, to provoke or excite*; knaptō, *to comb
or card wool*; *later Attic,* 'gnaptō.' 'Ah see an hear eneaf o flitin **natterin**
wimin adoot bein tied to yan . . . that dov I.'—*Al.*, 1880.

**NATERABLE,** *natural.*

**NATUR,** *nature, essence, essential qualities.* 'It's took all the **natur** out
of it.'

**NAY,** *no*; *O. N.* **Nei,** *Wel.* na, *Gael.* ni, *Dan.* and *Swed.* nei, *Goth.* ne,
*Ger.* nein.

**NEEAN, NEEA,** *no*; *Goth.* **Niu,** *O. N.* neinn, *A. S.* næn, nen, nin,
*none*; contr. from *ne, ean, not one.* '**Nea** matter to what he wer yooaked.'—
*Bla.*, p. 13.

**NEAF,** *fist*; *O. N.* **Hnefi,** *the fist*; *Swed.* näfve, *Dan.* nœve.

**NEÄK,** *nick, nook*; *O. N.* **Hnjúkr.** '**Neäk**' is a Ramsgill form (*see* pp. 92
and 113, also **Newk**).

**NEÄN,** *nine*; *Goth.* **Niun,** *A. S.* nigon, *Dut.* negen, *Swed.* nio, *Dan.* ni,
*Ger.* neun, *Gael.* naoinear, naoi, nao.

**NEAR,** *stingy*; *O. N.* **Nœr,** *close, sharp.* A man who has money, and is
careful of it, is said to be 'near.' (*Dan.* nœrig, *Swed.* närig, *Atk., Cl. Gl.*)

**NEARHAND,** *near, nearly*; *Dan.* **Nœrhaand,** *A. S.* neah-hand, *near.*
A common expression in Niddersdale.

> ' Makine, adieu, the sun goes west,
>     The day is **neirhand** gane.'
>                     —*Robin and Makyne,* l. 52 (printed 1568).

**NEATHER,** *nearer*; *A. S.* **Neheh,** *near*, would form a *compar.* nehehra,
which guttural may be repres. by '**neather.**' Only those who know the bleak
four miles round Greenhow Hill can appreciate all that is expressed in the line,

> ' Ah wish the'y wark laid **neather** heame.'—*Bla.*, p. 15.

*Goth.* (*Ulf.*) nehw, *near*; nehwis, *nearer.*

**NEEAWHAR,** *nowhere*; *A. S.* **Náwar, náhwær.** 'He'd nivver been
**neeawhar** fra heeame.'—*Bla.*, p. 13. When I was at Lofthouse in 1871, it
was said that there was an old woman up there who had never been out of the
dale, not even climbed the sides to look over. I remember a man in possession
of a good farm, whose age was 60 years, who had never slept but two nights out
of the house, and those two nights not together, and who had never been farther

than Ripon. Formerly there were plenty who never moved from home from the cradle to old age.

**NEEBER, NEABER,** *neighbour*; *A. S.* **Neah gebúr, neahbúr.**

**NEET,** *night*; *A. S.* **Neaht, neht.** 'Siththan ane **neaht**,' after one night.' —*L. Hlothær*, 10. ' Yah **neet**,' one night.—*Colloq.*

**NEB,** *beak*; *A. S.* and *Dut.* **Neb,** *Dan.* **nœb,** *Swed.* **näbb,** *O. N.* **nef.** 'Gif mon othrum thæt **neb** ofaslea,' If a man cut off another's *nose*.—*L. Ælfred*, c. 40. At Lodge (1871), a bird caught in a brick trap was said to have been 'caught by its little **neb**.' Connected with NEAF, NIP, NEP.

**NEKT,** *naked*; *O. N.* **Nekt,** *nakedness.*

**NEPPIN,** *nipping, cropping grass* (see KNEP).

**NESHT,** *next.* As with 'HISHER' and other words given in this Glossary, the 'sh' in **nesht** represents a guttural found in *Ger.* **Nächst,** lost in *O. N.* **næst,** *Swed.* **näst,** *Dan.* **noest,** *Dut.* **naast, naaste**; *A. S.* **nexst,** *next.*

**NEWK,** *nook*; *O. N.* **Hnjúkr,** *a knob, peak, eminence.* At Lodge and *locality*, as distinguished from NEAK at Ramsgill. Near Lodge is a high field, named 'Bewtcher Newking'='Butcher's *ridge-field*'—portion of the ridge (see pp. 92 and 113).

**NIP,** *pinch*; *Dut.* **Nijpen, Knijpen.** The ramifications of this root are most various, *e.g.*, *O. N.* **hneppa,** *to cut short*; *O. H. G.* **knyppen, nippen,** *to snap the fingers*; *Ger.* **kneipen,** *Swed.* **niupa,** *Dan.* knibe, *Russ.* shchěpoke, *to nip* (see NEAF, NEB, NEP).

> ' But ever shee droopeth in her mind
> As, **nipt** by an ungentle winde,
> Doth some faire lillye flowre.'—*Sir Cauline*, 2, 39.

**NIVVER,** *never*; *A. S.* **Næfre,** contr. from ne, sefer.

**NOBBUT,** *only.* ' It's **nobbut** us'= not but.

**NODDLE,** *head* (slang); *O. E.* nodile, 'nodil, nodle.'—*Prompt.*, 357. *Wel.* cna, *that is rounded*; *O. N.* hnúdr, *a knob, ball*; hnoda, *a clew*; *Icel.* hnod, *a rivet-head*; *Dan.* knude, *a knot,* and many others; *Lat.* nodus, for gnodus; *Gr.* gnathos, *a tooth.*

**NOO,** *now*; *O. N.* **Nú,** *Dan.* nu; *O. N.* 'Sommeren er **nu** over' (in *Cleas.*); *Goth.* nu, *Dut.* nu, *Ger.* nuh, nun; *Gr.* nûn, *Lat.* nunc.

**NOOSE,** *nose*; *O. N.* **Nös,** *A. S.* nosu; *Swed.* näsa, *Dan.* nœse, *Ger.* nase, *Russ.* and *Eng.* nose, *Dut.* neus.

**NOPE,** *a blow*, properly the *effects* of a blow, *a lump*; *O. N.* knappr, *a knob*; hnappr, *a button*; *Gael.* and *Wel.* cnap, *a knob*; *A. S.* cnæp, *Ger.* knopf, *Dut.* knop, *Eng.* knob; *Wel.* cnipws, *a fillip* with the finger; *Dut.* nópen, *to spur, prick, encourage.*

**NOR,** *than*; *Gael.* **Na,** *Wel.* no, *than.* 'Bigger **nor** me.'—*Bla.* p. 36.

**NOWT,** *nothing*; *A. S.* naht, contr. from ná-wuht, ná-wiht; no-whit, *not a whit.* 'Gif other eare **nawiht** gehereth,' if the other with his ears **nowt** heareth.—*L. Æthelbert*, 40 (561-616). '**Nawiht** on thæm wite.'—*L. Æthelstan*, 21 (924-940). 'Ac se Abbot nolde thæs **naht**,' but the Abbot would have **nowt** of it.—*Sax. Chron.*, 1083. 'Haveth he **nout** of Walingford oferlyng,' he has **nowt** of the Wallingford honours ('overling,' opposed to 'underling ').—*Rich. of Almaigne*, l. 10. 'When they had ascertained his liabilities they ass'd him what his assets amoontid tew. He said, "**Nowt.**"'—*Al.*, 1880. ' Liza may say it's gud, bud ah reckon **nowt** on't.'—*Ib.*

**NUT,** *not.* A further contr. of 'nowt.' Nawuht, naught, naht, nowt, **nut,** not. 'T' moor's **nowt** like itsen.'—*Bla.*, p. 39. 'A thing at's **nut** reet.'— *Ib.*, p. 13.

# O.

**OADE, OWD,** *old*; *Dut.* **Oud.** 'Een oud man'='an owd man,' 'eene oude vrouw'='an oade ooman.'

**OFT,** *often*; *O. N.* **Opt, oft**; *A. S.* **oft,** *Goth.* (*Ulf.*) **ufta,** *Swed.* **ofta,** *Dan.* **ofte.** 'Se cýrlisce man the **oft** betogen were thyfthe,' the rustic man who has been **oft** accused of theft.—*L. Ine,* c. 37 (688-728).

'**T' OADE MAN,**' or 'the old man,' *i.e.* 'the old *mine.* *Gael.* **Méin, méinn, meun,** *a mine, mineral;* *Wel.* **maen,** *a stone, mineral;* **màn,** *a space, what holds or contains.* The lead miners of Greenhow on striking into old workings underground say they have come upon 'the old **man,**' which is clearly the old *mine,* as shown above, but this being forgotten they sometimes express the same by saying 'the old **man** has been there.'

**ONT,** *aunt*; *O. Fr.* **Ante.**

**ONNY, ONY,** *any*; *A. S.* **ánig,** as 'any,' from 'ænig.'

**ONNYWERES,** *anywhere.*

**ONTUV,** *on to.* 'To mak back at neet **ontuv** Hardcastle Moor.'—*Bla.,* p. 39.

**OOR,** *our*; *A. S.* **úre,** *our,* would suggest an unaccented form [ure]; *Goth.* **unsar.**

**OOT,** *out*; *O. N.* **út.**

**OP,** *up*; *Dan.* and *Dut.* **Op.**

**OPPEN,** *open*; *O. N.* **Opinn.**

**OUT, OWT,** *anything, ought, aught*; *A. S.* **out,** contr. from **awuht, awiht,** *a whit.* 'Oththe his landes **awuht,**' owt of his land.—*L. Ælfred, Introd.* 26. 'Minra **awuht** feala,' my *somewhat* numerous.—*Laws,* Ib. 'Nage heo his yrfes **awuht,**' she has not *a whit* of his estate.—*L. Ælf,* c. 8. 'Wordes ne weorces **owiht** dón,' by word or deed to do **owt.**—*L. Æthelst.,* pt. 2, c. 2. 'And gif ther is **out** to eadwiten,' and if there is **owt** to blame.—*Ancren Riwle,* pt. IV. 'Ah like it far better nor **owt** at's i t' hoose.'—*Bla.,* p. 42.

**OUT, OWT,** *ought, should.* 'Ought 'for 'owed.' 'Proud he **owt** to feel hissen.'

**OV,** *on*; *Dut.* **Over,** *of, about, upon, &c.* 'Fer they'd seeame reight as us up **ov** Hardcastle Moor.'

**OWER,** *over*; *A. S.* **Ouer.**—*Sax. Chron.,* 1137. 'Comin **ower** t' moor,' '**ower** neet,' 'gie **ower,**' *leave off,* &c., are common colloq.

'She wor awlus ageeat, an' scarce ivver gav **ower.**'—*Bla.,* p. 37.

# P.

*Grimm* VI.—*Goth.* P = *O. H. G.* Ph. or f; *Gr., Lat., Celt., Slav.* B; *Sans.* B or V.

---

**PALLY,** *Polly*—as a place name, 'Pally's Crags.'

**PARK,** *an enclosure, field for horses,* in Coverdale (*see* pp. 32, 34).

**PASHY,** *wet underfoot*; *Ger.* **Patsche,** *sludge, mud.*

'T'weather's been **pashy** this spring.'—*Bla.,* p. 21.

**PASTOOR,** *pasture*; *O. Fr.* **Pasture** (*Cot.*). The *O. Fr.* pron. is well preserved at Lodge, and generally near the Dalehead (*see* p. 31).

**PATE,** *the badger.* The *Gael.* is broc, brochd; *O. N.* brokkr (?), *Dan.* brok, *Wel.* broch, *Eng. Dial.* brock, *Mod. Gr.* trochos (*Swed.* gräfling, *Dut.* das, *Ger.* dachs). 'Pate' is a very local name, 'brock' being the usual word. 'Pate,' *the* *badger*, does, I believe, give its name to 'Pateley,' which used to be spelt 'Pait-ley.' I cannot find any source or origin for the name of 'pate,' meaning the *badger*, in any of the languages contributing to this Dialect. Guided by the well-established case of 'peat,' from 'bete,' I am led to identify the 'bad' in 'badger' with 'pate'; but what is 'badger'? (1.) *Wel.* **Baedd,** *a boar* = **Pate**; baeddu, *to wallow; to tumble about in the dirt;* **baeddwr,** one who *tumbles about in the dirt* = 'badger'; *Fr.* bedoüe, bedouer. (2.) **Pate,** *might* = *Fr.* **Bête,** as 'peat' = 'bete'; but I think the former explanation preferable in the absence of positive evidence, and because the latter does not explain 'badger' at the same time. The 'pate' is now extinct—for an account of the last *see* INTROD. (3.) *Note.* 'Bite, *a fox*,' among gypsies on Mitcham Common (1880).

**PEAT,** *peat*; *A. S.* Bétan, *to better, to improve*; bétan fýr, *to mend or repair* a fire (*Bos.*); *O. E.* béten, *O. Fris.* béta, *O. N.* bœta. 'Fíres béte.'—Chauc. *Cant. Tales*, 2,253. 'A brighte fír wel bett.'—*Sir Perceval.* 'Thornton Romances.' Yorks, early 15th cent. (*Stratm.*). 'Bete the fire,' gave the name of 'betes,' or 'peats' to the sods with which the fire was 'beted' (*Wedg.*); *Gael.* foid.

**PEAT-CREEL,** *a basket for holding peats*, which stands in the room.

**PEWDER,** *pewter*; *Gael.* peòdar, pleodar; *Dut.* peauter, speauter (*Spelter*); *Icel.* piátr, *Low. Lat.* peutreum, *O. Fr.* peutre (*Bra.*), *Ital.* peltro, *Span.* peltre.

'**PIN-FOLD,**' a *pound*; *A. S.* Pinn, *a penn, pound.* '"Pund" and "pound," from the "pin" of the ancients, whence "pinfold."'—Wilkins *Gloss. to A. S. Laws. s. v.* Pundbrece.

**PLEEACE,** *place*; *A. S.* **Plæce** occurs in the Cotton MS. of the Gospels, written about A.D. 900. The A. S. was interlined between the Lat., which was written about 680 (*Somner*). We cannot therefore have taken our word straight from the Fr. as is commonly represented. *Lat.* platea, *Span.* plaza, *Ital.* piazza, *Fr.* place, *Wel.* plâs.

**PLEAF,** *plough*, at Ramsgill.

**PLIF,** or **PLEW,** or **PLEUGH,** *plough*, at Lodge. With **plif** and **pleaf** compare *Dan.* plov; with **plew, pleugh,** *A. S.* plou. *O. N.* plógr, *Swed.* plog, *O. Dut.* plog, ploug; *Dut.* ploeg. *Russ.* plyge (ploog), *O. H G.* ploh, phluog; *M. H. G.* phluoc, pfluoc; *Gr.* pflug; *Gr.* ploion, *to sail*; *Sans.* plava. 'Sulh' is the word used in the A. S. Laws, 'plough' never. In *O. N.* arthr is the genuine word, according to Cleasby. Nor is plough *Goth.*, for Ulf. uses hoha, *hoe*—something like the breast-plough of the Cotswolds probably. Plough is therefore *O. H. G.*, probably from the *Russ.* Sulh, the *A. S.* word—*Pers.* kulba, *a plough*; *Lat.* sulcus, *a furrow*—is still in use in Somerset.

**PODDISH,** *porridge*; *O. Fr.* Potage, *pottage.* **Poddish** is nearer the parent form than 'porridge.'

**POODER,** *powder*; *O. Fr.* Puldre, *Fr.* poudre; formerly poldre, originally puldre, from *Lat.* pulver (*Bra.*), *Dut.* poeder, poeijer, pulver; *Ger.* pulver. Fr. pron. well preserved.

**PORE,** *poker.* I suppose Po'er, like brea'r, briar, from breaker (*see* p. 25).

**PRETHA,** *prithee.* I pray thee.

# Q.

**QUALITY,** 'gentlemen,'— too often flash persons wholly unworthy to buckle the shoes of the Dalespeople, some of whom annually look forward to the grouse season, 'when t'quality cums up t'Daäl.'

# R.

**RAKE,** *n.* (1.) The *line of heaps* on the surface, made by working a lead vein; the heaps on the 'back of a lode.' The *Pers.* (and *Hind.*) **Rak,** *a row or line*; *Russ.* **draka,** *Dan.* **række,** *a row*; *O. N.* rakr, *straight*; rak, *the rakings of hay* in a field; *Atk. Cl. Gl.* gives RAITCH, *a white line* down a horse's face (also Hall). (2.) *A footpath, Pers.* **rak,** *a row or line*; rãh, *a road, way*; *O. N.* **rekstr,** *a beaten track,* originally that made by a drove of sheep or cattle. (3.) A 'sheep-rake,'* *sheep-track.* Huntley (*Cotswold Gloss.*) gives 'RACK, *a path*, chiefly applied to the paths made by hares; *Dut.* **racke,** *a track*.' I find *Dut.* **rak,** *a part of the road.* We have ' een goed **rakje,** 'a good *part of the road* behind us.—*Holtrop.* 'At Buckden,' writes Mr. Dakyns, 'we have "**Rakes** Wood," a wood through which goes the *old straight road* which is itself called "Buckden **Rake.**"' **Rake**=road, in *Sir Gawayne*, Lancash., about 1360. Also Alex., 3384, ' Out of the **rake** of rightwisness renne suld he nevire.'—*Stratm.* 4. *A dog's name.* ? *O. N.* **reki,** *driver* (see p. 13 and *Erratum* to ditto).

**RAKE,** *v.* (1.) Sheep on the moors are said to ' **rake out,**' when they form single file, as they do on being first disturbed. 'To **rake in row,**' in the passage—

> ' But keip my sheip undir yon wod;
> Lo quhair they **raik** on raw.'—*Robin & Makyne*, l. 12.

*Gael.* **rach,** *to go, walk, travel*; *O. N.* **rekja,** *to spread out,* unfold; *Goth.* **rakjan,** *to reach, stretch*; **rikan,** *to reach, collect, heap up*; *Dut.* reiken, *Swed.* räcka, *Dan.* roekke, *Ger.* reichen, *Lat.* rego, *Gr.* orego, *Gael.* rùig, *to reach*; *O. N.* **reika,** *to wander, walk,* in a *wavering, unsettled manner*, as sheep. 'To raik on raw.' (2.) *To drive*; *Gael.* ruaig, *O. N.* **raka,** originally vreka (*Cleas.*), *to drive, to wander*; *Wel.* rhacu, *to put forward, to advance, to take the lead*; *Goth.* (*Ulf.*) wrikan, wrakjan, *to persecute*; *Dut.* wreken, *A. S.* wrecan, *Eng.* wreak, *O. H. G.* rechan, *Ger.* rächen, *Swed.* vräka, *Dan.* vrage, *Lat.* urgere (*Cleas. Skeat.*).

**RAM,** *adj., stinking, fetid, offensive*; *O. N.* **Ramr,** *strong, bitter, &c.*, *Dan.* **ram.**

**RAMPS,** *garlic*; *A. S.* **Hramse** (? meaning), *Swed.* **rams,** *garlic*, prob. from the *O. N.* **ram,** *neut.* ramt, *bitter, strong*, like an onion. **Ramtgras** (*Elucidarium*, 141, in Cleas), is no doubt *garlic.* Somner, followed by Bos. renders *A. S.* **hramse, hromse,** by ' Henbane,' *but* ? (*see* BELLONED). ' Ramsgill ' may take its name from **rams,** *garlic*, which is freq. in the woods, covering the ground like a carpet, to the exclusion of all other plants.

**RANDOM,** the *direction* of a lead vein. ' We're following the **random** now,' used by the miners of Greenhow Hill.

**RANG,** *wrong*; *O. N.* **Rangr,** *A. S.* **wrang.**—*Sax. Chron.*, A.D. 1124.

**RANNELBOAK,** *beam* in the old chimney; *O. N.* **Rann,** *the house*; bálkr, *beam*; ranns-bálkr, *house-beam* (*see* pp. 21-24).

**RATTEN,** *a rat*; *Gael.* **Radan;** *a water rat*, ' radan uisge.' *O. N.* rotta, with *def. art.* **rotta-inn;** *Dan.* rotte, with *def. art.* **rotten;** or *Swed.* ratta, rotta, with *def. art.* **rotten,** might indeed be the source of the Gaelic word, especially when we have regard to the history of the Norwegian rat, which has spread from thence. *A. S.* ræt, *O. H. G.* rato, *Ger.* ratte, ratze; *Fr.* rat. The *Prompt. Parv.* has ratun or ratón.

**RAY** enters into several place names up dale, of which instances are given p. 82, with a suggestion as to meaning of **ray.** Since printing that sheet, however, I find that **rae** is *Gael.* for *a pasture* (*see* Introductory Commentary).

---

* Sheep-rakes—In Sweden, Ulleráker, lit. ' Wool-rakes,' formerly a realm of Sweden, in the present Province of Westmanland. There is still a village so called (*Frithiof.*, cant. 3, note p. 48). With this compare ' Flock Rake,' now enclosed, on plateau 1,700 feet, east of Malham Tarn; where ' flock,' however, may be *O. N.* **Flaki,** *an elevated flat moor* (p. 92).

**REEAN=REIN,** *a strip of grass* left unploughed around a ploughed field; but *see* Study VIII., pp. 60-68.

**REEAST,** *rest*; *A. S.* Reost, ræst, rest, *rest.*

**REEASTED,** *restive, fresh, skittish.* I think this must be *A. S.* **Rested,** *pp.* of restian, restan, hrestan, *to rest*—'**rested,**' therefore ' eager.' ' Ay, Shoo's reästed, thoo mun let her gan oop t'bank a bit, t' tak t'joomp oot of her.'—*Colloq.*

**REEATS,** *roots.* ' T'tree-reats.'

**RECKLING,** *the youngest* or *smallest of a brood* of chickens, ducks, &c.; *O. N.* Reklingr, *Icel.* ' rekningr,' and rekingr'; *Dan.* **rekling,** *an outcast,* lit. ' the *little driven* one'; from ' reka,' *to drive.* Atk. *Cl. Gl.* finds in Kok, *S. Jutland,* vrássel, vrásling, for vrágsel, vrágsling, in the same sense as above. Kok quotes Outzen for vrág, vrágling (*see* p. 30).

**RECKONS,** *toothed sticks,* now of iron, on which the pothooks are hung. *Wel.* **Rhignez,** *a notched stick* (*Ow.*). The ' reckons' hang on the ' swape' or ' beak' (p. 20), which Atk. *Cl. Gl.* calls the ' reckons.' *Wel.* rhig, rhigyn, *a notch, groove.* Rhignez, *a notched* or *furrowed part* of anything, render's Atk.'s suggestion, ' Reek-airn,' ' smoke-iron,' unnecessary; moreover, ' reckons,' the ' notched stick,' probably existed ages before iron was known here.

**REDSTAKE,** *the post* in a bewce *to which the cow is tied* or fastened. *A. S.* **Wræd,** *a band, tie;* **stáca,** *a stake;* wræde, *a latch, buckle, control, handle, &c.;* ' writha,' *a band, rein, thong, bridle.* The beasts were formerly *tied up* with *twisted bands* of willow, ash or hazel, still the fastening of the COW-BOW, *q.v.;* also p. 31.

**REEK,** *n., smoke, fog* or *mist, drizzle;* *Swed.* Rök, *Dan.* rög, *Dut.* rook, *O. E.* roke, *Ger.* rauch, *smoke;* *Goth.* (*Ulf.*) rekwis, rikwiz, *darkness;* rign, *rain.*

**REEK,** *v., to smoke, to be misty;* *O. N.* rjúka, *Swed.* röka, *Dan.* röge, *to smoke;* *Ger.* riechen, *to smell;* *A. S.* reócan, récan, *to smoke;* (*Gr.* brëssō, hrëgnumi, *to break;* hrëgmin, hrëgmis, *breakers,* the ' reek' of the sea. ' Epi hrëgmïni thalassës.' *Il.,* I., 37. *Russ.* berege, *the shore;* *Eng.* breakers; *Goth.* rikwizjan, *to become dark.* ' Why it rain'd and it reekt, barn, ye nivver saw sike weather.'—B. Bailey, in Grainge's *Hist. of Nidderdale,* p. 224.

**REET,** *right;* *A. S.* Reht, riht, *right.*

**REWL,** *rule;* *A. S.* Rewl, *e.g.* ' Ancren Riwl.' The ' g' in *Lat.* **regula** must have been pronounced as ' y.'

**RID,** *to clear;* *A. S.* Riddan, *O. N.* rydja, *Dan.* rydde, *A. S.* hreddan, *to rid;* *Scot.* red or redde (*Cleas.*). On Saturday night ' all's ridded up.'

**RIDDING,** *a clearing;* *O. N.* Rjódhr, *a clearing,* open space in a forest (*Cleas.*). See RUDDING, ROYD.

**RIDDING** or **RHYDDING,** *a ford;* *Wel.* Rhŷd, rhydle, *a ford;* rhydiad, *a forming a ford;* rhydiaw, *to form a ford.*

**RIDDLE-CAKE,** *a kind of oatcake;* *Gael.* Rideal, *W.* rhidyll; *A. S.* hriddel, *a sieve, riddle.*

**RIG** (1), *back;* *O. N.* Hryggr, *Swed.* rygg, *Dan.* ryg, *A. S.* hrycg (from the *O. N.*), rig; *Russ.* kryazhe, *O. H. G.* hrucki, *Ger.* rücken, *Gr.* hrachis. The farmers never speak of a sheep's *back,* but of his '**rig.**' (2.) *A ridge,* common in names of hills; *O. N.* hryggr, Fjall-hryggr, *a mountain ridge.*

**RIGGERT,** *a close tup;* *O. N.* Ríg-gyrthr, *tight-girt,* *part.* of ríg-gyrtha, *to girth tightly, from* rígr, *stiffness.* In a R. the testicles are under the back, whence some have supposed ' rig, girt.'

**RILE,** *disturbance.* Hall. has ' RILE, *to disturb, to vex.*—East.'

  ' Froons are ruffled temper's shaddas
   Issuin' fra sum hidden **rile.**'—*Bla.,* in *Al.,* 1880.

**RIPE,** *to grub up wood, scrubs, bushes, &c.;* *A.S.* Rīpan, *to ripe or reap.* ' When " Turner Carr" was **riped** a few years ago there were brears, chewps, &c.'—*Colloq.*

**RIS'D,** *raised.* 'Ther rent'll be **ris'd.**'

**RIVE,** *tear, split;* O. N. **Riúfa, rifa;** *Swed.* **rifva;** *Dan.* **rive,** *to rip up.*

**ROVEN,** *torn;* O. N. **Rofinn,** *part.* of do. '**Roven** up to the grain.'— p. 108.

**ROAT,** *bray* of an ass; *Gael.* **Raoic,** *a bellow, roar,* the voice of a deer; *Wel.* **rhoch,** *a grunt;* hence *Fr.* ruit, rut; *Eng.* rut, 'the **rutting** season'; *Swiss,* rüden, *to bellow;* *Ger.* ranzen, *to rut;* rauschen, *to roar;* *Bret.* ruda, *to be on heat;* *Gael.* rnoichd, *to bell* as a deer, *to roar;* *Wel.* rhochain, *to grunt* like swine; rochi, *to grunt, to growl;* *Dut.* ruchelen, *to bray, grunt.* ' Pooer Jerry' [to his donkey] 'to which Jerry replied wi' a **roat** at wad hev alarmed onnybody bud his maister.'—*Al.,* 1880.

**ROWANTREE,** *mountain ash;* O. N. **Reynir,** *Swed.* **rön,** *Dan.* **rönne,** *Lat.* ornus, *Goth.* runa, O. N. rún, *a mystery, a written character;* raun, *a trial, experiment,* and reyna, *to experience,* are all kindred. The original notion is scrutiny, mystery (*Cleas.*). R. so called from being supposed to contain a magic power against witches (Carr., *Crav. Gloss.,* and Atk. *Cl. Gl.*).

**ROOAD,** *road.*

**ROOSE,** *rush on to ruin;* A. S. **Hreósan,** *to rush, waver, fall;* O. N. hrjósa, *to shudder;* *Swed.* rysa; *Wel.* **rhwysaw,** *to flourish, wanton;* rhwys, *adj., vigorous, wanton;* rhwys, *n., vigor, wantonness;* rhwy, *that runs out, excess.* The word is therefore from the *Wel.* in the sentence, 'The rich may romp an **roose** away.'—*Blu.,* p. 9.

**ROYD,** *a clearing in a wood;* O. N. **Rjódhr** (*see* RIDDING, RUDDING).

**RUCKLE,** *a stack of peats* on the moors (p. 119). '**Ruckle,**' 'little rick.' *Gael.* **ruchdan,** *a little conical rick* of hay or corn. '**Ruchd,** a conical rick of hay or corn' (*Armstr.*). This is exactly the shape of the ' peat ruckles.' *A. S.* hreac, *a rick;* O. N. hrúga. On the moors as a place name, 'High **Ruckles.**'

**RUDDING,** *a clearing;* O. N. **Rud,** *a clearing in a wood;* with *def. art.* inn, rudinn, *the clearing.* Ormerod = ' Orme's *clearing*' (*see* RIDDING and ROYD). ' Rudd' occurs as a place name, and as a man's name.

**RUDDLE,** *red paint* for marking sheep; *Wel.* **Rhuzell,** *red ochre* or ruddle; rhydlyd, *rusty;* rhwd, *rust,* rhwdawg, *rusty;* **rhwzeli,** *a red salve;* O. N. **ryd,** *rust;* rydga, *to become rusty;* *Goth.* rauds, *Dut.* rood, *Ger.* roth, *red.*

**REW, RUE,** *to repent;* A. S. **Hreówan, reówan,** *to repent, rue;* hreówsian, reówsian, *to be sorry for, to grieve for* (*Bos.*); O. N. **hryggja,** *to be grieved,* also *to grieve;* A. S. 'Mid sóthre **hreowe,**' with true *penitence.*—*Canons, Eadg.,* ' Be Bétan,' c. 18.

> ' And thow hast brent Northomberlond
> Full sore it **reweth** me.'—*Otterb.,* l. 44.

> 'Sair, sair, I **rew** the deed.'—Ld. Barnard, in *Gill Morrice,* l. 194.

**RUNG,** *a round* of a ladder; O. N. **Röng,** same. From rangr, *crooked, not straight;* originally, no doubt, applied to the *branch* or *stumps of branches* which formed the steps of the ladder. A ship's rib is called ' röng' or 'ranga.'

> 'His owen hand then made he ladders three
> To climben by the **rangës** and the stalks.'—*Cant. Tales,* v. 3625.

**RUNNEL,** *a sike or grip,* open drain in a field; *Dan. Dial.* **Rönnel.**

# S.

**SA AH,** *shall I.*

**SAAH,** *so.*

**SAAN'T,** *shall not.* ' Ah **saan't,** sa ah noo.'—*Al.,* 1880.

**SAAIKE**, *sake*. *Goth.* **Sakjo**, *strife*; sakan, *to rebuke, strive*; *A. S.* **sæc**, *war, battle*; **sacu**, *a lawsuit, &c., a cause, accounts*; 'for his **sake**,' for his *cause, side. interest.*

**SAIM**, *lard*; *M. Lat.* **Sagimen, sain, sayn**, *fat*, especially *fat* which the monks used (*Du Cange*); hence *Gael.* saim, *rich*; *Wel.* saim, *grease*; *Ital.* saime, *lard*; *O. Fr.* 'sain, *seam, the tallow, fat or grease* of a hog.'—*Cot.* *Sax.* seme.

**SAMMEL**, *gravel* (Westmoreland. *J. R. Dakyns*).

**SAMMEN**, *a mass of conglomerated gravel.* Some well diggers near Bedale told me that they came upon a 'salmon' at 25 feet. *Goth.* saman; *O. N.* **saman**, *acc. sing.* of samr, *together*; *Dan.* **sammen**, *Gr.* hama, *Lat.* simul.

**SARVANT**, *servant.*

**SAT**, *seated*; *O. N.* **Sat**, *pret.* of sitja, *to sit*, incorrectly used as a participle.

**SATTAL**, *v., to settle*; sattal'd, *settled.*

**SATTAL**, *n., a settle*; *A. S.* **Sætel.**

**SCADDLE**, *unsteady*; *O.N.* **Skadligr**, 'scathely,' 'scaddle,' *noxious, hurtful*; skæthr, *scatheful, noxious*; *A. S.* scæthig, *noxious, criminal.*

**SCALE**, *n., shale, laminated* indurated clay; *A.S.* **Scala.** As a place name, 'Scale Gill,' 'Scale Hill' near Leathley. S. so called because it *separates.*

**SCALE**, *v., to scatter* molehills; *O. N.* **Skilja**, *Swed.* skilja, *to separate.*

**SCOOR**, *scour*; *Dan.* **Skure**, *to scour*, *Dut.* schuren, *O. Fr.* escurer.

**SCOPPERDIL**, *a button mould.* 'In former years, when farmers dressed in drab breeches and gaiters, the **scopperdill** was covered with the same material as the garment. It is made of bone, with a hole in the centre. Boys used to fix a piece of stick through the hole and spin it with finger and thumb; hence to 'spin like a **scopperdill**.''—*T. Thorpe.* *O. N.* **skapdr, skaptr, skapid**, *shaped*; *part.* of skepja, *to shape.* Kennett has 'A **scoppering** or **scopperell**, a little sort of spinning top,' &c. The term occurs in a MS. Dict., dated 1540 (*Hall.*).

**SKRAT**, *to scratch*; *Dan.* **Kratte, kradse**, *to scratch.*

**SCREEAM**, *scream.*

**SCROGGS**, *stumps, low rough bushes*; *Dan.* **Skrog**, *stump*; *O. N.* skrukka, *a shell*; *Gael.* sgrog, *a skull cup, hat*, a ludicrous term for the *head* or *neck.* 'Scroggs' may still be seen on Thrope Edge (*see* p. 117). A valley in the chalk near Basingstoke is called 'Scroggs.'

**SCUM**, *a film on water*; *Dan.* **Skum**, *froth or foam.*

**SCUMFISH**, *v., to stifle, suffocate*, especially with smoke; *A. S.* **Scymfian**, *to cover*; (? from) *Gael.* **cum fodha**, *to stifle*, lit. *to hold beneath.* Not the 'scumfit' of *Jam.* or the *Ital.* sconfiggere of *Jam.* and *Brock.*

**SEEA**, *look here.* Often used to call attention when addressing a person.

**SEEA**, *so*; *A. S.* **Swǽ** begets 'seea,' as 'swá' begets 'so.'

**SEEAF**, *safe*; *Lat.* **Salvus**, *Fr.* sauf.

**SEÄGAR**, *sugar* (Ramsgill); *Gael.* **Siucar**, sucar; *Wel.* suȝyr, *Dan.* sukker, *Swed.* socker, *Dut.* suiker, *Fr.* sucre, *Ital.* zucchero, *Lat.* saccharum, *Pers.* shakar, *Sans.* sharkara, *Arab.* sukker. The *Dial.* word seems to evidence a tendency to pron. like the *Gael.*, though of course of later introd. than Gaelic times in this locality.

**SEALH**, *a kind of willow*; *A. S.* **Seal**, sealh; *Gael.* seileach, *O. N.* **selja**, *Goth.* salh, *O. H. G.* salaha, sala; *Fr.* saule, *Lat.* salix; *Gr.* helikē, in Arcadia, *the willow* from its pliant nature (*L.* and *S.*); connected with the root of *Gr.* elisso, eilo, *Lat.* volvo, *Ger.* wälzen, *Eng.* willow, *Goth.* valvjan, *O.H.G.* wellan —the primary meaning being *to turn round, twist*; *A. S*, sala, *Eng.* sallow.

**SEEAM**, *same*; *Goth.* (*Ulf.*) sama, sasama; *A. S.* sama, *same, same*; *Finnish*, sama, *same*; *Sans.* same, *like, equal*; *Gr.* hama, *Lat.* simul (*see* SAMMEN).

**SEEAN, SEAN**, *soon*; *O. N.* **Senn**, *soon* (*see* SEUN).

*d* 2

**SEÄP**, *soap* (Ramsgill); *Dut.* **Zeep**, *Gael.* **siabunn, siopunn**; *Wel.* sebon, *Ger.* seife, *Lat.* sapo, *Ital.* sapóne, *Fr.* savon, *Bret.* soavon, suan. The remark under SEAGAR applies to this word.

**SEAVES**, *rushes*; *O.N.* **Sef, *Dan.* siv.** As a place name, 'Fleet Seaves' (*see* SIEVE, and pp. 27, 28).

**SEEAVE**, *save*; *Lat.* salvare, *Fr.* sauver.

**SEESTA**, *seest thou.*

**SEET**, *sight*; *A.S.* ge-siehd, *sight.*

**SET**, to *set* peats (*see* p. 119); *A.S.* **Settan**, *O.N.* **setja**, *Dan.* **sœtte**, *Swed.* **sätta**, *Dut.* **zetten**, *Goth.* (*Ulf.*) **satjan**, *Gr.* tithenai; setō, *Laconian* for thetō (Aristophanes, *Lysistrata*, 1080).

**SETTLE**, fireside *seat* with high back; *A.S.* **Setl, gesetl** (*see* p. 25).

**SEÜN** or **SEWN** (pron. seoon), *soon.* A true form [seóna] (?) the parent of *A.S.* sóna, *soon; Goth.* suns, *immediately; Dut.* saen, *soon.* 'Soon,' *i.e.*, the *about to be*, appears to be connected with the root of *Goth.* sind, *A.S.* seon, synd, *are*, and *Ger.* seyn, *to be.*

**SEUER, SEWER**, *sure*; *O.Fr.* **Seür**, later **seur**, now **sûr**; *Prov.* segur, *Span.* seguro, *Lat.* securus. O. Fr. pron. well preserved.

**SFETTLE**, to *infect, convey infection.* 'You'll **sfettle** me with your cold.' —*Colloq.* A farmer was said to have been '**sfettled** by his own beästs.' Mr. Dakyns writes 'SMITTLE,' a common, but less correct, form. **Sfettle**, to *communicate* the means of killing, to *make ill*; *O.N.* **svelta**, to *kill, to starve; Dan.* sulte, to *starve, suffer hunger; Goth.* (*Ulf.*) **sviltan**, to *be put to death, to die; A.S.* **sweltan**, *O.E.* **swelte**, *O.L.G.* sveltan, *O.H.G.* svelzan. For O. E. examples *see* Stratm. *O. E.* svelte, by transpos. svetle, whence **sfettle**; *Gr.* sphatto, *Att.*, pres. for sphazō, *I slay, kill*; *imperf.* esphatton.

**SHAFT**, *handle; O.N.* **Skaft**, skapt, lit. that which is *shaved*, a *shaved* stick; *A.S.* sceaft; *Dan.* skaft, *Dut.* schacht, *Ger.* schaft, schacht. In the *Laws of Ælfred*, c. 32, 'If they are both equal in length, ord & hindweard sceaft,' where 'sceaft' means the part of the cusp of the spear which was fastened on to the stem. The circumference of a shaft which the hand would just surround became a standard measure with the Saxons. 'ix sceafta munda.'—*L. Æthelst.*, Pt. 2, c. 2.

**SHAK**, a hollow in the surface of the ground, left after the falling in of the crust in the carboniferous limestone districts, and in the salt bearing 'new red' marls near Ripon. The largest is 'The Great **Shak**,' on Barden Fell. Smaller ones are commonly called **Shak-holes**. They are sometimes caused by old workings. *O.N.* **skakkr**, *distorted.*

**SHAM**, *shame; O.N.* **Skamm**, usually **skömm**, *Ger.* skammar, *shame.*

**SHAMFUL**, 'It's fair **shamful**, and can't be stoodened any longer.'— *Colloq.*

**SHANK**, *handle; Dan.* **Skank**, *A.S.* sceanca, scanca; sceonca, soonca. *Dut.* and *Ger.* schenkel. 'Gif tha earm **scancan** (arm bones) be both broken.' 'Gif se **scanca** (leg bone) be stabbed below the knee.'—*L. Ælfred*, c. 40.

**SHAP**, *shape; O.N.* **Skap**, *shape; A.S.* gesceap.

**SHAW**, a boggy place on the moors frequently has the name 'Shaw' (*see* p. 107; also my Papers on the 'Vestiges of the Ancient Forest on part of the Pennine Chain,' *Transac. of Brit. Assoc.* (York Meeting), 1881; and *Trans. Geol. and Polytechnic Soc. of West Riding of Yorkshire*, 1881) where I have shown there were formerly *trees. O.N.* **Skógr**, *Swed.* skog, *Dan.* skov, a *wood; A.S.* scúa (*shower*), *O.N.* skuggi, *Dut.* schawe, *shade, shelter; Gr.* skeuē, *Lat.* scutum (*Cur., Sk.*).

**SHE'Y**, *she; A.S.* **Seó**, *she; see* SHOO. 'She'y' written by *Bla.* (*Greenhow*).

**SHIPN**, *cowshed, stable, small barn; Wel.* **Ysguboran**, a *small barn.* See pp. 106-107 for *A.S.* forms, **scipen**, &c. 'To neate **scypene**.'—*Bede*, IV., 24.

**SHIVE,** *n.,* *a slice;* *O. N.* **Skifa,** *a shaving, slice;* *Ger.* scheibe.

**SHIVE,** *v.,* *to slice, laminate;* *O. N.* skifa, *to slice.* 'The stone . . . shives off with frost.'—*Colloq.,* p. 17.

**SHIVER,** *shale* (Lancashire, *Dakyns,* MS.).

**SHOO,** *she;* *A. S.* **Seó** (pron. shoo), near the Dale Head (*see* SHE'Y).

**SHOON,** *shoes;* *A. S.* Sceón, Scón (*pl.* of sceó, scó), *shoes.*

**SHOOR,** *shower;* *A. S.* Sceór; *A. S.* scúr gives *shower.*

**SHOOT,** *shout;* **Shootid,** *shouted.*

**SHU,** *she; see* SHOO.

**SHUN,** *shoes* (see SHOON).

**SHOWL,** *shovel;* *Wel.* **Ysgubell,** *a broom;* ysgub, *a sheaf, broom;* *A. S.* sceofl, scofl, scobl, *a shovel;* scóf, *dust;* *Gr.* skaptō (*Cur., Sk.*).

**SIDE,** *to move aside;* *O. N.* Sida, *to side.* 'I'se gitten all **sided** up,' *e.g.,* on Saturday night. Near Dale Head.

**SIDER,** *longer;* *O. N. compar.* of sid, *late;* **Sidarr,** *longer, later;* **sidr,** *less;* *A. S.* sidor, *longer, later, compar.* of sid, *late.*

**SIEVE,** *a rush;* *O. N.* Sef, *Dan.* siv, *A. S.* sife, syfe (*see* SEAVE); *O. H. G.* sib; *A. S.* sibi, *a sieve,* because made of *rushes* (*see* SILE, SINE). S. so called because they grow in *wet* places (*see* SIPE, SOFT).

**SIKE,** *a small stream or gutter, an open field drain;* *O. N.* Sík, *a ditch;* *A. S.* sich, sic, *a gutter, watercourse* (*Somn.*). A word especially used on upland pastures and moors (*see* pp. 81 and 104).

**SIKE,** *such;* *A. S.* Swylíc, contr. from swá, líc, or ilíc, *so like, such;* swilc, swylc, contr. 'such' is contr. from swá, ilc, ylc or ilíc.

**SILE, SAHL,** *n., a sieve;* *Gael.* Siolachan, whence *O. N.* sáld, *Dan.* sle, sold (*Gr.* ikmas, *Cur. Sk.*); (*see* p. 28).

**SILE, SAHL,** *v., to strain;* *Gael.* sioladh, *O. N.* sálda, *Swed.* sila, *Pl. D.* silen.

**SINE,** *v., to strain;* *A. S.* Sihan, seon, *to strain;* sile. 'Sine,' contr. from sifan or sivan, as 'sen' from 'seven,' 'aboon' from 'abufon,' &c. *O. N.* sía, for 'síva' or 'sífa'; *Gr.* Ikmas (*Cur. Sk.*), (*see* SIPE); *O. H. G.* sihan, *O. Dut.* sijghen, *O. E.* sihen (*Stratm.*), (*see* p. 28).

**SINE,** *n., a sieve;* *O. N.* sía, *O. Dut.* sijghe, *O. H. G.* síha (*Prompt.,* 79).

**SIN,** *since;* *A. S.* Síththan, sýthan, sýththan, sýththon, seothan, seothon; *O. N.* sithan, *Dan.* siden. 'Thonne siththan.'—*L. Æth.,* 52, and in the beautiful verses *Sax. Chron*, A.D. 938 :—

| | |
|---|---|
| 'Siththan eastan hither<br>Engle and Saxe<br>Up becomon<br>Over brymum brad.' | 'Sin from the east hither<br>Engle and Saxon<br>Up came<br>Over the broad sea.' |
| . . . . . . | . . . . . . |
| 'Syththan sunne up<br>On morgen tid.' | ' After sunrise<br>In early morn.' |

N.B.—'Sunne up' opposed to 'sundown,' still in use.

' And **syne** my logeyng I have take.'—*Otterb.,* ver. 39 (fought 1388).

'**Sen** God he sendis bute for bale.'—*Robin and Makine,* l. 37 (about 1571).

'Bairne **sin** thy cruel father is gane.'—*Lady Anne Bothwell's Lament,* l. 36.

In Nidd. common as 'some time **sin**.' Fabian, 1493, uses the uncontracted forms. 'And **sethen** that time.'—*Chron.,* c. 134, and again, 'Benet, that was in good favour with King Oswy, went sythes to Rome.'—c. 134.

**SINGLET,** *a 'jersey.'* Opposed to 'doublet,' or 'guernsey.' A flannel worn next the skin.

**SIPE,** *to drip;* *Pl. D.* Sipen, *Dut.* zipen (*Atk., Cl. Gl.*); *Dan.* sive, *to drip, to give out drop by drop;* but *Wel.* sipian and *A. S.* sipan, *to take in drop by drop* (*see* SINE).

**SKEEL,** *a milk pail or can*; *O. N.* **Skjóla,** *a pail* (*see* p. 31). Formerly a shallow wooden pan, with one of the staves left longer than the rest (the 'Beild.') Now any milk pail.

**SKIFT,** *shift*, *O. N.* **Skipta,** *Dan.* **skifte,** *A. S.* **scyftan,** *to shift.* At Lodge, a farmer from Melmerby, Coverdale, remarked, 'They'll happen have got **skifted** to-day' (1871).

**SKRIKE,** *v.*, *to shriek*; *O. N.* **Skríkja,** *Dan.* skrige, *Russ.* krēchate, za-krechate (*see* p. 137).

**SKRIKE,** *n.*, *a shriek*; *Wel.* **Ysgreç,** *a shriek*; (2.) Name of a bird.

**SLACK,** *a hollow boggy place*; *Wel.* **Llaca,** *mire* (*see* p. 70); *O. N.* **slakki,** 'Dan. slng, *hollows* of some length and breadth in a road or track' (in Atk. *Cl. Gl.*). 'cp. *Dan.* slank, *Ger.* schlank.'—*Cleas.* As a place name, 'Foulcauseway **Slack**,' near the Bolton end of the B. and Harrogate Road.

**SLANG,** *slung*; *A. S.* **Slingan,** *to sling.* ' An thar we lang switchers we **slang** taty crabs,' And there with long swishes (bendable sticks) we **slang** potato tops.—*Bla.*, p. 38.

**SLAPE,** *slippery, thin, weak*; *O. N.* **Sleipr,** *slippery.* When the 'hippings' are wet with rain they are said to be '**slape**,' *i.e.*, *slippery*, but *weak* tea and *thin* 'hasty-pudding' are also said to be **slape**.

**SLATE,** *flagstone.* 'Slate' means *flat.* *Goth.* **Slahits,** *O. N.* **sléttr,** *Dan.* **slet,** *flat*; *Gael.* sglent, sgliat, *a slate*, is, no doubt, a borrowed name. *Shale is* also called **slate,** *e.g.* 'Blue slate.'

**SLECK,** *to slake, quench*; *O. N.* **slökva, slecthi, slecqua**; *Dan.* slukke, *to slake*; *Swed.* **släcka,** *Dut.* lesschen, *Eng. lush.* 'Hann slcæktti thar nu thorsta sinn.'—*Barlaams Saga*, 198, *Cleas.*

**SLED,** *a sledge*; *Gael.* **Sladd,** *Wel.* **ysled,** *O. N.* **sledi,** *Dan.* **sloede,** *Dut.* sledde, sledde; *Ger.* schlitten, whence *Ital.* sliscio, *Russ.* salazkhe, *a sledge*; *Gael.* slaod, *O. N.* slæda, slæda; *Ger.* schlittern, *Ital.* slisciare, *to drag, to sled*, perhaps the original of to 'lead' peats, &c., in Nidd. There are four kinds of **sled** in Nidd., of which one, sketched on Witton Fell, is shown below.

'He smote the **sledded** Polack on the ice.'—*Hamlet*, Act I., sc. 1.

**SLEET,** *a flat* meadow or moor. *O. N.* **sléttr,** *a plain*; *Dan.* **slette,** *level field*; *Goth.* slahits, *flat*; (*see* p. 91, also SLATE). Allied to 'slide' and 'sled.'

**SLITTER,** *adj.*, *careless, slippery*; *A. S.* **slidor** or **slithor,** *slippery.*

'And to a drunken man the way is slider.'—*Cant. Tales*, v. 1266.

**SLITTER,** *v.*, *to slip through*; *A. S.* **Slitherian,** *to slip out.* 'Ah didn't carr hoo ah did it, nobbut ah gat **slittered** through it.'—*Colloq.*

**SLOP,** *a loose garment*; *Gael.* **Slapar,** *a skirt*; *O. N.* **sloppr,** *A. S.* **slop,** *a gown, loose garment*; *Ger.* schleppe; akin to *Dan.* sloebe, *train, trail*; *O. N.* slapa, *Dan.* sloebe, *to hang loose.* 'Blue lin slop.'—*Bla.*, p. 18.

**SLOTT-BAR,** a moveable bar sliding horizontally on the Branderi (*see* p. 18, and Fig. 2, p. 19).

**SLOUNGEING.** ' If thee desn't gie ower, ah'll gie thee a **sloungeing** bat,' a heavy blow. *O. N.* **Slaung,** *pret.* of slöngva, slyngva slengja, *to sling*; *part.* slunginn.

**SLY**, *to act slily*; *O. N.* **Slægja**, *to cheat*, act *on the sly*. Of a girl, 'An **slyed** oot ta meet him.'—*Bla.*, p. 18.

**SMEAK**, *smoke*; *A. S.* **Smeóc**, *smoke*; smeócan, *to smoke*.

**SMEAKIN**, *smoking*; *A. S.* **Smeócend**, *smoking*.

**SMELLER**, *a heavy or sharp blow*; *O. N.* **Smellr**, *a smack*. 'Ah'll gie thee a smeller.' *O. N.* smella, *Swed.* smälla, *Dan.* smœlde, *to crack a whip*.

**SMOWL**, *smile*. 'Billy smowled an sed, "Thoo oade madlin."'—*Al.*, 1880.

**SMOWLIN**, *smiling*. 'Ahve seen yer smowlin leaks at yan another.'—*Ib.*

**SOFT**, *wet*, *rainy*, especially a *fine*, *wet*, *warm rain*. From the climate, the salutation, ''Tis soft,' is heard more frequently than any other. *A. S.* Soft, seft, connected with Sipe, *to drip*, *q.v.*; also Sieve.

**SOOND**, *sound*; *Dan.*, *Swed.* and *Ger.* Sund.

**SPEER**, *to ask*; *O. N.* Spyrja, *Dan.* spörge, *A. S.* spirian, spýrian, *to ask*. 'Thonne mot man smeagan and geornlice spirian,' then should one enquire and diligently *ask.*—*Lib. Constit.* Æthelred, § *Be Cyric Grithe*. 'And laga smeagan and spýrian oft,' and search the laws and *consult* them oft.—*L. Cnute*, (1017-35), c. 21.

> 'And bid hir cum to Gill Morice
> Speir nae bauld baron's leave.'—*G. M.*, l. 38.

**SPELL**, *a piece*, *splinter of wood*; *O. N.* **Spölr**, *a bit*, *short piece of wood*, or of anything; spjall, spell, *a flaw*; *Swed. Dial.* spjäle, *strips of wood*, *laths*; *Dan.* spile.

**SPYRTLE**, *a flat stick* for stirring porridge. 'Gull-spyrtle.' *A. S.* **Sprýtle**, *a stick*, *a sprout*; spyrtan, *to sprout*; sprote, *a sprout*; spyrta, spirta, spyrd, *a basket*, from being made of *sprouts* of willow, hazel, &c.

**SQUAB**, *the settle*. Originally *a stuffed cushion*, from which the name passed to the seat (*see* Settle, also p. 25).

**SQUIRT**, *to dart quickly*. 'An lile bonny askerds wad squirt amang t' ling.'—*Bla.*, p. 38.

**STAG**, *a colt*; *O. N.* **Steggr**, *a mounter* (*see* p. 32).

**STAK**, *stuck*; *O. N.* **Stakk**, *pret.* of stinga, *to stick*.

**STAN**, *stone*. In the name 'Stangate,' in How Stean Basin. 'Rubbin stans.'—*Bla*, p. 7. Stane, *O. N.* steinn, is not used here.

**STANG**, *a pole*, *post*, *stick*; *O. N.* **Stöng**, *gen.* stangar, *pl.* stangir; *Dan.* stang, *Ger.* stange, *A. S.* steng, *Wel.* ystang, *Gael.* stang, *a peg*, *pin* (*see* p. 90).

**STARE**, *strong*; *O.N.* **Sterkr**, *Dan.* stœrk; *Swed.* stark, *A. S.* stearc; *Gr.* stēr, stēriktos, *stark*; stērizo, *to stand fast*; stear, stēr, *stiff fat*; *O. N.* stórr, *big*; *compar.* stæri or stærri, *super.* stærstr; *Gr.* steiros, *hard, barren*; steira, *a barren cow*, (? *a steer*); *A. S.* steor, *a steer*; *Lat.* sterilis, *sterile*.

**STARVE**, *to shrivel with cold only*; *A. S.* **Steorfan**, stearfian. 'Starved' in the ord. sense is given by 'hungered.' **Starved** meant an effect of *cold* first, as a phrase given in *Bos.* specifies 'stærf of hungor.'

**STAWL**, *falter*, *fail*, *give in*; *O. N.* **Stallra**, *to halt*, *falter*; staulask, *to walk infirmly*. 'Hjarta drepr stall,' the heart *fails* (*Cleas.*). 'Ah's fairly beginnin to stawl.'—*Bla.*, p. 25. Cleasby says, 'Metaphorically from stallr, *the step of a mast*.'

**STEAD**, *stood*.

**STEÄN, STEEAN**, *stone*; *A. S.* **Stœn** (*see* Stan), *Goth.* stains, *Gr.* stîon, stía, *a pebble* (*Cur.* 225, *Sk.*); *Later Gr.* steïon, steía (*L.* and *S*); *Pers.* sang.

**STED**, *place*; *e.q.* 'Doorsted.'

**STEE**, *a ladder*; *O. N.* **Stí**, stigi, *a step*, *steep ascent*, *ladder*; *Dan.* Stige, *ladder*; sti, *path* (whence 'Sty Head Pass'); stige, *to climb*; *A. S.* stigan, *Gr.* steichō, *Sans.* stigh, *to climb*; *O. H. G.* stega, *an ascending* (*Cur.* 177), (*see* Stag). In place names Braisty = Brae-sty, Cattersty (in Cleveland), and perhaps Swinsty, Washburndale.

Studies in Nidderdale.—*Lucas.*

**STEE-STOWER**, *ladder-stalk* (see STOWER).

**STEAL**, *stool*; *A.S.* **steal, steall, stœl**, *a seat*.

**STINT**, *to limit*; *O.N.* **Stytta**, *to shorten*. Those who have experienced the good-natured hospitality of some remote farmhouse will have heard the frequent injunction, ' Don't **stint** yersel,' and doubtless responded thereto in true English fashion. The word as used in the Ballads is *A.S.* **stintan**, *to be weak, faint*. Thus :—

> ' He never **styntyde** ne never blane
> Till he came to the good Lord Persè.'
> —*Anc. Chevy Chase*, Fit. 2, l. 69.

> ' I wys he neither **stint** ne blanne
> Till he his ladye see.'—*Sir Cauline*, l. 151.

Commons, *i.e.* moors, here, as elsewhere, are **stinted** and **unstinted**, on which the commoners can turn out a *limited* or an *unlimited* number of sheep (see pp. 9 and 65).

**STIRK**, *a year old calf*; *A.S.* **styrc, stirc, stiorc**, *a stirk*; **sterc, stearc**, *strong, stark* (see also STARK, STRONG and STOWER). A **stirk** is either a ' stott-stirk ' or a ' heifer-stirk.'

**STOCK**, *cattle*. On a farm, ' We keep the gate shut lest the **stock** should get through.'

**STOOP**, *a post*, e.g., ' Yek yet **stoop**,' *oak gate-post*. ' Long **stoop**,' *tall stone way-post* (see p. 98).

**STOOR**, *dust, disturbance*; *Wel.* **Ystwr**, *O.N.* **styrr**, *Dan.* **stöi, stir**, *tumult, brawl, fight, war*; **stör**, *dust*; *Gael.* **strìgh**, *stir*. ' Ah raised sike a **stoor**,' made such a *noise.*—*Bla.*, p. 66. ' If ther owners had seen us thar'd been a nice **stoor**.—*Ib.*, p. 38. Obsolete in the sense of *fight*, as in the Ballads—

> ' And Estmere he and Adler yonge
> Right stiffe in **stour** can stand.'—*King Estmere*, l. 272.

Connected with next word.

**STORM**, *snow*. ' Summat ta burn again a **storm** of ayther frost or snow. —*Al.*, 1880.

**STORMY**, *snowy, ' like snow*.' The sense is remarkable. The salutation, ' 'Tis **stormy**,' is a greeting only heard in reference to *snow*. ' 'Tis rúff ' (rough), being applied to *wind*. ' 'Tis wild,' *to wind, wind and rain, &c.* If a man says, there will be ' a **storm** afore neet,' he means there will be a fall of *snow*. But it is only near the Dale Head and up on the plateaux that folk are so correct. In the corrupt dialect of Pateley Bridge, no doubt, the word may frequently be heard in its general sense. To my mind this word affords the key to the solution of the problem so ably and beautifully handled by Prof. Max Müller (*Lect. on Science of Language*, XI., v. 2, p. 506 *et seq.*), as to the meaning of **Saramâ**, and clinches the argument of Prof. Kuhn, ' who was the first to analyse the meaning and character of **Saramâ** [and who] arrived at the conclusion that **Saramâ** meant **storm**, and that the Sanscrit word was identical with the Teutonic *storm* and with the Greek *hormē*.' If the proper and original meaning of **storm** was *frost and snow*, and **storm** be etymologically identical with **Saramâ** (as *Eng.* ' stone'; *Pers.* ' sang '), then the query of the learned Professor, ' But admitting that **Saramâ** meant originally the *runner*, how does it follow that the *runner* was meant for **storm** ?' is intelligibly answered, in the appearance of *snow* driven before the northern blast. If **Saramâ**, the **storm**, meant *frost and snow* in countries lying to the north of India, we can understand why **Saramâ**, ' discovered the cleft of the rock,' . . . . . . and how she ' crossed the waters of the Parâ,' and why the Panis say ' Thou art come in vain to this bright place,' as well as why they ask Saramâ about Indra (*Jupiter Pluvius*) (108th Hymn of the last book of the Rigveda, pp. 508-9, Max Müller's *Lect.*). **Saramâ** is called 'the dog of the gods,' and said to have been 'sent by Indra,' in an Indian Commentary cited by M. Müller (p. 510), 'to look for the cows,' who 'were carried off by the Panis from the world of the gods and thrown *into darkness*'—*ergo*, towards the *north*, the land of *frost and snow*. Saramâ, the Dog of Indra, was mother of the Sārameyau, the two four-eyed brindled watch dogs of Yama (conjectured by some to have been originally Indra and Agni (*fire*), and Sārameya to be the Greek Hermeías). **Saramâ** is made to mean the 'dawn' by Max Müller, by others the 'wind,' by Williams the 'runner.'—*Sans.-Eng. Dict.*, 1872, p. 1092, col. 2, and p. 1110, col. 1. We can understand why **storm**, in the sense of '*frost* and *snow*,' hugs the north, where the storms are of that character, and why it should mean *rain* and *wind* in more southern climes. It would be a curious point, if the sense of **storm**, preserved on part of the Pennine Chain, should be found by any other evidence to bear out Kuhn in his identification of **storm** and **Saramâ**, and that **Saramâ** dates back to a northern 'land of darkness,' and first meant '*frost and snow*.' I have deemed it my duty thus, with much diffidence, to draw attention to the issue arising upon this word **storm**. *Swed.*, *Dan.* and *Dut.* **storm**, *Dan.* stormvind, *Dut.* stormwind, *Ger.* sturm, sturmwind, *Russ.* shchtorme, *Wel.* ystorm, *Gael.* stoirm, *A.S.* **storm, steorm, stearm**, which looks like a locative **storum**, 'in the stoor' (as they say 'stoor and drive') *i.e.*, 'in the stir.' *A.S.* stirian, styrian, *to stir*, &c. (see 'STOOR'). Jamieson has 'STORM, *snow*, Aberd.' This use of the term is pretty general in S'[cotland].

**STOTT**, *a bull-calf*; *A.S.* Stotte; *Dan.* stud, *an ox.* Lye has *A.S.* stotte in one passage only, where he renders it by *equus vilis* as a contemptuous term for a horse, like *Icel.* stoti, a nickname occurring in Landnamabok; *O.N.* stod, *a stud* (of horses).

**STOTT-STIRK**, *a year old bull-calf.*

**HEIFER-STIRK**, *a year old cow-calf.*

**STOYT**. 'They pointed an said, "What a girt stoyt is he."'—*Bla.*, p. 36; of a little boy. *O.N.* staut, *a stuttering* in reading; staut-færr, *able to read a little.*

**STOWER**, *the stalk* of a ladder, *a stake, paling*; *O.N.* staurr; *Gr.* stauros, *a stake, paling*; *Sans.* stavaras, *firm*; *Lat.* in-stauro, *to erect*; *Goth.* stiurjan, *to fix*; *Dut.* sturen; *Ger.* steuern, *to steer* (see STEE-STOWER).

**STRAIT**, *narrow*; *Ital.* stretto, *O. Fr.* estroit, *Mod. Fr.* étroit, from *Lat.* strictus.

**STRANG**, *strong*; *A.S.* Strang, *O.N.* strangr, *Swed.* sträng, *Dan.* and *Ger.* streng, string, *O.H.G.* strang, *Lat.* stringo, *Gr.* strangō, strangenō (*Cur.*, 577). 'Tham strangan and tham unmagan,' the strong and the weak.—*Canons*, temp. Eadgar, § *De Confessione*, 3.

**STRANGER**, *stronger.*

**STREET**, *straight.*

**STREEAN**, *strain*; *O. Fr.* Estraindre, estreindre; *Mod. Fr.* étreindre, *to bind, tie up*; *Lat.* stringere, *to hurt, injure.*

**STRUKE** *struck*; *O.N.* Struku, pret. (*plural*) of strjúka, *to strike*; *Dan.* stryge. 'Away she struke off at full trot.'—*Bla.*, p. 14. *Icel.* 'Hestrinn strauk fra mer,' the horse *run away* from me. **Strok-hestr**, *a runaway horse* (*Cleas.*).

**STREIGHT**, *straight*; *A.S.* Gestreht, *part.* of streccan, *to stretch.* 'And streight came out.'—*St. George for Engd.*, Grubb. 1688, l. 59. *O. Dut.* strack, *A.S.* stræc, strac, *straight*; *O. Dut.* stracks; *Dan.* strax (*Eng.* straightways), *immediately.*

**STREIGHTEN**, *to straighten*; *A.S.* Stregdan, stredan, *to spread, strew*; strægan, *same*; streccan, *to stretch, make straight.*

> 'Cum don on thi' bonnet an' shawl,
>     An' streighten thi' cap an' thi' hair.'—*Bla.*, p. 24.

**STRETCH**, *to exercise*; *A. S.* **Streccan**, *to stretch over.*

'Capered and **stretched** up an doon.'—*Bla.*, p. 36.

**STROTH**, in Lang*stroth*dale = Lang **strath** Dale, and in Col*ster*dale = Coal, **strath** Dale. *Gael.* **Strath** (Scot. and Cornwall); *Ir.* **srath**, *a valley, mountain valley, &c.*; *Wel.* **ystrad**, which latter is, in Eng. place names, common, *e.g.*, **Stroud, Strood, Stroud** Green, Hornsey, Middlesex, and near Croydon, Surrey, &c. (*see* also p. 1, note).

**STUDY** (pron. **stoody**), *to think, ponder, think out*; *Lat.* Studeo, *to apply the mind to*; *O. Fr.* **Estudier**, *Mod. Fr.* étudier. Always used in the sense of *think*. The response to an enquiry may often be, 'Let me **stoody**' = let me *think*. 'He's varra mitch gean [gi'en] tn **studdin**. What he *thinks* aboot ah nivver can tell.'—*Al.*, 1880. *Russ.* chydo (pron. Chooda, Riola), *wonder.*

**STUFFLE**, *stew, fume.* 'Oade Snarle gat inta a reg'lar **stuffle**.' *Gael.* **stuadh**, *a wave*; stuadhmhor, *stormy, proud*; or **sturt**, stuirt, *sulkiness, pride*; sturtail, *sulky, sullen, proud.* As stubh = *stuff*, and stuth = *stuff*, so stuadh or sturtail = *stuffle.*

**SUD**, *should*; *A. S.* **Sceolde**, *imperf. potent.* and *fut. part.* of scealan, *ought, shall.*

**SUER**, *sure* (see SEUER).

**SUNSIDE**, *the south, towards the south*; *Norweg.* **solsiden**, same sense. Used by the miners of Greenhow.

**SUP** (pron. **soop**, like 'cook'), *to drink*; *O. N.* **Supa**, *A. S.* **supan**, **suppan**; *Dan.* **söbe**, *to sup drink.* *cf.* *Soup* and *Supper.*

**SUTE**, *suit*; *O. Fr.* **Siute**, **sieute**, **seute**; *Mod. Fr.* suite.

'He had a **sute** of silk
About his middle drawn.'—*Boy and Mantle*, l. 9.

'Cooarderoy **sute**.'—*Bla.*, p. 35.

**SWANG**, 'a fresh piece of green swarth *lying in a bottom* among arable or barren land, a dool.'—*Grose.* In place names freq., *e.g.*, 'Brown Beck **Swangs**,' Colsterdale. *O. N.* **Svangr**, *a hollow*, the belly. **Swangs** are *hollow places* in high ground, or on plateaux.

**SWAPE**, *a crane over the kitchen fire*; *O. N.* **Sveipr**, *an oar*; *A. S.* **sweop**, swope, swiopa, suiop, *a whip*; *Norw.* svöbe, *a whip.* **Swape**, llt. *the sweep* or *sweeper*; thus 'the handle of a pump' is so called in Norfolk; 'a long pole used in drawing water out of a well,' in the North (*Grose*); 'an oar,' on the Tyne (*see* p. 19). *Wel.* ysgub, *Gael.* sguab, *a broom.* Connected with next word.

**SWAP**, *v.*, *to exchange, barter*; originally, *to exchange blows*, confirming Grimm's explanation of Cowp, *q.v.* *A. S.* **Swapan**, *to sweep round, to swap*; *Goth.* sweipan, *to swipe*, sweep; *Gael.* sguab, *to sweep*; *Wel.* ysgubaw, *to sweep.* 'Swapte,' 'swapped,' in the Ballads; *A. S.* **sweop**, swept, p. of swapan.

'At last the Douglas and the Persè met,
Lyk to Captayns of myght and mayne;
The' **swapte** together till the both swat
With swordes that wear of fyn myllàn.'
—*Anc. Chevy Chase*, F. 2, 25-28.

'They **swapped** together whyll that they swette
Wyth swordes scharp and long.'—*Otterb.*, F. 2, l. 101.

'And to the wits of Glaucus away stole Jove Divine;
Who with Tydides Diomede made **swap** and barter fine.'
—C. Merivale, *Iliad*, 1869, VI., 235.

**SWARBLE**, *to swarm, i.e.* to climb up a pole or a tree by the legs and arms;

*Russ.* vzbērat'sya, *to climb,* comes nearest pres. word, but **swarble** = swarmble = *scramble;* *Dut.* grabbelen, *Fr.* grimper, agripper, *to scramble;* *Dut.* grabbel, *Ger.* krabbel, *a scramble.*

  'To **swarble** up t' trees an late birds' nests t' day lang.'—*Bla.,* p. 38.

  **SWAT,** *squat, flat.* 'Till ah fell we'y me'y noddle full **swat** ageean t' yoon.'—*Bla.,* p. 34. *Wel.* **yswad,** *a throwing down, a falling flatly;* ystwatiad, *a squatting down;* yswatiaw, *to squat, lie flat.* As to line 26 in *Anc. Chevy Chase:—*
        'The swapte together till the both **swat,**'
that might mean till they both *fell down* or *sweated.*'

  **SWATH** prop. **SWARTH,** *to convert arable into grass land,* a verb formed from the noun; *O. N.* **svörthr,** *Swed.* **sward,** *Dan.* grön-swœrd, *Ger.* schwarte; *Dut.* zwoord, *skin of bacon;* grœne zóde, *greensward.* Sward originally meant the *skin,* hide.

  **SWEEL,** *to gutter, waste,* of a candle; *Wel.* **Ysweiliaw,** *to waste, consume;* *A. S.* swélan, *to burn.* Connected with next word.

  **SWELTED,** *overpowered with heat;* (1) *O. N.* **svelta,** *Goth.* (*Ulf.*) swiltan, *A. S.* **sweltan,** *to die;* *O. E.* **swelte** (*see* SFETTLE), *O. L. G.* sveltan, *O. H. G.* svelzan (*Stratm.*); suilizon, *to perish by heat;* *M. H. G.* swiltan, *to die* (Atk. *Cl. Gl.*); (2) *O. N.* **svelta,** *causal* to preceding, *to put to death* (*Cleas.*); *O. E.* **swelten.** For O. E. instances *see* Stratmann. 'Ah's fair **swelted.**'—*Colloq.,* after a walk on a hot day.

  **SWITCHER,** '*a slender stick* something like the shape of a whipstock,' *a swish.*   'An thar we'y lang **switchers** we slang táty crabs.'—*Bla.*

# T.

*Grimm* V.—(*Eng.*) *Goth.* T; *Lith., O. Slav., O. Ir., Lat., Gr., Sans.,* D; *O. H. G.* Z.

  **T',** *the;* *A. S.* **Te,** *the.* 'Thæt **te** ryht æwe,' that t' right laws.—*Ine,* A.D. 688. 'Thæt **te** nænig ealdormanna,' that no alderman. First appears in the *Sax. Chron.* after A.D. 1138 contr. for 'the,' which also appears in the *Chron.* same date, contr. for theó for seó, heó, for se, seó, thæt, *he, she, it.*

  **TA,** *to.* 'Ah thowt he're [he war = was] gine **ta** dee.'—*Bla.,* p. 16.

  **TA,** *thou;* *Lat.,* whence *Fr., Gael.* and *A. S.* **Tu.** In *O. N.,* after verbs, tu, as skal-tu, mun-tu, vil-tu; *A. S.* wilt-tú. 'Wil-ta gan wi' me.'—*Bla.,* p. 15. *Russ.* tei (pron. *ty* or *tea*) (*see* THOO).

  **TAISTRILL.** In *Brock.* taistrel, testril; in *Atk.* tastrill; in *Leeds Gloss.* tarestrill, *a mischievous, ill-behaved boy.* *Gael.* (from taisdeal, *a journey*) **tais-dealach, taisdealaiche,** *a saunterer, lounger.*

  **TAK,** *take;* *O. N.* **Taka,** *to take.*

  **TAK ON,** '*take on,' grieve, to lament, be low-spirited.* 'Dooan't **tak on** like that.'

  **TATY,** *potato.*

  **TATY CRABS,** *potato tops.*—*Bla.,* p. 38.

  **TAV,** *to.* 'It's been proved **tav** a gert fact.'

  **TAINE,** *the one* (*see* TEEAN). 'What **taine** did tother did.'—*Al.,* 1880.

  **TEEA, TEEAN,** *the one;* *A. S.* **Te ean.** Correctly used in the verse—
    'Tone day to marry King Adland's daughter
        Tother day to carrye her home.'—*K. Estmere,* l. 109.

But reduplicated in the following—

    'Therfor the ton of us shall de this day.'—*Anc. Chevy Chase,* l. 72.

    'The tone of us schall dye.'—*Otterb.,* F. 1, l. 48; F. 2, l. 8.

Or, perhaps, 'the tone' is 'thæt one,' with the 't' misplaced.

**TEEA,** *to; Wel.* Tua.

**TEEABLE,** *table; Fr.* **Table,** *Lat.* **tabula,** *Guel.* taibhle (from the *Eng.*).

**TEEALE,** *tale; A. S.* **Teale, tealde,** *told;* tenllan, *to tell; O. N.* tal, *talk;* tala, *a tale;* tala, *to talk; Swed.* tala, *Dan.* tale, *to tell; Dut.* taal, *speech, &c.; Ger.* erzälung, *a tale.*

**TEEAP** (Ramsgill), *tup,* ram; *O. Fr.* Toup, *a ram,* from *L. Ger.* topp (*Bra.*). Generally pron. 'toop,' like 'cook' or 'book' (short).

**TEEASTY,** *tasty,* agreeably flavoured. *O. Fr.* **Taster,** *to feel; Ital.* tastare. *Lat.* taxitare (frequentative of tastare), *to touch frequently.*

**TEEM,** *to pour; A. S.* **Teeámian,** *to produce in abundance.* In Nidder. *to rain heavily, to empty a cart.*

**TELLED,** *told.* 'Noo, ah **telled** ye nut ta due it.' *A. S.* tealde.

**TEMSE,** *a hair sieve; Dut.* **Tems,** *Dan. Dial., N. Fris.* tems, *Swed. Dial.* tämms, *Mid. Lat.* tamisium. *It.* tamiso, tamigio; *O. Fr.* tamis, which gives *S. Eng.* tammy (see p. 15).

**TENGS,** *tongs; Swed.* **Täng;** *O. N.* töng. taung, *tongs;* tengja, *to tie or fasten together; Dan.* tang, *Dut.* tanghe, *A. S.* tange; *Ger.* zange, *tongs* (see p. 25).

**TENG,** *to sting; Guel.* **Teum,** *to bite, sting;* **teumta,** *bitten,* which is no doubt the **betwenged** which forms the subject of a note on p. 4, and which in this Gloss. I was tempted to connect with the erroneous notion of witchcraft entertained by my informant, for want of a better explanation. I heard **betwenged** at Lofthouse and Middlesmoor applied to cattle suffering from a disease.

**TENT,** *show, teach; A. S.* **Teon,** *to tug, pull, lead, educate.* 'And to cræftan **teon,**' and *induce them to learn* a craft.—*Canons, Eadg.,* 51. 'Ah'll **tent** thee,' I'll *teach* thee.

**TEW,** *to; Wel.* **Tua.**

**TEWK,** *took.*

**TEWFIT,** *peewit; Prov. Dan.* **Tyvit,** from the bird's note.

**TEWT,** *to it.*

**THACK,** *n., thatch; O. N.* **Thak,** *A. S.* thæc, *Dan.* tœkke, *Swed.* halm-tak, *O. H. G.* dakyu; *Ger.* dach, *thatch; Lat.* tectum; *Gr.* stegos, tegos, *a roof.*

**THACK,** *v. To thatch; O. N.* **thekja,** *A. S.* theccan, *Dan.* tœkke, *to thatch; Lat.* tegere, *Gr.* stégō, *Ger.* decken, *Dan.* dœkke, *Sans.* sthagámi, *to cover* (*Cur.* 155). 'Ye'll see a oade **thakt** buildin i t' loanside.'

**THAR, THARR,** *there; O. N.* **Thar,** *A. S.* thar, *Goth.* (*Ulf.*) thar, *O. H. G.* darot, *Ger.* dort, *Dut.* daar, *Dan.* and *Swed.* der.

**THARF,** *adj., slow, unwilling, afraid; Goth.* **thaurfts,** *O. N.* **Thörf,** *A. S.* thearf, *need, poverty;* thearfa, *poor; Goth.* (*Ulf.*) thaurfts, *needy, poor.* A man acts unwillingly because he is *obliged* to; *slowly* because he is *unwilling;* *reluctantly* he makes a journey on foot by night in *fear* from *necessity.* A very common word in the A. S. Laws. 'Gif he **thurf,**' if there is *need.*—*Ine,* 54. 'Ne **thearf,**' no *need.*—*Ælf.,* Introd., *Exod.* xxii. 2. 'Ne **thearf** ic N. sceatt ne scyllig,' I do not *owe* N. a 'scot' or a shilling.—*Æthelst.,* pt. 2, c. 21.

**THEE,** *thou, you.* 'Thee read it.' *Dan.* **De.**

**THEE, THE'Y,** *thy.*

**THEEASE,** *those; O. N.* **Thessir, thessar, thessi** (*masc., fem.* and *neut. plu.* of thessi), *these; Dan.* **disse.** 'Those' is *A. S.* thás, *nom. and acc. plu.* of thes, for which reasons 'these' for 'those' prevails in N.E. and Scotland.

**THENK,** *thank; A. S.* **Thænc.**

**THERSENS,** *themselves.*

**T'THICK END,** *the greater part.* 'T'thick end of hofe an hoor.'— *Bla.,* p. 15.

**THINK-ON,** *remember; A. S.* **Thincan, gethencean,** *to think.* 'Ah'll try and **think-on,**' really is, 'Ah'll try and **thincan,**' *remember.* 'On thisum anum dóme man mæg **gethencean.**'—*L. Ælf.,* Introd. 'Utan **gethencan** hú

Jacob,' &c.—*L. Æthelst.*, Introd. 'We moton eac **thencan,**' we mun eke **think-on.**—*Ib.* *See* also my *History of the Gypsies,* Rutherfurd, Kelso, 1880, for a play upon this word and Zingáno.

**THIRR,** *these*; *O. N.* **Their,** *they, them.*

**THOO,** *thou*; *O. N.* **Thú.** '**Thoo** knaws,' thou knows. 'Thou' is *Goth.* and *A. S.* thú, *Ger.*, *Dan.* and *Swed.* dû; *Lat.* and *Gr.* tu; whence I regard the forms 'ta,' 'tu,' as in reality *Lat.* For *Lat.* 't' we expect *Goth.* 'th,' by Grimm's law, and for 'tu' find *Goth.* 'thú.'

**THOWT,** *thought*; *A. S.* **Thúhte,** *p.* of thincan. 'Thane Halgan Gaste wæs gethúht.'—*L. Ælf.*, Int. from Acts xv., 28. 'Me rihtest **thúhton,**' seemed most just to me.—*Ib.* '*Thonne* **thúhte** us ærest most thearf,' then it seemed to us first most needful.'—*L. Edmund,* c. 6.

**THRANG,** *busy*; *O. N.* **Thröngr,** thraungr, thrængr, *close, tight*; *O. Swed.* **thranger,** *Dan.* trang, *Swed.* tráng, *A. S.* **thrang,** *pressed*, *p.* of thringan, *to press, crowd, throng.* 'If tn be **thrang** we'll be back in an hoor.'—*Bla.,* p. 17. *Goth.* threihan, *to throng*; *O. E.* thring, *Ger.* drängen, *Dut.* dringen.

**THRAW,** *throw*; *A. S.* **Thráwan,** *to throw.* 'Sat **thrawin** t'shuttle weavin.' *Goth.* thragjan, *to run,* *A. S.* thrægian; *cf. A. S.* thrah, *a space of time, a season*; *O. Eng.* throw.

**THREAP,** *to argue*; *A. S.* **Threapian,** *to threap, reprove*; **threapung,** *a threaping, chiding, &c.* (*Bos.*), but ? other meanings; *Gael.* **dearbh,** *to prove, try, certify, attest, put to the test, &c.*; *O. N.* thrap, thrapt, *a quarrel,* which seems to be connected with threp, *a ledge, a footing,* formed by a projecting stone in a wall, whence *a logical basis, an argument*; threifa, *to touch, feel* with the hand; thrífa, *to clutch, grip, take hold of.* The *Gael.* dearbh, *to prove*; *Wel.* darbwyllaw, *to persuade,* seem to have been the innocent cause of the *argument.* *Argument* leads to *quarrelling, quarrelling to killing,* whence *Dan.* drœbe, *to kill, slay.* 'Drœbe med snak,' *to bore to death with talking*; drab, *manslaughter.*

'It's not for a man with a woman to **threape**
Unless he first give o'er the plea.'
—*Take thy old cloak about thee,* l. 61.

**THREAVE,** '*a measure* containing 12 *sheaves straw,* or 24 *ling*' (*Grainge*); *Gael.* '**Treabh,** *two cocks of corn* consisting each of 12 *sheaves*' (*Armst.*); **treabh, treibh;** *Lat.* tribus, *Eng.* **tribe** or clan, *a farmed village,* '*village community,*' from treabh, *to till, plough, cultivate.* Out of '**treabh-talamh,**' *the ploughed land of the tribe,* or *the village community,* the Romans made 'Triptolemus' (*Vallancey*), *the ploughman*; *Wel.* **drefa,** '24'; '**drefa** o yd,' 24 *sheaves* of corn; **dref,** *a bundle*; whence *Mid. Lat.* dreva, *O. N.* **threfl,** *Nor.* trœve, *Swed.* **trafwa,** *Dan.* **trave,** *A. S.* **thraf,** *a thrave*; *M. H. G.* trava, *a heap*; *Mid. Lat.* trava; *Russ.* trava, *grass*; *Ital.* and *Lat.* draba, *whitlow grass*; *Span.* drava; *Wel.* drefu, *to bundle or tie together*; *O. N.* thrífa, *to thrive,* and *thrift.* '**Dreva** manipulorum unius vinculi de avena.'—*Cambro-Britannic Laws,* in Spelm.

**THROOAT,** *throat*; *A. S.* **Thróte,** *Dut.* strot; *O. H. G.* droza, drozza; *Ger.* drosssel, drostel, *the throat.* 'Throte-golle.'—*Prompt. Parv.,* with the note, 'throte-gole,' or 'throte-bole,' 'neu de la gorge, gosier.' *A. S.* throt-bolla, *the windpipe.* '**Throt-gole** '= *Gr.* trachēlos, *throat.*

    *A. S.* Th = *Gr.* T; tra[d]-chēlos (*Gr.* chēilos, chelumon, *the chest*).

    *A. S.* G = *Gr.* CH; throa t-gole (*Lat.* gúla, &c., *see* GULL).

    *A. S.* Th = *Ger.* D; drost el (for drotsel, *O. H. G.* droza).

'Throat-golle' contracts into 'throttle,' 'throte-bolle' into the Cleveland form 'thropple.' Of the same origin is the next word.

**THROSTLE,** *thrush*; **Moor-throstle,** *Ring-Ousel*; *A. S.* **throstle, throste;** *O. N.* thröstr, *Dan.* trost, *Russ.* drosde, *Ger.* drossel, *Lat.* turdus.

**THYVEL** or **THYBEL,,** *a flat piece of beechwood* used for stirring porridge; *A. S.* **Thyfel,** *a shrub, thorn* (*Bos.,* but ?). Also called '**gull-thyvel.'**

**THYTHEL**, *same; A. S.* **Thythel**, *a bush, bough, branch.*

**THYSEN**, *thyself.*

**TIDER**, *tidier; O. N.* **Tidari**, *comp.* of tidr, *customary, &c.*, from tid, *time.* The *compar.* tidier in *Eng.* is *A. S.* tidigere, tidiggere. Tidy means lit. *timely, seasonable, &c.*

**T'L, TIL**, *to; O. N.* til, *Dan.* til, *Swed.* till, *to* (*see* **TUL**).

    'And quhat a hauld sall we draw **till**
      My mirry men and me.'—*Edom O'Gordon,* l. 5.

**TIV**, *to*, used before a vowel (*see* **TUV**).

**TOFF**, *tough.*

**TOFT**, *a homefield; O. N.* **Toft**, topt, *a piece of ground,* messuage, homestead; *A. S.* toft (*see* p. 32).

**TOKE**, *talk.* 'They wok'd alike an they tok'd alike.'

**TO MORN**, *to-morrow.*

**TOPPIN**, *hair on the head; Wel.* **Topyn**, *a tuft of hair; Gael.* top; *O. N.* toppr, *a tuft of hair.* The following passage, 'Hest hvitr at lit, raudh eyrun ok **topprinn**,' a white horse with *red* ears and *forelock,* toppin (*Laxdæla Saga,* 194, in *Cleas*), is strikingly like 'He'd a carrotty **toppin**.'—*Al.,* 1880.

**T'TOTHER**, *the other; A. S.* **Thæt other** with the 't' misplaced.

    'A the tothar syde that a man might se.'—*Anc. Chevy Chase,* F. 2, l. 25.

    'The tone of them was Adler yonge
      The tother was King Estmere.'—*K. Est.,* l. 5.

**TOV IT**, *to it*; (*see* **TIV, TUV**).

**TORFLE, TURFLE**, *to die a natural death; Gael.* **Torchair**, *to perish, happen;* torchar, *a mortal fall, death; O. N.* thverra, *to be drained, ebb out; part.* thorinn, thurr, *Wel.* twyr, *A. S.* thyrr, *dry;* thyrran, *to dry up, wither;* thurh, thruh, thryh, *a coffin.* A horse dying in a field is said to **torfle**; if at night, 'he torfled i t' neet.' *Russ.* soknyte, *to wither.*

**TREEACE**, *trace; O. Fr.* **Tralot**, *a teame-trace or trait* (*Cot.*); *Lat.* tractus.

**TRET**, *treated, badly used; A. S.* **Dréht**, *troubled, vexed, grieved, p.p.* of dreccan, *to oppress, use badly.* 'The his leodscýpe swýthe **dréhte**,' which greatly *harassed* his country.—*L. Eadgar, Suppt.* 'I never was so **tret**,' in the matter of rent by a landlord.—*Colloq.*

**TREWTH**, *truth; A. S.* **Treówth**. The ord. pron. of truth is nearer *O. N.* tryggth, 'whence *Mid. Lat.* treuga, *Eng.* truce' (*Cleas.*); *O. N.* tryggr, *Goth.* (*Ulf.*) triggws, *true.*

**TROOSERS**, *trousers; O. Fr.* **Trousses**, *Mod. Fr.* trousse, *breeches;* trousser, *to tuck up; Lat.* tortiare, a verb formed from tortus, *p.p.* of torquere, *to turn, &c.*

**TUE, TEW**, *too.*

**TUL**, *to; O. N., Swed., Dan.* **Til**, *to.*

    'Gilderoy was a bonny boy,
      Had roses **tull** his shoone.'—*Gilderoy,* l. 2.

    'He gained the love of ladies gay,
      Nane eir **tull** him was coy.'—*Ib.,* l. 13.

Gilderoy was hanged at Edinburgh, July, 1638.

    'When he'd gitten **tul** her ageean.'—*Bla.,* p. 14.

**TUV**, *to*; before a vowel or 'h' mute. 'He's gaine **tuv** his warke.'—*Al.,* 1880. 'Fra his tail **tuv** his heead.'—*Bla.,* p. 12.

**TWANG**, *whip; A. S.* **thwang**, thwong, *a thong.* Our *dial.* form would be written t'wancg, as thincg, thing. 'Ah'll gie thee t' twanc.'—*Lodge*. 'Ah'll gie thee a **twanck**.'—*Pateley*.

**TWEA**, *two*; *A. S.* **Twio**, *two*.

**TYKE**, 'a Yorkshire tyke.' *O. N.* tík, *O. Swed.* tik, *a bitch*; *Swed. Dial.* tik; *Dan. Dial.* tiig, *a bitch* (*Atk*.). Blackah calls a favourite horse an 'oade tyke,' and a 'horse-cowper' is so styled in the following humourous little excursion :—

### T'Oade Yorkshire Tike.

Bane ta Clapham town-gate liv'd an owd Yorksher tike,
Who i dealing i horseflesh had ne'er met his like;
'Twor his pride that i au the hard bargains hede hit,
Hede bit a girt monny, bud nivver bin bit.

This oud Tommy Towers (bi that naam he wor knaan)
Hed an oud carrion tit that wor sheer skin an baan;
Ta hev killed him for t'curs wad hev bin quite as well,
Bud 'twor Tommy's opinion hede dee ov hissel !

Well, yan Abey Muggins, a neighbourin cheat,
Thowt ta diddle oud Tommy wad be a girt treat;
Hede a horse, too, 'twor war than oud Tommy's ye see,
For t' neet afoare that hede thowt proper ta dee !

Thinks Abey, t'oud codger 'll nivver smoak t'trick,
I'll swop wi' him my pooer deead horse for his 'wik,
An' if Tommy I nobbut can happen ta trap,
'Twill be a fine feather i' Aberram cap!

Soa to Tommy he goas, au' the question he pops:
'Betwin thy horse an' mine, prithee, Tommy, what swops ?
What wilt gi' me'y ta boot ? fer mine's t'better horse still !'
'Nout,' says Tommy, ' I'll swap ivven hans, an ye'y will.'

Abey preeached a long time about 'summat ta boot,'
Insisting that his war the liveliest brute;
Bud Tommy stuk fast where he first had begun,
Till Abey shook hands, an sed, 'Well, Tommy, dun !'

'O ! Tommy,' sed Abey, ' ah's sorry fer thee,
Ah thout thow'd a hadden mair white i the'y ee;
Good luck's wi' thy bargin, fer my horse is deead.'
'Hey !' says Tommy,' my lad, so is mine, an' it's fleead ! '

—*Nidd. Al.*, 1873.

# U.

**UPHOD**, *uphold = warrant, be bound*, in the line. 'They're ganning fer scooring steeans too, ah'll **uphod** 'em.'—*Bla.*, p. 18.

**URCHIN**, *hedgehog*; *A. S.* **Erscen**, *ircing*; *Belg.* horta, *hurts*; *Lat.* ericius, *M. Lat.* erinaceus, *Franco-Gall.* herisson, *Mod. Fr.* hérisson (from the *Lat.*), oursin, *urchin*. On Mitcham Common the gypsies call it **archie** and **archie-witchin**, or **aitchéwitchin**, which is the *Dut.* ijzerwerken (lit. ironwork), *a hedgehog*; *Russ.* ezhenoke, *Ger.* egel (*see* also my *Hist. of the Gypsies*, Rutherfurd, Kelso, 1882).

## V.

**VARRA, VARY,** *very*; *O. Fr.* **Verai,** vray; *Chaucer,* **veray;** *O. Eng.* verai, verrai, verray, verrei, verri (*Stratm.*); *Dut,* waar, *Ger.* wahr. ' Nut **varra** lang efter.'—*Bla.,* p. 39.

**VAST,** *n., a large quantity.* 'There war a **vast** o' money spent over that job.'—*Colloq. Fr.* **Vaste** (*subst.*), *Ger.* wüste; *Lat.* vastus (*adj.*).

## W.

**WAD,** *was*; *Goth.* **Vardh,** *1st, 2nd* and *3rd pers. sing.,* pret. of vairdhan, *to be*; *O. N.* vard, pret. of verdha, *to be*; *A. S.* weard, pret. of weorthan, *to be.*

**WAD,** *would*; *A. S.* **Wolde,** *would.* 'They thowt they **wad** hev a lark.'

**WAE,** *woe*; *A. S.* **Waa, wæ;** *Dut.* wee, *Ger.* wehe, *Wel.* gwae, *Lat.* væ, *Gael.* wo, *O. N.* Vá, *A. S.* wá.

**WEA WORTH,** *woe worth*; *A. S.* **Weá,** *woe*; **weorth,** *imperat.* of weorthan, *to happen.*

1. 'Gif muth oththe eage wo weordeth,' if to mouth or eye *woe happen.*—*L. Æthelbert,* 45 (561-616).

2. **Woe worth, woe worth** *thee,* wicked wood,
   That ere thou grew on a tree,'
remarked Little John, when his bow broke.—*Rob. Hood & Guy of Gisborne,* l. 69.

3. '**Woe worth, wae worth** ye, Jock, my man.'—*Edom O'Gordon,* l. 69.

4. '**Woe worth, woe worth** thee, false Scotland.'
   —*Murder of Darnley,* (1567-8).

5. 'Howl ye, **woe worth** the day.—*Ezek.,* xxx., 2.

6. '**Wae worth** the loun that made the laws,
   To hang a man for gear.'—*Gilderoy,* l. 65 (1638).

7. '**Wheea worth** 'em they'll hear what we say.'—*Bla.,* p. 18.

**WAKE,** *weak*; *A. S.* wác, wæc, but our form would be written wæc.

**WAKKEN,** *waken*; *A. S.* **Wæcan,** *Dut.* waken, wekken, *Ger.* wachen, wechen.

**WALE,** *to hurry*; *A. S.* weallan, *to boil*; *Dut.* Ijlen, overijlen, *Ger.* eilen, übereilen, *to hurry.* ' Ah did **wale** it when ah startid.'—*Colloq.*

' Seea ah **waled** on as fast as i' cud.'—*Bla.,* p. 27.

**WALSH,** *insipid*; *i.e.,* **Welsh** to a Saxon; *A. S.* **Walahiso, wæliso,** wylisc, wilisc, *foreign*; wealh, *pl.* wealhas, wealas, weallas; Walas the *Welsh*; *anything not Saxon.*

**WANDTA,** *warrant thou* (see WEEST).

**WANKLE,** *weak*; *A.S.* **Wancol,** woncol; *Ger.* wankel, *unsteady*; *fluc-tuating*; *Dut.* wankelen, *to totter* (see WENCLE).

**WAR, WARR,** *was*; *O. N.* var, *1st* and *3rd pers. sing.* pret. of vera, *to be.* ' They fand him quiatly grazin' o' t'rooadside, as if nowt **warr.**'

**WARK,** *ache, pain*; *O. N.* **Verkr,** *Dan.* værk, *pain.* 'A bit o nice fatty-caike . . . a glass of beest beertult, an a bit o' heeame fed bacon (some o' wer awn feedin) . . . it seems varra hard it sud bring t'stummark **wark** like this.'—*Al.,* 1880.

**WARK, WARKE,** *work*; *A. S.* **Wearc, wæarc,** weorc; *Goth.* vaurkjan, *to work*; *O. N.* verk, *Dut.* and *Ger.* werk, *Dan.* værk, *work.*

' And bids me leave my wearye **warke.**'—*Aged Lover,* l. 35.

' Ah'll **warke** na mair.'—*Colloq.*, Lofthouse. ' He's gaine tuv his **wark.**' — *Al.*, 1880.

**WAR,** *worse*; *O. N.* **Verr,** *Swed.* värre, *Dan.* vœrre, *A. S.* wærra, *worse.*

**WARSE,** *worse*; *A. S.* **Wærsa.**

**WARRANT,** *was not*; *O. N.* **Var'at,** *was not* (*Lodbrok. Quid., see* p. 85).

' Still he **warrant** a thief.'—*Bla.*, p. 12.

**WARP,** *threads that run with the length* of a piece of cloth, &c. (*see* p. 216).

**WATH,** *a ford*; *O. N.* **Vath,** *a ford*; *A. S.* **wath,** *a way*; wad, *a ford*; *Dut.* watte; *Lat.* vadum, *a ford.* ' **Wath** ' as a place name occurs several times, *e.g.*, three miles above Pateley and near Ripon. In Surrey ' Waddon ' occurs twice; on the Wandle, near Croydon; and on the Wey, near Farnham.

**WATTHER,** *water.* Like ' fadther.'

**WE, WI', WE'Y,** *with*; *A. S.* **Wid;** *O. N.* vid, vidr, or vith, vithr, *with*; *Goth.* withra, *Dan.* ved.

**WEÄM,** *stomach*; *O. N.* **Vömb,** *the belly.*

' Yah neet this week lile Mat began
Ta plean aboot his **weame.**'—*Bla.*, p. 16.

**WEANT,** *will not.*

**WEE,** *with* (*Bla.*).

**WEEAR,** *wear*; *O. N.* **Vera,** *A. S.* **werian,** *to wear.*

**WEEL,** *well*; *A. S.* **Wæl,** well, *well.*

' An slyed oot ta meet him as **weel** as ah cud.'—*Bla.*, p. 16.

**WEEST,** *wilt be*; *A. S.* **Wyrst,** contr. from weorthest, wurthest, wyrthest, 2nd pers. *sing. pres.* of weorthan, *to become.* ' Ah'll wandta **weest** seun be all reight,' I'll warrant thou wilt soon, &c.—*Bla.*, p. 29. **Weest** is here used in a future sense. Weorthan had no *future,* therefore this was expressed by the *pres.* tense, as in the example.

**WELL,** *a spring, a natural outflow of water*; *A. S.* wyl, wyll, wil, **well,** weall, *a spring,* lit. that which *bubbles up*; wyllan, weallan; *Goth.* wulan, *to well up, flow*; ' wiel, *whirlpool*; *Lat.* volvo; *Gr.* cluō, *to roll round* ' (*Cur.*); *A. S.* wyl = **wylm,** *a boiling, bubbling*; **æwylm** (Ewelme, a place name, lit, ' water-well '; in the *locative* case, *the place where the spring breaks out.* ' Oth hire **æwylm,**' up to its *source.*—*Treaty of Ælfred and Guthrun,* 1 (A.D. 878). This is ' Ewelme,' in Bucks, and ' Ewell,' in Surrey, at both of which places large chalk springs issue. The Domesd. form, ' Etwelle,' for ' Ewell,' does not weigh against such evidence; the ' t ' is probably a mistake for Eawelle (*see.* **HELL,** and in ref. to that art. *cf. A.* and *M. Gr.* helos, *a marsh, i.e., a spring* bog; *Mod. Gr.* heleos, *a marshy field* by the side of a river; (f)elos; *Lat.* vallis (*Cur.* 530); *O. N.* kelda, *Swed.* källa, *Dan.* kilde, *M. H. G.* qual and quil, *Ger.* quelle).

**WENGBY,** *leathery, tough.* ' As toff as **wengby.**'—*Al.*, 1880.

**WER,** *was.* See **WAR,** and add *A. S.* **Wære,** 2nd pers. *sing. perf.* of wesan.

**WER,** *were*; *A. S.* **Wæron,** *plu.* of do.

' And some unseen **wer** present there.'—*Fair Bridges,* 1577. ' Altho he **wer** nobbut a hoss.'—*Bla.*, p. 12. ' Er we **wer** flit away.'—*Ib.*, p. 14.

**WER,** *our*; *O. N.* **Vár,** várr; *Icel.* vor, *Dan.* vor, *Swed.* vár our. ' We like to see **wer** barns at neet.'—*Bla.*, p. 10.

**WERSELS,** *ourselves.* ' We streean **wersels** all at we can.'—*Bla.*, p. 22.

**WERSENS,** *ourselves* (*see* **WER** and **SEN**). ' An then we sal git **wersens** streight.—*Bla.*, p. 29.

**WESH,** *n., a wash*; *A. S.* **Wæsc,** wesc; *Dan.* vask, *Dut.* vasch, a wesh, wash. ' Let's have a **wesh** ' (*Colloq.*), *i.e.,* ' water'; *Gael.* uisge, *water.*

**WESH,** *v.*, *to wash*, that is, to 'water'; *Gael.* **uisgich**, *to water*; *A. S.* wascan, *to wash*; *Dut.* waschen, *Dan.* vaske. 'Ah **wesh'd** an then sanded the floor.'—*Bla.*, p. 27. The River **Wash**burn is called '**Weshburn**,' and with 'Kirkby **Wiske**' and the **Esk** (Cleveland) must be classed as a remnant of Gaelic nomenclature (*see* BURN).

**WEWTAL,** *to whistle*; *Gael.* **Fead**, *to whistle*, to **wewt**; **feadailich, wewtaling**, *whistling*; *A. S.* hweosan, *to blow*; hweotherung, *murmuring*; *Gael.* feadaireachd, *whistling*; *A. S.* hweotha, hwiotha, hwitha, *a breeze*, from its *whistling*. 'A lile bird **wewtaled** up in a tree.'—*Al.*, 1880. Yarrell, followed by Atk. (*Cl. Gl.*), is mistaken in associating the name 'whew duck,' or 'whewer,' a name of the widgeon, with this word (*Yarrell*, III., 193). 'Whewer' is *Wel.*: çwiwell, *the widgeon* from its flight, the female salmon; gwiwell, *a widgeon, the female salmon*, from their movements; cwiwiaid, *widgeons*. 'Whews '= cwiws, *widgeons* —all from çwiw, *a whirl* or *quick turn*; çwiwian *to turn, dart about, fly here and there.* So also gwiwer, 'whewer,' *the squirrel* (*Ow.*).

**WHAM,** *a swamp* on the moors; *O. N.* **Hvammr**, *Swed.* kvammen, *Dan.* suomp, sump; *Alam.* suam, *Goth.* svamms, *a sponge*; *A. S.* svam, *Belg.* svamme, *fungus*; *Gr.* somphos (*Cur.*).

**WHAR,** *where*; *Goth.* **Hwar**, *O. N.* hvar, *Dan.* hvor, *A. S.* hwar, *Ger.* wo. 'Fer let me . . . be whar I like wi him.'—*Bla.*, p. 18.

**WHELK,** *a lump*. *Prompt. Parv.* gives 'Whele or whelke, soore whelle, qwelke (wheel).' *Russ.* polosa.

**WHELP,** *a pup*; *A. S.* **Hwelp**, hweolp, **welp**; *O. N.* **hvelpr**; *Dan.* hvalp, *a whelp, pup*; *Goth.* wulfs, *A. S.* wulf, *Eng.*, *Dut.* and *Ger.* wolf; *O. N.* úlfr, *Dan.* ulv, *Lat.* lupus, *Gr.* lukos, *wolf*; *Lat.* vulpes, *fox.* Cleasby is mistaken in connecting 'North E. *Ulf* in pr. names, Ulpha, *Ulverston*,' directly with úlfr, *wolf.* ' Ulfr,' a well-known historical character is responsible for that (*see* p. 95).

**WHEML,** *to overturn, empty a cart*, lit., *to turn up on its wheels*; *A. S.* hweol, hweowol, hweogl, hweohl, that which *revolves, a wheel*, gave a vb., hwiolan, *to wheel*, and **hweolum**, contr. [hwelm] **whelm**, *to turn up on its wheels.* Hweolum is the *dat. plu.* made into a verb, lit., *on the wheels.* **Wheml** by transpos. from **whelm.** A story is told of an old woman who, at last over-coming her aversion to travel by rail, proceeded in a train with a basket of eggs to market. A slight accident occurred by which she and her basket were thrown out on to the line and all her eggs broken. She, being more ruffled than hurt, picked herself up, enquiring in an injured tone of voice, 'Do they aye **whammel** us out this gate?' *O. N.* hjól, *Swed.* and *Dan.* hjul, *Dut.* wiel, *Russ.* koleso, *A. S.* hweol, *Eng.* wheel, *that which turns* = *Goth.* hweila, *a while time, turn.*

**WHILE,** *until* (*see* WAL).

**WHINNY, WINNY,** *to neigh*; *Wel.* **Wihi**, *the whinnying of a horse*; **wihiaw**, *to whinny* (*Ow.*); *Lat.* hinnire; *Fr.* hennir, *to neigh*; *Lat.* hinnus; *Gr.* ginnos, gīnos, *a mare, a mule's foal, &c.* 'He'd set up a **whinny** an run.' —*Bla.*, p. 13.

**WHITTLE,** *a carving knife*; *A. S.* **Hwitel**, **hwitle**; thweotan, *to cut off*; *Lat.* cultellus.

**WHYÁ,** *why.*

**WILTA,** *wilt thou* (*see* TA, *thou*). 'Wilta gan wi' me?' 'Wilta wed me?'—*Bla.*

**WINGE.** 'What is ta **wingein** and cryin at?'—*Colloq.*, to a crying child. Lit. **winge** means to act as one under the *whip. O. N.* **thvinga**, *to weigh down, oppress*; *Dan.* tvinge, *O. H. G.* dwingan, *M. H. G.* twinge, *Ger.* zwingen; *A. S.* thwingan, *to force, constrain, compel.*

**WINNAT,** *will not.*

**WISHIN,** *cushion*; *Gael.* bog-shùidheagan, *Russ.* polyshchka; *Lat.* culcitra, *dim.* culcitinum; *Ital.* cuscino, ooscino; *Fr.* coussin, whence *Ger.* küssen, *Dut.* kussen. The *Dial.* form seems a corrup. of the *Ital.*

**WISHT!** *hush, be quiet*; commonly said to a child. *Gael.* éisd!

'The winds with wonder whist.'—Milton, *Ode to the Nativity*, Hymn. V. v.

**WITH,** *a wood* (see p. 107); *O. N.* **Vithr,** *a wood; A. S.* withige, withie, withthe; *Eng.* withy, *Ger.* weide, *Lat.* vitta, *Gr.* 'itus (*Cur.*).

**WITHER,** *vicious; Wel.* **Gwydiawg,** *Gael.* guineach, *vicious.* Of a mare, 'She seazed him full **wither** by t'neck.'—*Bla.,* p. 14.

**WITTALED.** 'Ah've gittan fas'en'd ta t'sod if ah aint gittan **wittaled** ta t'tree.'—*Al.,* 1880. *Wel.* **Gwÿzaw,** *to grow woody;* gwyzen, *a tree;* **gwyzawl,** *rudimental;* so '**wittaled,**' means 'rooted' to the tree, so as to form part of its wood, grafted.

**WO,** *who; Dan.* **Hvo,** *A. S.* hwá, huá; *Gael.* lo, *Russ.* kto.

**WOKED,** *walked.*

**WOR,** *was* (see WAR, *was*).

**WORSER, WUSSER,** *worse; A. S.* wýrsa, *worse.* 'The **wýrsa sý,**' be the worse for it.—*L. Eadg.,* c. 4, A.D. 959-75.

**WRANG,** *wrong; O. N.* **Rangr,** older form **vrangr;** *Swed.* vráng, *Dan.* vrang, *Goth.* wraikws, *wry, crooked; A. S.* wringan, *to wring.*

**WUR,** *was* (see WER, *was*).

**WUTS,** *oats; Fris.* **Oat,** pron. as a contracted dissyllable. 'Oat,' *i.e.,* that which can be *eaten. O. N.* áta, *food,* but only of beasts, *a carcase* (because it is *eaten*); æti, an *edible* thing, *oats; A. S.* áten, *oats;* áta, œt, *an oat.*

# Y.

**YA,** *you; A. S.* **Eow,** *dat., acc.* and *abl. plu.* of thú.

**YAAL,** *ale; A. S.* eal, eala, ealo, ealad, ealod, eolod, *ale; Dan.* öl, *Dut.* ail or eel (from the *Eng.*).

**YAH,** *one; Gael.* **Aon,** haon; *A. S.* ean, *an.* 'Ya' for 'yan,' as 'a' for 'an.'

**YAK, YEK,** *oak; Gael.* **Darach,** darag, *oak; A. S.* ác. The *Dial.* form (corrup. from the *Gael.*) would be written 'eac,' and supplies the noun from which *A. S.* eácen, *great, mighty, strong,* may be formed. '**Yak** yat stoop'=*oak* gate post.

**YALLO,** *yellow.*

**YAM,** *aim.*

**YAN,** *one; A. S,* ean. 'Where **yan** went t'other went.'

**YANCE,** *once; A. S.* eanes, *gen. sing.* of ean, used adverbially. 'Ofter than æne,' oftener than *once* (lit. *that one time*).—*L. Ine.,* where the *neut. def.* is used.

**YAT,** *gate; A. S.* **Geat.** '**Yak** yat stoop,' oak *gate* post, and in the name **Yetholm,** Roxburghshire.

1. 'And whan they came to King Adland's hall,
   Untill the fayre hall **yate.**'—*King Estmere,* l. 172.

2. 'And hir **yates** all locked fast.'—*Edom O'Gordon,* l. 34.

3. 'Seest thou not yonder hall, Ellén?
   Of redd gold shines the **yate.**'—*Child Waters,* l. 74.

4. 'He knew ivvery **yat** at rooadside.'—*Bla.,* p. 12.

**YE, YE'Y,** *you, thou.* 'See'ah **ye'y** mun sit **ye'y** doon.'—*D. and M. Dale.*

**YERSEN**, *yourself* (*see* SEN).

**YEWN**, *to bully*; *Wel.* **Hewian**, *to defy continually or often, to hector*; **ewn**, *powerful, impetuous, overbearing*; **ewni**, *to become so.*

**YIT**, *eat.* Intermediate between *A. S.* etan and hitadh; *Eng.* Eat, and *Dial.* HIT, which *see.*

**YON**, *yond, yonder*; *A. S.* **Geond.** ' I think that's him comin **yon**.'— *Colloq.*

**YOON**, *oven*; *Swed.* **Ugn**, *Goth.* (*Ulf.*) auhns, *Dan.* ovn, *A. S.* ófen, *Ger.* ofen, *Dut.* óven, *Gael.* àmhuinn, uamhainn.

**YOOAK**, *yoke*; *A. S.* **Iuc**, *a yoke*; *Lat.* jugum; *A. S.* iucian, iugian, *to yoke.*

**YOOAKED**, *yoked.*

**YULE**, *Christmas*; *O. N.* **Jól**, *A. S.* geól (*see* pp. 42-5).

**YULE-CLOG**, *yule log* (*see* CLOG and p. 42).

--------

More than half the above Glossary of 957 words consists of *O. N.* and *A. S.* elements—*O. N.* 262 and *A. S.* 241 words. Next come *Gaelic* 43, *Wel.* 37, *Dan.* 34, *O. Fr.* 28, and *Dut.* 15. The *O. Norsk* or *Scandinavian* element is the characteristic of the Dialect, and carries with it one or two *Lapp* and *Russian* words. The *O. N.* and *A. S.* bring down several *Old Gothic* forms ; besides which, the Dialect preserves a very remarkable series of seven *Gothic* words not found in *O. N.* or *A. S.* Dicts. These *Gothic* words form one of the most interesting features of the Dialect. The *Welsh* element proves the survival of descendants of the ancient Cymry here resident, beyond all question ; but by far the most striking feature is the presence of a large number of *Gaelic* words, which it will only be necessary to enumerate to show that some of them also prove the survival of descendants of a still more ancient *Gaelic* speaking population upon this area. They are **Ask**, **Beäst**, **Bink** (*Ga.* Beinc), **Brat** (also *W.* and *A. S.*), **Burn**, **Shag** (in Buttershag), **Cabin** (also *W.*), **Cambril**, **Cloot** (also *W.*), **Deea**, **Dud**, **Fair**, **Far**, **Fog** (?), **Fratch**, **Gay**, **Glasp**, **Haining** or **Hainish**, **Hog**, **Jowl**, **Kail**, **Lick**, **Loaning**, **Nangin**, **Nor**, **Pewder**, Rake (also *Goth.*), **Ratten**, **Ray**, Riddle (also *W.* and *A. S.*), **Roat**, **Ruckle**, **Scumfish**, **Seägar** (in sound), **Seäp**, **Sile**, **Slate** (?), **Stroth**, **Stuffle**, **Taistrill**, **Teng**, **Threave**, **Torfie**, **Wesh** (through *A. S*), **Wewtal**, **Yah** (?), **Yak** (cor. of Darach). In addition to these, there are ten *Monastic Latin*, and five *German* words; and a few ancient Oriental forms, such as Biggin, Fell (1), Fettle, Gang, Anters and Ananters, which have come, with 'Boskab' and others that have stopped short of England, along the northern route.

CPSIA information can be obtained at www.ICGtesting.com
Printed in the USA
BVOW03s1527190814

363415BV00023B/1169/P

9 781295 846238